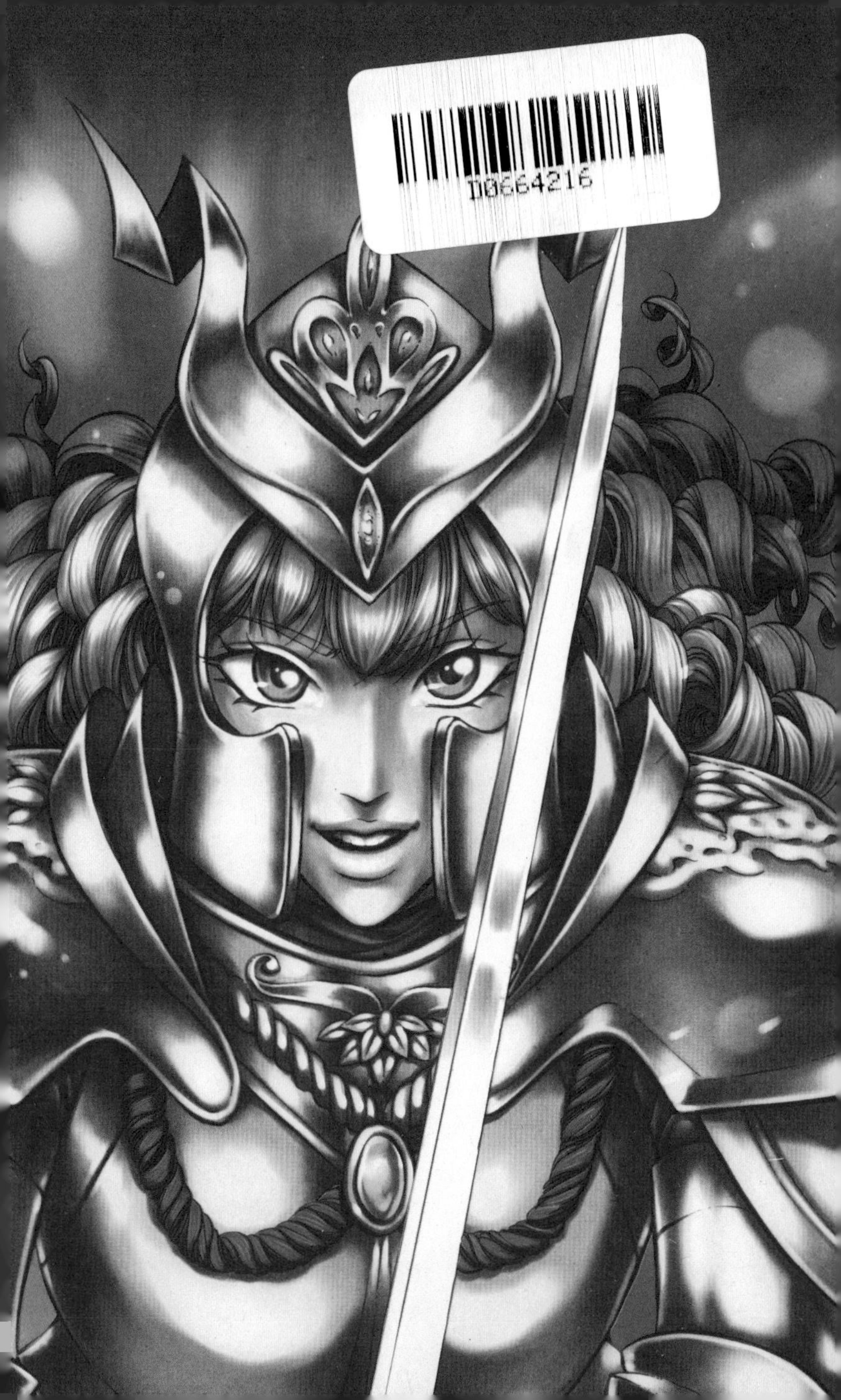

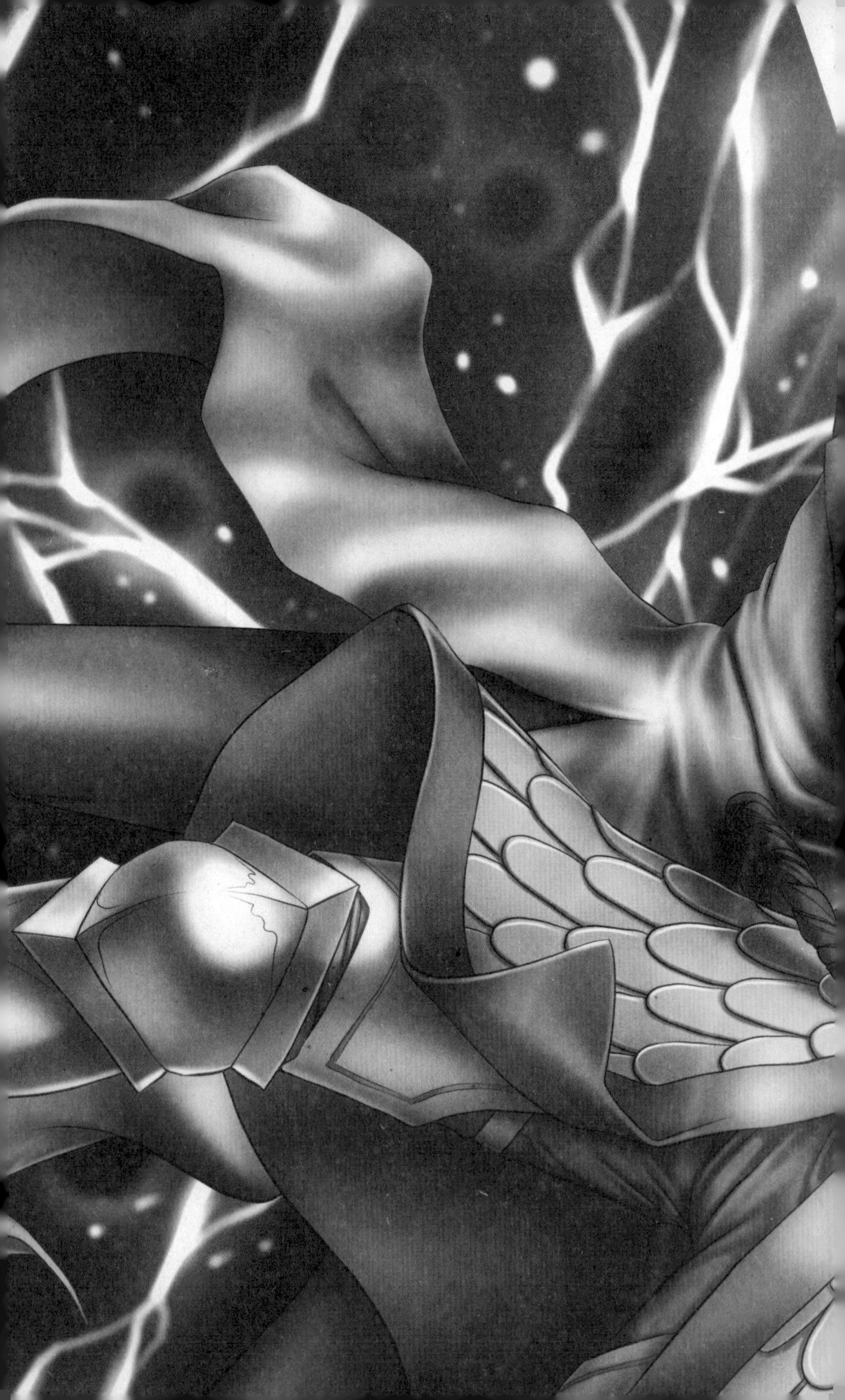

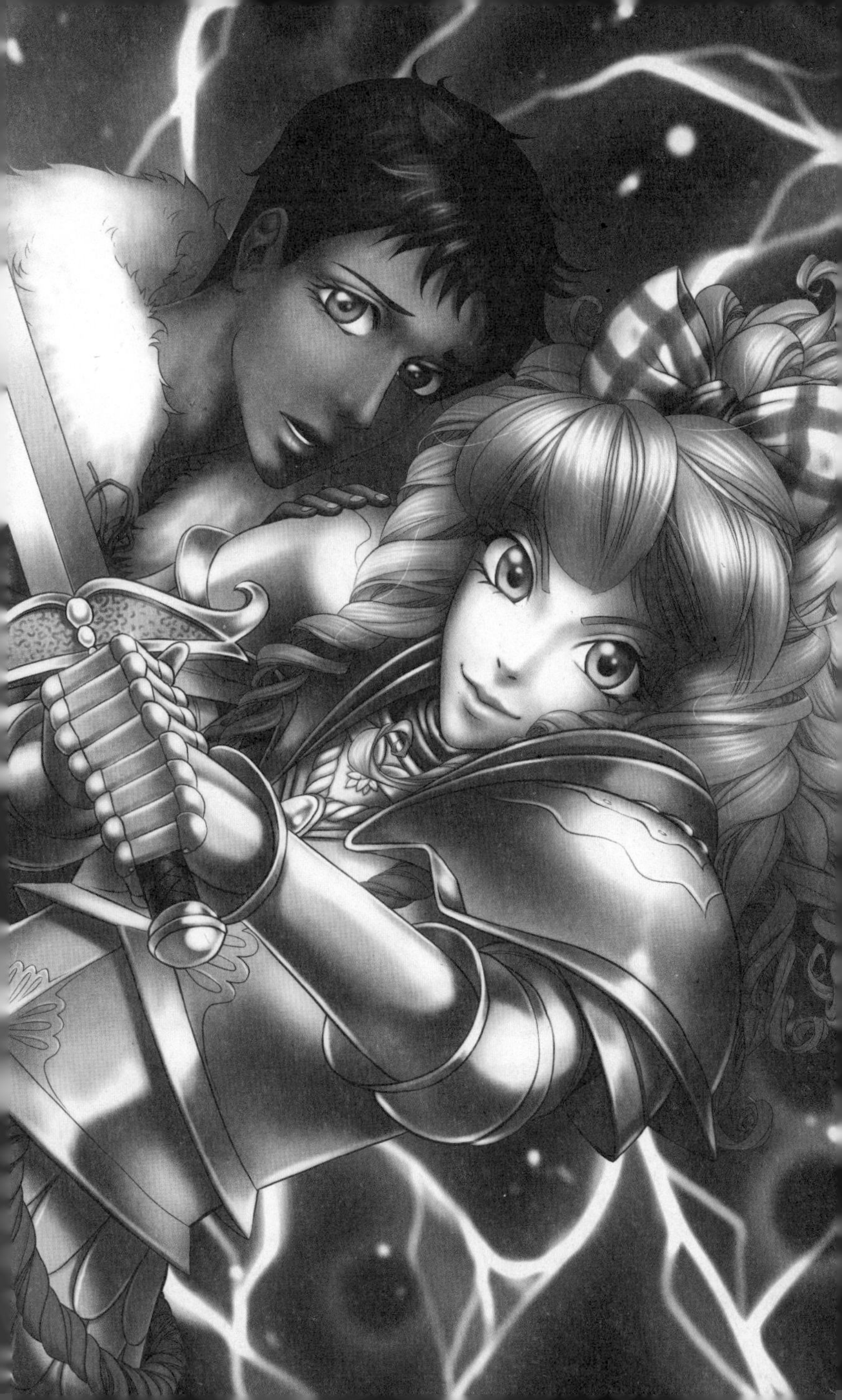

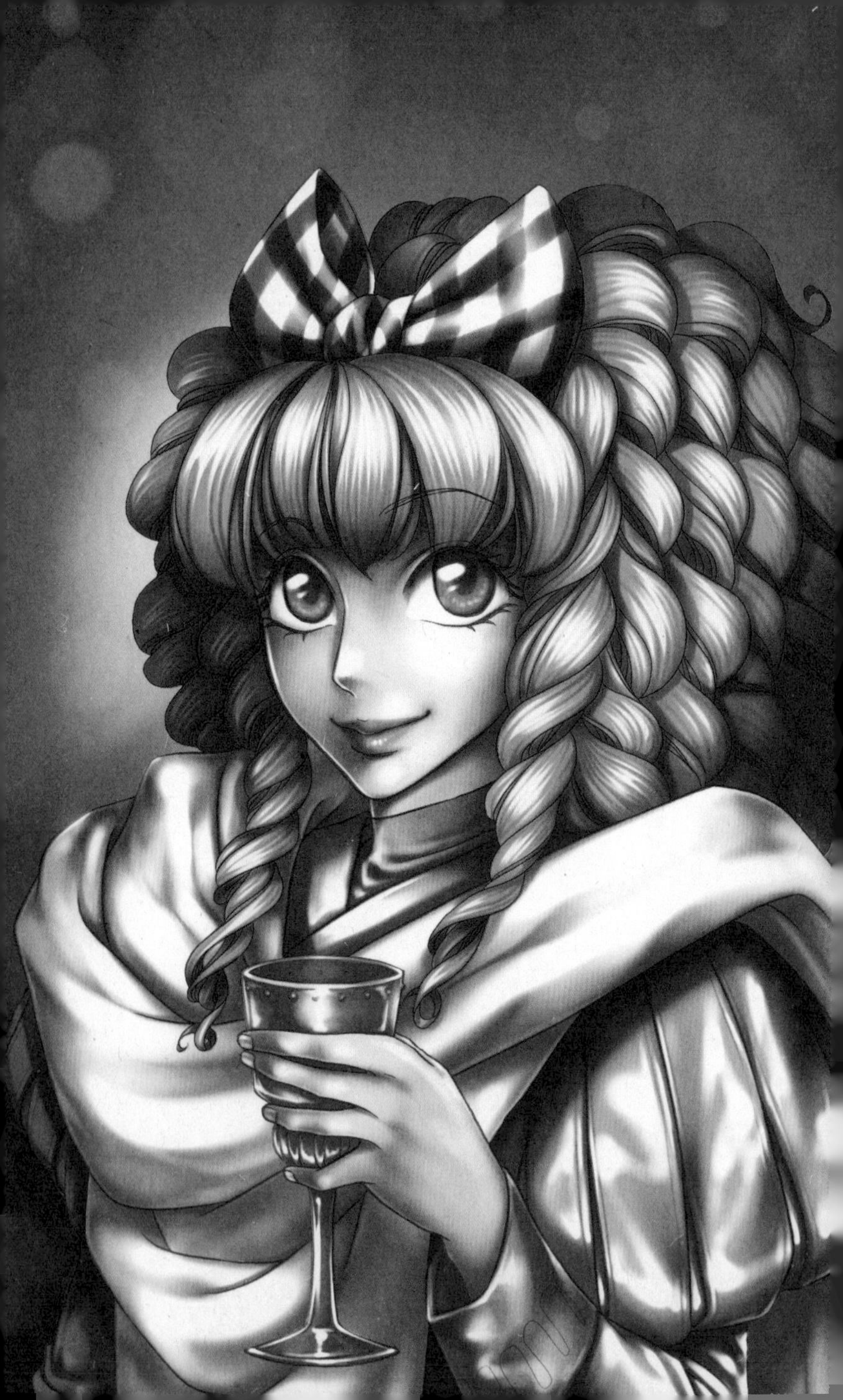

Sword Princess AMALTEA

3

Natalia Batista

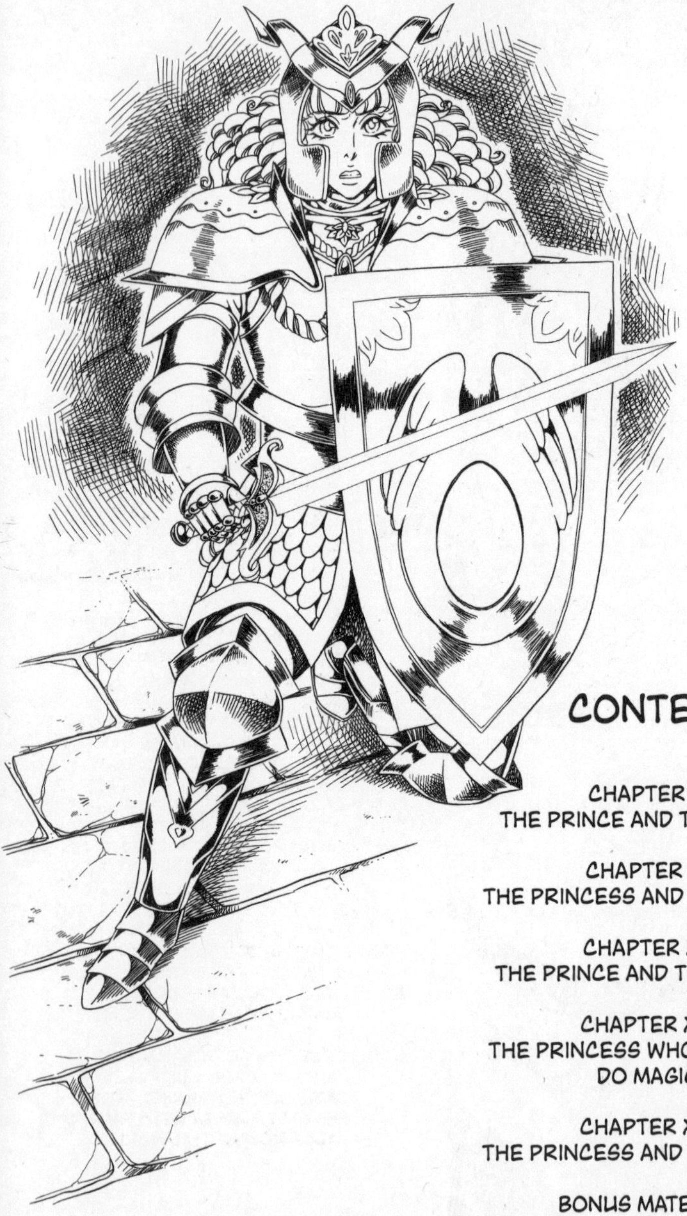

CONTENT

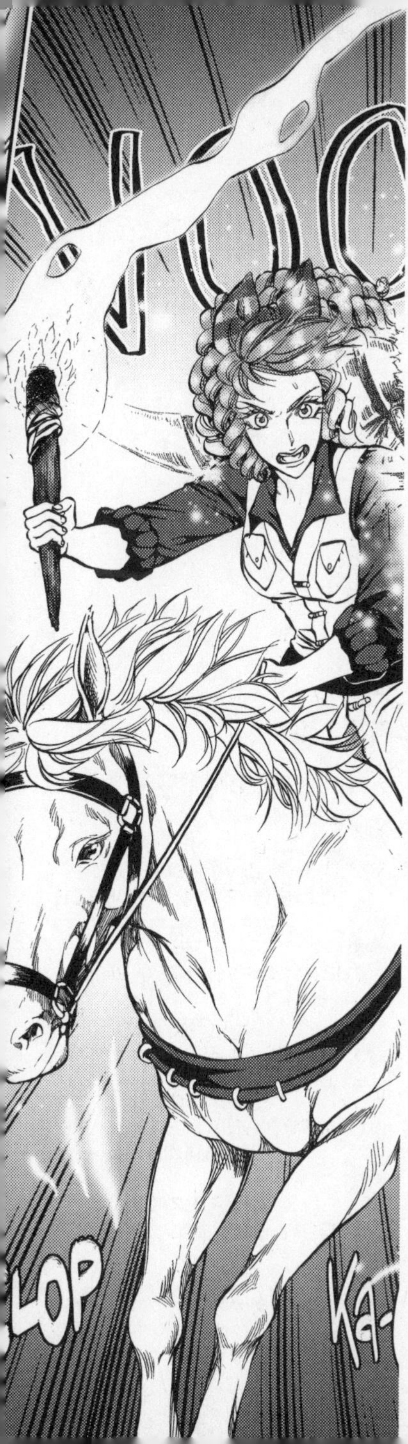
LOP
Ka-

PREVIOUSLY ON...

SWORD PRINCESS AMALTEA

WITH PRINCESS AMALTEA AND PRINCE OSSIAN'S FEELINGS FOR ONE ANOTHER SLOWLY BLOOMING INTO SOMETHING MORE THAN JUST A CONVENIENT PARTNERSHIP, THE APPEARANCE OF A POWERFUL CHALLENGER FROM OSSIAN'S PAST THREATENS THEIR FUTURE TOGETHER. BUT AMALTEA STILL HAS TO PROVE HER WORTHINESS AS A SUITOR AND HEIR TO THE THRONE OF THE GREY MOUNTAINS QUEENDOM IN A BATTLE TO THE DEATH. HAS SHE GROWN ENOUGH TO EARN PRINCE OSSIAN'S HAND... AND HEART? CAN THE TWO OF THEM FIND A PLACE IN A WORLD STACKED SO UNFAIRLY AGAINST THEM?

SEE THE ACTION-PACKED CONCLUSION IN NATALIA BATISTA'S GENDER-FLIPPED FANTASY MANGA WITH FANS ALL AROUND THE WORLD!

Characters in Book Three:

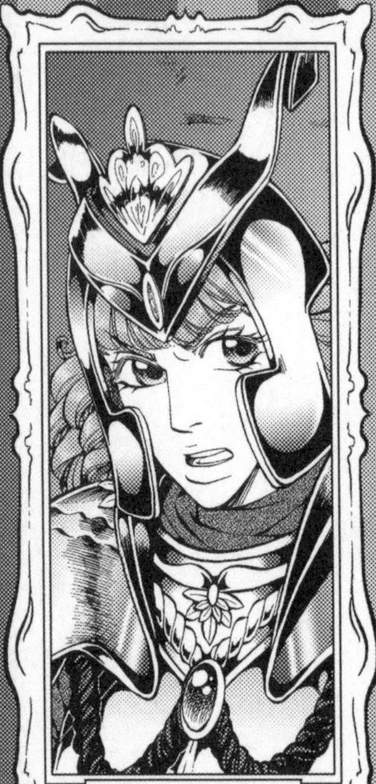

Princess Amaltea

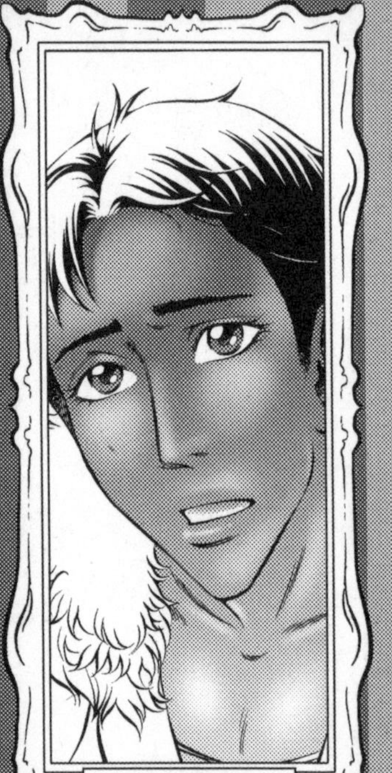

Prince Ossian

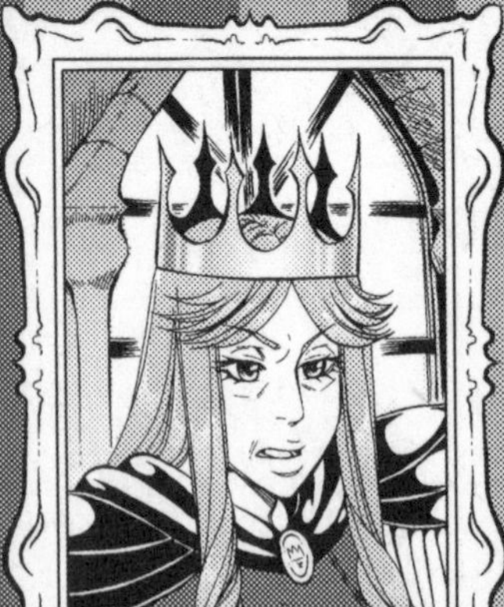

Queen Galatea

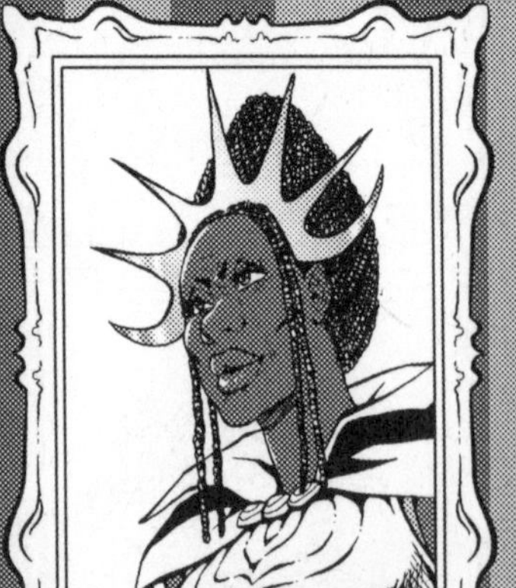

Queen Ylvasin

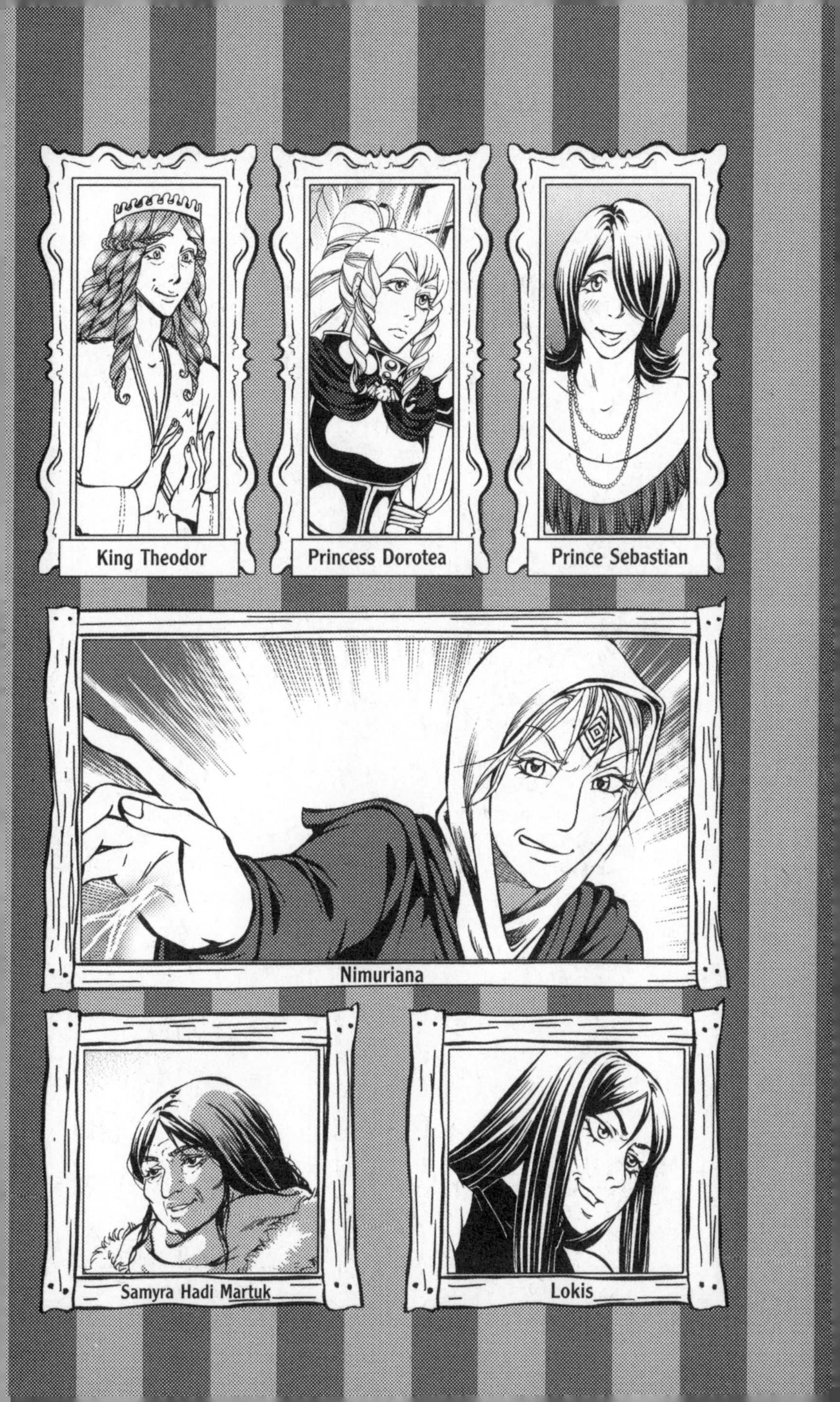
Prince Sebastian
Princess Dorotea
King Theodor
Nimuriana
Lokis
Samyra Hadi Martuk

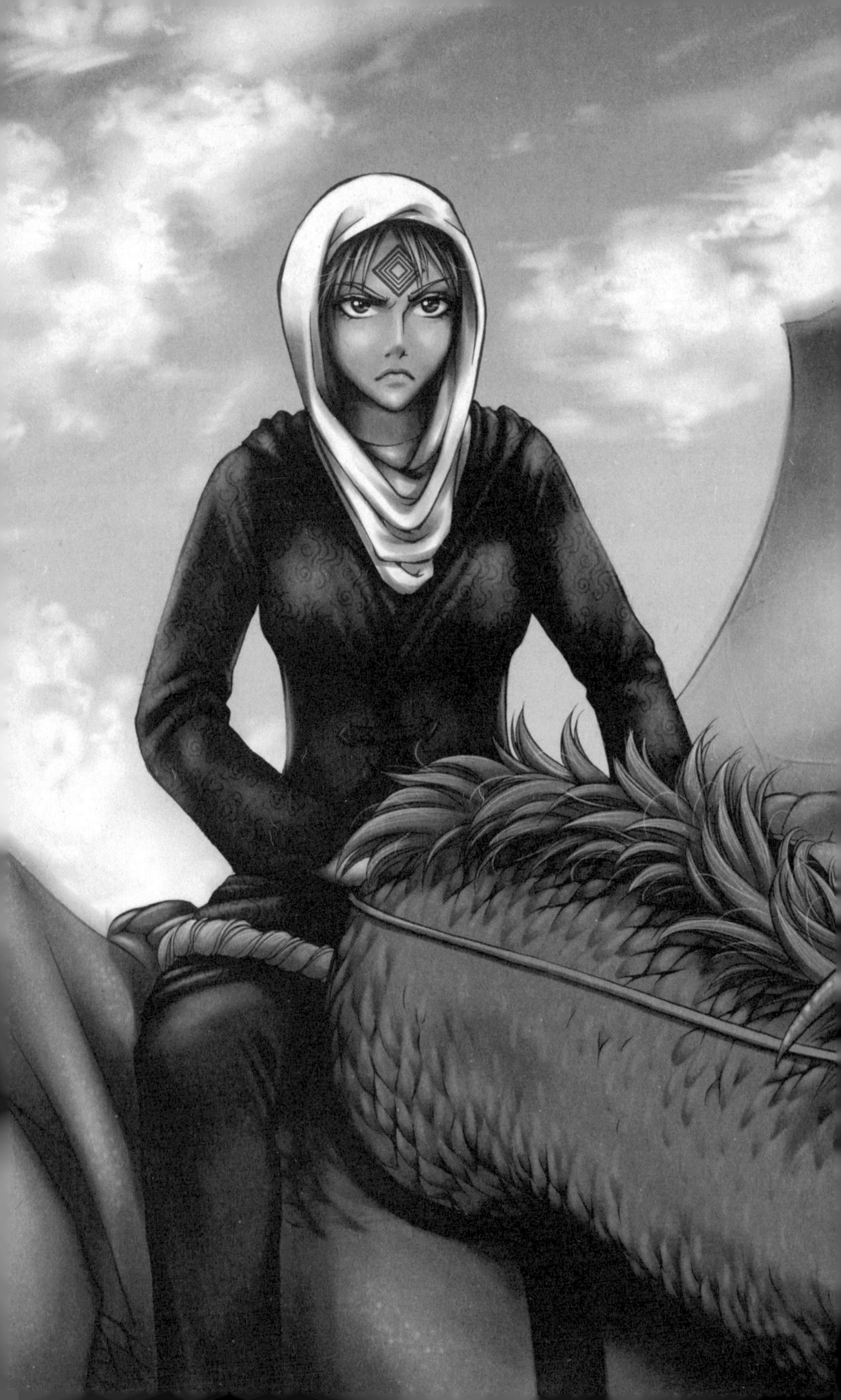

Chapter X

The Prince And The Witch

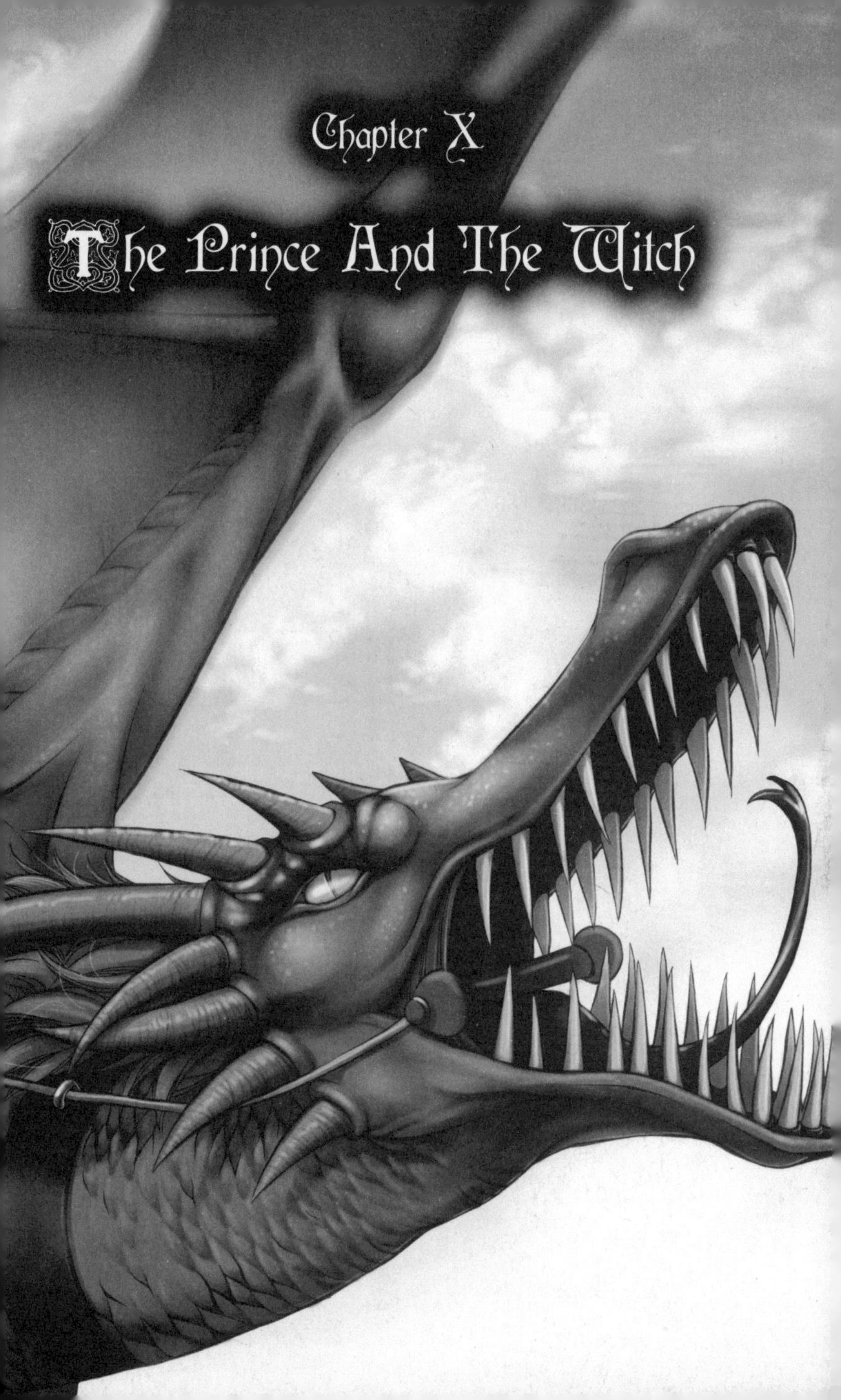

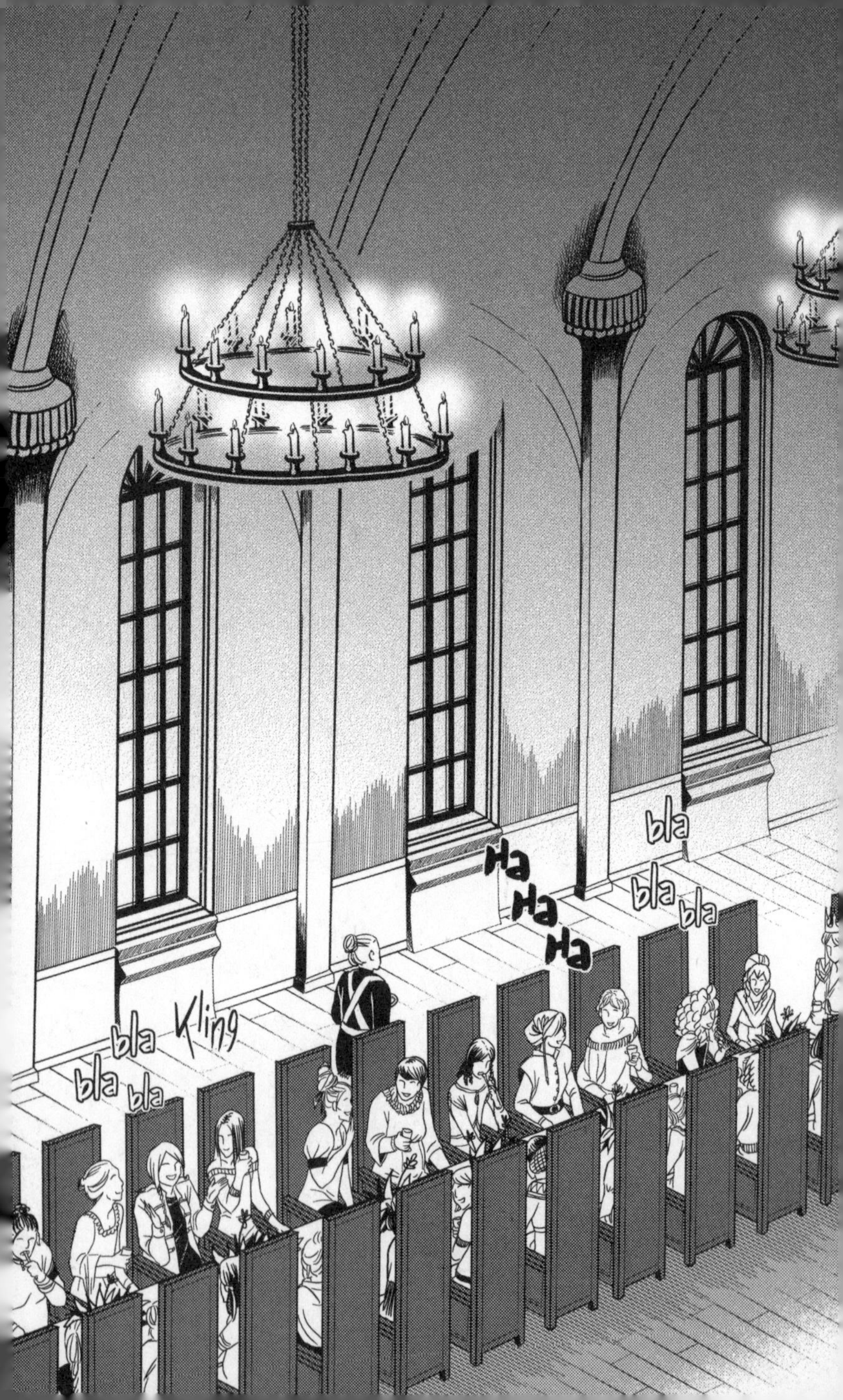
bla
bla bla
Ha
Ha
Ha
Kling
bla
bla bla

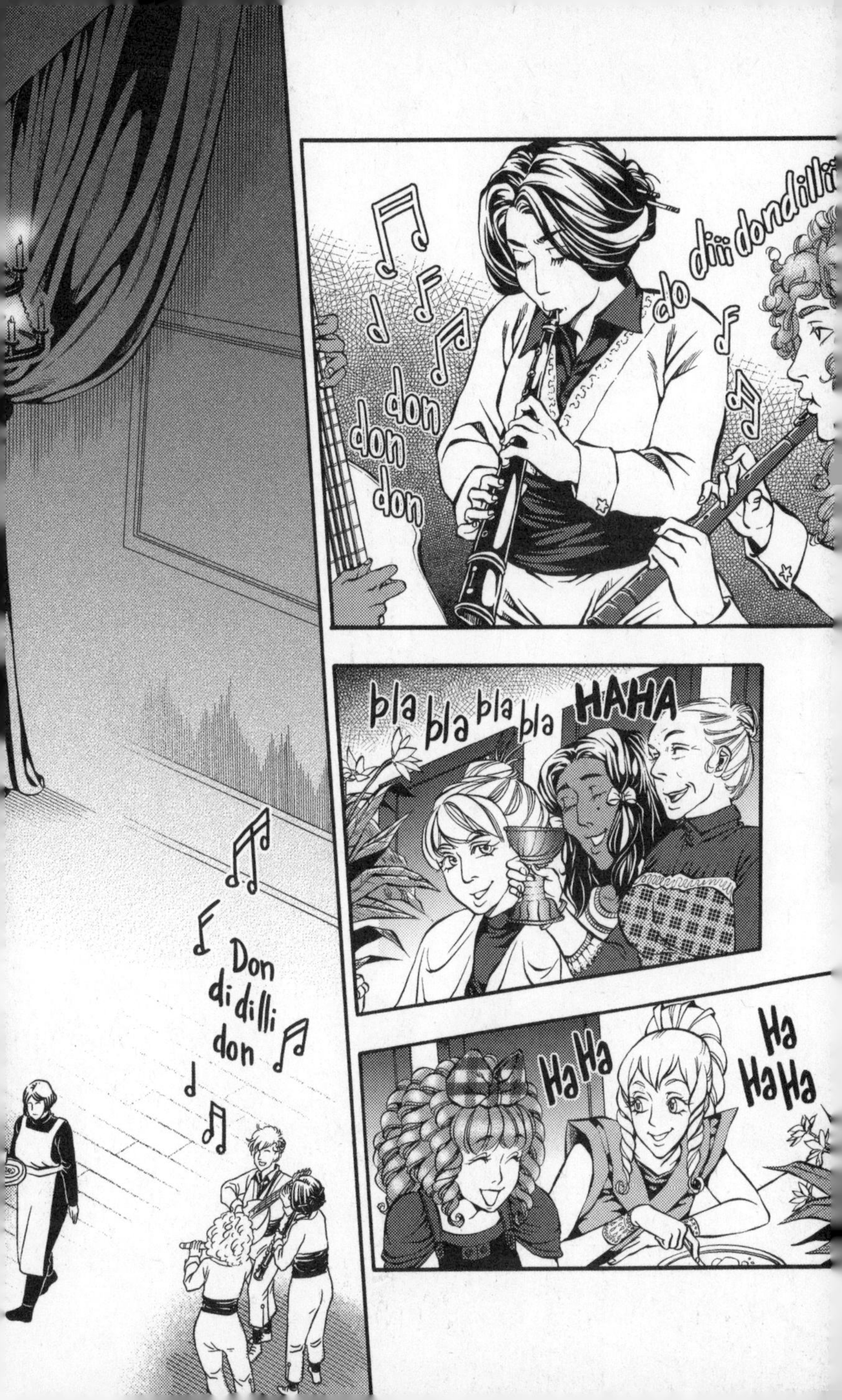
do diii dondilli
don
don
don
HAHA
bla bla bla bla
Ha
HaHa
HaHa
Don
di dilli
don

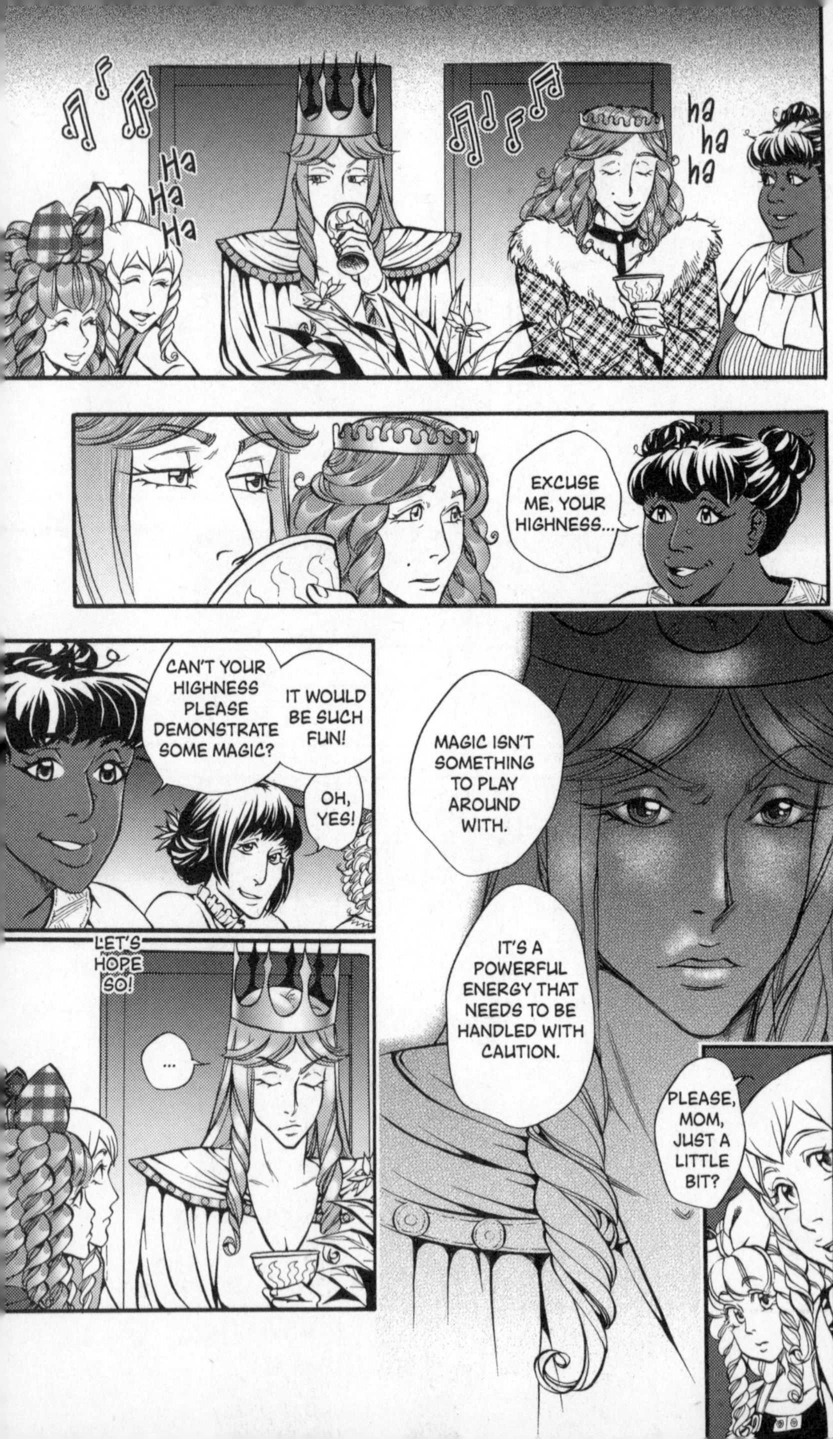
Ha Ha Ha
ha ha ha
EXCUSE ME, YOUR HIGHNESS...
CAN'T YOUR HIGHNESS PLEASE DEMONSTRATE SOME MAGIC?
IT WOULD BE SUCH FUN!
OH, YES!
LET'S HOPE SO!
...
MAGIC ISN'T SOMETHING TO PLAY AROUND WITH.
IT'S A POWERFUL ENERGY THAT NEEDS TO BE HANDLED WITH CAUTION.
PLEASE, MOM, JUST A LITTLE BIT?

PLEEEASE?

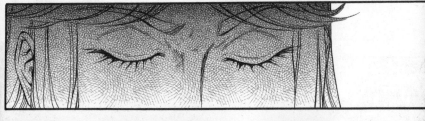

Dsh~

Tak
Tak
Tak

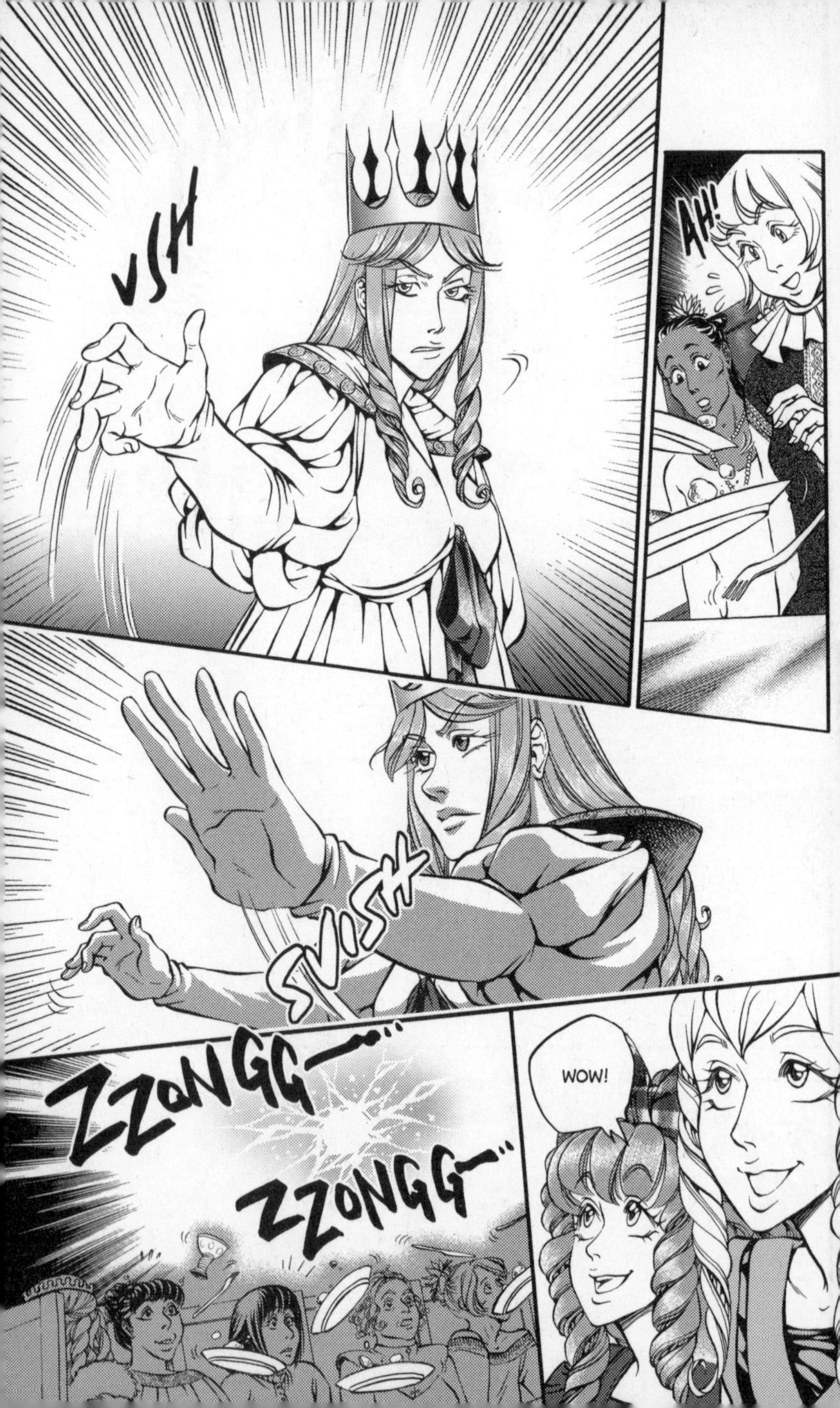
AH!
VSH
SWISH
WOW!
ZZONGG—
ZZONGG—

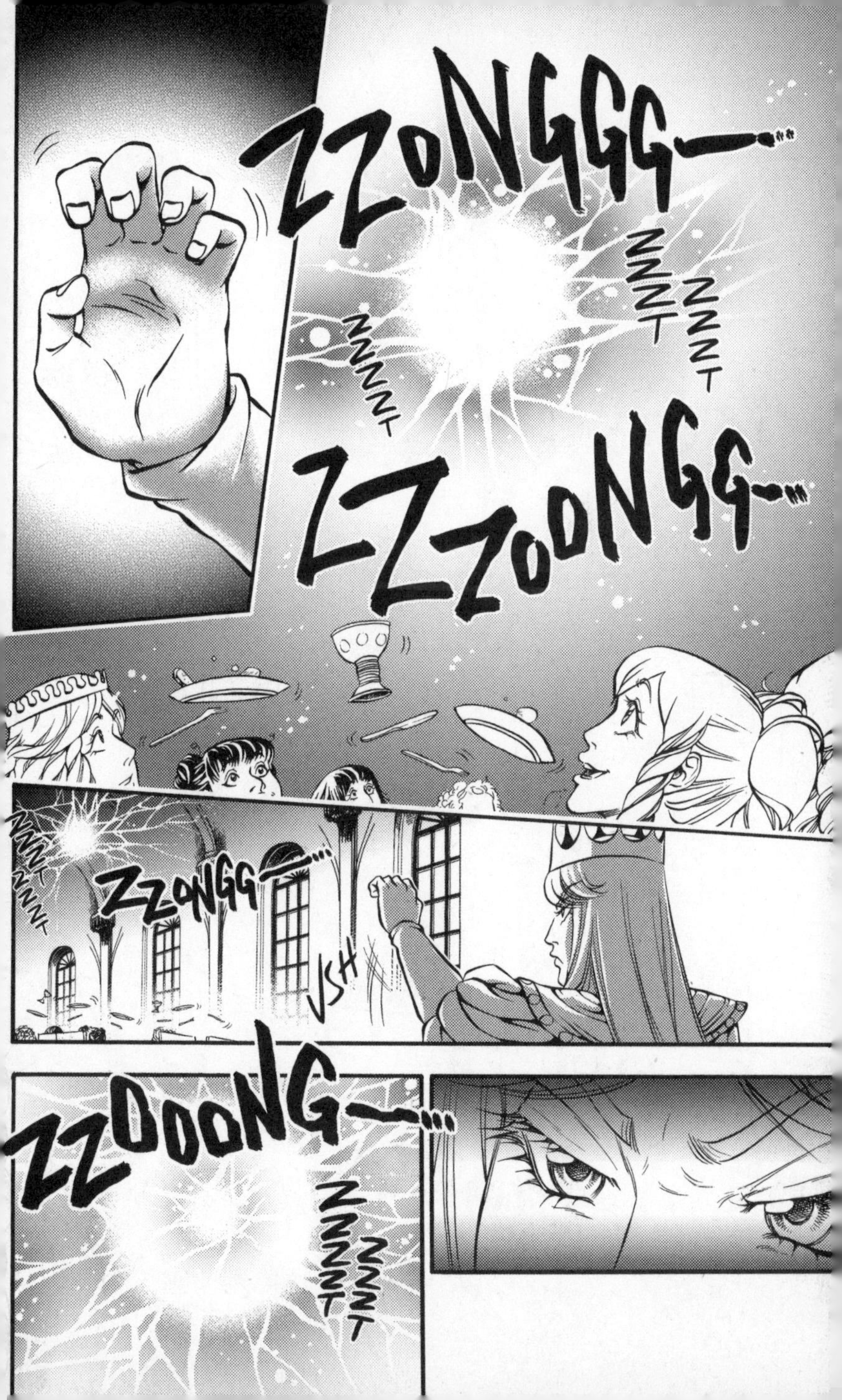
ZZONGGG—
ZZZZT
ZZZZT
ZZZZZT
ZZZOONGG—
ZZONGG—...
VSH
ZZOOONG—...
ZZZZZT
ZZZZT

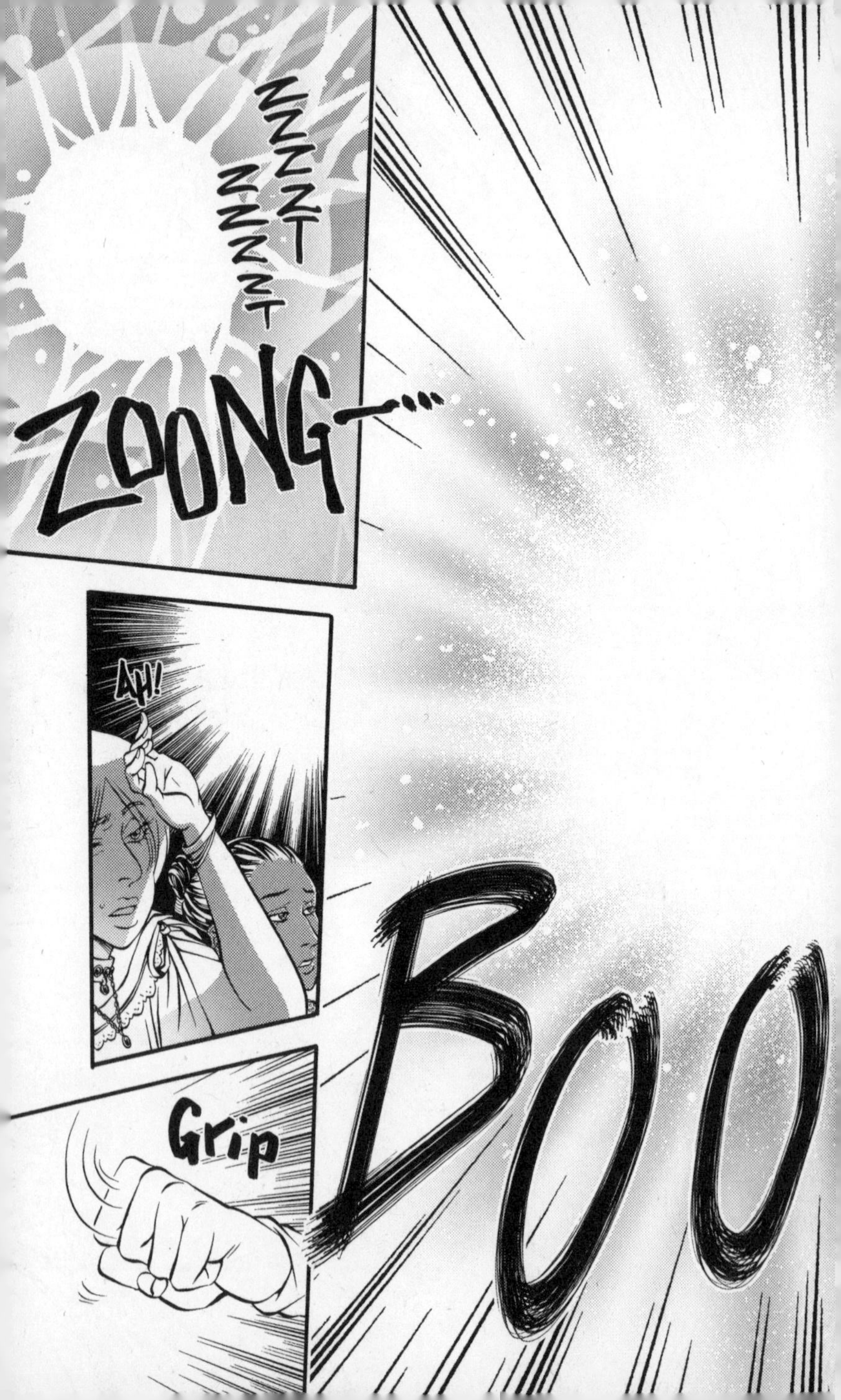
ZZZZZT
ZZZZZT
ZOONG—
AH!
Grip
BOO

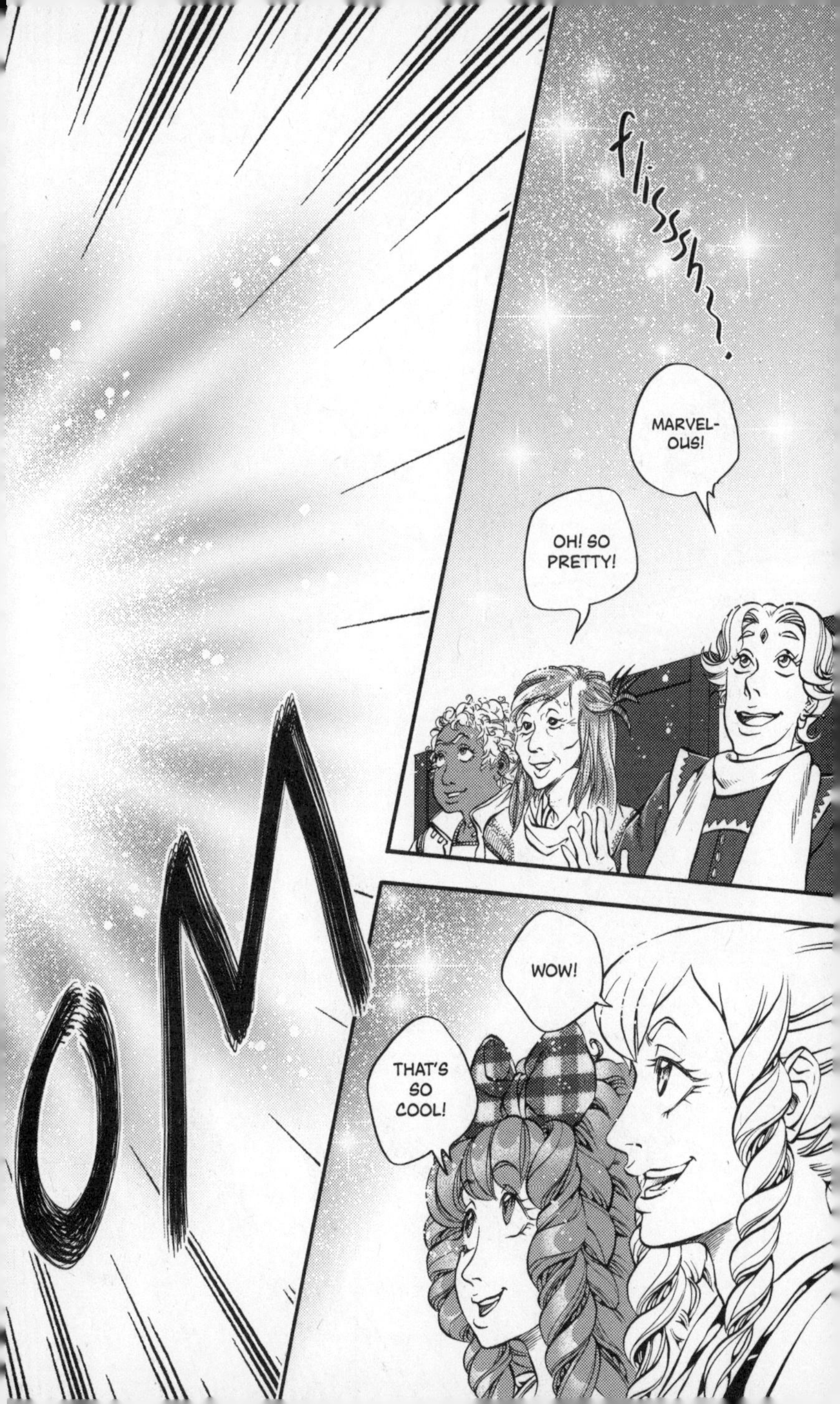
flisssh~~.
MARVEL-OUS!
OH! SO PRETTY!
WOW!
THAT'S SO COOL!
OM

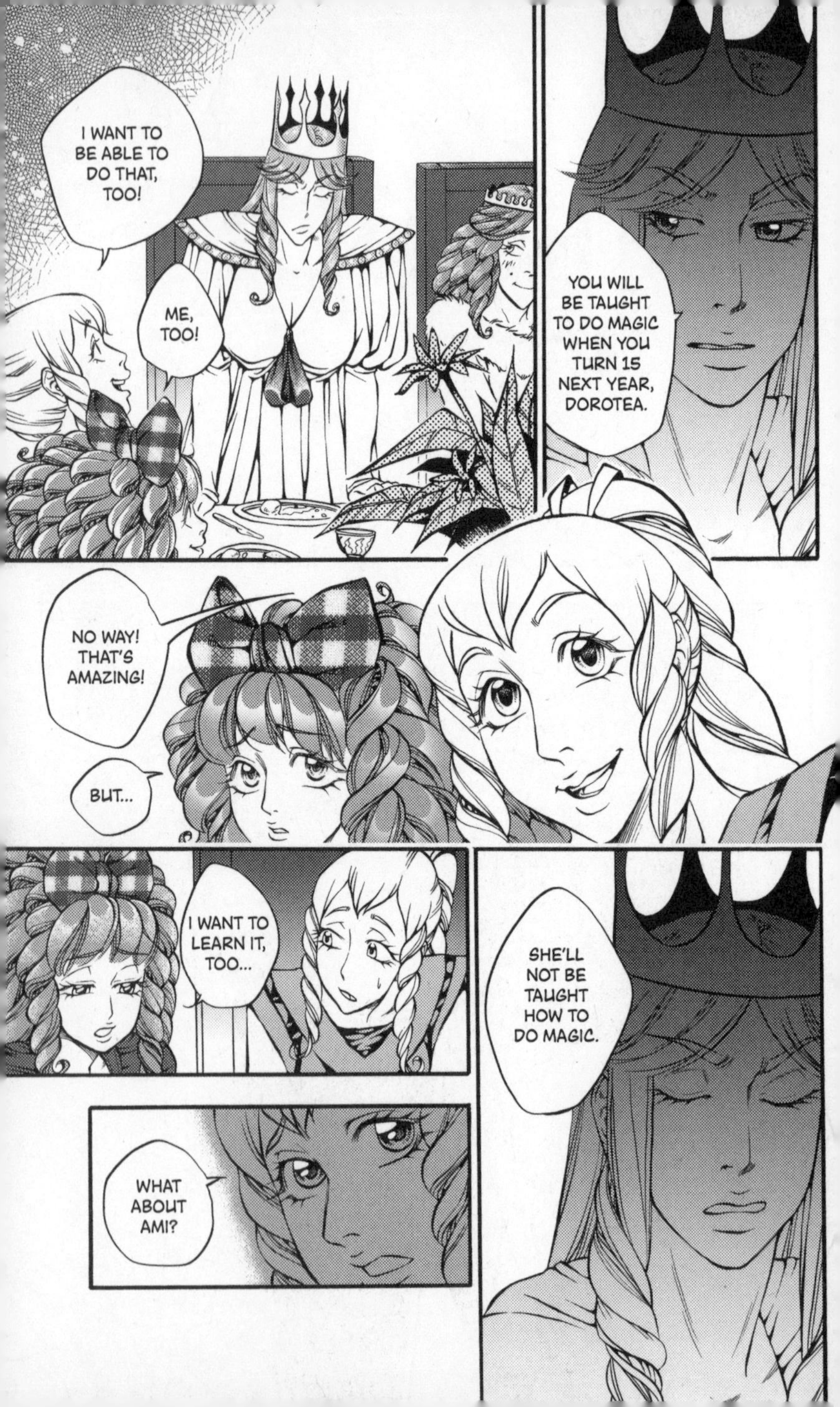
I WANT TO BE ABLE TO DO THAT, TOO!
ME, TOO!
YOU WILL BE TAUGHT TO DO MAGIC WHEN YOU TURN 15 NEXT YEAR, DOROTEA.
NO WAY! THAT'S AMAZING!
BUT...
I WANT TO LEARN IT, TOO...
WHAT ABOUT AMI?
SHE'LL NOT BE TAUGHT HOW TO DO MAGIC.

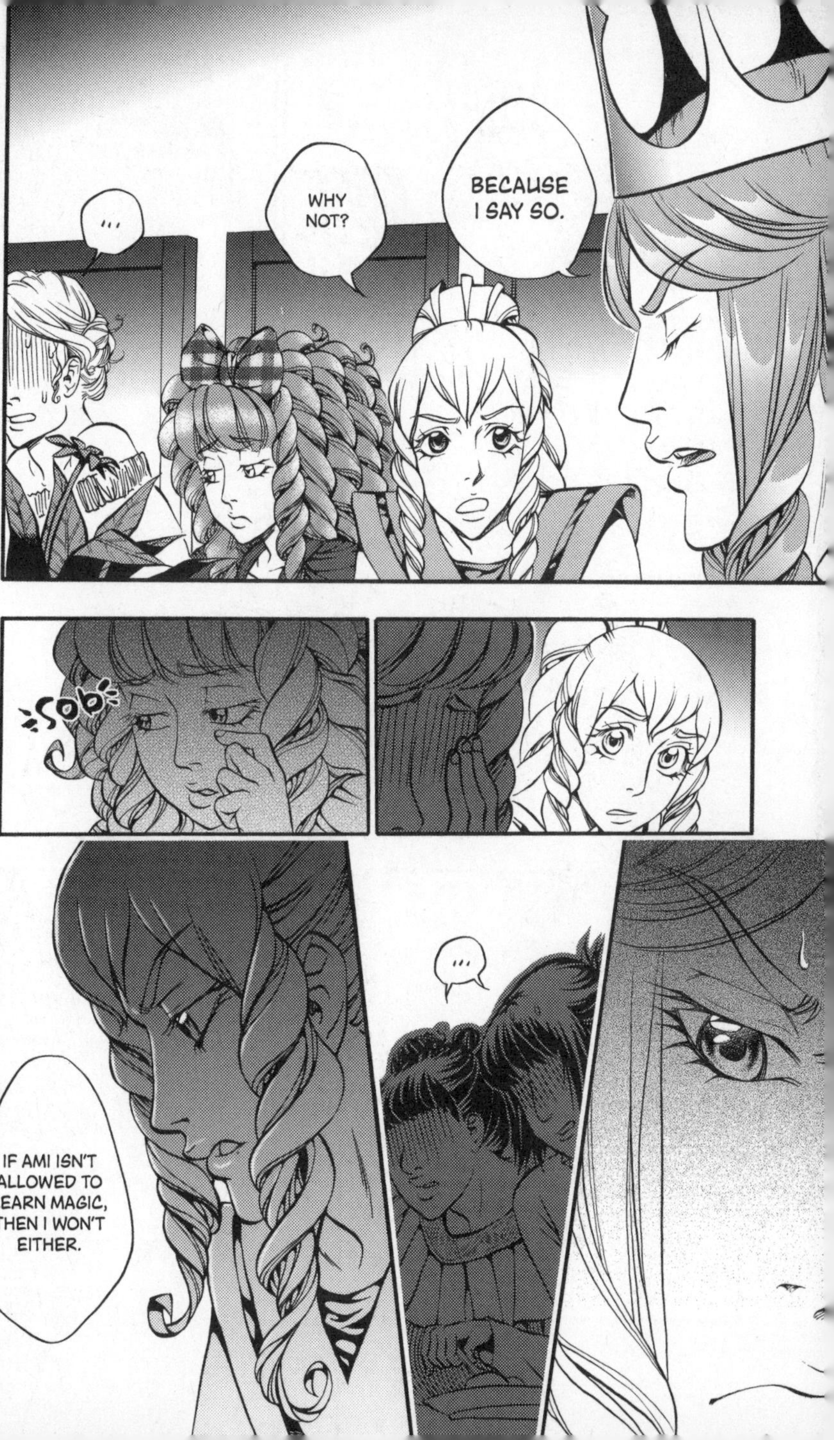
BECAUSE I SAY SO.
WHY NOT?
...
SOB
...
IF AMI ISN'T ALLOWED TO LEARN MAGIC, THEN I WON'T EITHER.

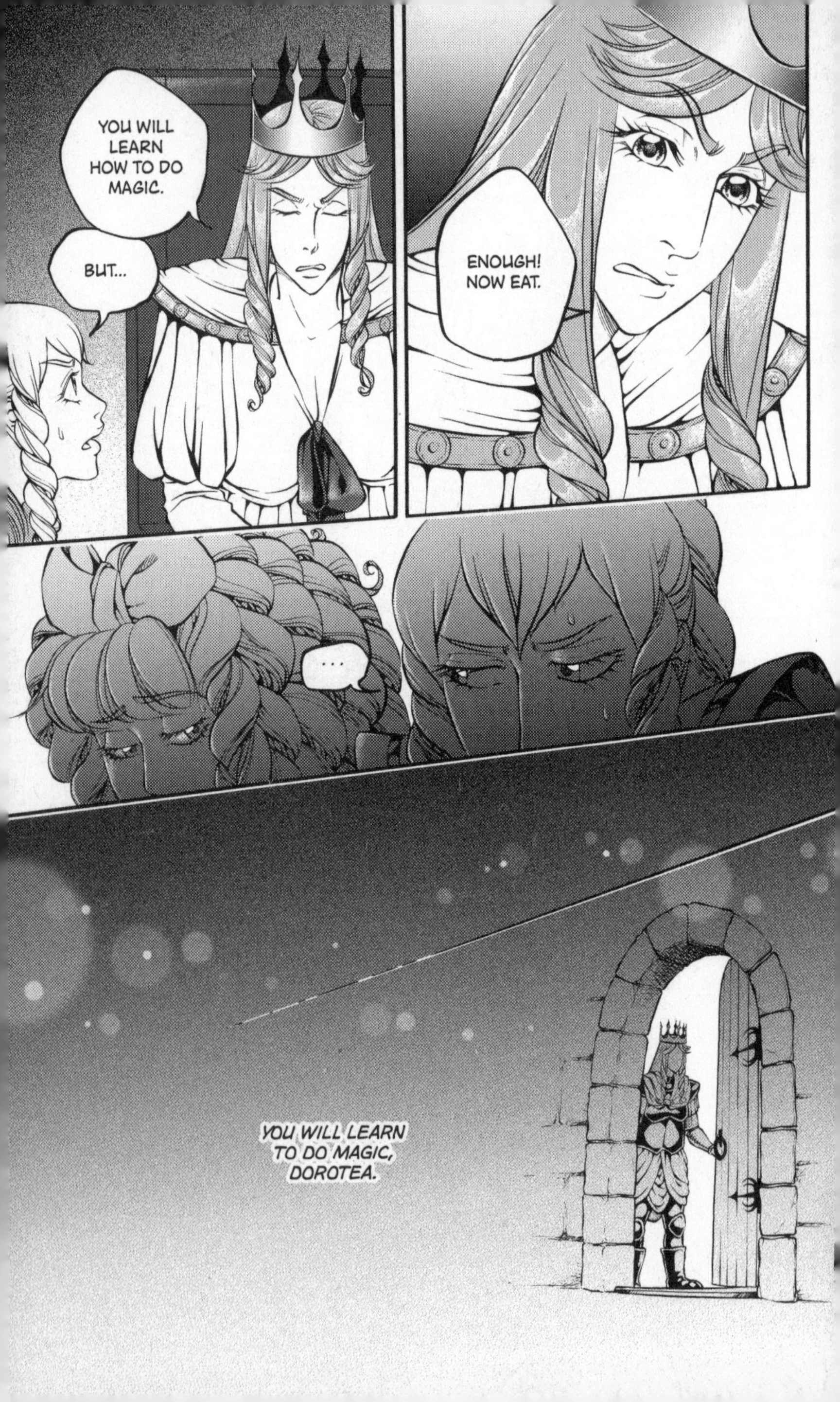
YOU WILL LEARN HOW TO DO MAGIC.
BUT...
ENOUGH! NOW EAT.
...
YOU WILL LEARN TO DO MAGIC, DOROTEA.

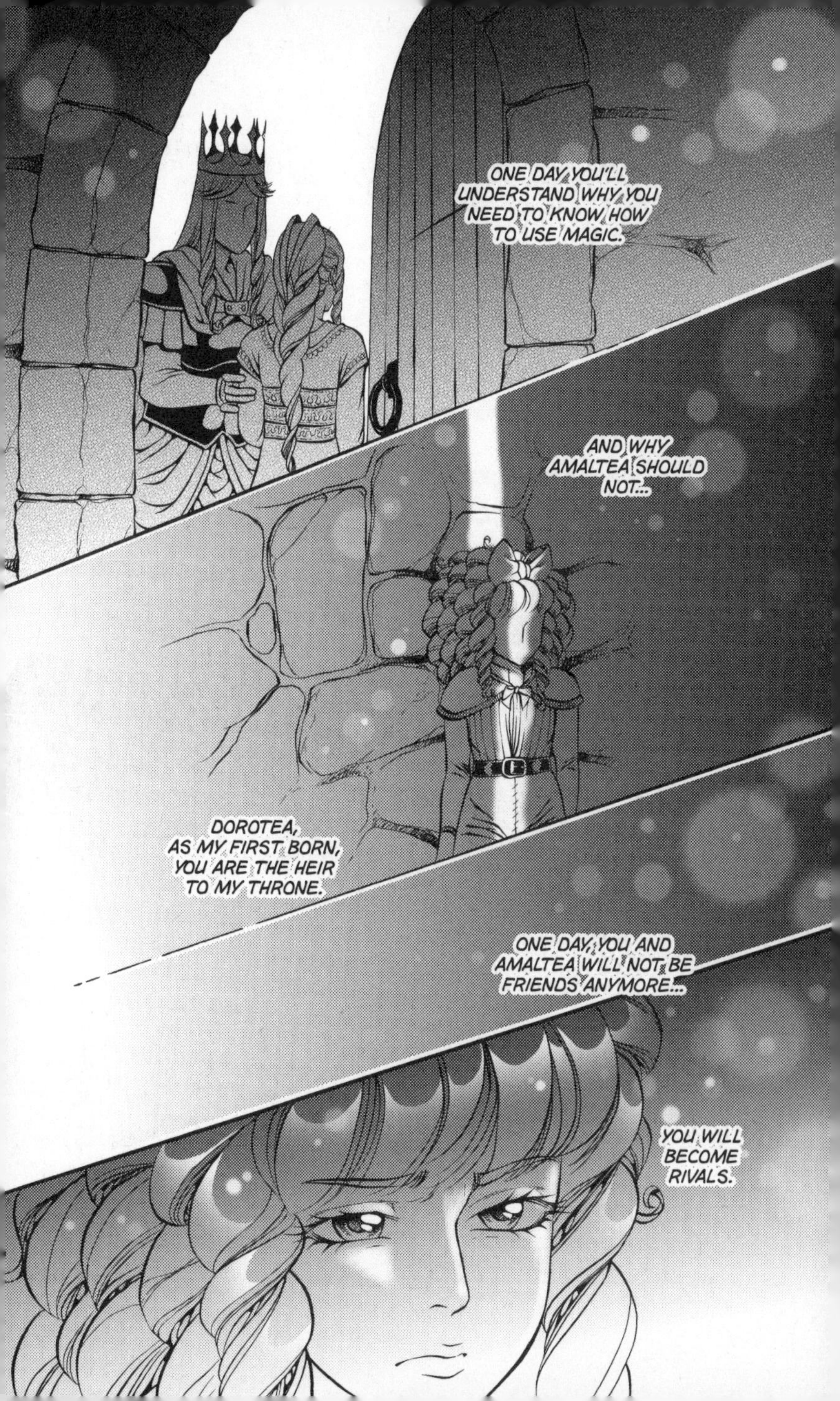
ONE DAY YOU'LL UNDERSTAND WHY YOU NEED TO KNOW HOW TO USE MAGIC.
AND WHY AMALTEA SHOULD NOT...
DOROTEA, AS MY FIRST BORN, YOU ARE THE HEIR TO MY THRONE.
ONE DAY, YOU AND AMALTEA WILL NOT BE FRIENDS ANYMORE...
YOU WILL BECOME RIVALS.

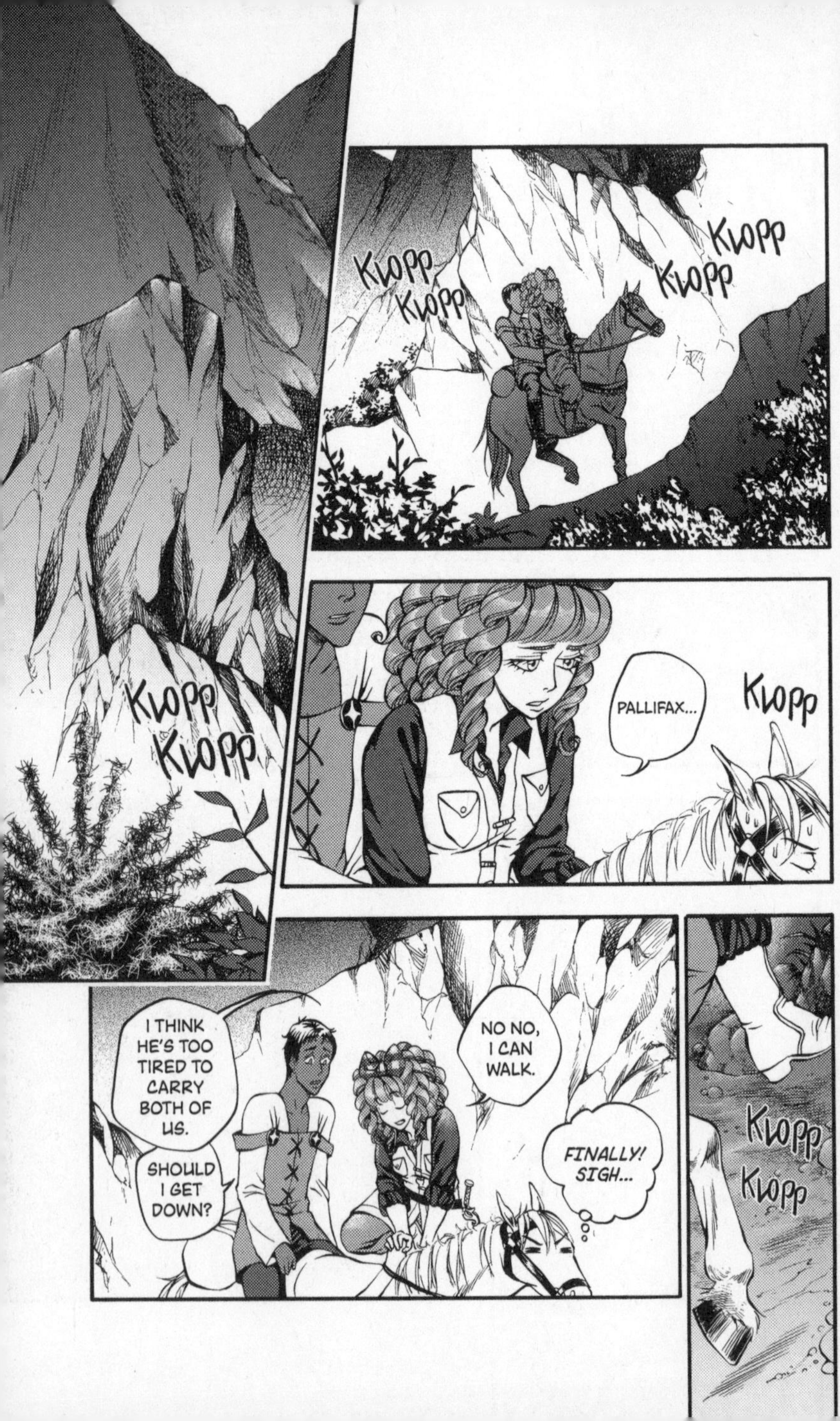
KLOPP KLOPP
KLOPP KLOPP
KLOPP KLOPP
PALLIFAX...
KLOPP
I THINK HE'S TOO TIRED TO CARRY BOTH OF US.
SHOULD I GET DOWN?
NO NO, I CAN WALK.
FINALLY! SIGH...
KLOPP KLOPP

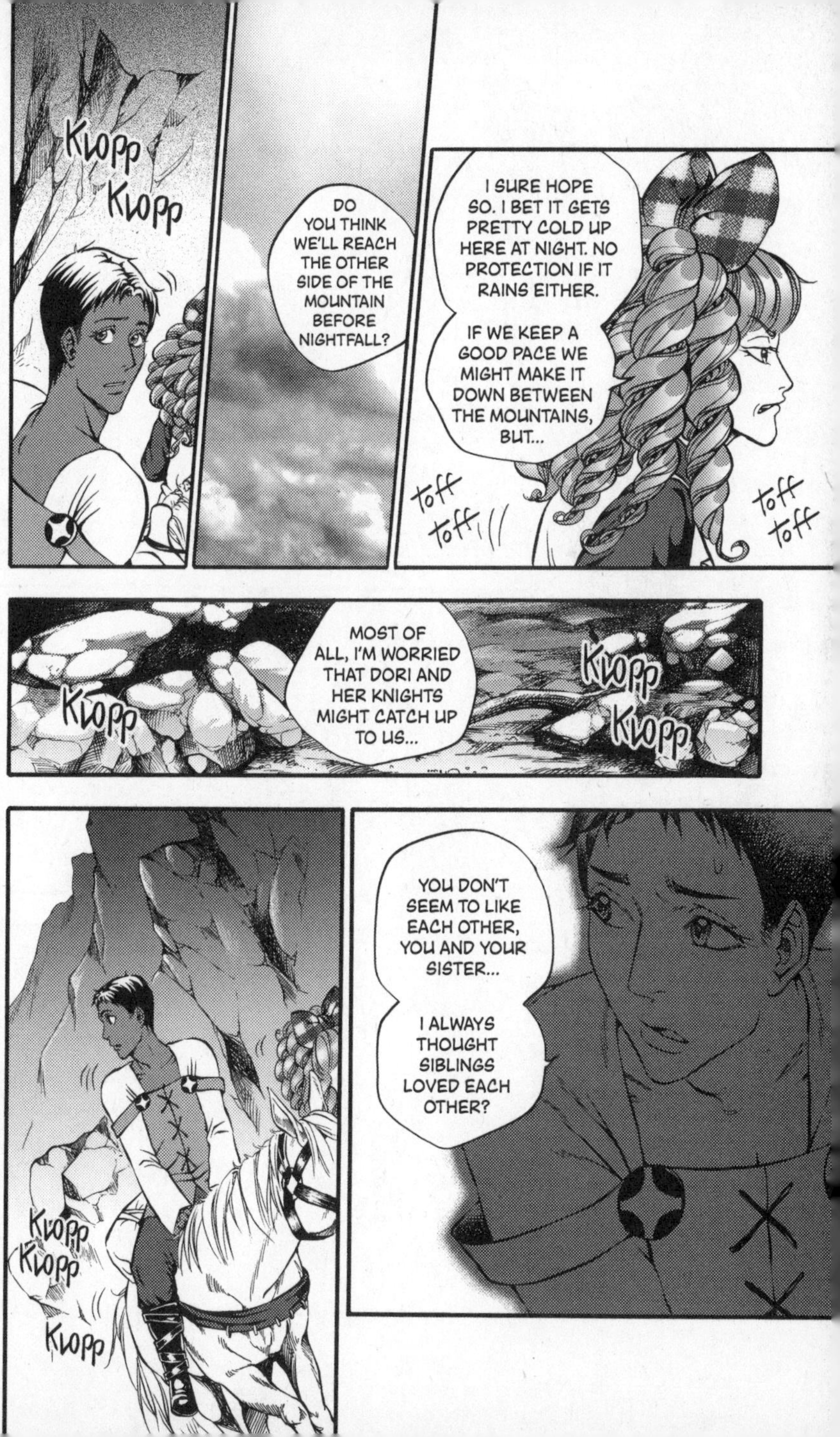
KLOPP
KLOPP
DO YOU THINK WE'LL REACH THE OTHER SIDE OF THE MOUNTAIN BEFORE NIGHTFALL?
I SURE HOPE SO. I BET IT GETS PRETTY COLD UP HERE AT NIGHT. NO PROTECTION IF IT RAINS EITHER.
IF WE KEEP A GOOD PACE WE MIGHT MAKE IT DOWN BETWEEN THE MOUNTAINS, BUT...
TOFF
TOFF
TOFF
TOFF
KLOPP
MOST OF ALL, I'M WORRIED THAT DORI AND HER KNIGHTS MIGHT CATCH UP TO US...
KLOPP
KLOPP
KLOPP
KLOPP
KLOPP
YOU DON'T SEEM TO LIKE EACH OTHER, YOU AND YOUR SISTER...
I ALWAYS THOUGHT SIBLINGS LOVED EACH OTHER?

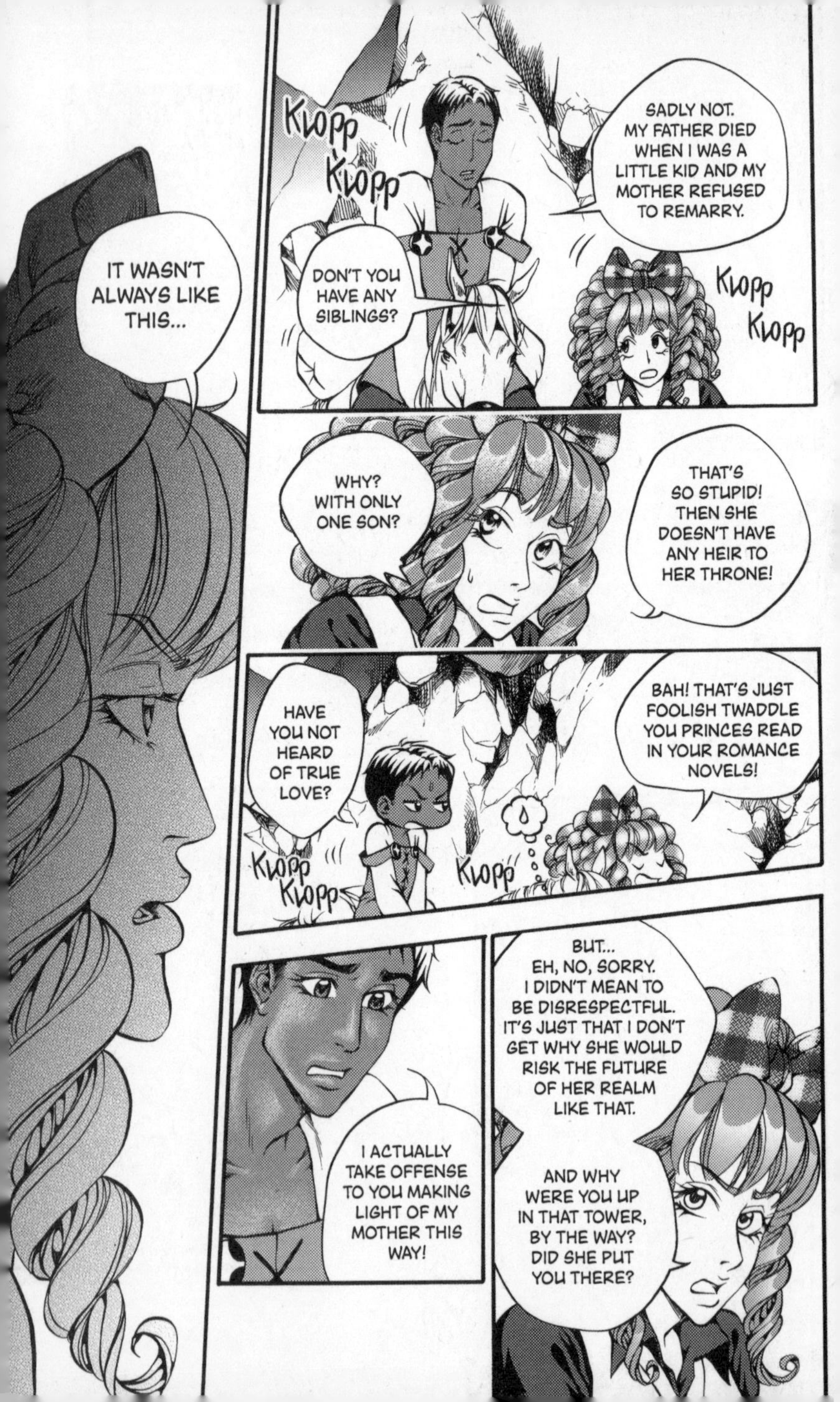
IT WASN'T ALWAYS LIKE THIS...
KLOPP KLOPP
DON'T YOU HAVE ANY SIBLINGS?
SADLY NOT. MY FATHER DIED WHEN I WAS A LITTLE KID AND MY MOTHER REFUSED TO REMARRY.
KLOPP KLOPP
WHY? WITH ONLY ONE SON?
THAT'S SO STUPID! THEN SHE DOESN'T HAVE ANY HEIR TO HER THRONE!
HAVE YOU NOT HEARD OF TRUE LOVE?
BAH! THAT'S JUST FOOLISH TWADDLE YOU PRINCES READ IN YOUR ROMANCE NOVELS!
KLOPP KLOPP
KLOPP
I ACTUALLY TAKE OFFENSE TO YOU MAKING LIGHT OF MY MOTHER THIS WAY!
BUT... EH, NO, SORRY. I DIDN'T MEAN TO BE DISRESPECTFUL. IT'S JUST THAT I DON'T GET WHY SHE WOULD RISK THE FUTURE OF HER REALM LIKE THAT.
AND WHY WERE YOU UP IN THAT TOWER, BY THE WAY? DID SHE PUT YOU THERE?

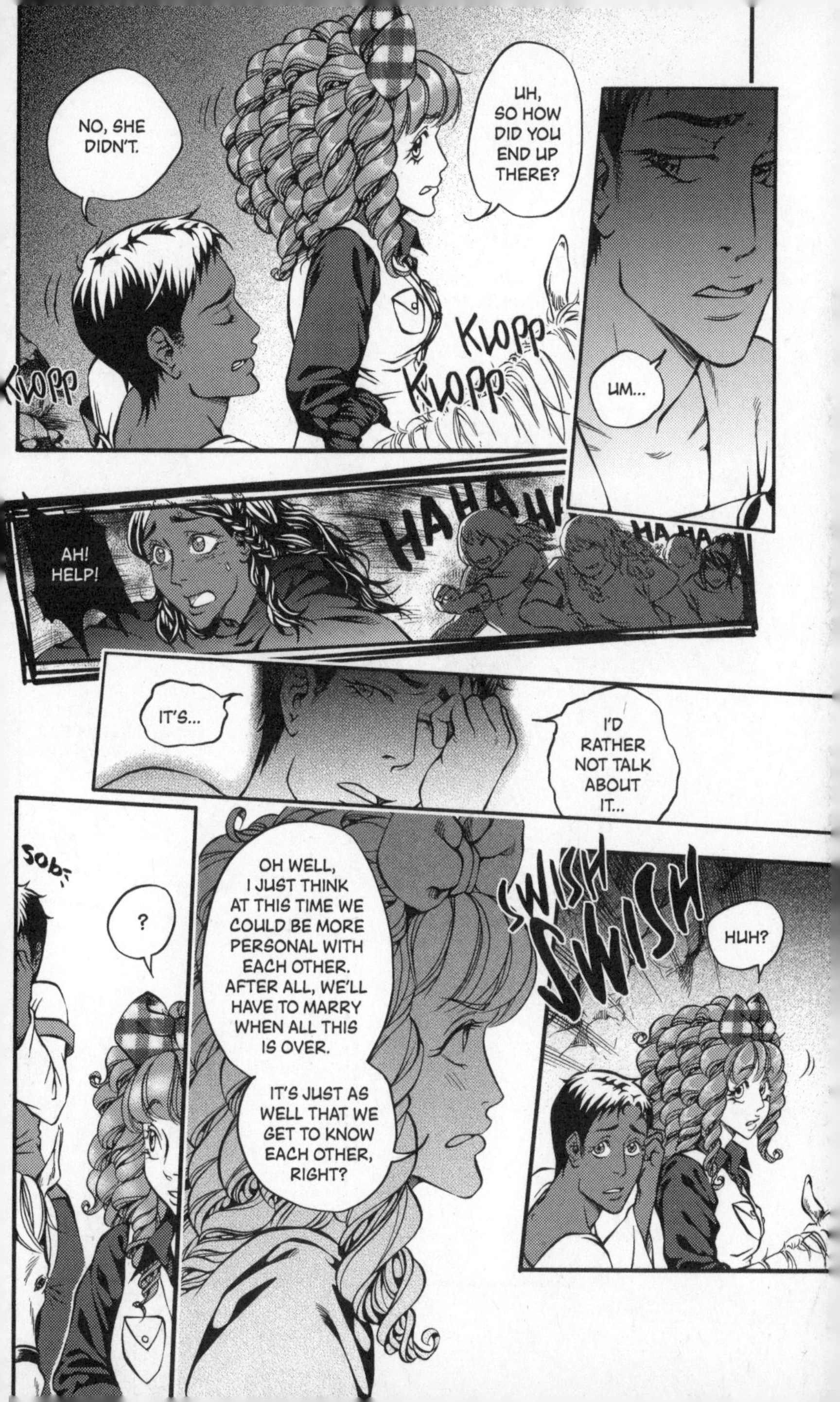
NO, SHE DIDN'T.
UH, SO HOW DID YOU END UP THERE?
KLOPP
KLOPP
KLOPP
UM...
AH! HELP!
HAHAHA
HA HA
IT'S...
I'D RATHER NOT TALK ABOUT IT...
SOB
?
OH WELL, I JUST THINK AT THIS TIME WE COULD BE MORE PERSONAL WITH EACH OTHER. AFTER ALL, WE'LL HAVE TO MARRY WHEN ALL THIS IS OVER.
IT'S JUST AS WELL THAT WE GET TO KNOW EACH OTHER, RIGHT?
SWISH SWISH
HUH?

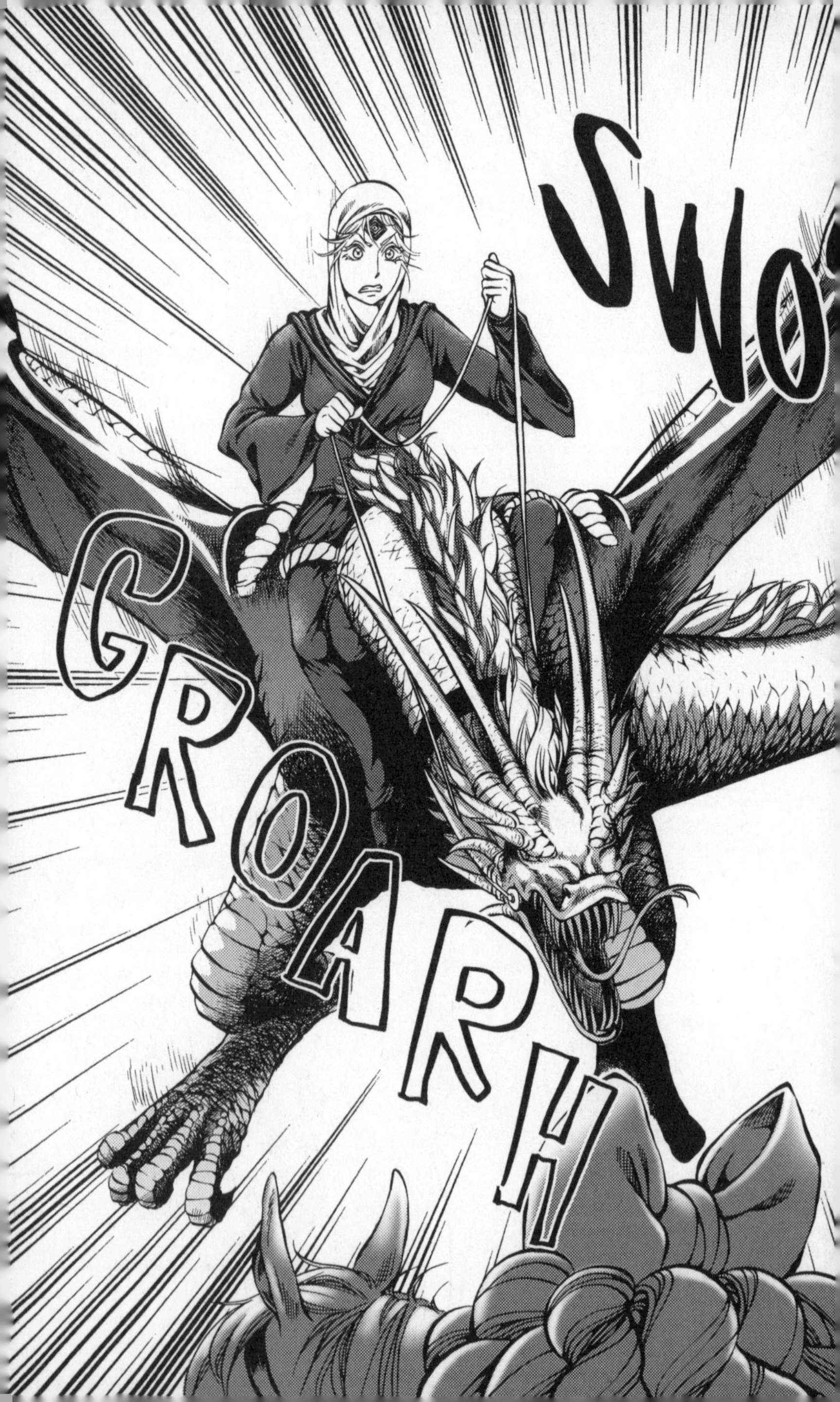
SWO
GROARH

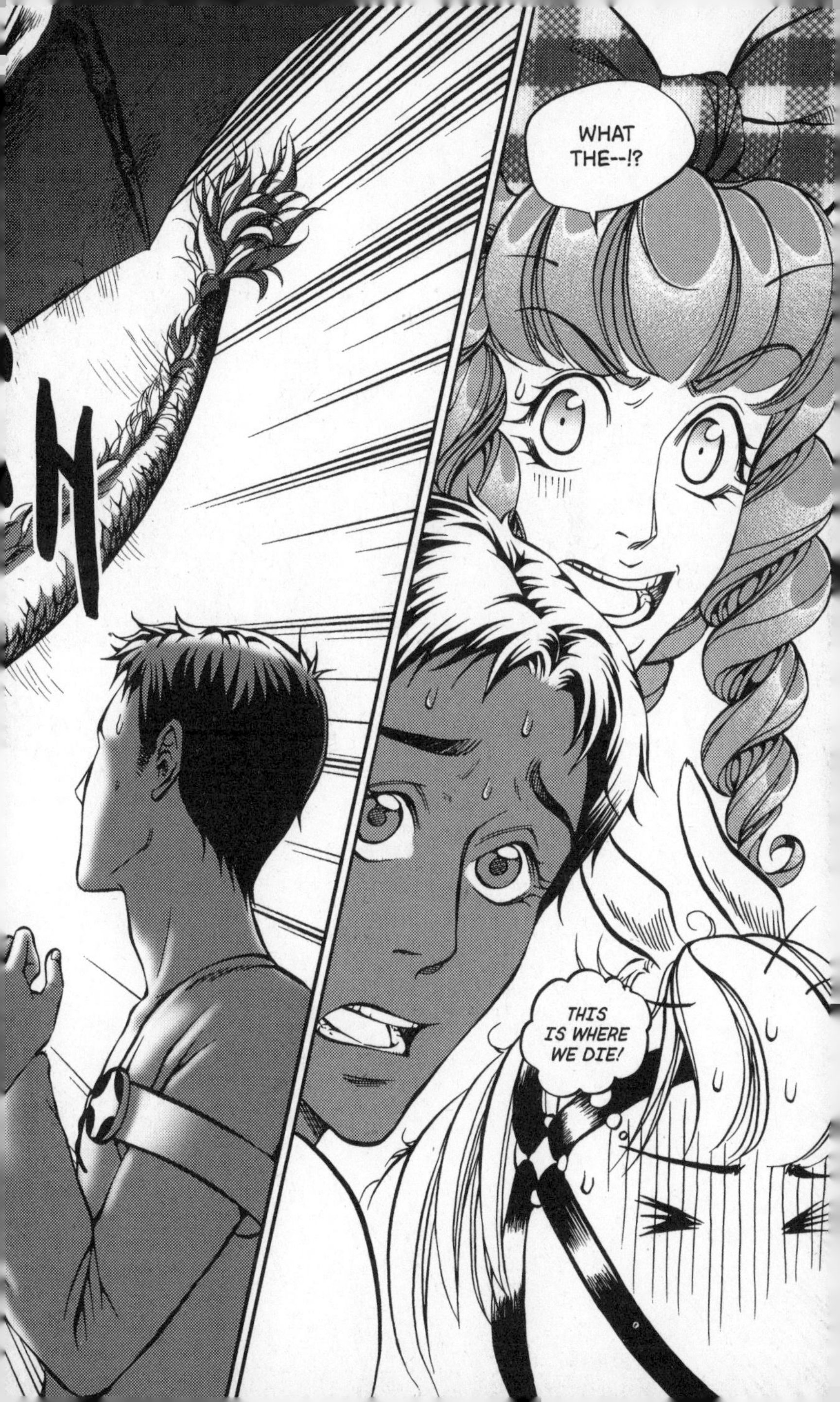
WHAT THE--!?
THIS IS WHERE WE DIE!

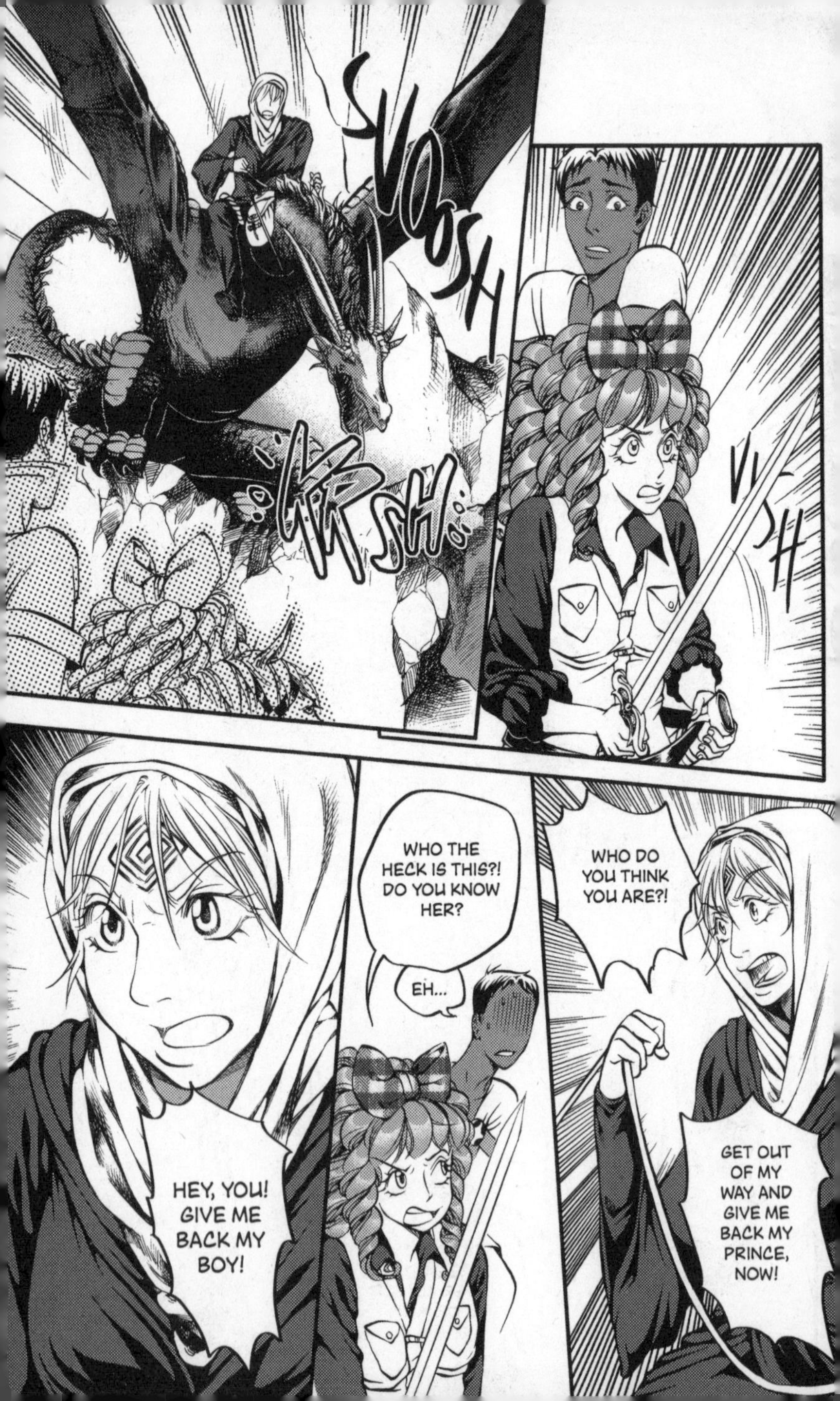
SWOOSH
KRSH
WHO DO YOU THINK YOU ARE?!
GET OUT OF MY WAY AND GIVE ME BACK MY PRINCE, NOW!
WHO THE HECK IS THIS?! DO YOU KNOW HER?
EH...
HEY, YOU! GIVE ME BACK MY BOY!

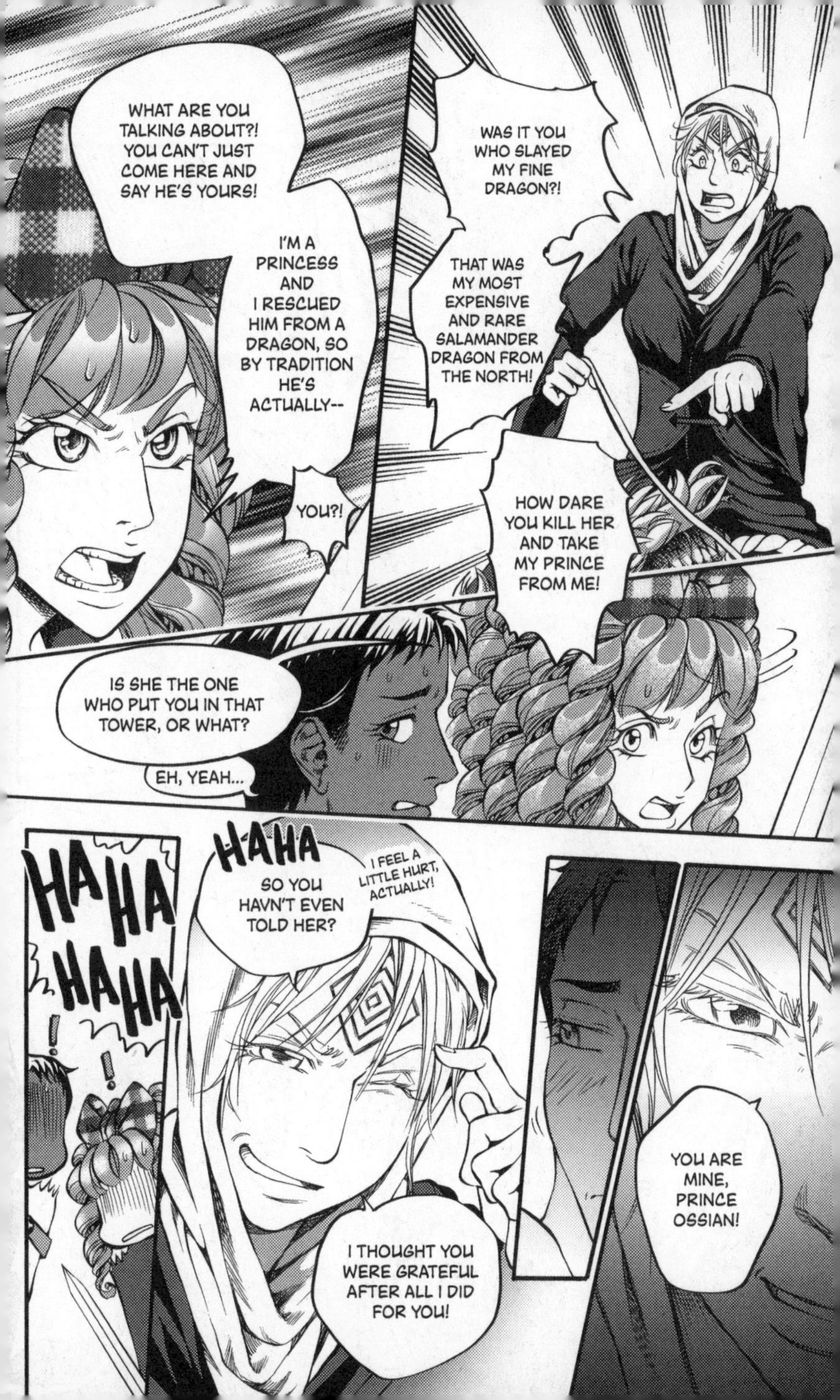
WAS IT YOU WHO SLAYED MY FINE DRAGON?!
THAT WAS MY MOST EXPENSIVE AND RARE SALAMANDER DRAGON FROM THE NORTH!
HOW DARE YOU KILL HER AND TAKE MY PRINCE FROM ME!
WHAT ARE YOU TALKING ABOUT?! YOU CAN'T JUST COME HERE AND SAY HE'S YOURS!
I'M A PRINCESS AND I RESCUED HIM FROM A DRAGON, SO BY TRADITION HE'S ACTUALLY--
YOU?!
IS SHE THE ONE WHO PUT YOU IN THAT TOWER, OR WHAT?
EH, YEAH...
YOU ARE MINE, PRINCE OSSIAN!
HAHA
SO YOU HAVN'T EVEN TOLD HER?
I FEEL A LITTLE HURT, ACTUALLY!
I THOUGHT YOU WERE GRATEFUL AFTER ALL I DID FOR YOU!
HAHAHAHAHA
! !

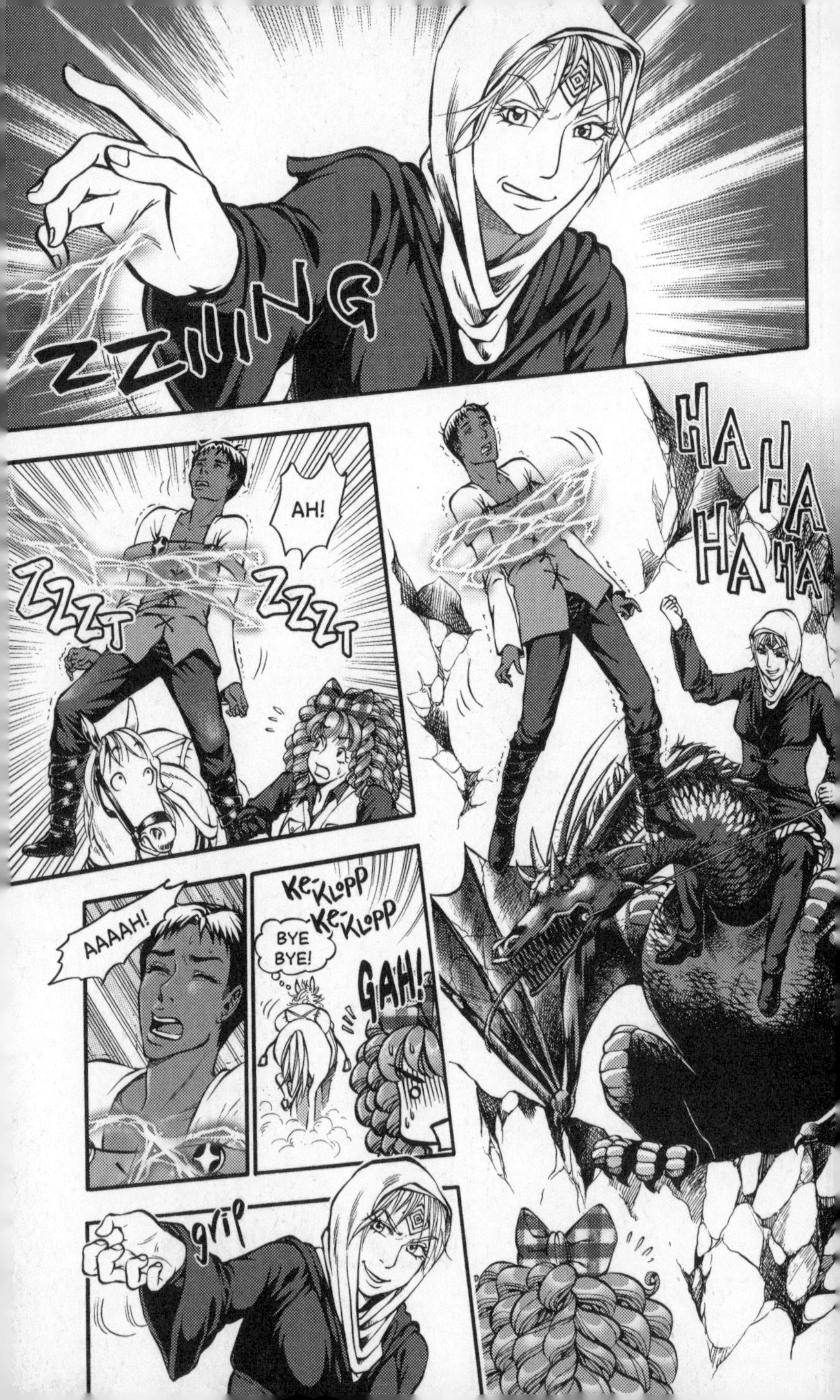
ZZIIIING
HA HA HA HA HA HA
AH!
ZZZZT
ZZZZT
KE-KLOPP KE-KLOPP
BYE BYE!
GAH!
AAAAH!
grip

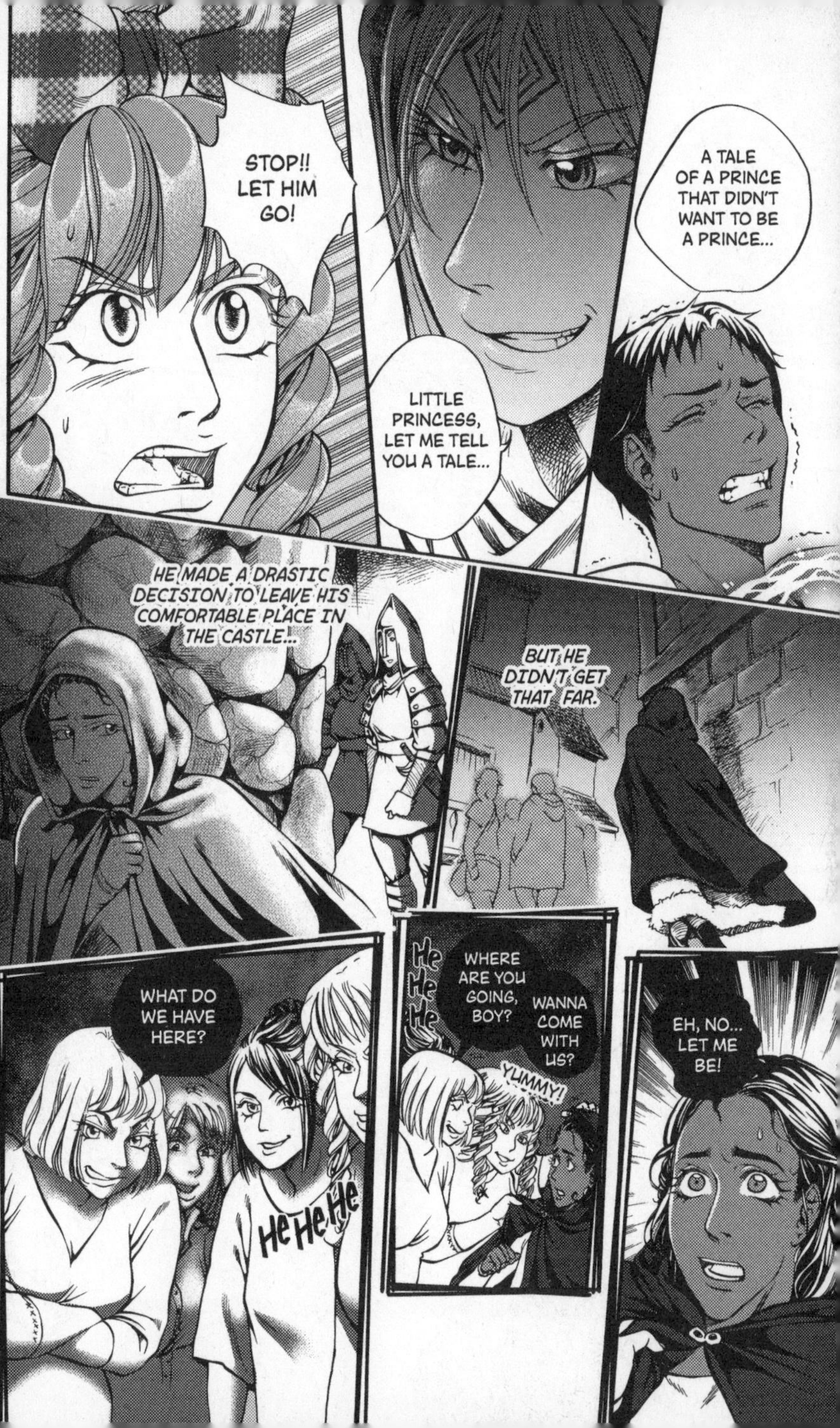
STOP!! LET HIM GO!
LITTLE PRINCESS, LET ME TELL YOU A TALE...
A TALE OF A PRINCE THAT DIDN'T WANT TO BE A PRINCE...
HE MADE A DRASTIC DECISION TO LEAVE HIS COMFORTABLE PLACE IN THE CASTLE...
BUT HE DIDN'T GET THAT FAR.
WHAT DO WE HAVE HERE?
He He He
He He He
WHERE ARE YOU GOING, BOY?
WANNA COME WITH US?
YUMMY!
EH, NO... LET ME BE!

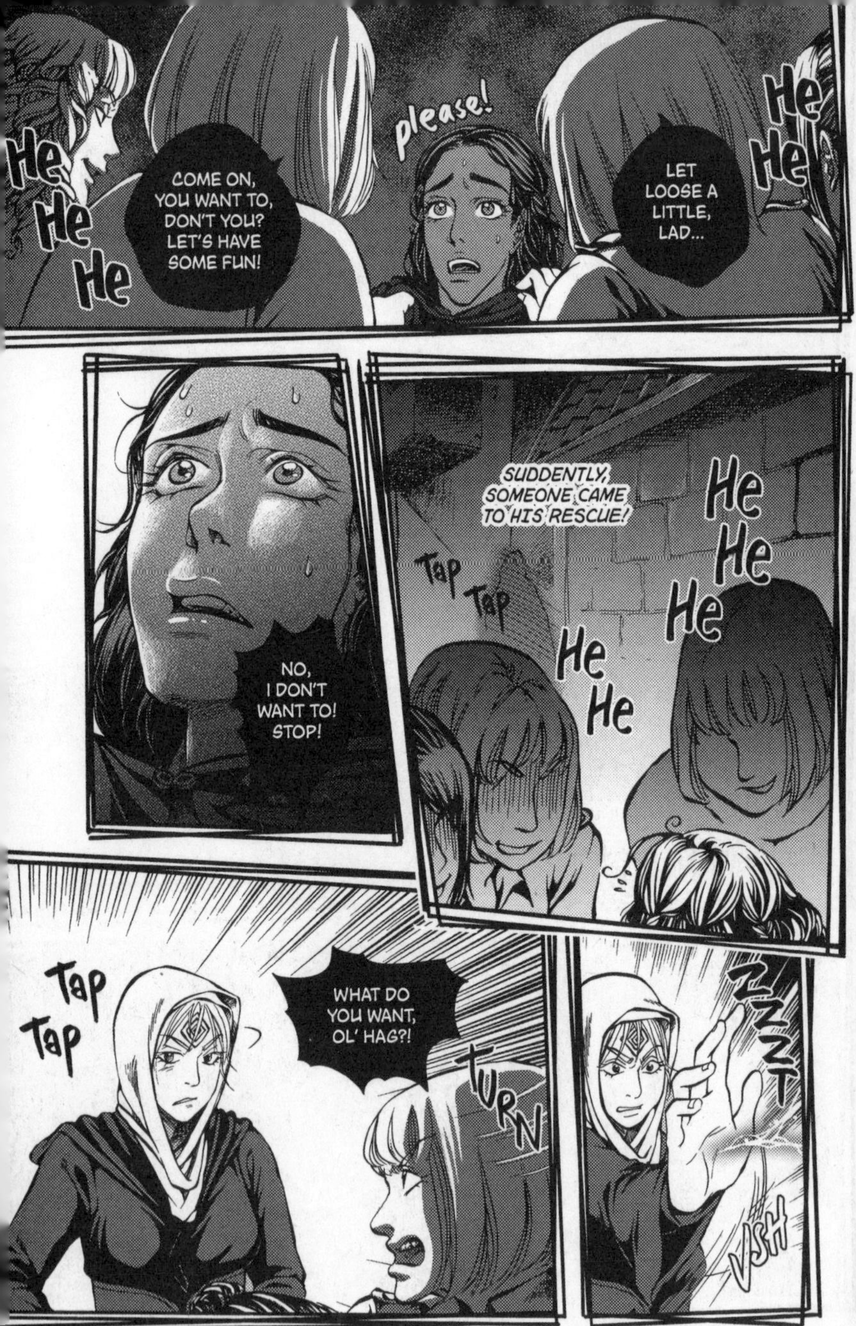
He He He
COME ON, YOU WANT TO, DON'T YOU? LET'S HAVE SOME FUN!
please!
LET LOOSE A LITTLE, LAD...
He He
NO, I DON'T WANT TO! STOP!
SUDDENLY, SOMEONE CAME TO HIS RESCUE!
Tap Tap
He He He
He He
Tap Tap
WHAT DO YOU WANT, OL' HAG?!
TURN
ZZZT
VSH

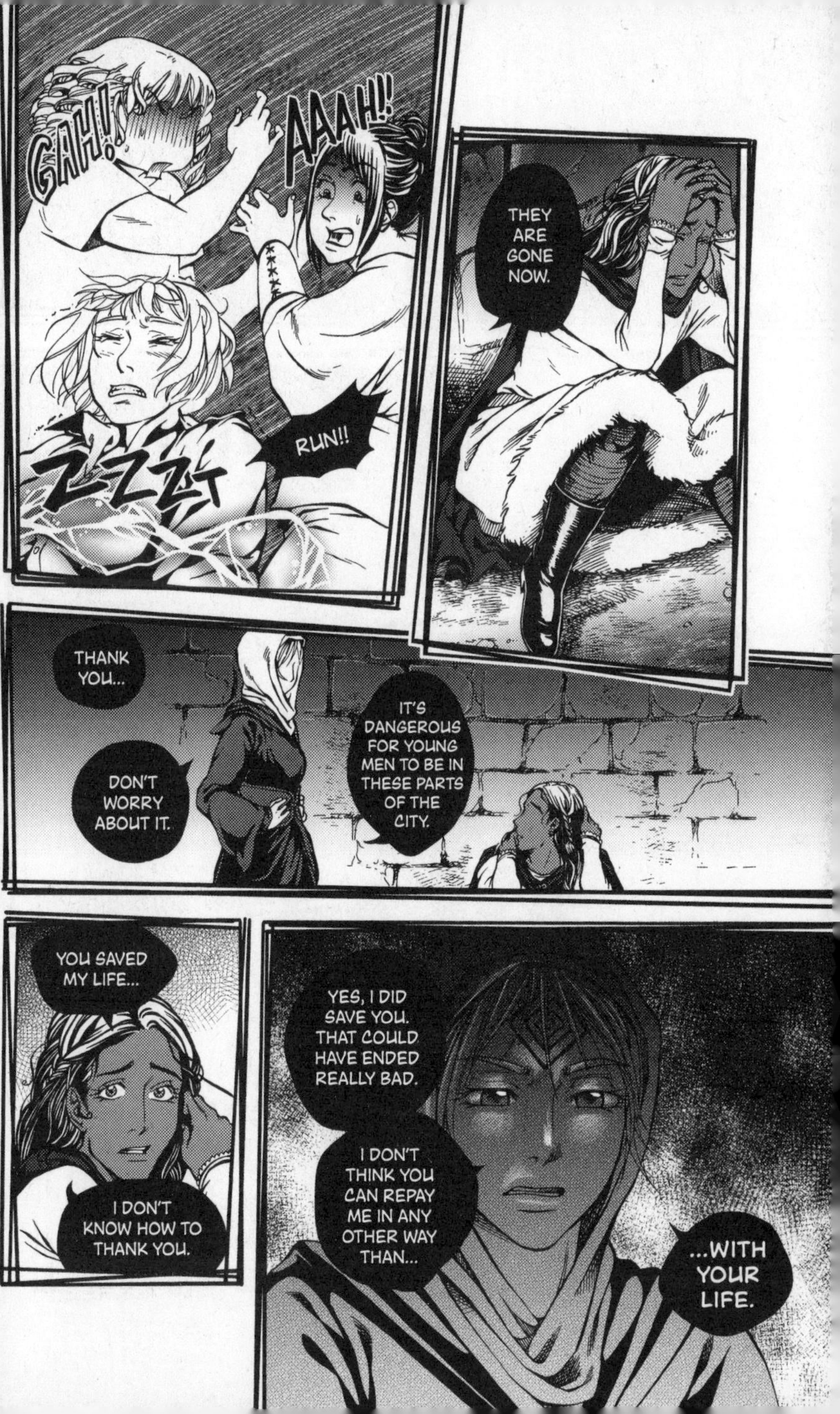
GAH!
AAAH!!
ZZZZT
RUN!!
THEY ARE GONE NOW.
THANK YOU...
DON'T WORRY ABOUT IT.
IT'S DANGEROUS FOR YOUNG MEN TO BE IN THESE PARTS OF THE CITY.
YOU SAVED MY LIFE...
I DON'T KNOW HOW TO THANK YOU.
YES, I DID SAVE YOU. THAT COULD HAVE ENDED REALLY BAD.
I DON'T THINK YOU CAN REPAY ME IN ANY OTHER WAY THAN...
...WITH YOUR LIFE.

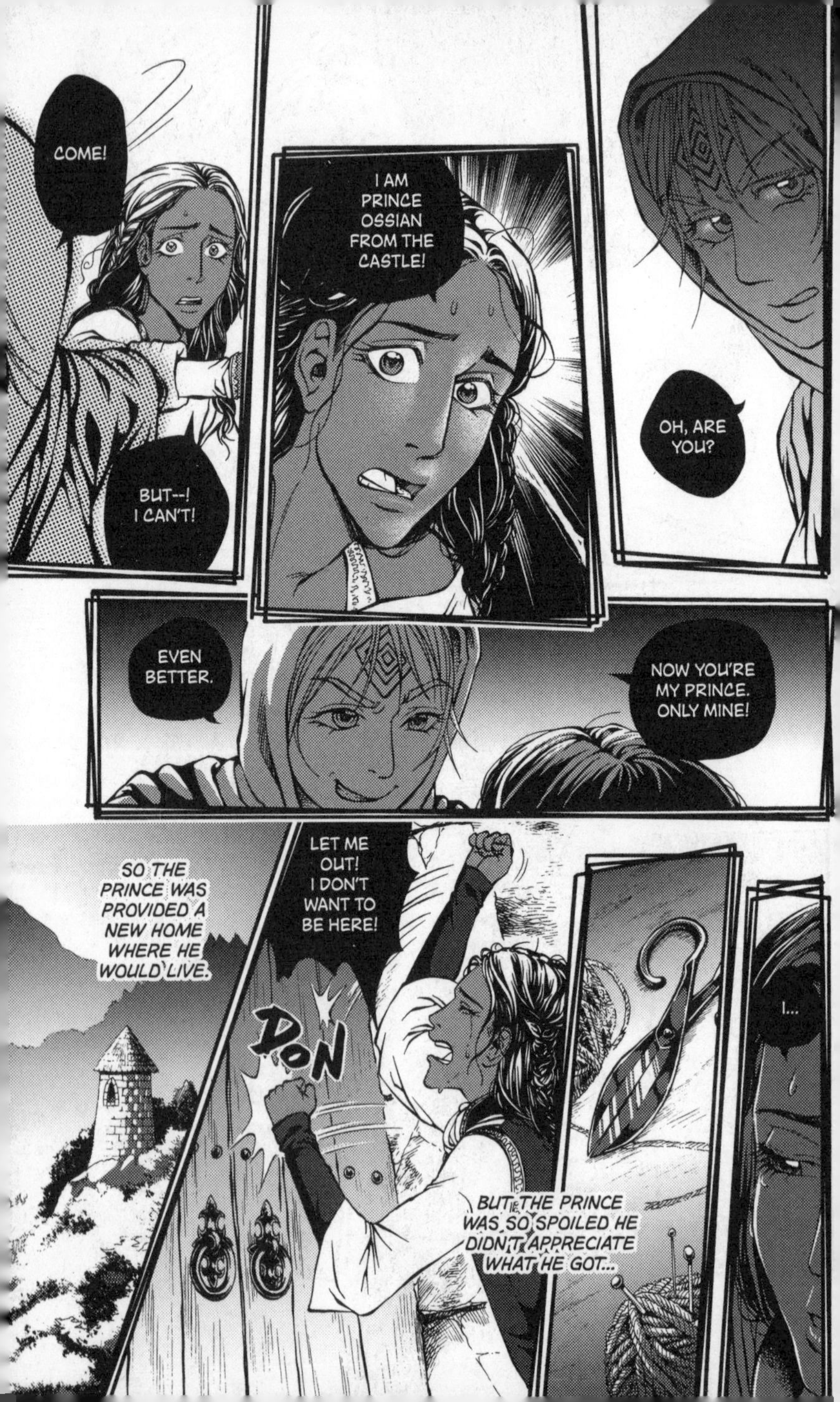
COME!
BUT--! I CAN'T!
I AM PRINCE OSSIAN FROM THE CASTLE!
OH, ARE YOU?
EVEN BETTER.
NOW YOU'RE MY PRINCE. ONLY MINE!
SO THE PRINCE WAS PROVIDED A NEW HOME WHERE HE WOULD LIVE.
LET ME OUT! I DON'T WANT TO BE HERE!
DON
BUT THE PRINCE WAS SO SPOILED HE DIDN'T APPRECIATE WHAT HE GOT...
I...

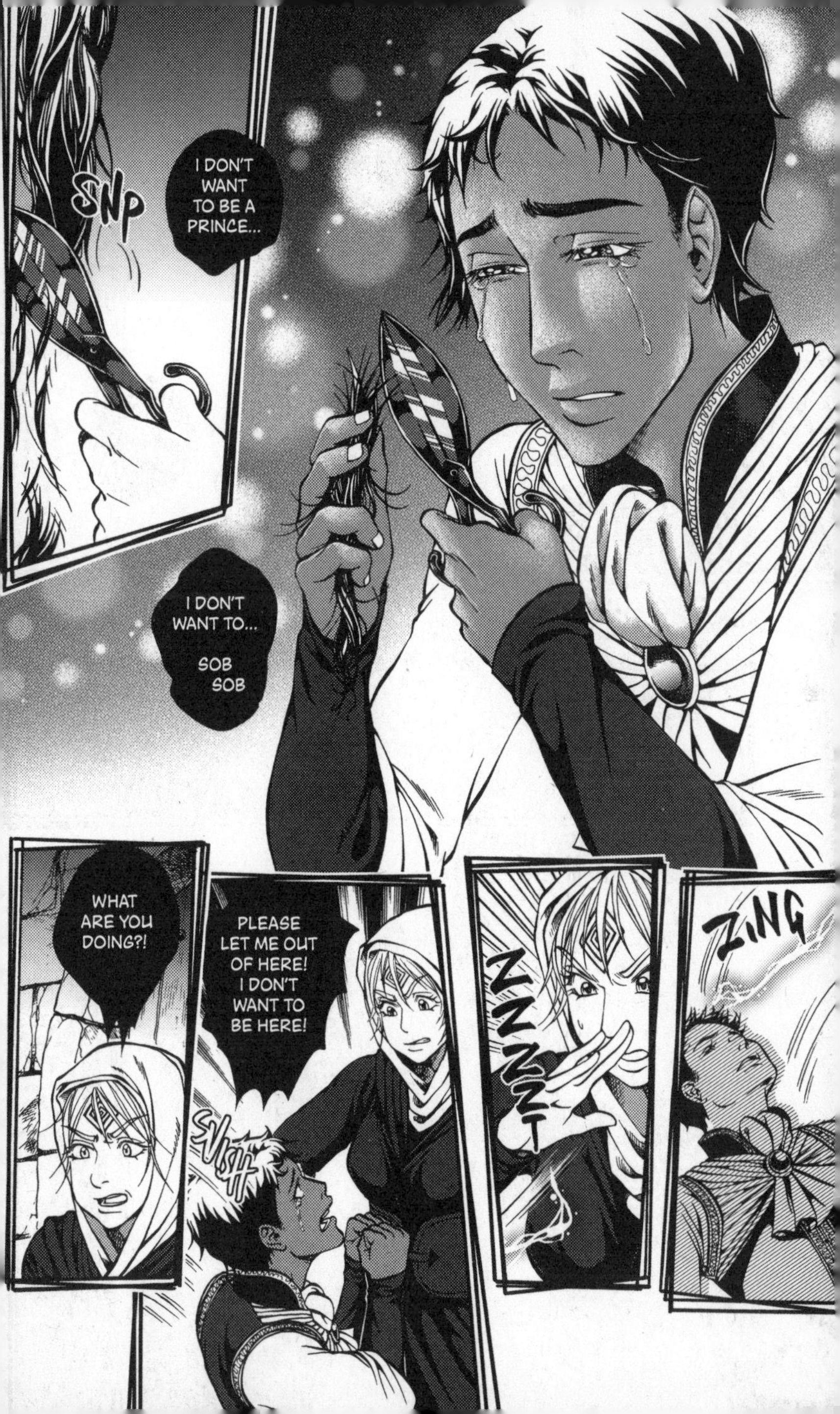
SNP
I DON'T WANT TO BE A PRINCE...
I DON'T WANT TO...
SOB SOB
WHAT ARE YOU DOING?!
PLEASE LET ME OUT OF HERE! I DON'T WANT TO BE HERE!
SWISH
ZZZZZT
ZING

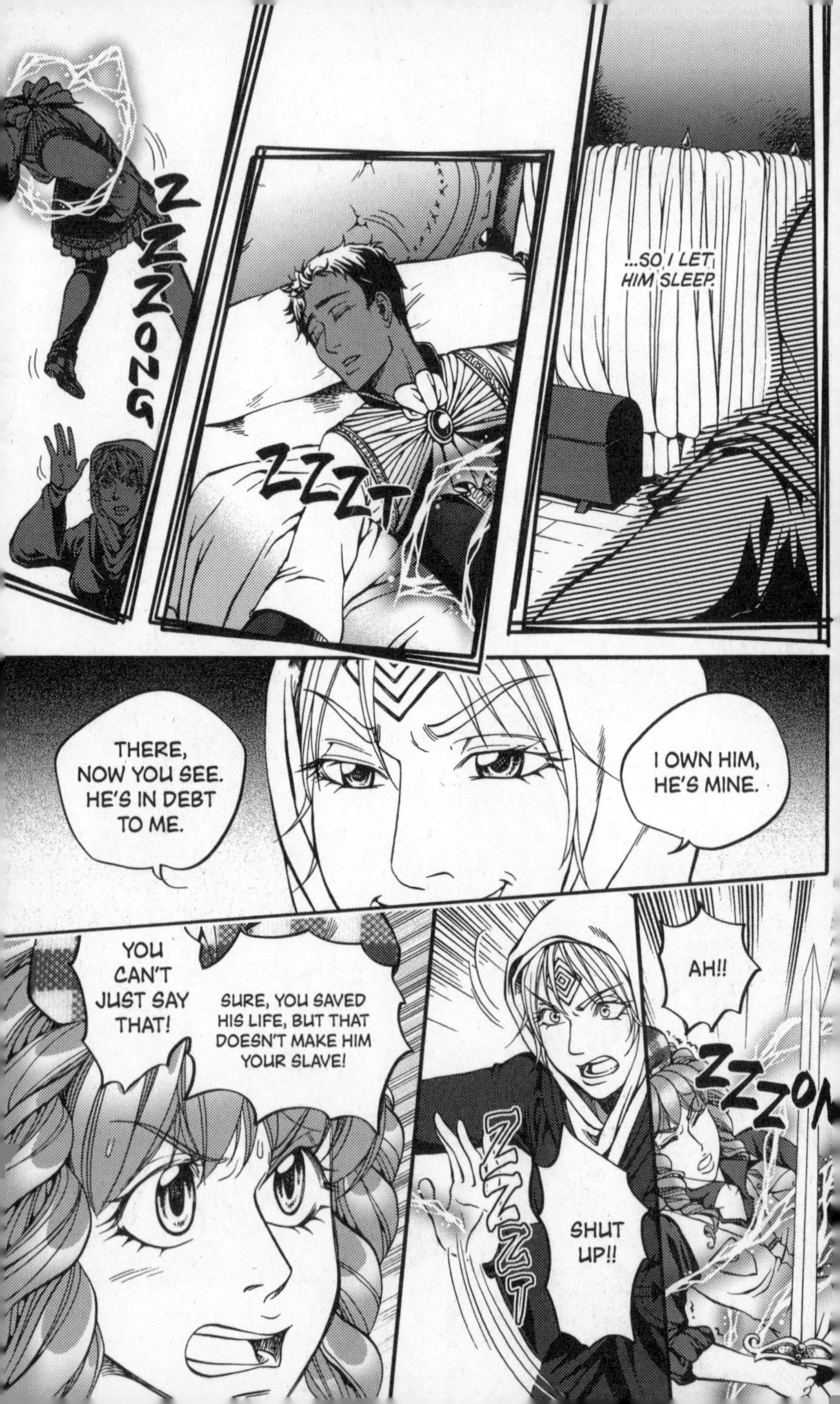
ZZZZONG
ZZZZT
...SO I LET HIM SLEEP.
THERE, NOW YOU SEE. HE'S IN DEBT TO ME.
I OWN HIM, HE'S MINE.
YOU CAN'T JUST SAY THAT!
SURE, YOU SAVED HIS LIFE, BUT THAT DOESN'T MAKE HIM YOUR SLAVE!
AH!!
ZZZONG
ZZZZT
SHUT UP!!

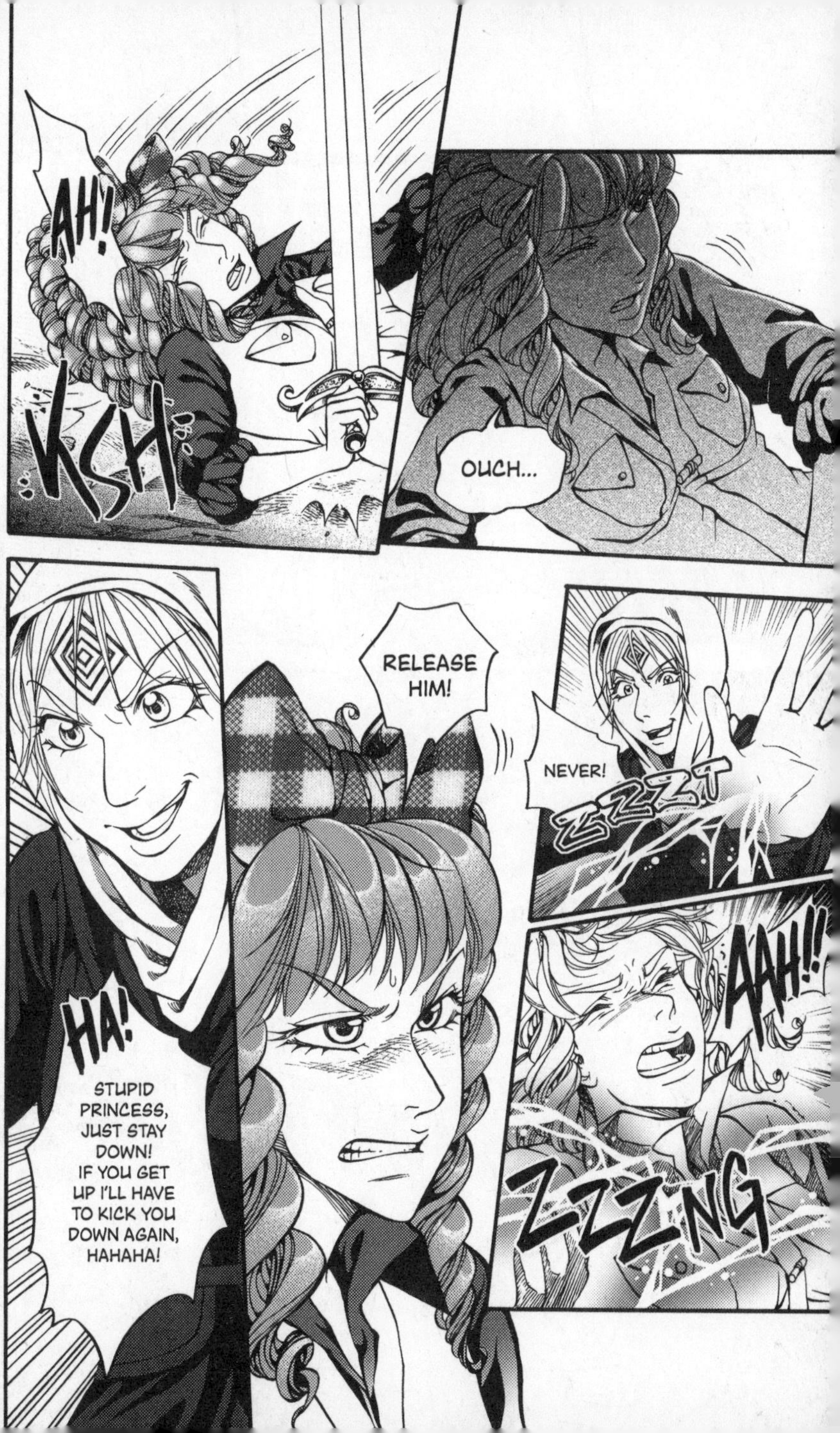
AH!
KSH
OUCH...
HA!
STUPID PRINCESS, JUST STAY DOWN! IF YOU GET UP I'LL HAVE TO KICK YOU DOWN AGAIN, HAHAHA!
RELEASE HIM!
NEVER!
ZZZZT
AAH!!
ZZZZNG

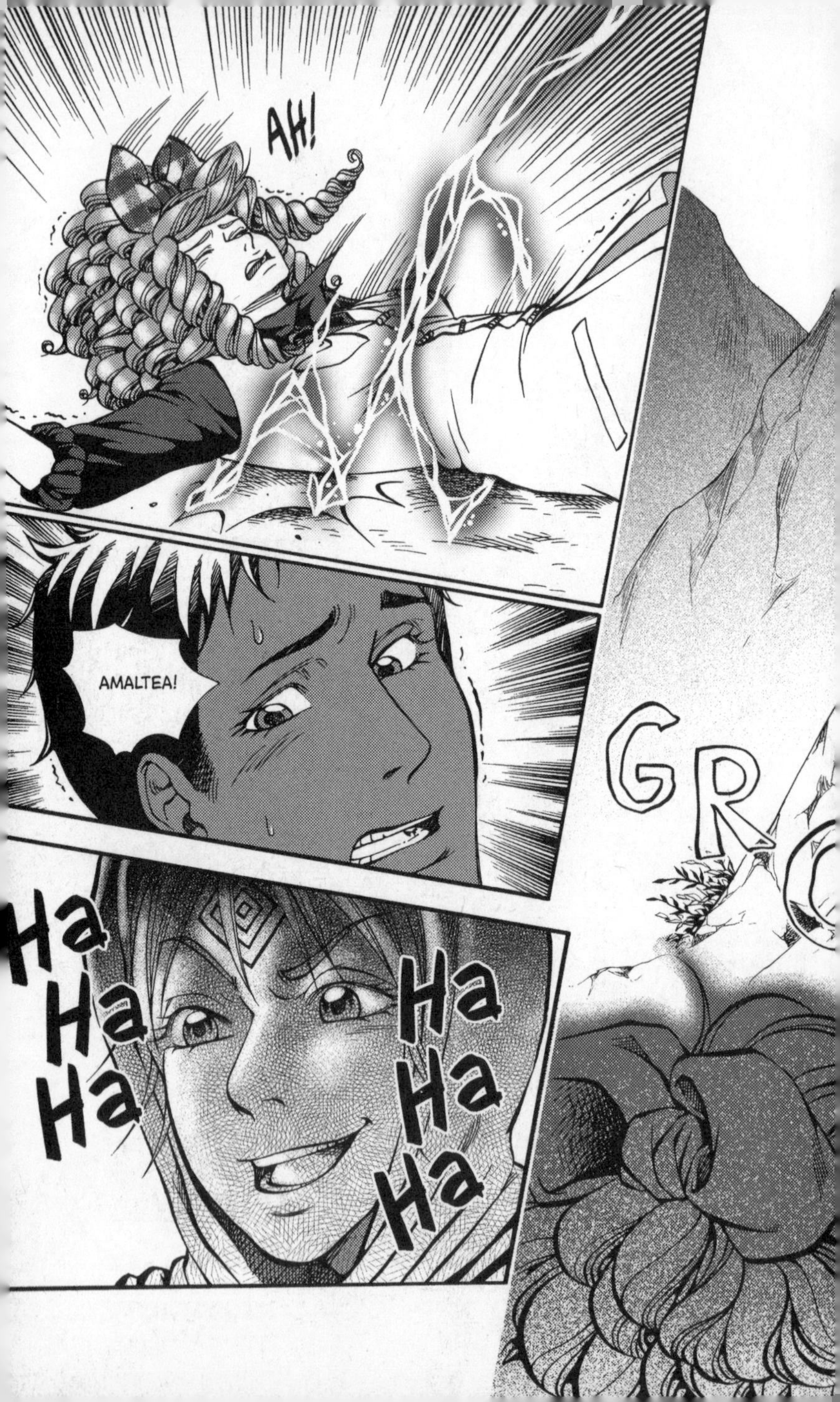
AH!
AMALTEA!
Ha Ha Ha
Ha Ha Ha
GR

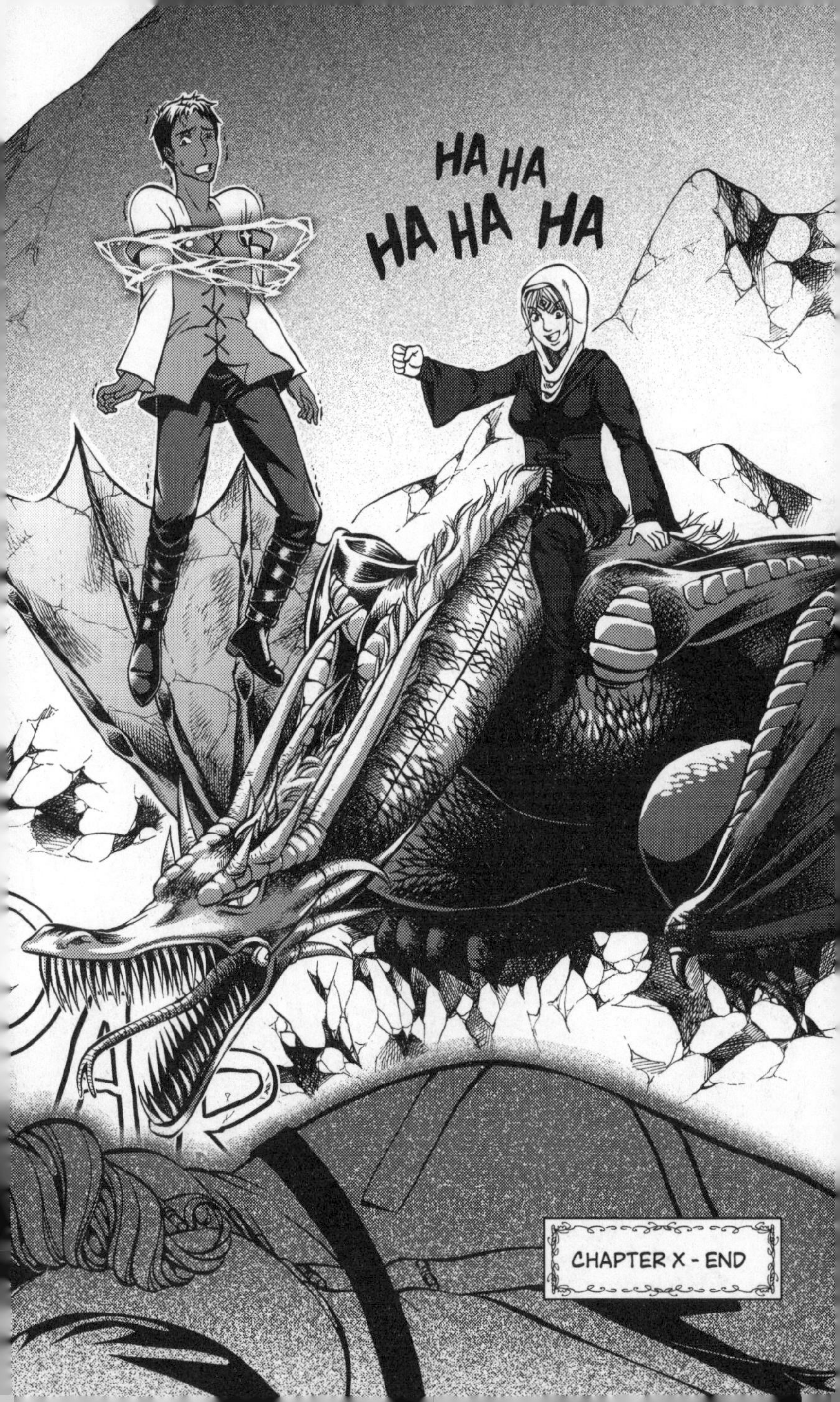
HA HA
HA HA HA
CHAPTER X - END

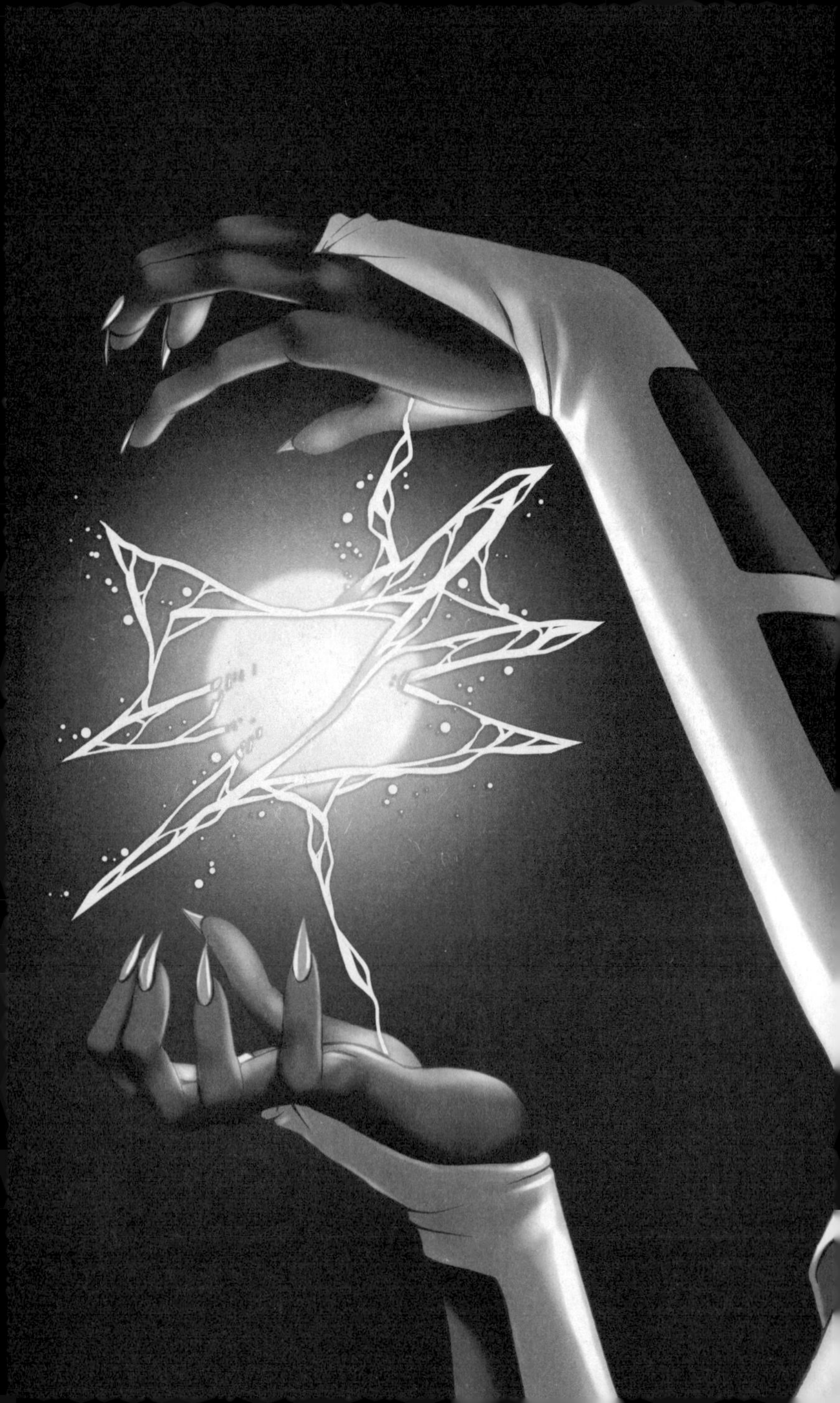

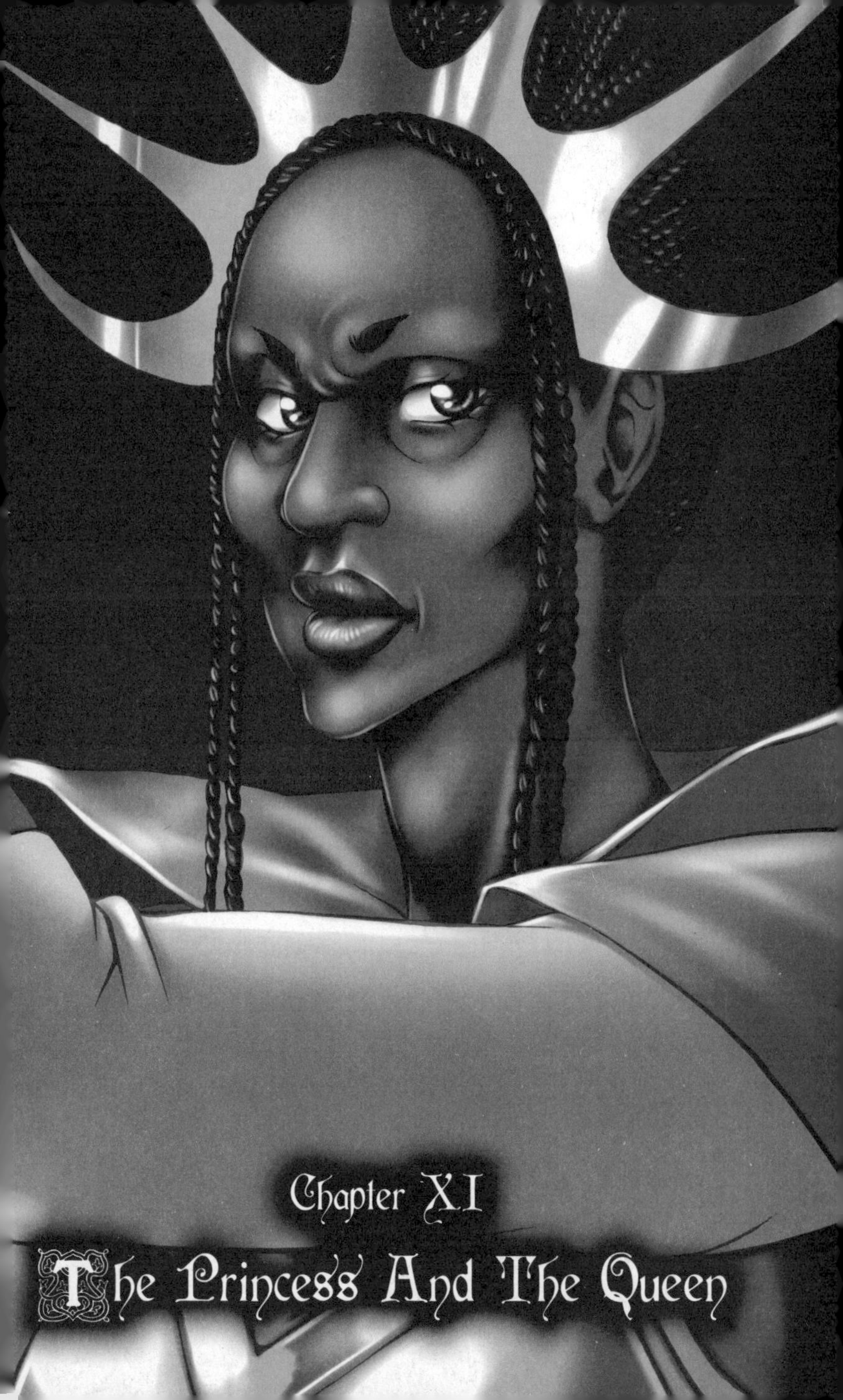

Chapter XI

The Princess And The Queen

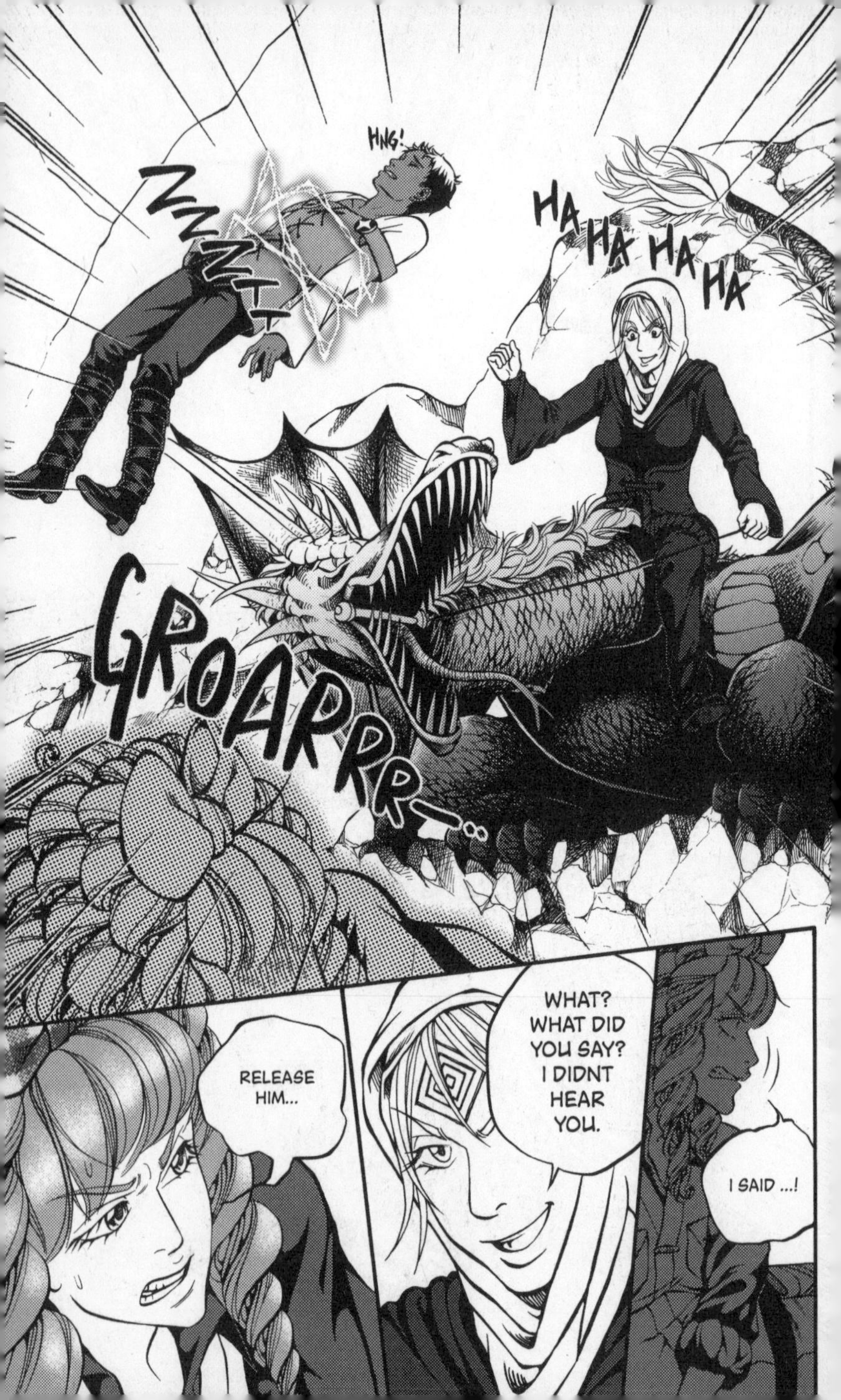
HNG!
HA HA HA HA HA
GROARRR–
RELEASE HIM...
WHAT? WHAT DID YOU SAY? I DIDNT HEAR YOU.
I SAID ...!

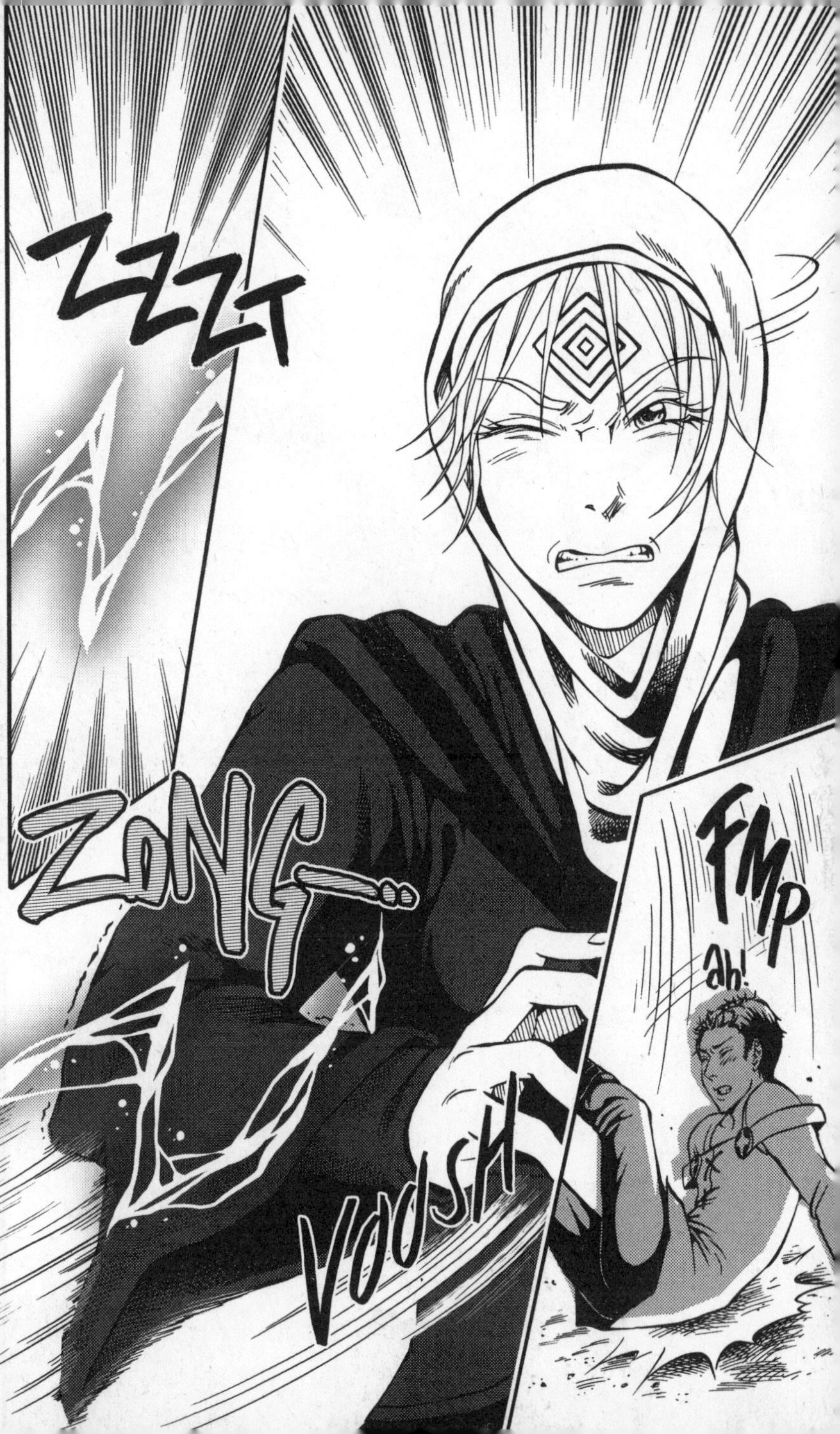
ZZZZT
ZONG...
VOOSH
FMP
ah!

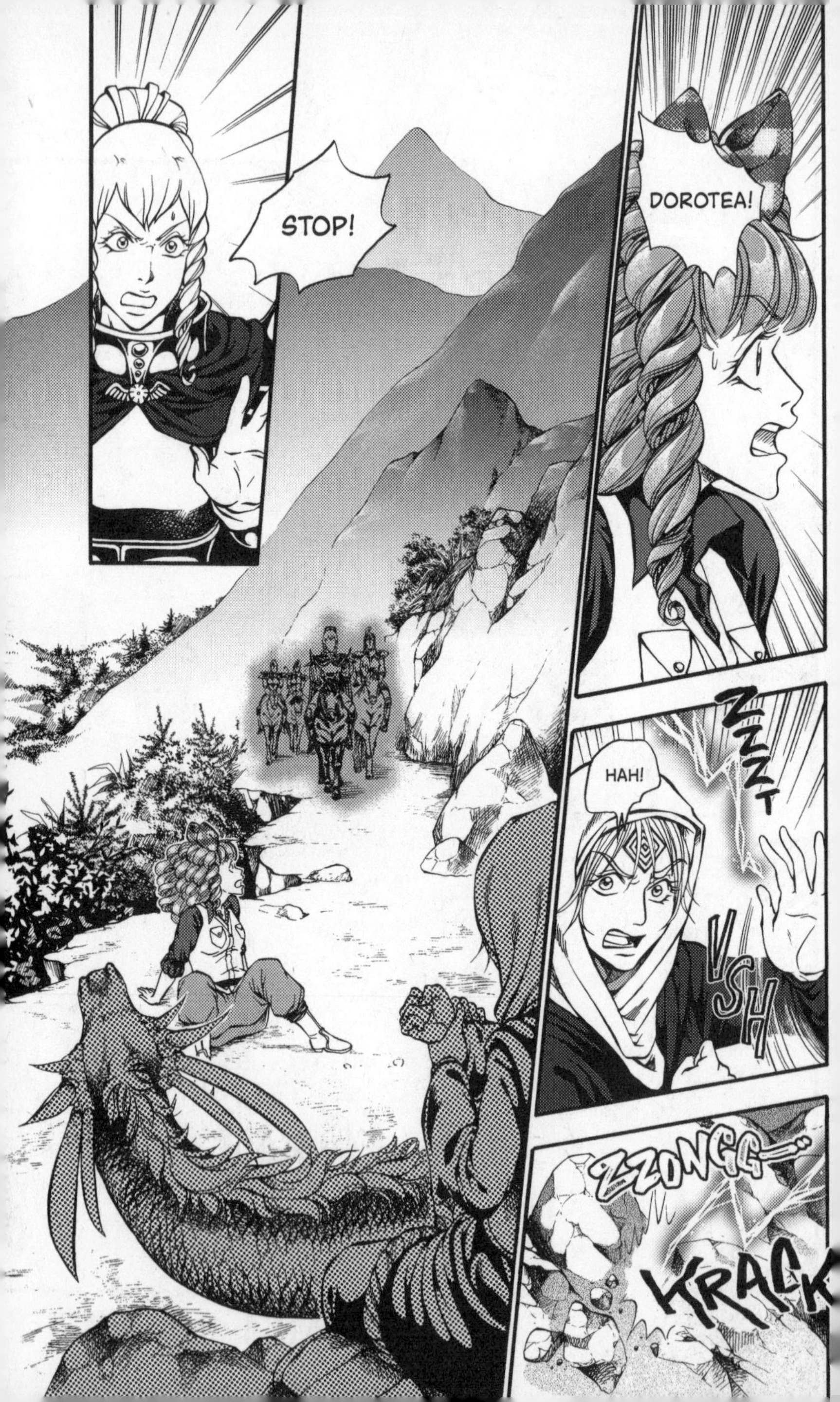
DOROTEA!
HAH!
ZZZT
VSH
ZZONGG
KRACK
STOP!

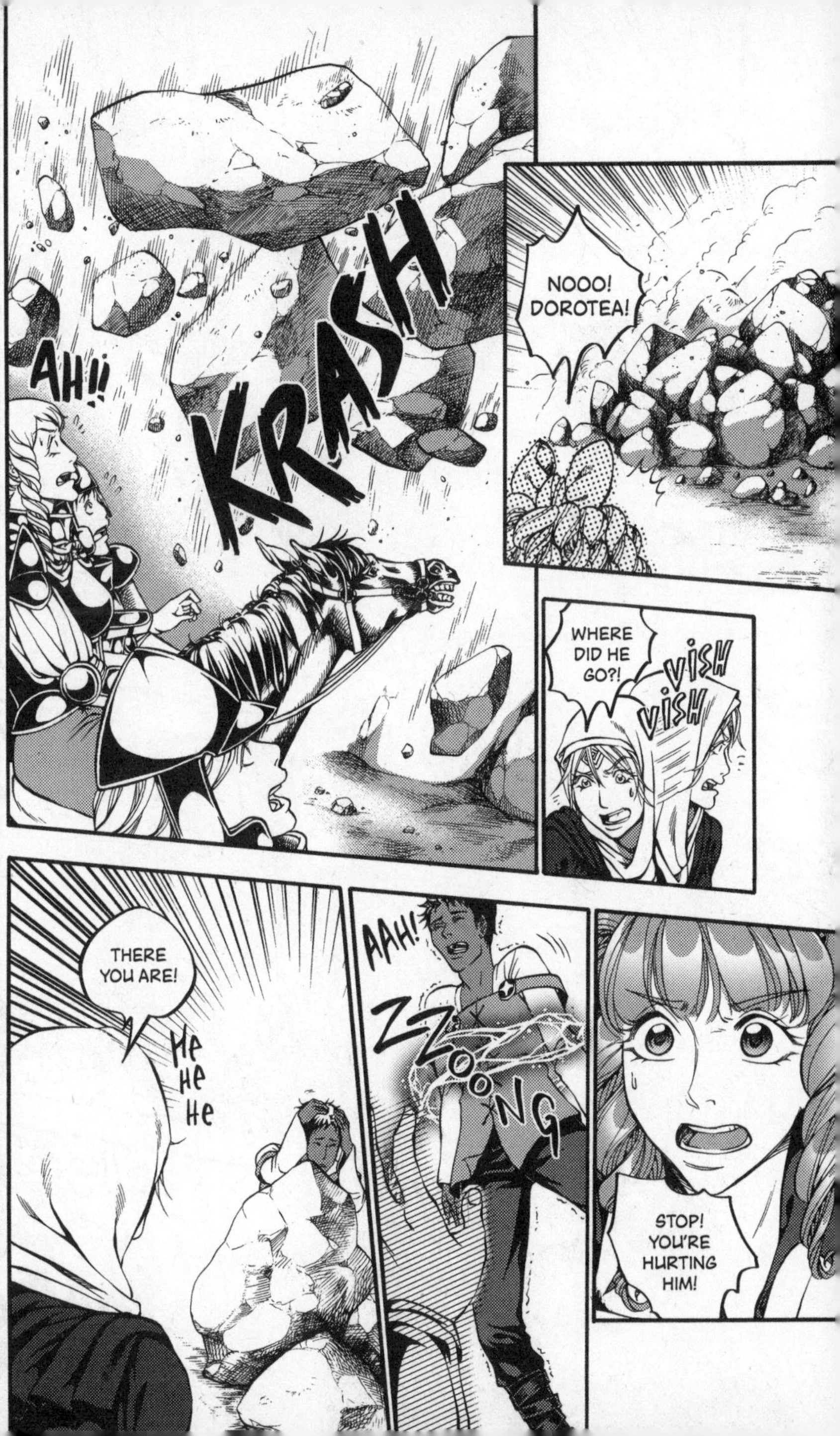
AH!!
KRASH
NOOO! DOROTEA!
WHERE DID HE GO?!
VISH VISH
THERE YOU ARE!
HE HE HE
AAH!
ZZOONG
STOP! YOU'RE HURTING HIM!

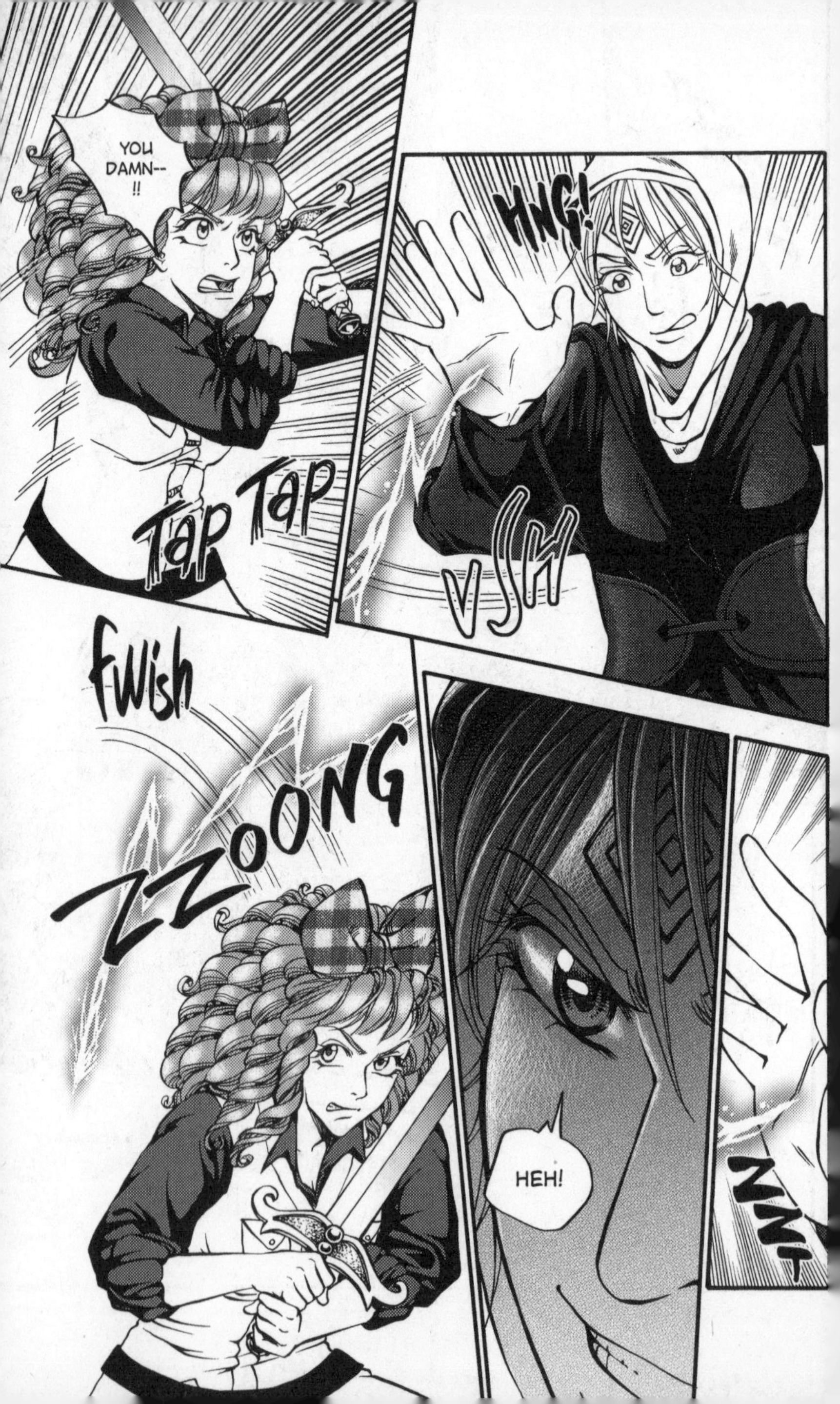
HNG!
VSH
YOU DAMN-- !!
TAP TAP
ZZZT
HEH!
FWISH
ZZOONG

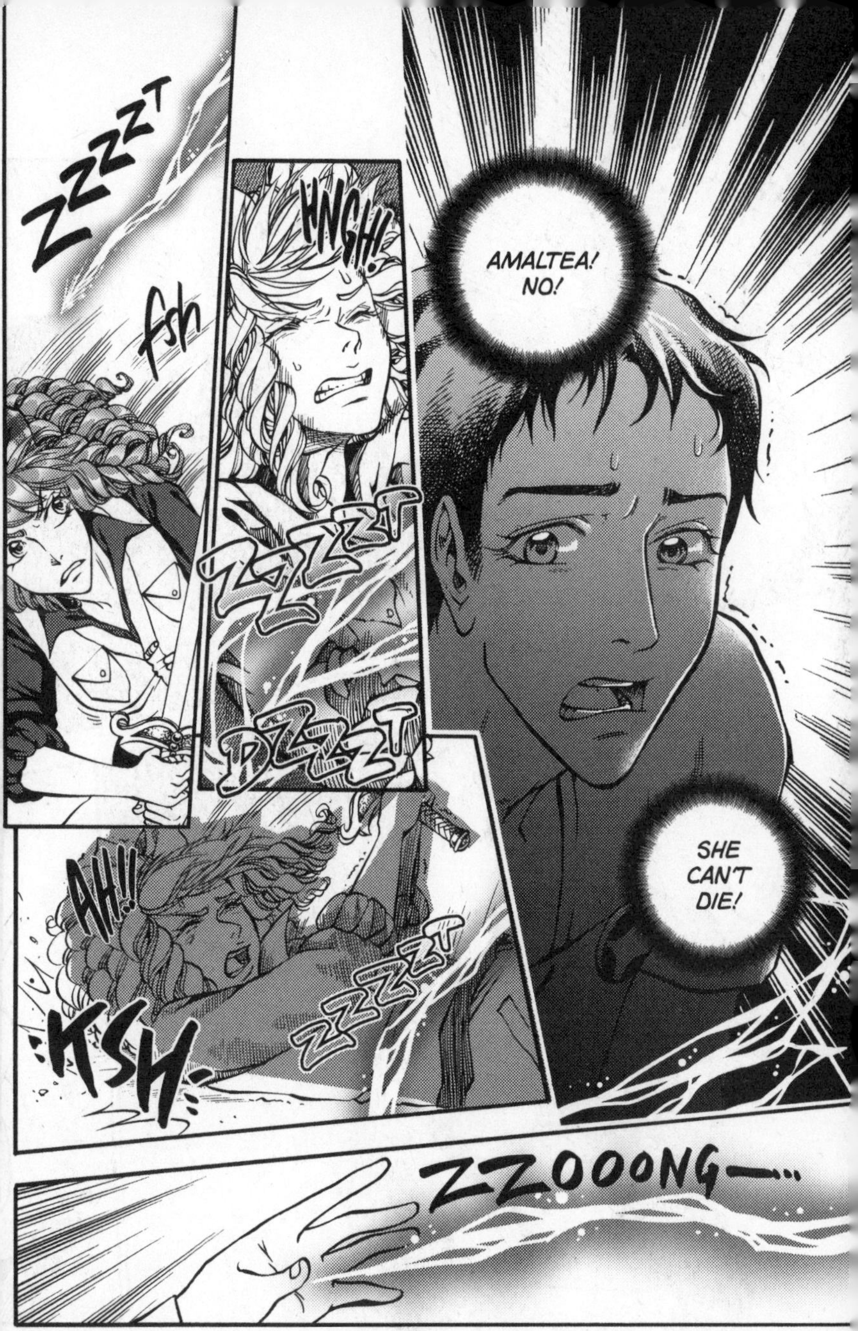
AMALTEA! NO!
SHE CAN'T DIE!
HNGH!!
ZZZZZT
DZZZZT
ZZZZZT
fsh
AH!!
KTSH
ZZZZZT
ZZOOONG

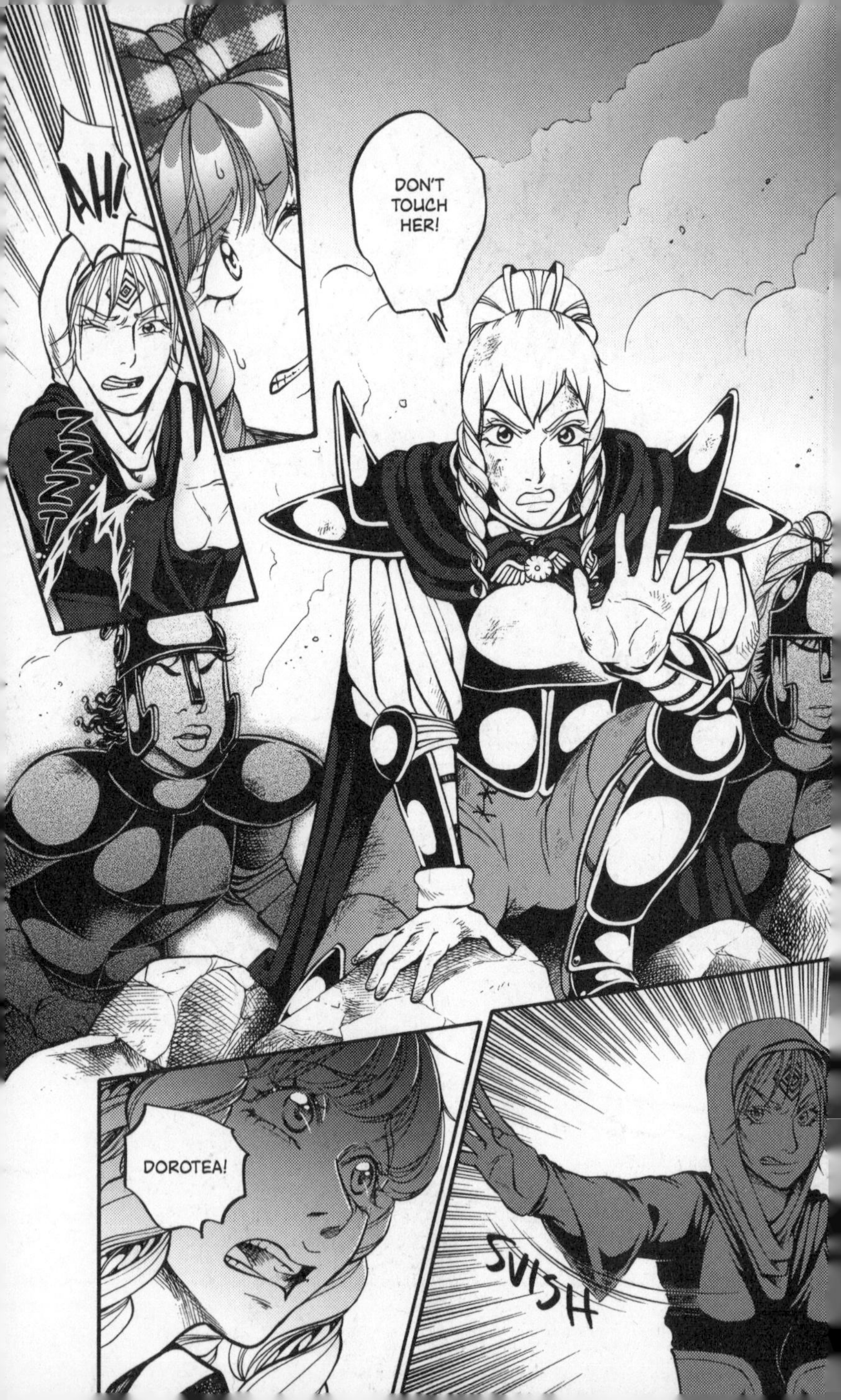
DON'T TOUCH HER!
AH!
TNNNN
SVISH
DOROTEA!

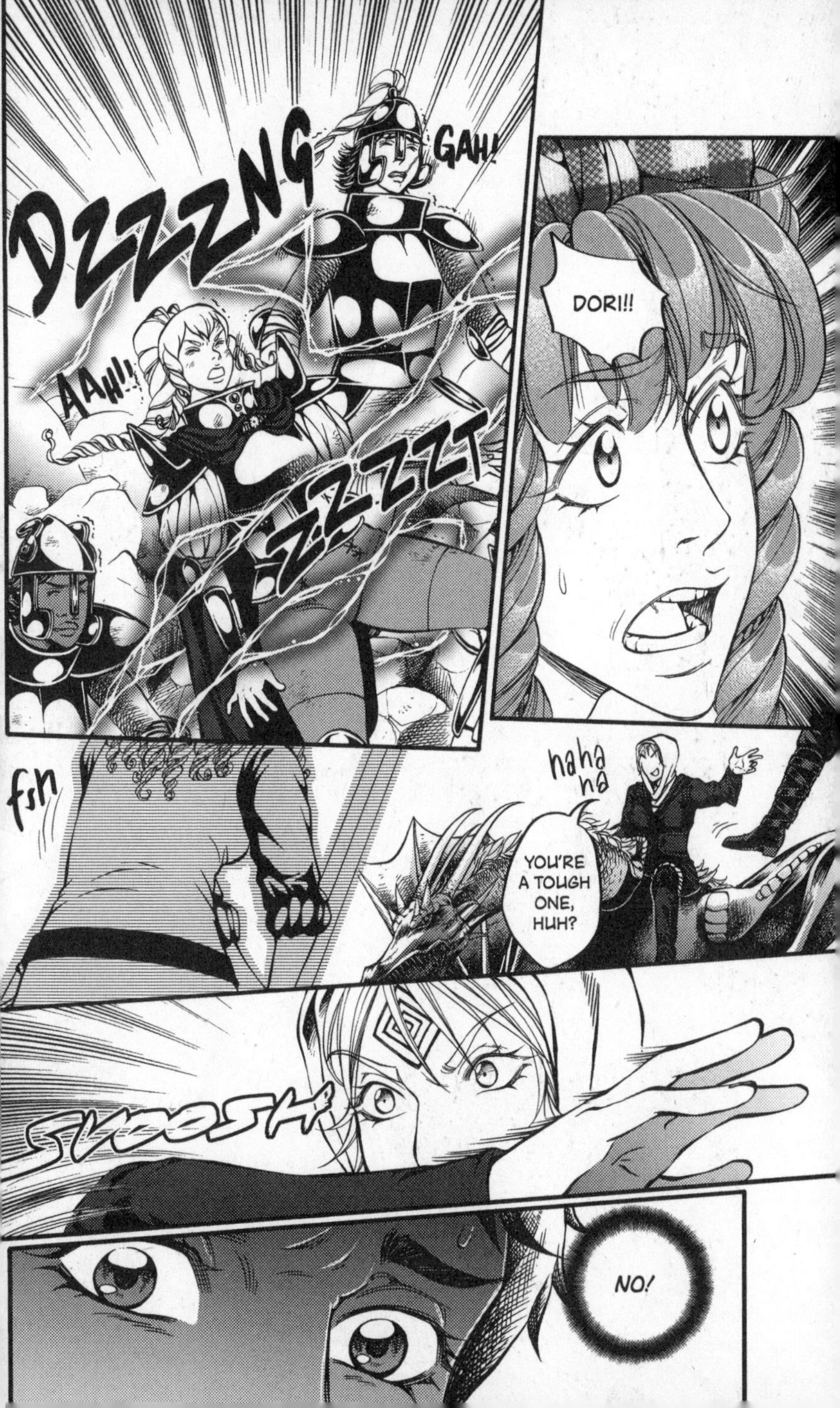
DORI!!
DZZZNG
GAH!
AAH!!
ZZZZZT
haha ha
YOU'RE A TOUGH ONE, HUH?
fsh
SWOOSH
NO!

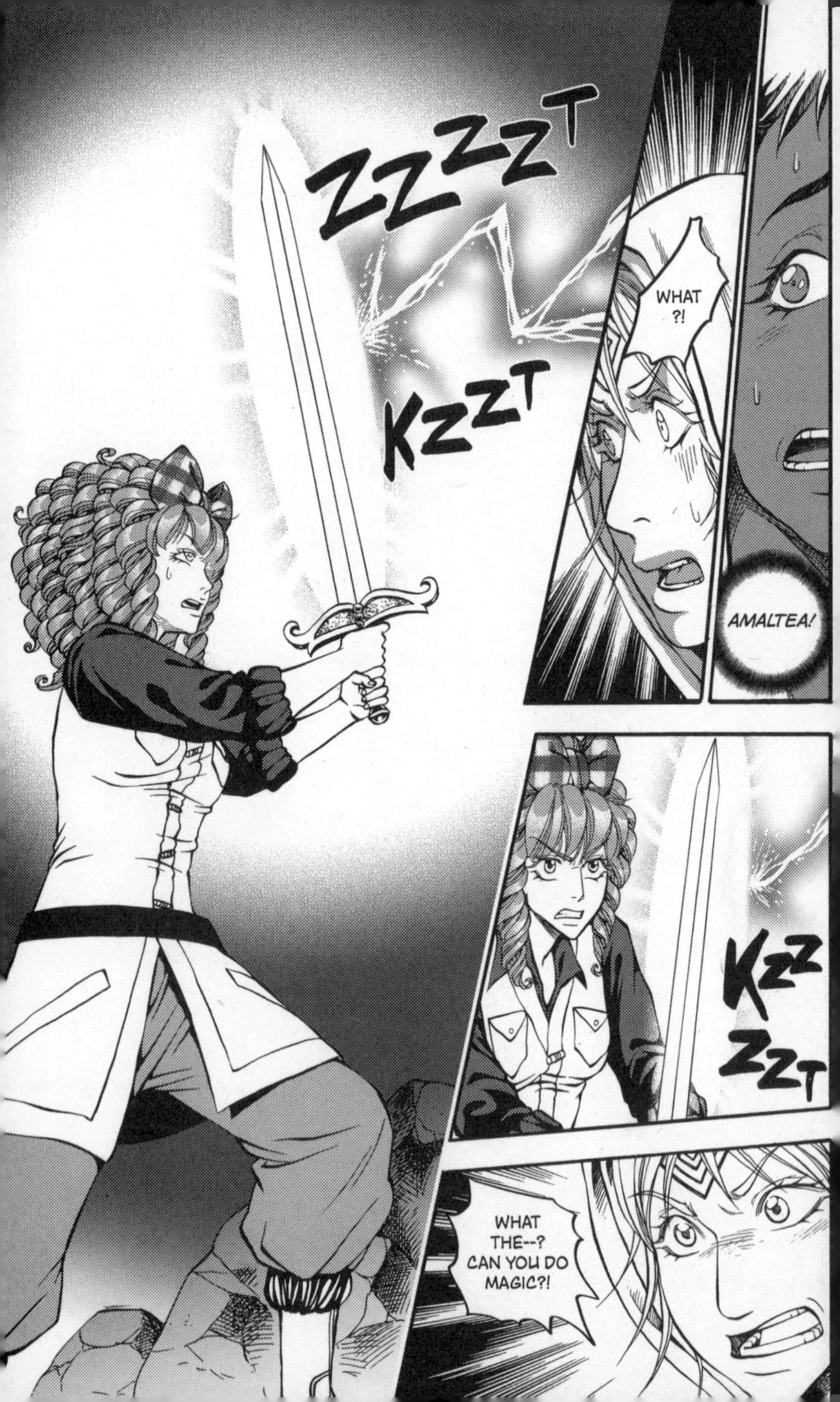
AMALTEA!
WHAT ?!
KZZ ZZT
WHAT THE--? CAN YOU DO MAGIC?!
ZZZZT
KZZT

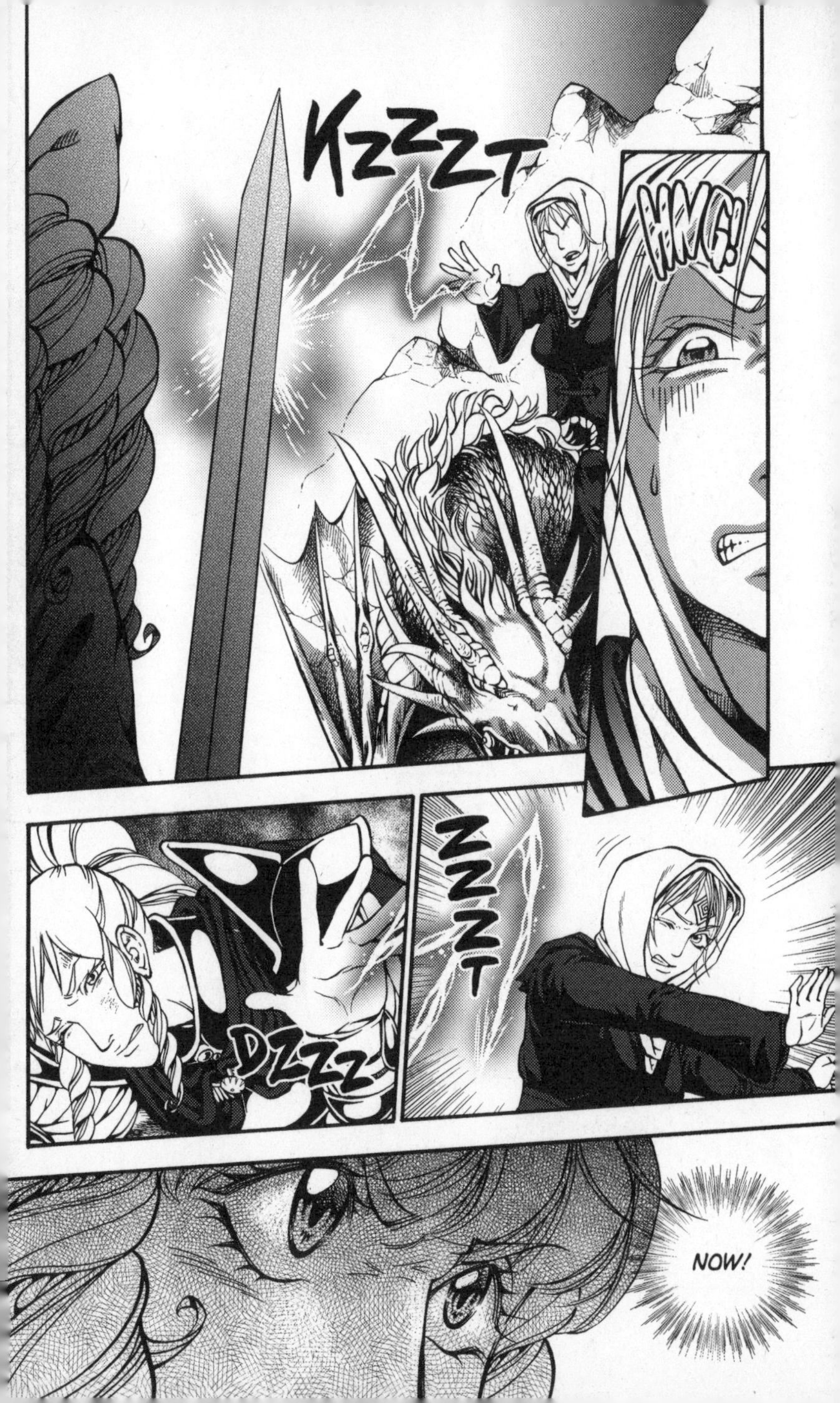

KZZZZT
HMG!
ZZZZT
DZZZZ
NOW!

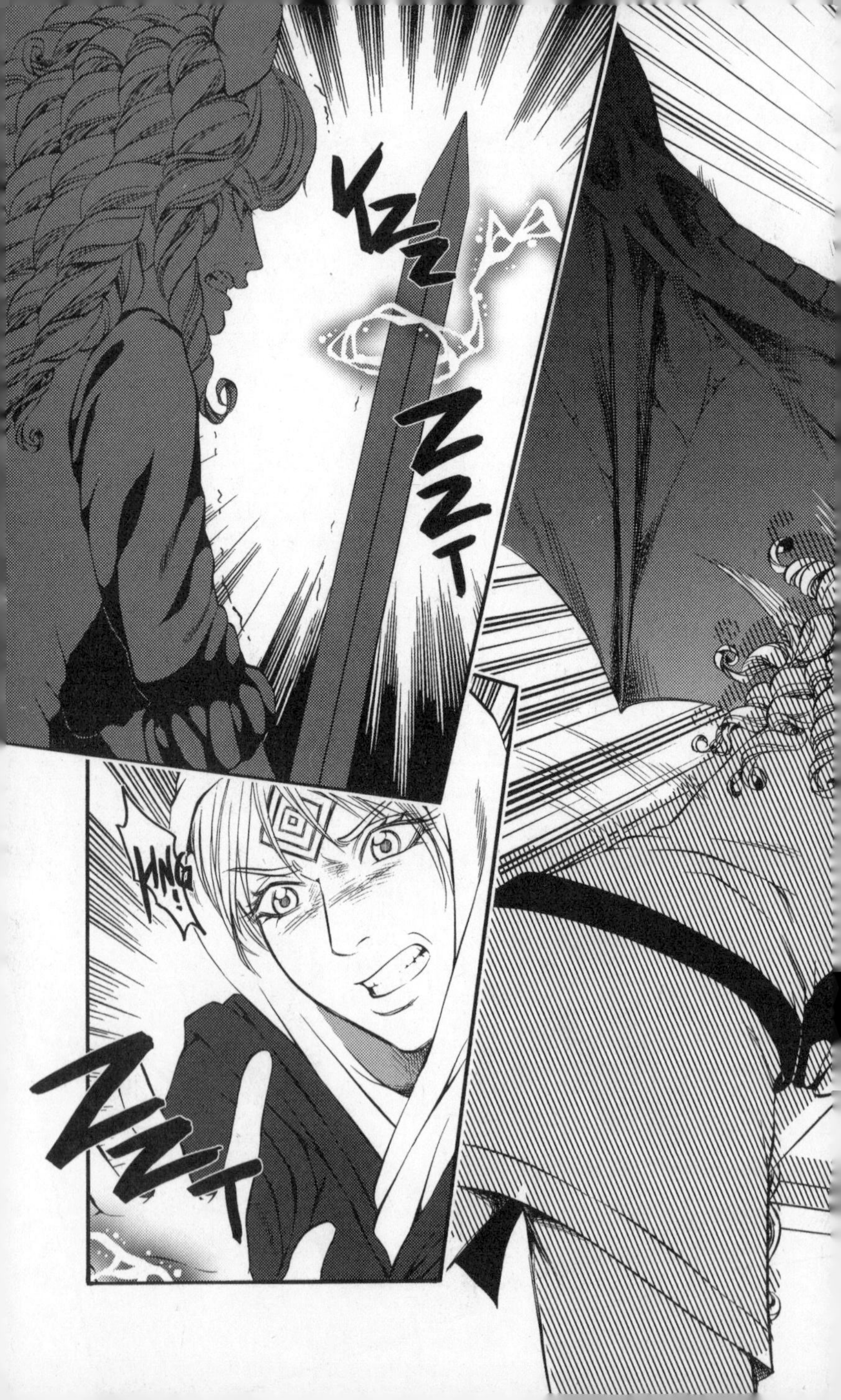
KZZZZZT
KING!
ZZZT

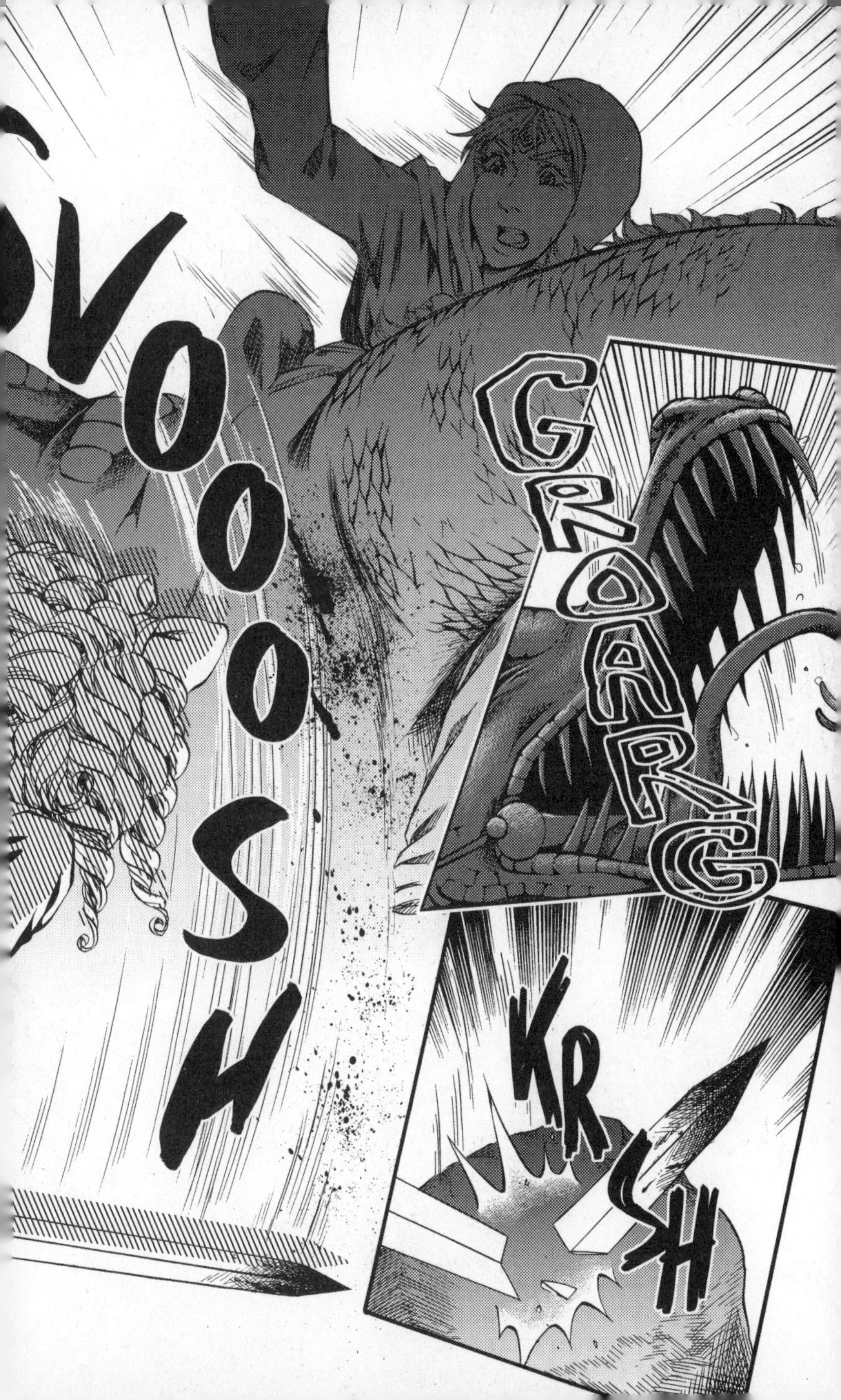
GROARG
VOOOSH
KRSH

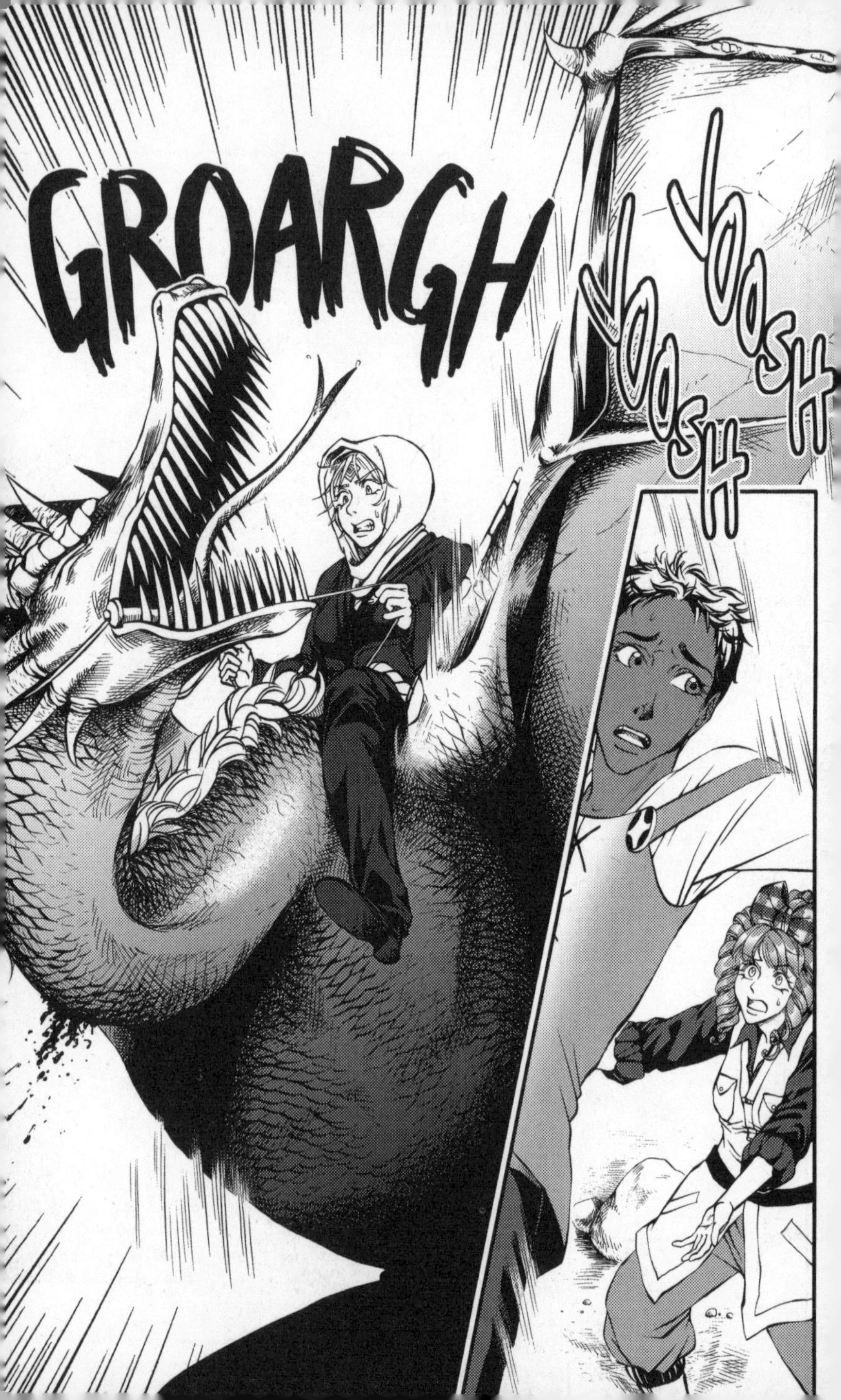
VOOSH VOOSH
GROARGH

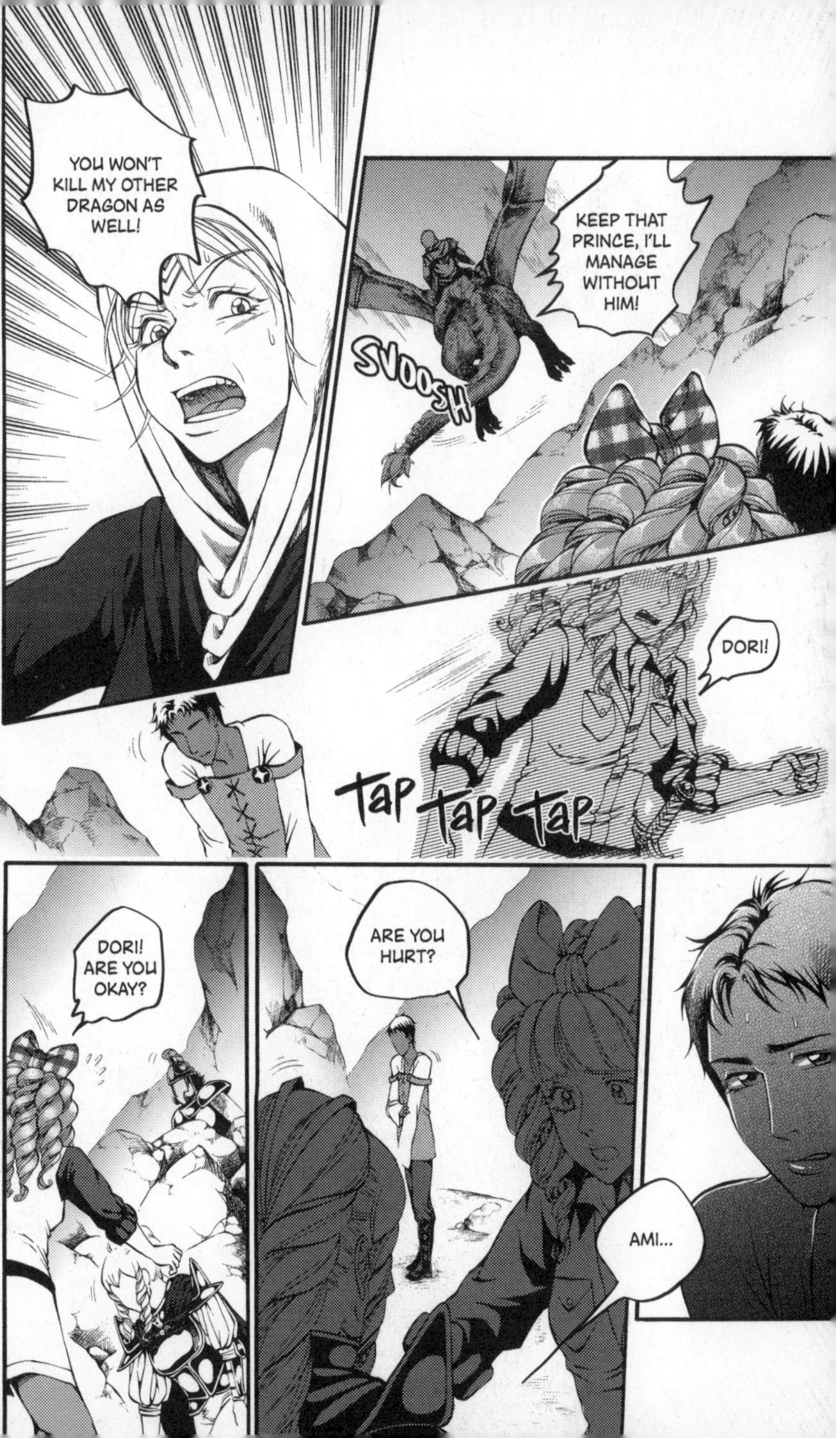
YOU WON'T KILL MY OTHER DRAGON AS WELL!
KEEP THAT PRINCE, I'LL MANAGE WITHOUT HIM!
SVOOSH
DORI!
TAP TAP TAP
DORI! ARE YOU OKAY?
ARE YOU HURT?
AMI...

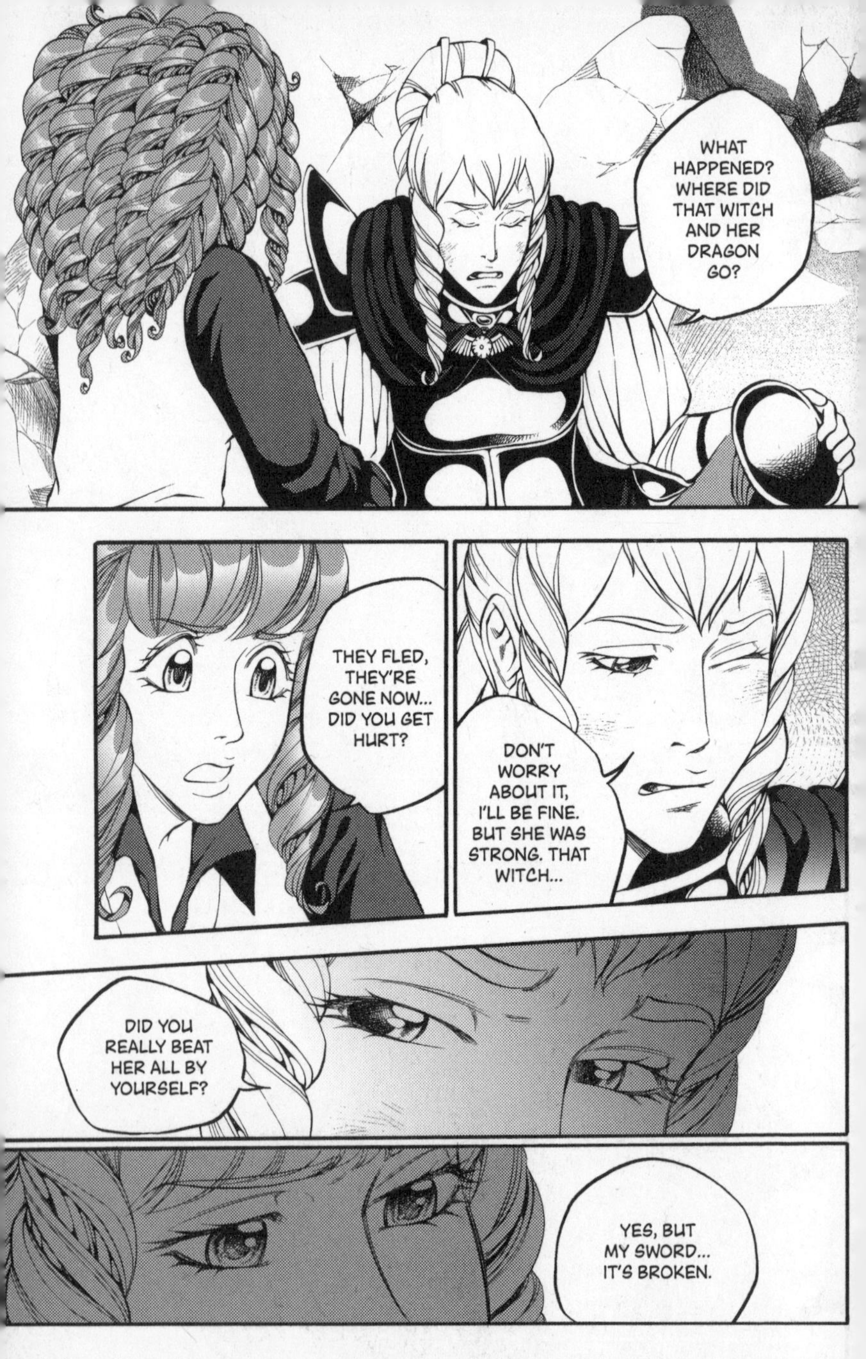
WHAT HAPPENED? WHERE DID THAT WITCH AND HER DRAGON GO?
THEY FLED, THEY'RE GONE NOW... DID YOU GET HURT?
DON'T WORRY ABOUT IT, I'LL BE FINE. BUT SHE WAS STRONG. THAT WITCH...
DID YOU REALLY BEAT HER ALL BY YOURSELF?
YES, BUT MY SWORD... IT'S BROKEN.

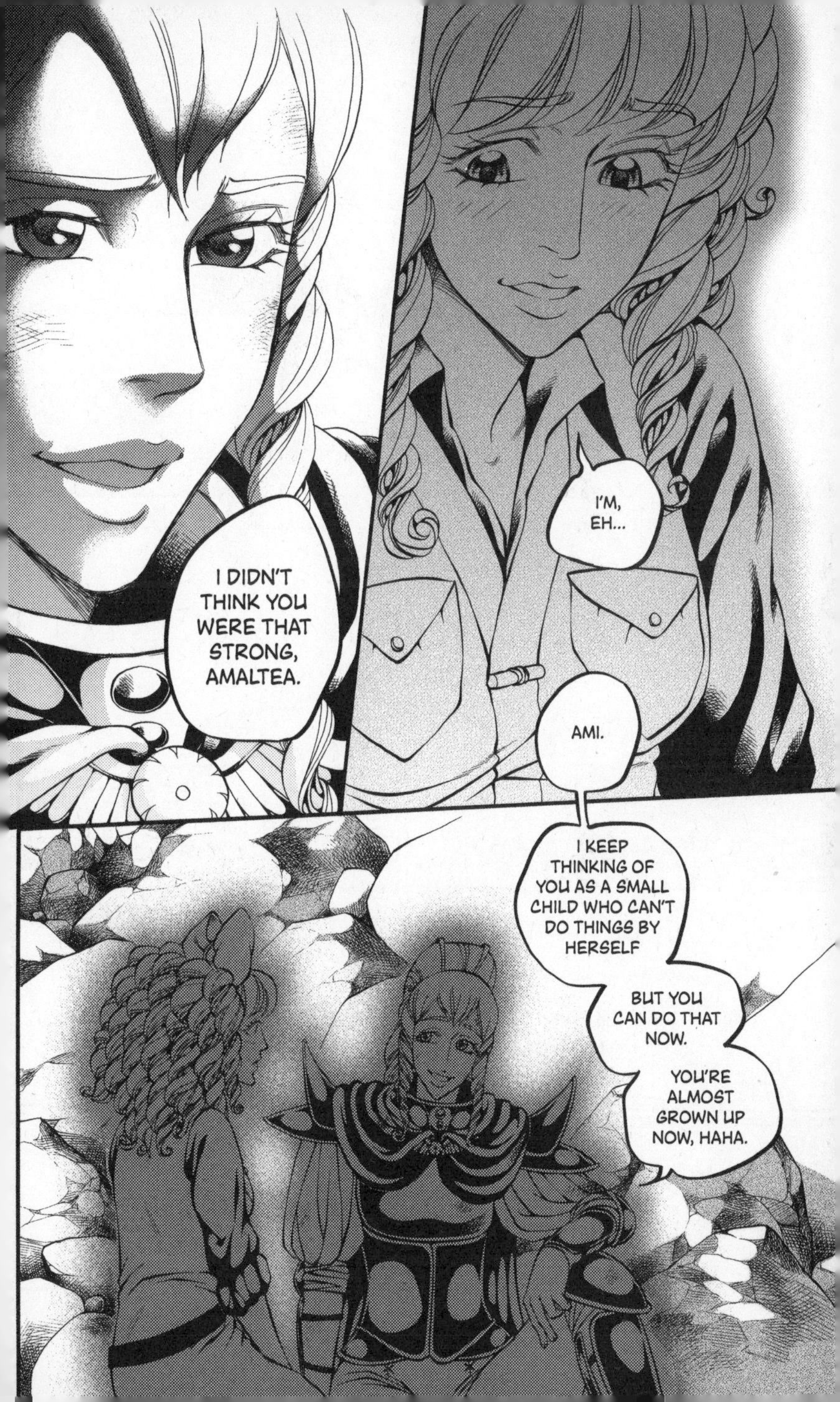
I DIDN'T THINK YOU WERE THAT STRONG, AMALTEA.
I'M, EH...
AMI.
I KEEP THINKING OF YOU AS A SMALL CHILD WHO CAN'T DO THINGS BY HERSELF
BUT YOU CAN DO THAT NOW.
YOU'RE ALMOST GROWN UP NOW, HAHA.

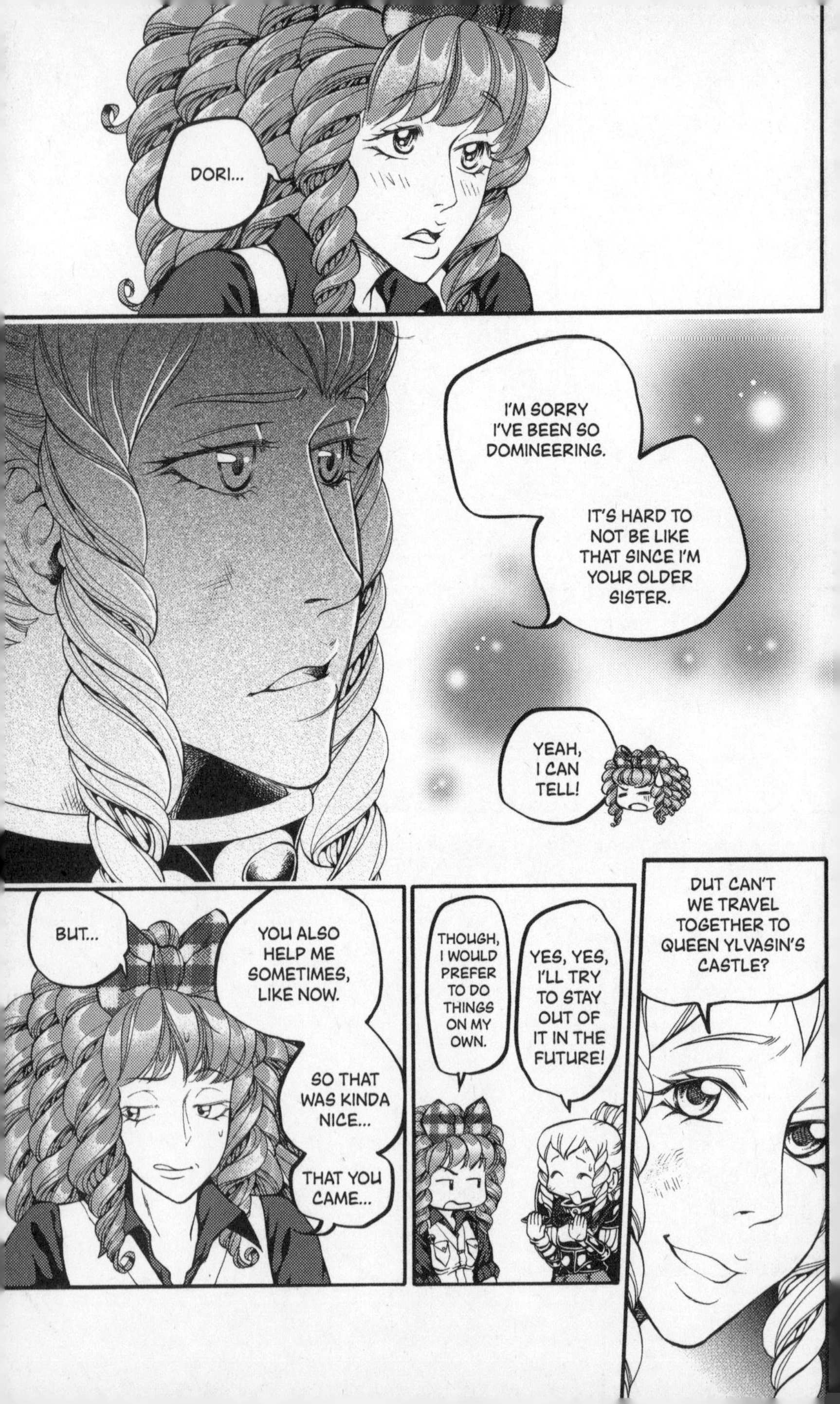
DORI...
I'M SORRY I'VE BEEN SO DOMINEERING.
IT'S HARD TO NOT BE LIKE THAT SINCE I'M YOUR OLDER SISTER.
YEAH, I CAN TELL!
DUT CAN'T WE TRAVEL TOGETHER TO QUEEN YLVASIN'S CASTLE?
YES, YES, I'LL TRY TO STAY OUT OF IT IN THE FUTURE!
THOUGH, I WOULD PREFER TO DO THINGS ON MY OWN.
BUT...
YOU ALSO HELP ME SOMETIMES, LIKE NOW.
SO THAT WAS KINDA NICE...
THAT YOU CAME...

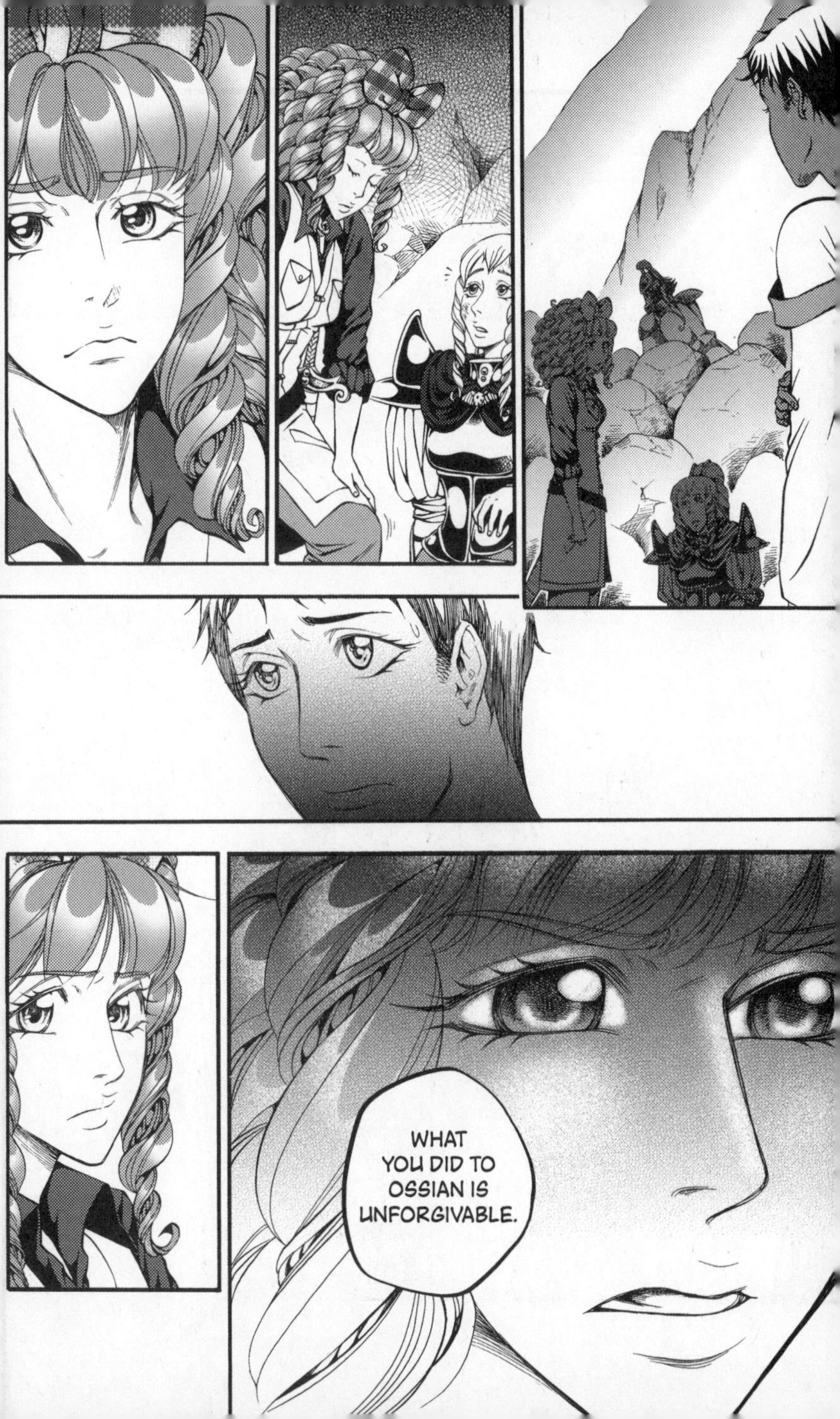
WHAT YOU DID TO OSSIAN IS UNFORGIVABLE.

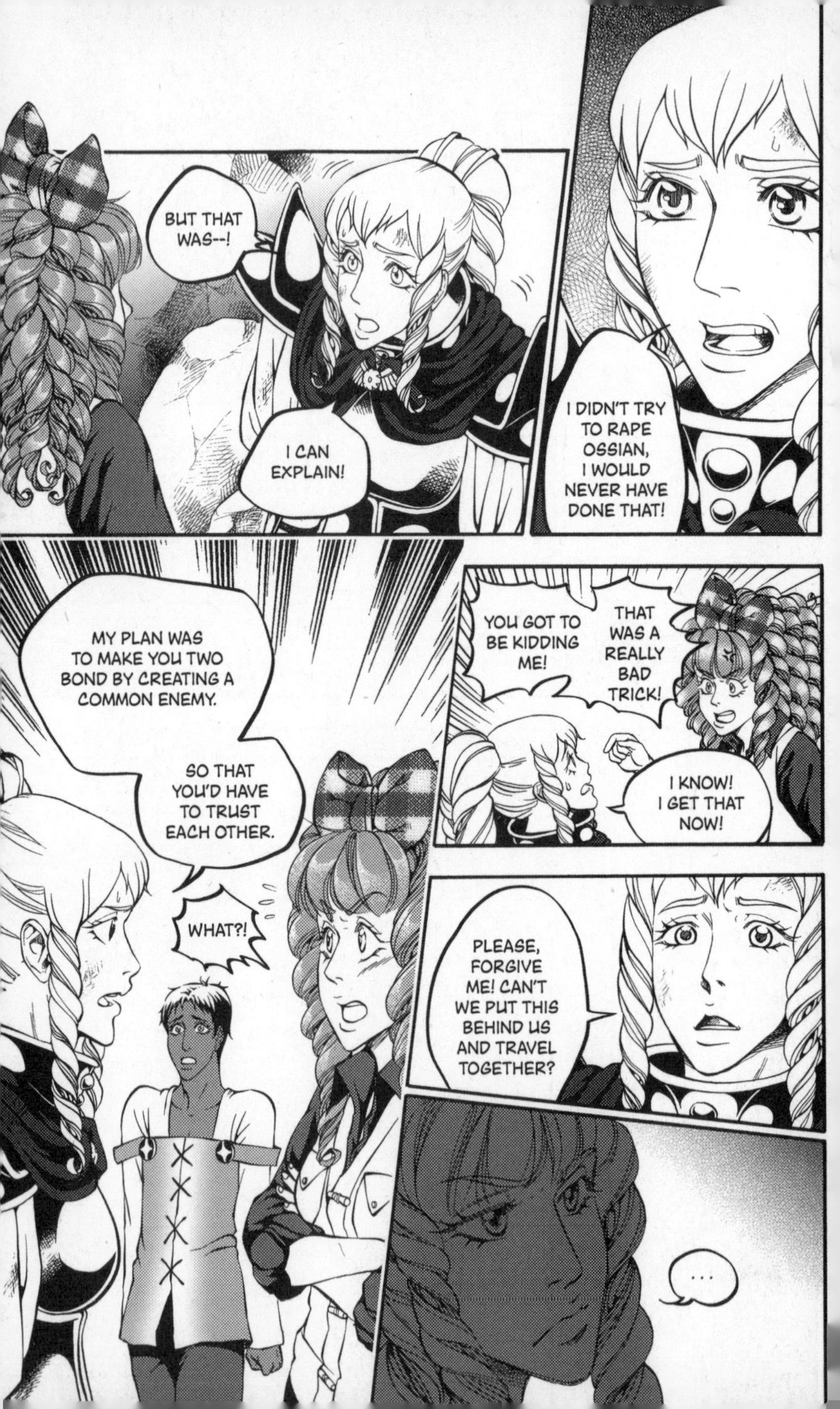
BUT THAT WAS--!
I CAN EXPLAIN!
I DIDN'T TRY TO RAPE OSSIAN, I WOULD NEVER HAVE DONE THAT!
MY PLAN WAS TO MAKE YOU TWO BOND BY CREATING A COMMON ENEMY.
SO THAT YOU'D HAVE TO TRUST EACH OTHER.
WHAT?!
YOU GOT TO BE KIDDING ME!
THAT WAS A REALLY BAD TRICK!
I KNOW! I GET THAT NOW!
PLEASE, FORGIVE ME! CAN'T WE PUT THIS BEHIND US AND TRAVEL TOGETHER?
...

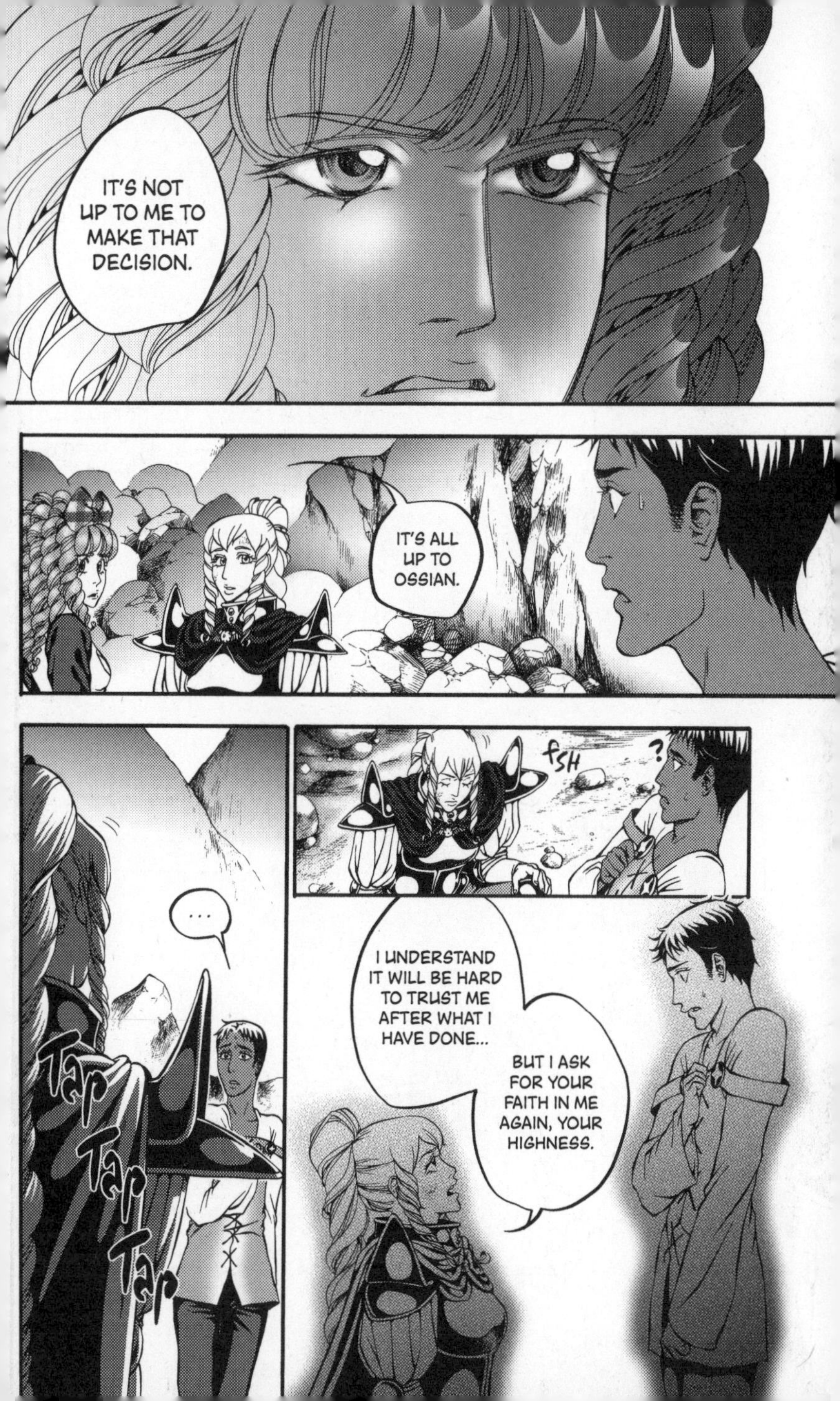
IT'S NOT UP TO ME TO MAKE THAT DECISION.
IT'S ALL UP TO OSSIAN.
fSH
?
I UNDERSTAND IT WILL BE HARD TO TRUST ME AFTER WHAT I HAVE DONE...
BUT I ASK FOR YOUR FAITH IN ME AGAIN, YOUR HIGHNESS.
...
Tap Tap Tap

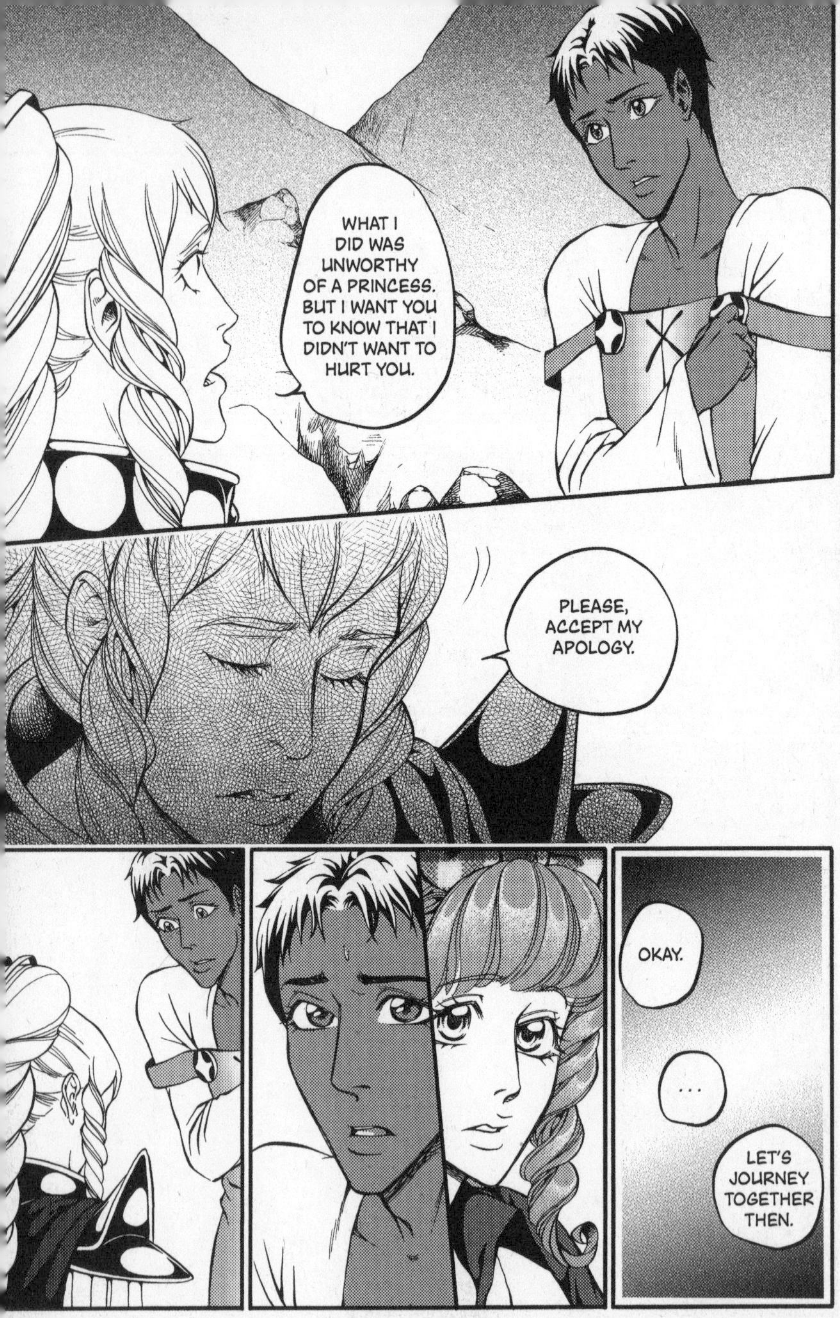
WHAT I DID WAS UNWORTHY OF A PRINCESS. BUT I WANT YOU TO KNOW THAT I DIDN'T WANT TO HURT YOU.
PLEASE, ACCEPT MY APOLOGY.
OKAY.
...
LET'S JOURNEY TOGETHER THEN.

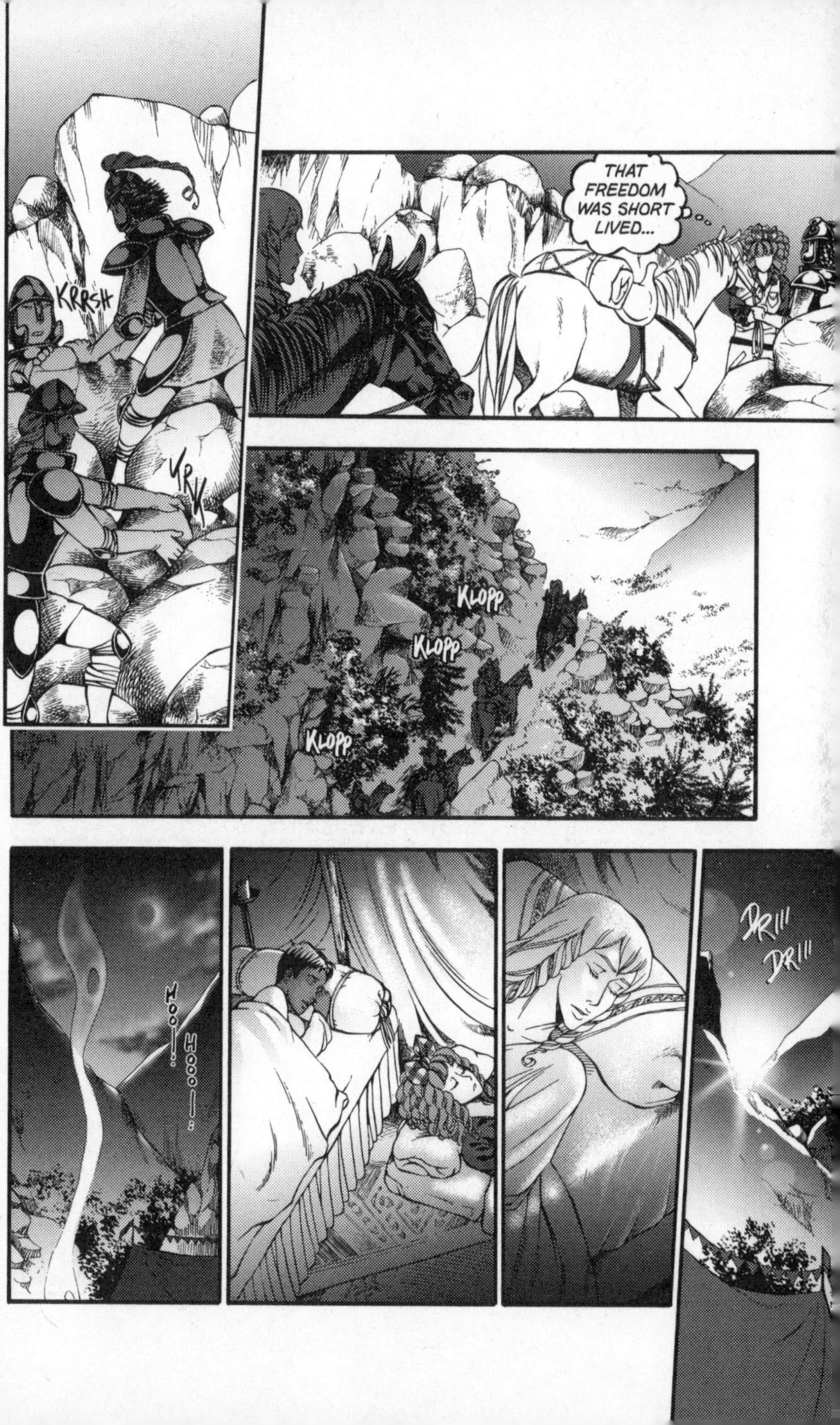
THAT FREEDOM WAS SHORT LIVED...
KLOPP
KLOPP
KLOPP
KRRSH
VRRK
DRIII
DRIII

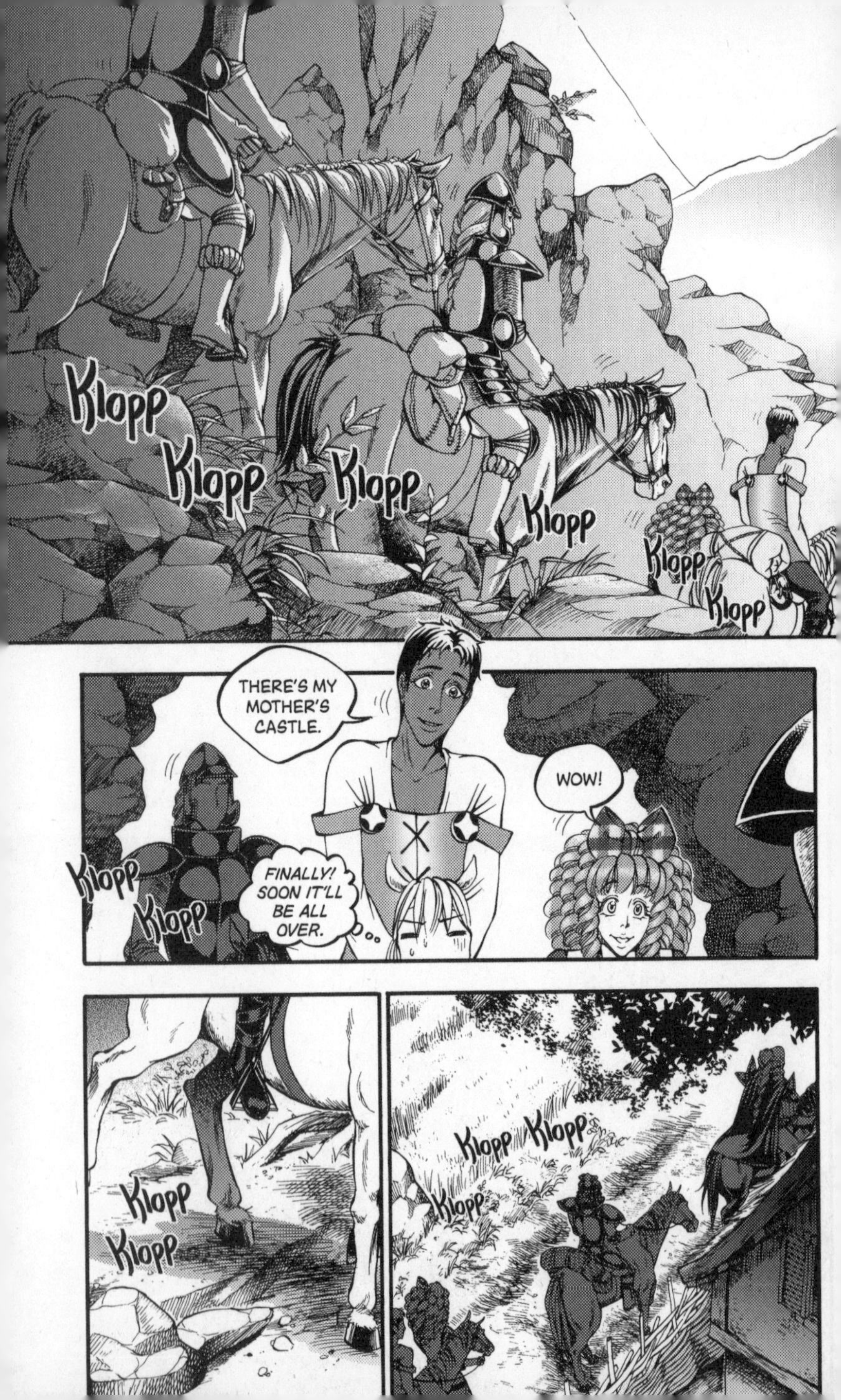
Klopp
Klopp
Klopp
Klopp
Klopp
Klopp
THERE'S MY MOTHER'S CASTLE.
WOW!
FINALLY! SOON IT'LL BE ALL OVER.
Klopp
Klopp
Klopp Klopp
Klopp
Klopp
Klopp

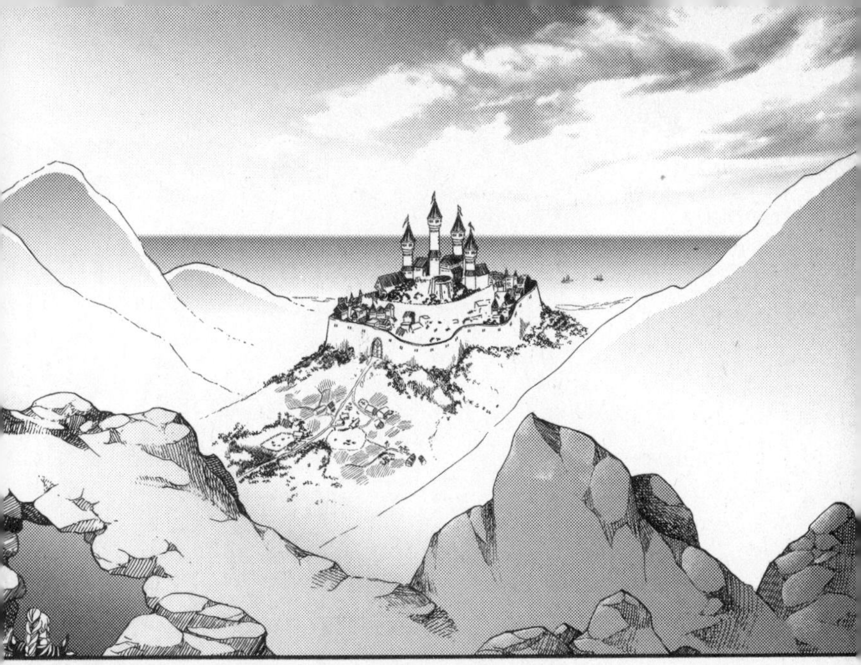

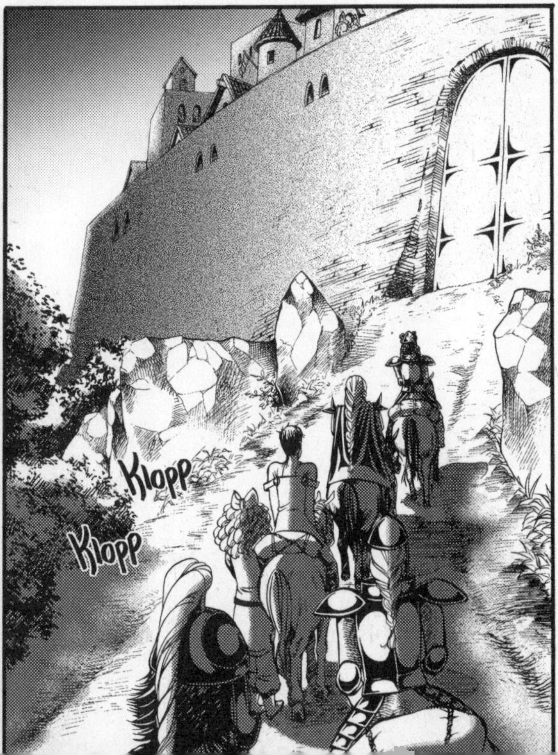
Klopp
Klopp

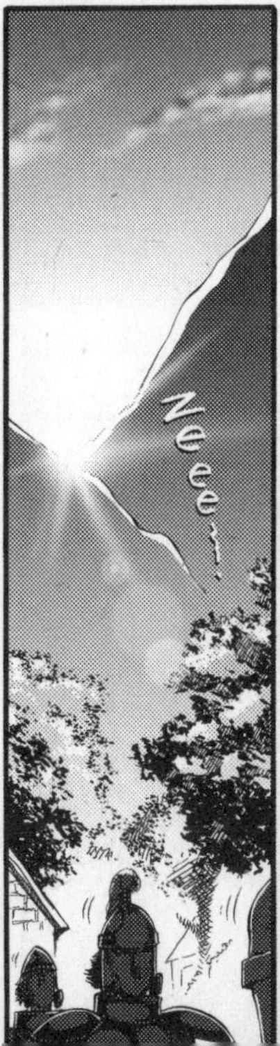
Neee...

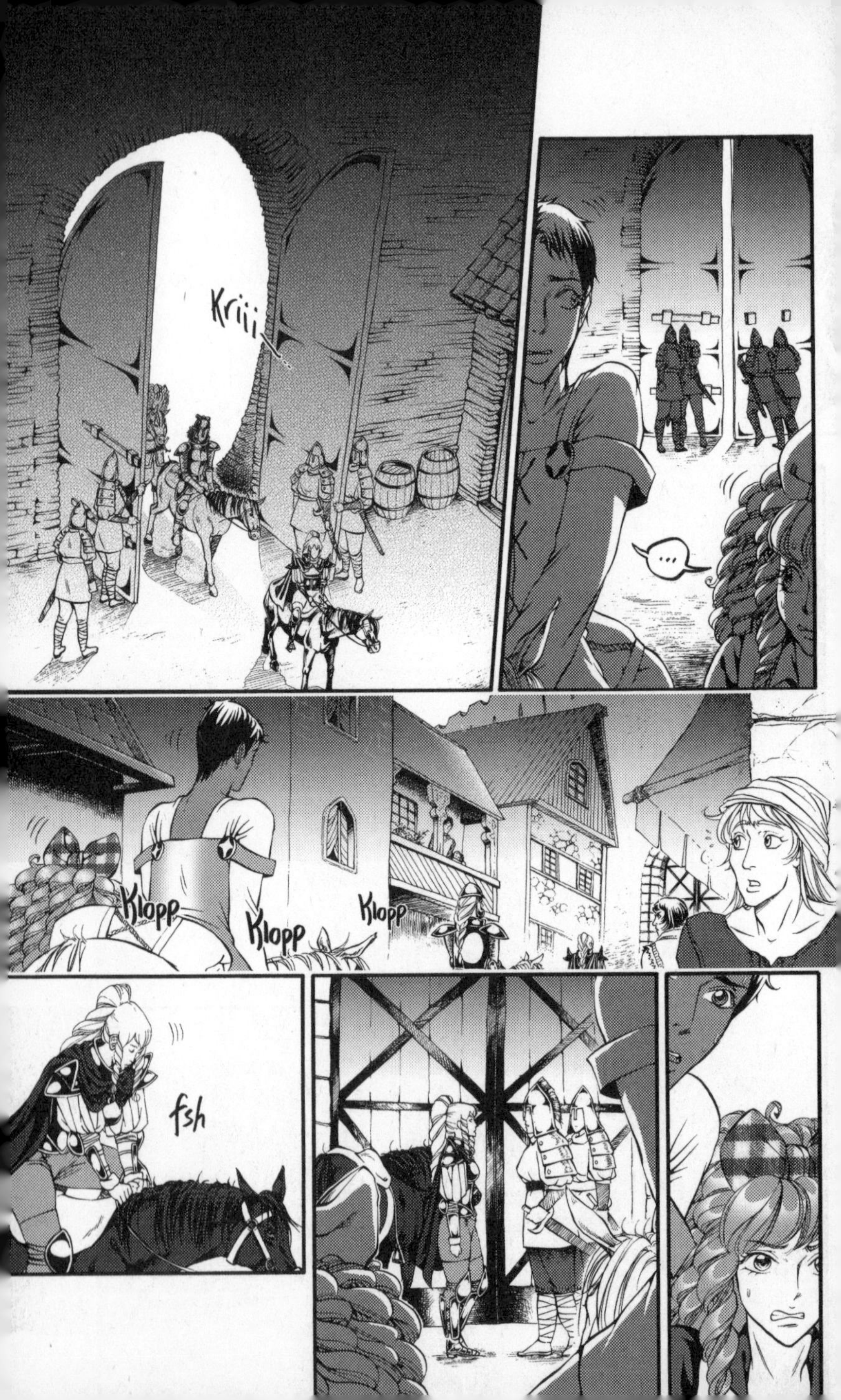
...
Kriii...
Klopp
Klopp
Klopp
fsh

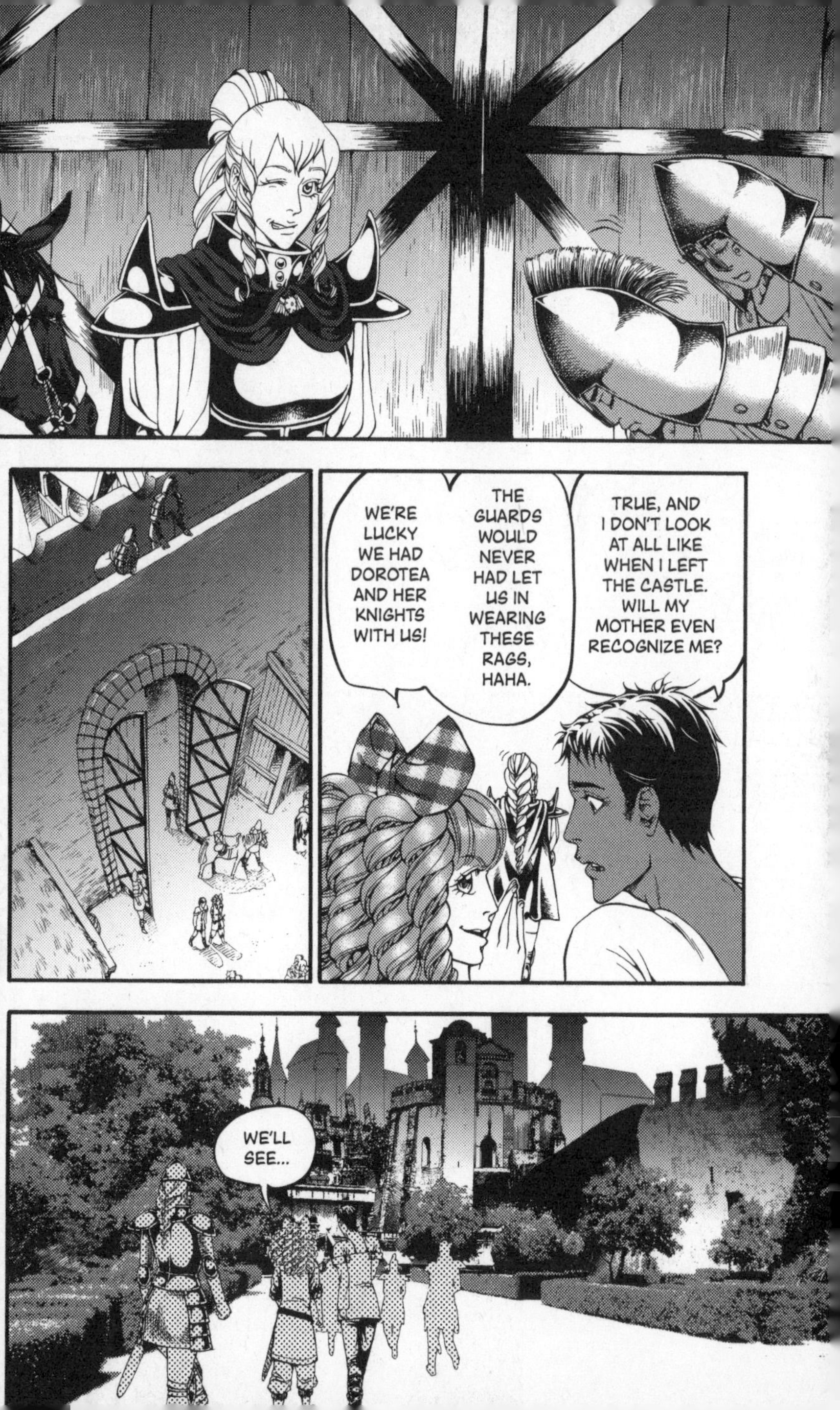
WE'RE LUCKY WE HAD DOROTEA AND HER KNIGHTS WITH US!
THE GUARDS WOULD NEVER HAD LET US IN WEARING THESE RAGS, HAHA.
TRUE, AND I DON'T LOOK AT ALL LIKE WHEN I LEFT THE CASTLE. WILL MY MOTHER EVEN RECOGNIZE ME?
WE'LL SEE...

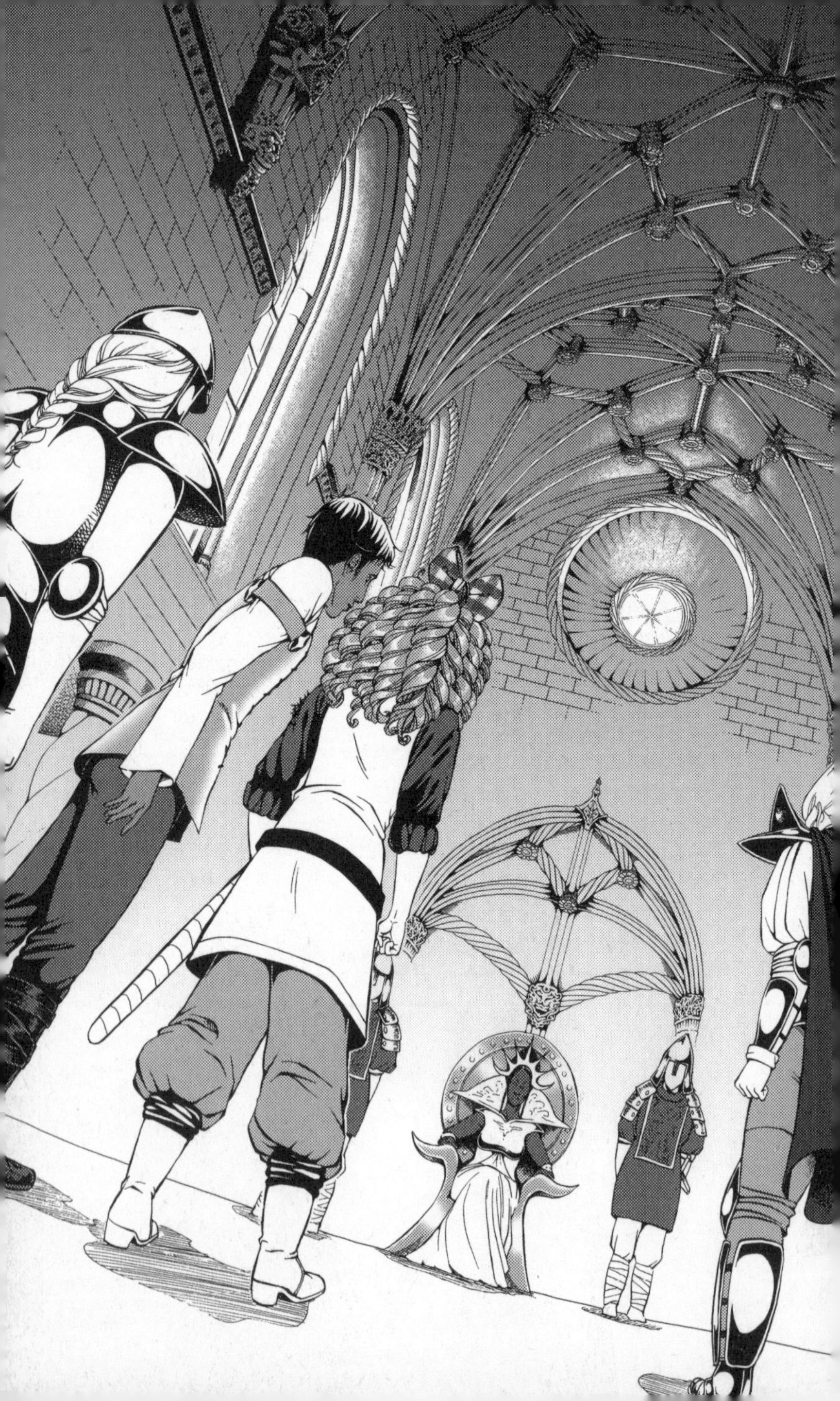

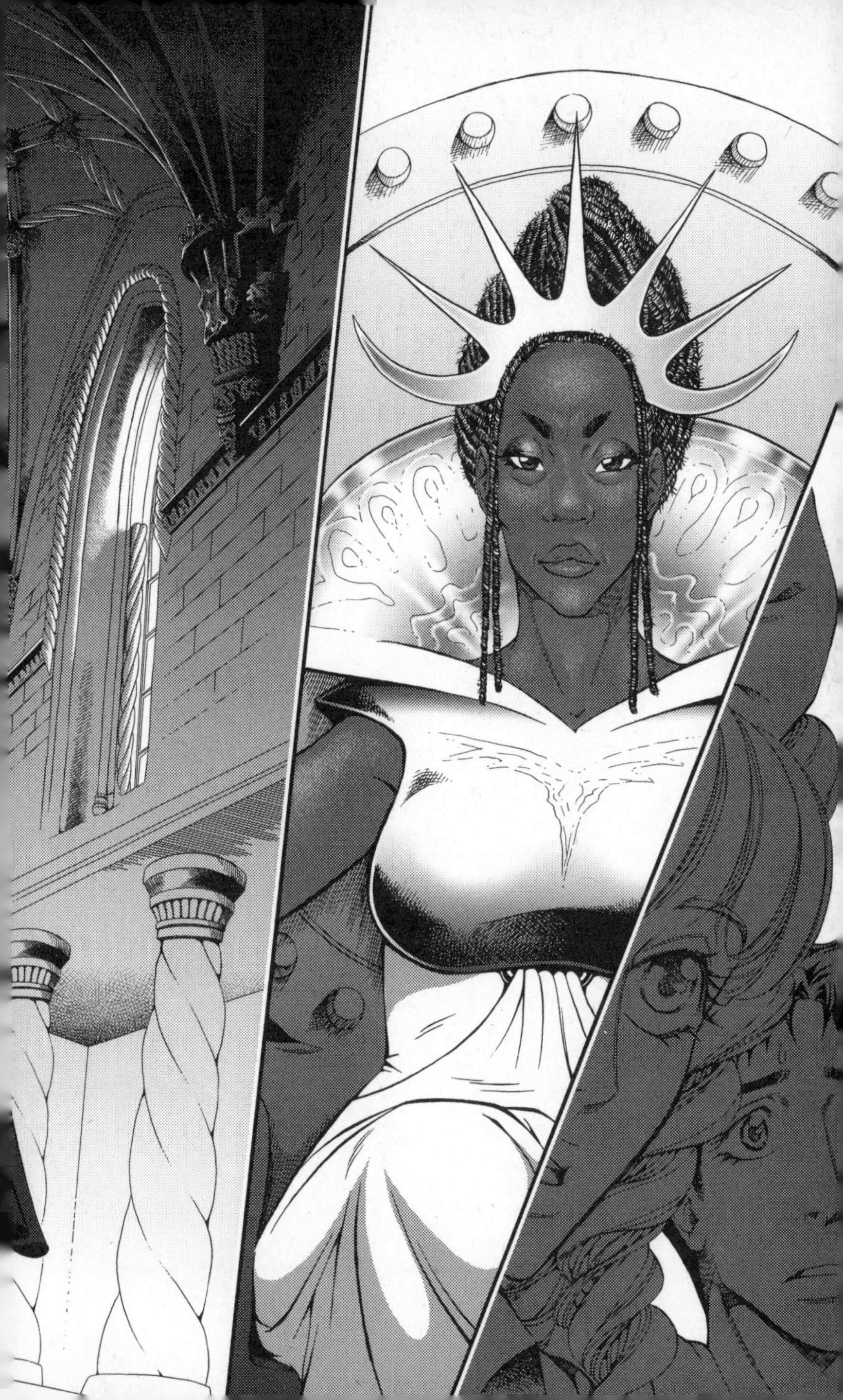

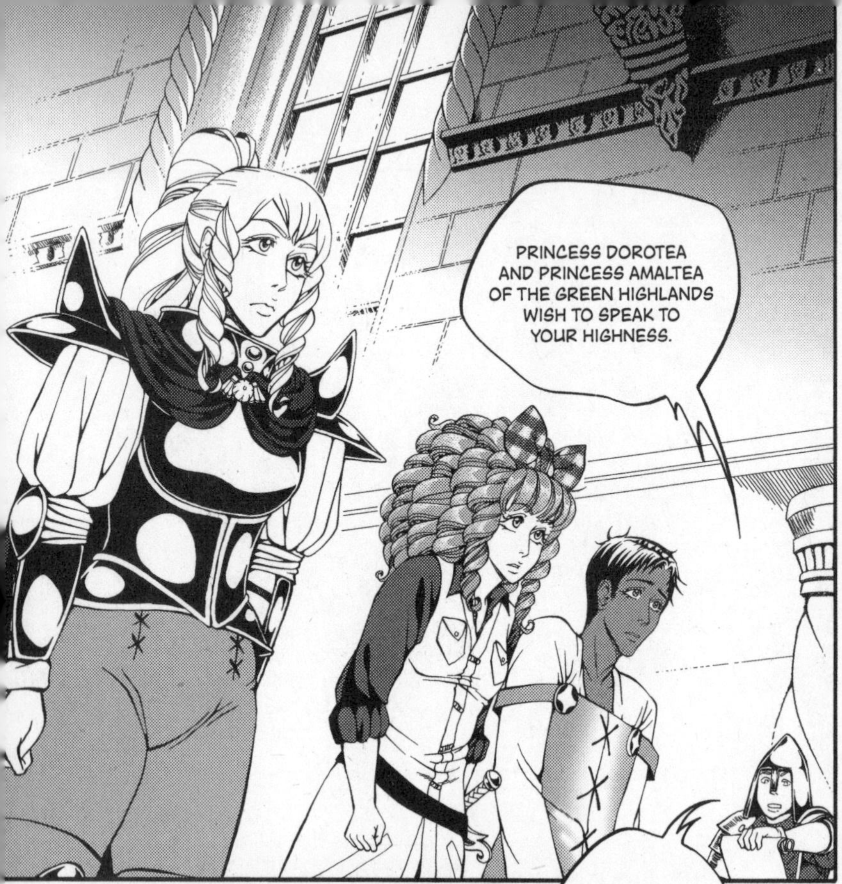
PRINCESS DOROTEA AND PRINCESS AMALTEA OF THE GREEN HIGHLANDS WISH TO SPEAK TO YOUR HIGHNESS.

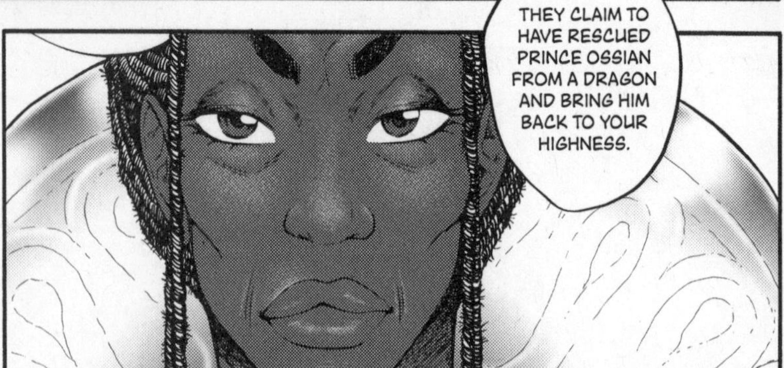
THEY CLAIM TO HAVE RESCUED PRINCE OSSIAN FROM A DRAGON AND BRING HIM BACK TO YOUR HIGHNESS.

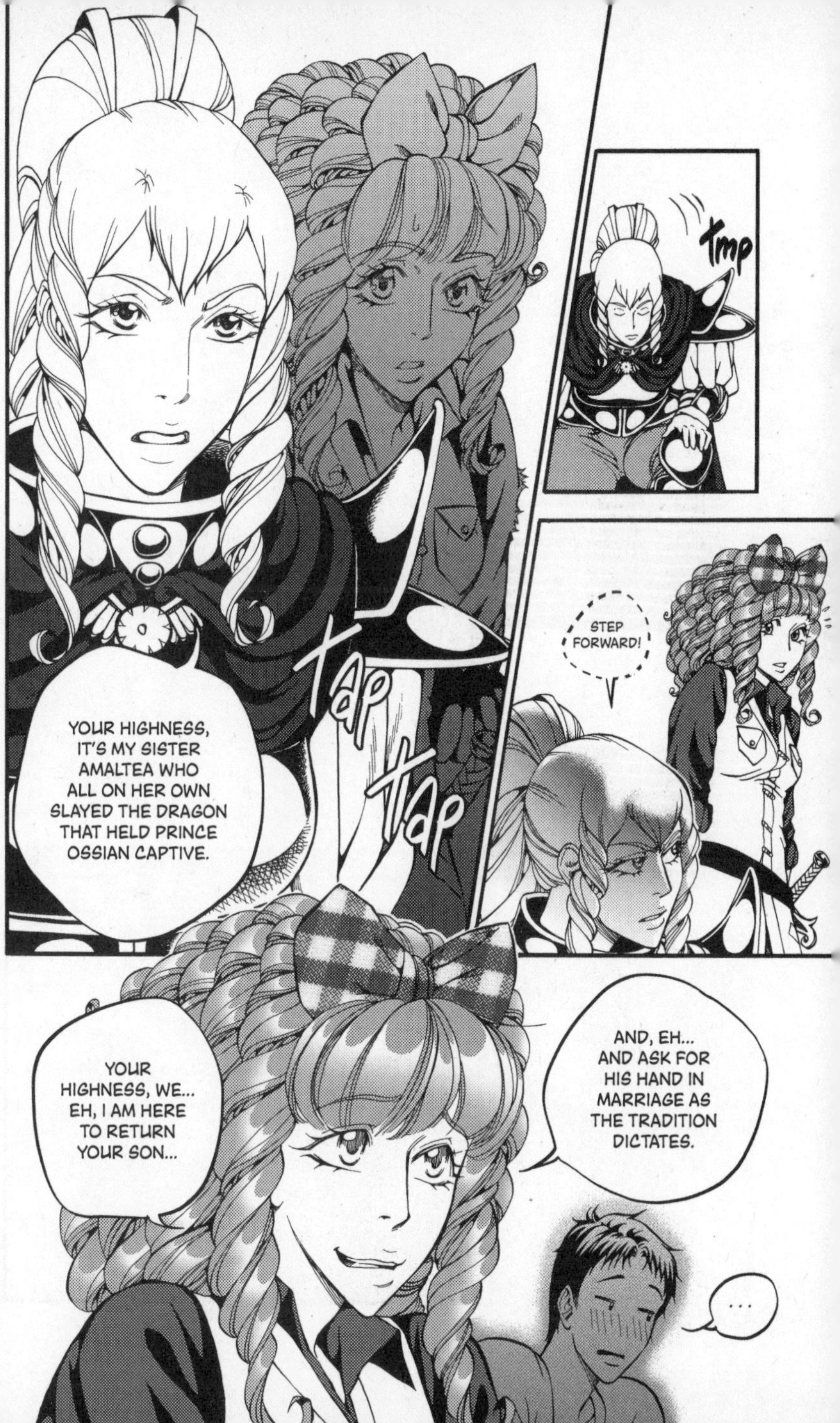
YOUR HIGHNESS, IT'S MY SISTER AMALTEA WHO ALL ON HER OWN SLAYED THE DRAGON THAT HELD PRINCE OSSIAN CAPTIVE.
TAP
TAP
TMP
STEP FORWARD!
YOUR HIGHNESS, WE... EH, I AM HERE TO RETURN YOUR SON...
AND, EH... AND ASK FOR HIS HAND IN MARRIAGE AS THE TRADITION DICTATES.
...

...

BOW!

RUCK

AH!

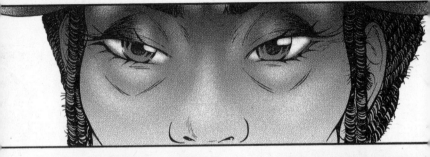

...

TOCK
TOCK
TOCK

TOCK TOCK TOCK

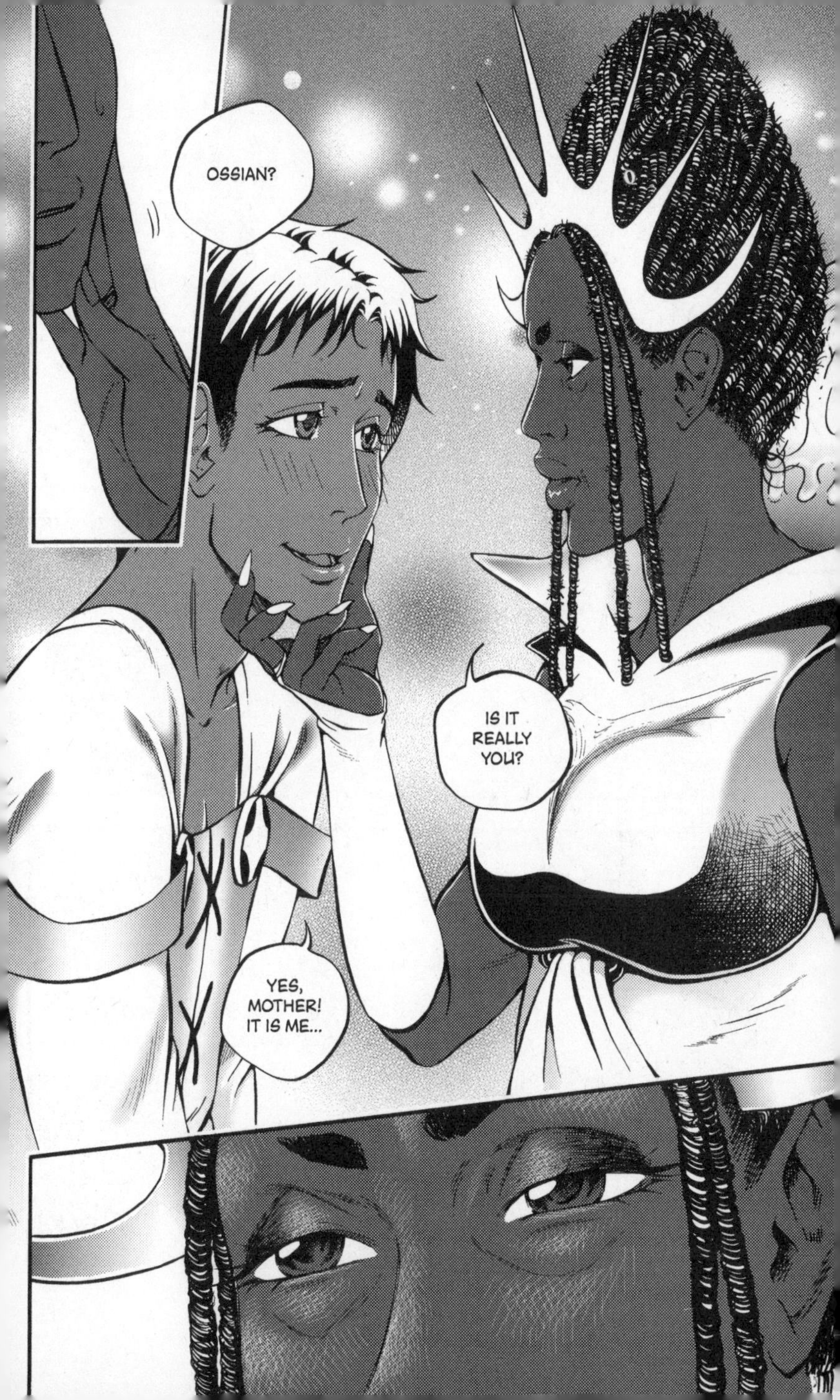
OSSIAN?
IS IT REALLY YOU?
YES, MOTHER! IT IS ME...

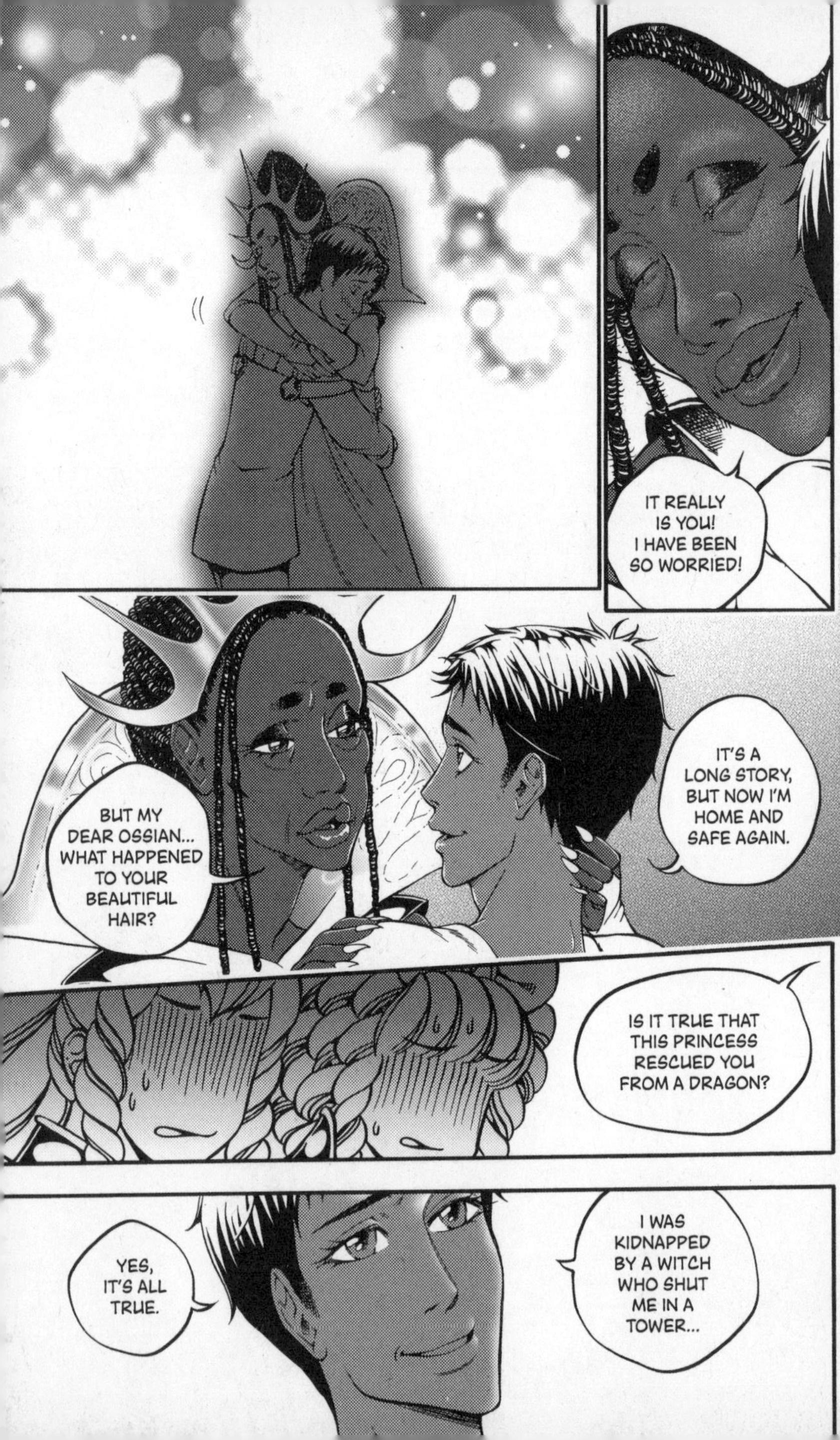
IT REALLY IS YOU! I HAVE BEEN SO WORRIED!
BUT MY DEAR OSSIAN... WHAT HAPPENED TO YOUR BEAUTIFUL HAIR?
IT'S A LONG STORY, BUT NOW I'M HOME AND SAFE AGAIN.
IS IT TRUE THAT THIS PRINCESS RESCUED YOU FROM A DRAGON?
YES, IT'S ALL TRUE.
I WAS KIDNAPPED BY A WITCH WHO SHUT ME IN A TOWER...

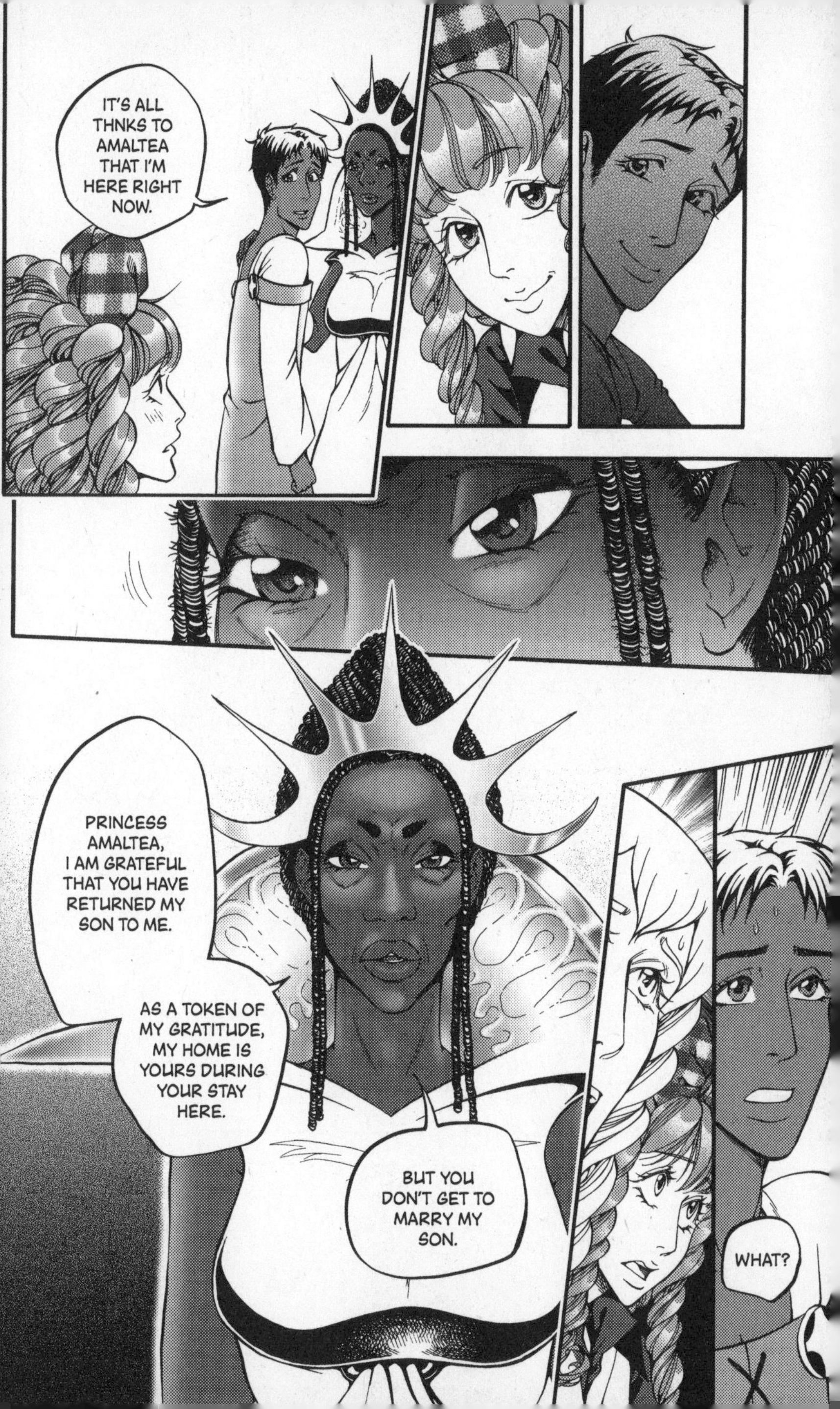
IT'S ALL THNKS TO AMALTEA THAT I'M HERE RIGHT NOW.
PRINCESS AMALTEA, I AM GRATEFUL THAT YOU HAVE RETURNED MY SON TO ME.
AS A TOKEN OF MY GRATITUDE, MY HOME IS YOURS DURING YOUR STAY HERE.
BUT YOU DON'T GET TO MARRY MY SON.
WHAT?

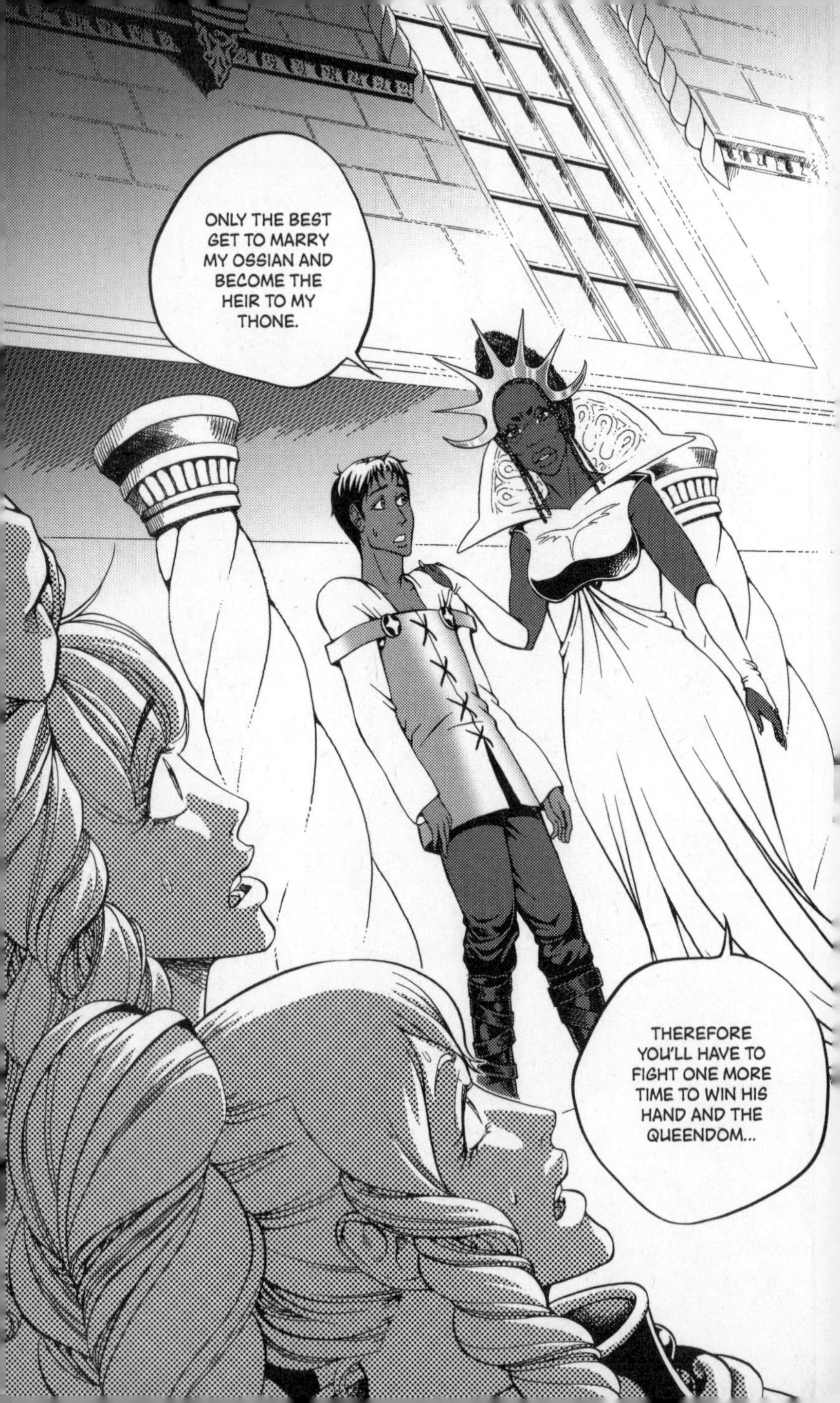
ONLY THE BEST GET TO MARRY MY OSSIAN AND BECOME THE HEIR TO MY THONE.
THEREFORE YOU'LL HAVE TO FIGHT ONE MORE TIME TO WIN HIS HAND AND THE QUEENDOM...

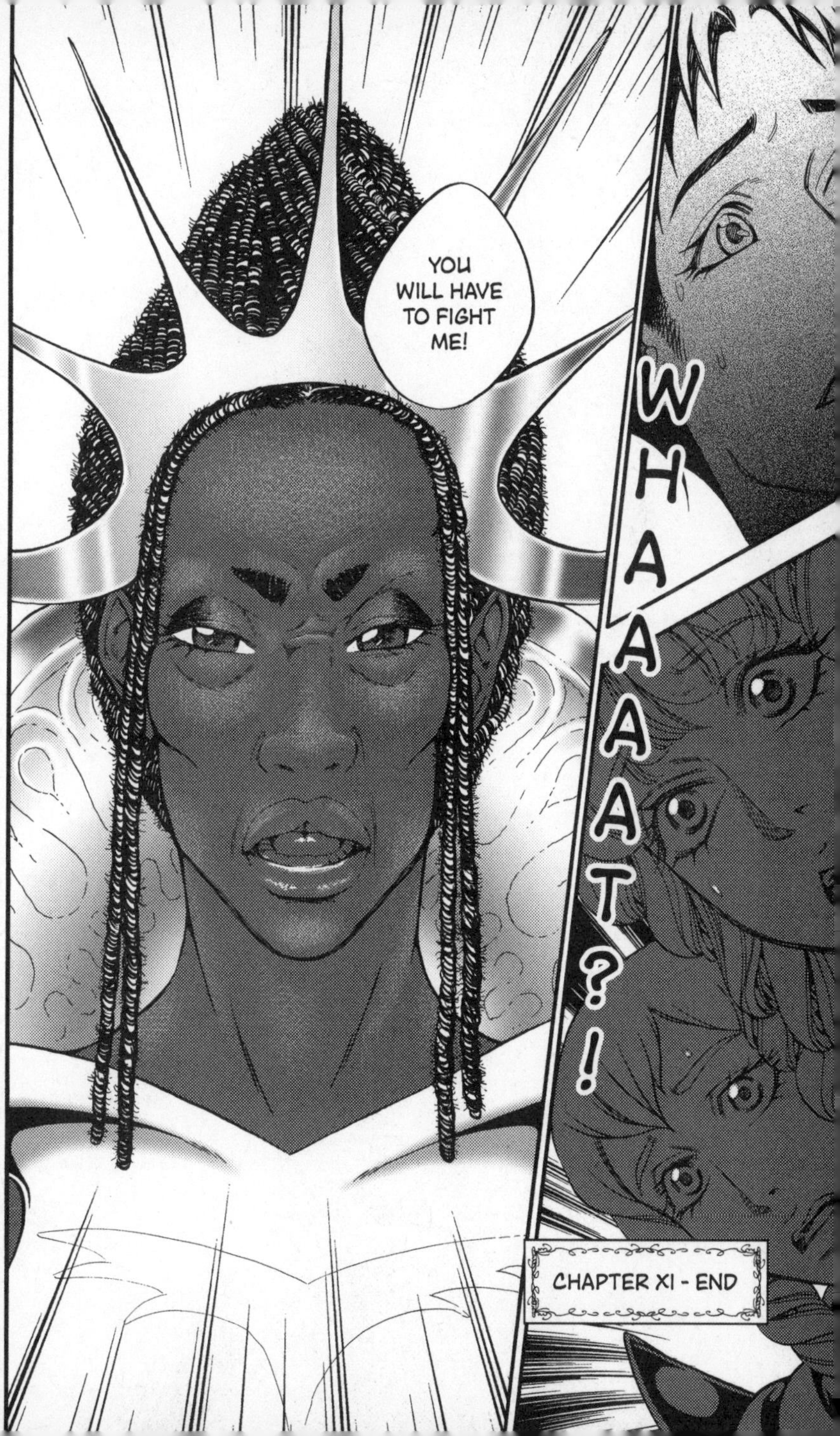
YOU WILL HAVE TO FIGHT ME!
WHAAAAT?!
CHAPTER XI - END

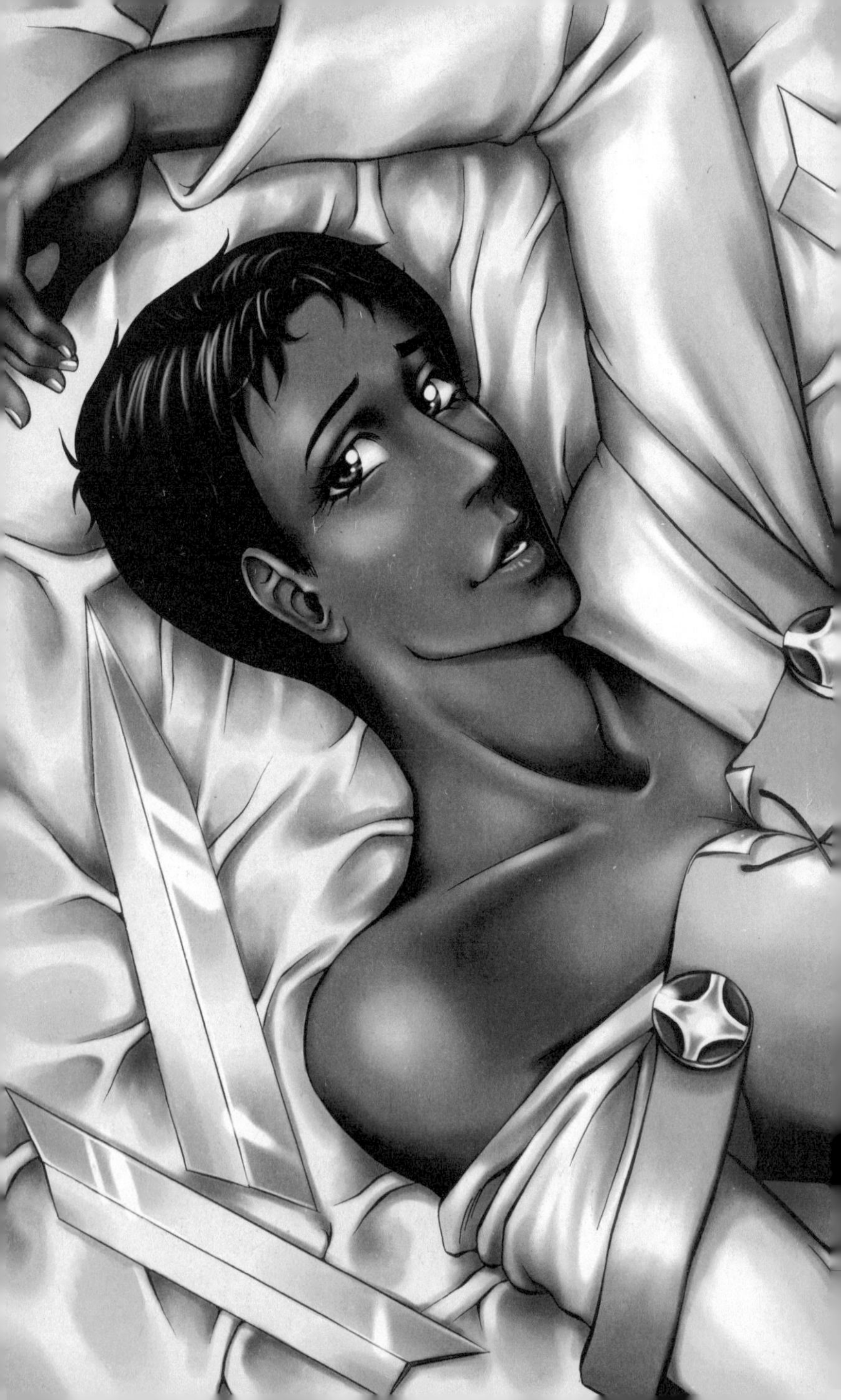

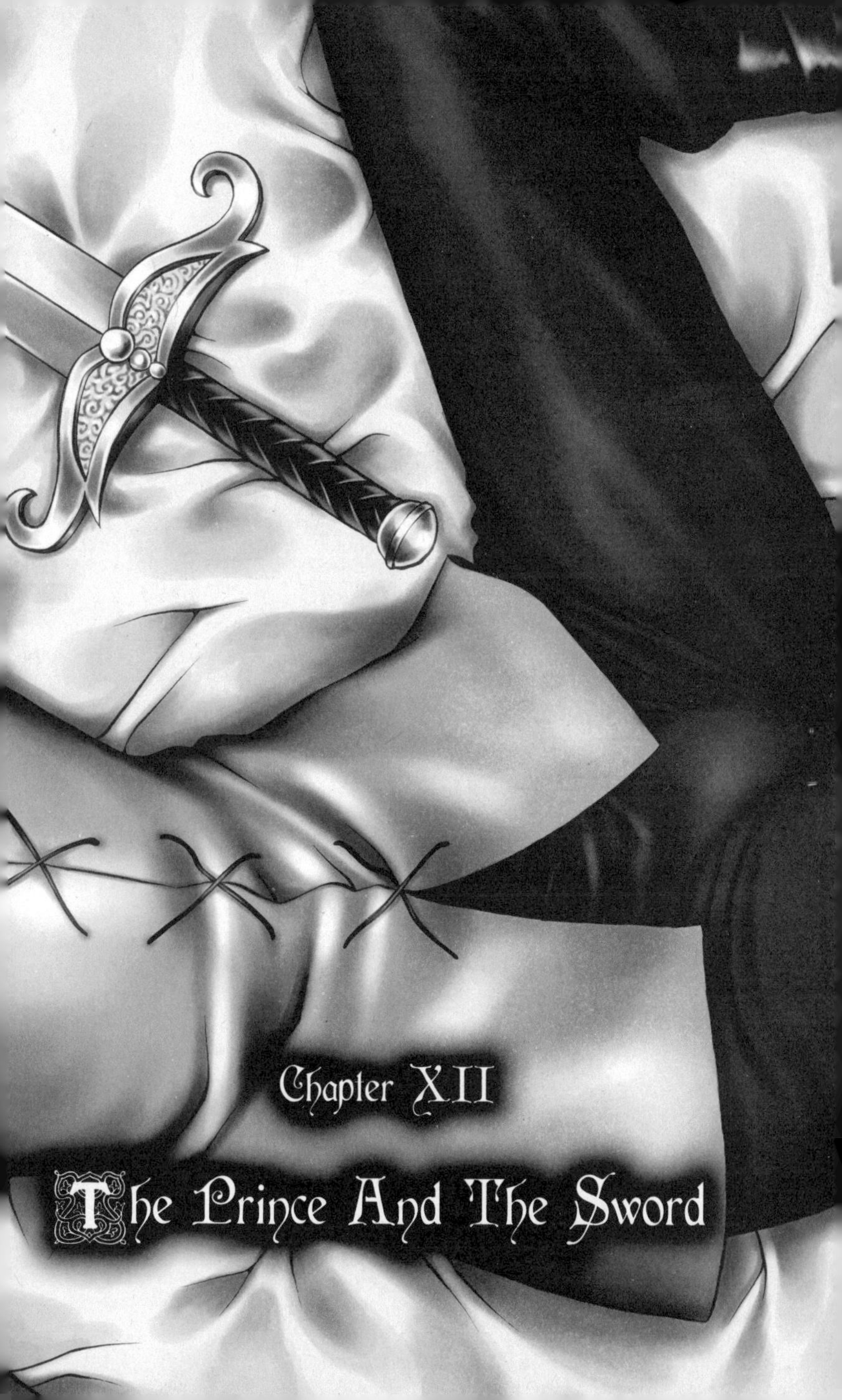
Chapter XII
The Prince And The Sword

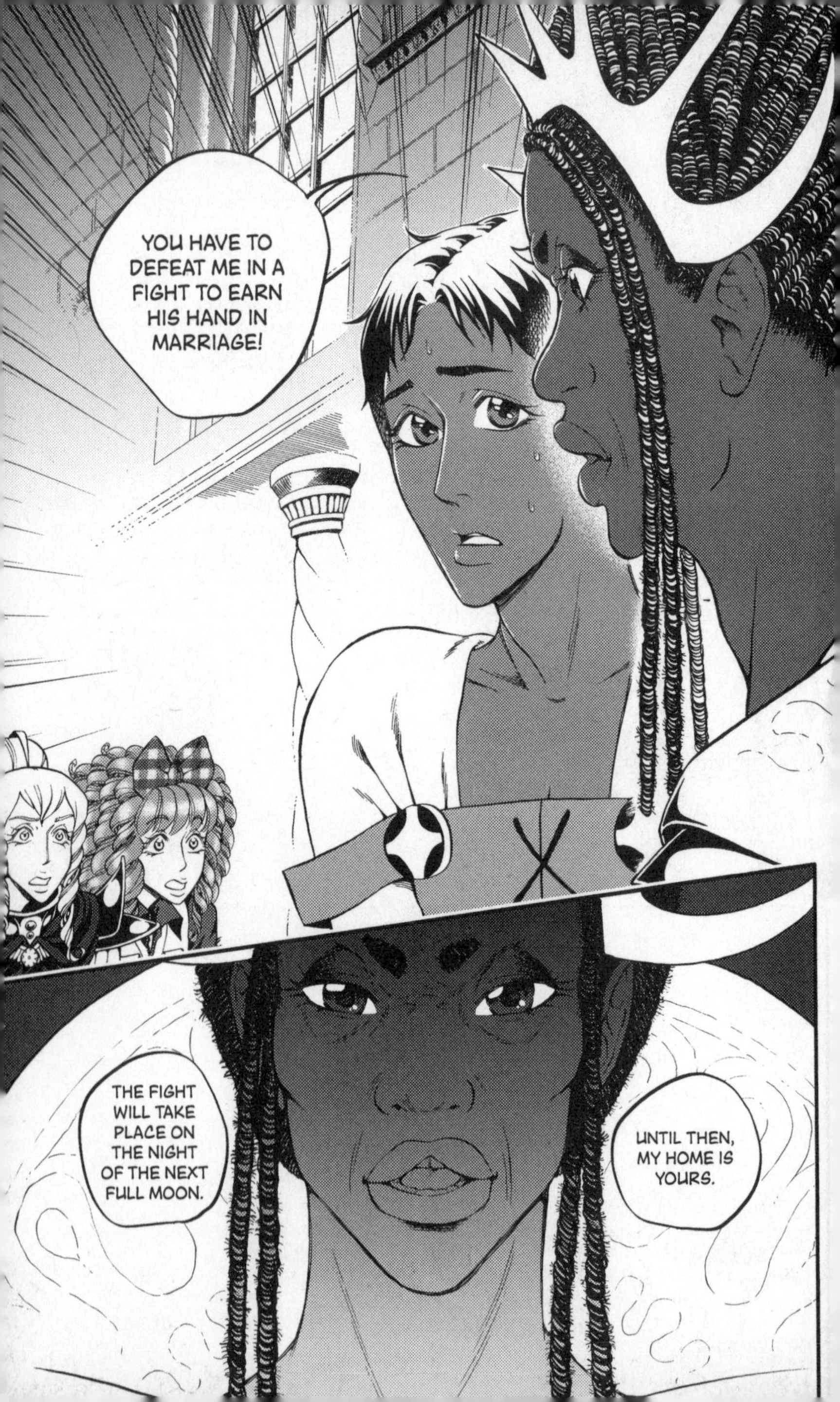
YOU HAVE TO DEFEAT ME IN A FIGHT TO EARN HIS HAND IN MARRIAGE!
THE FIGHT WILL TAKE PLACE ON THE NIGHT OF THE NEXT FULL MOON.
UNTIL THEN, MY HOME IS YOURS.

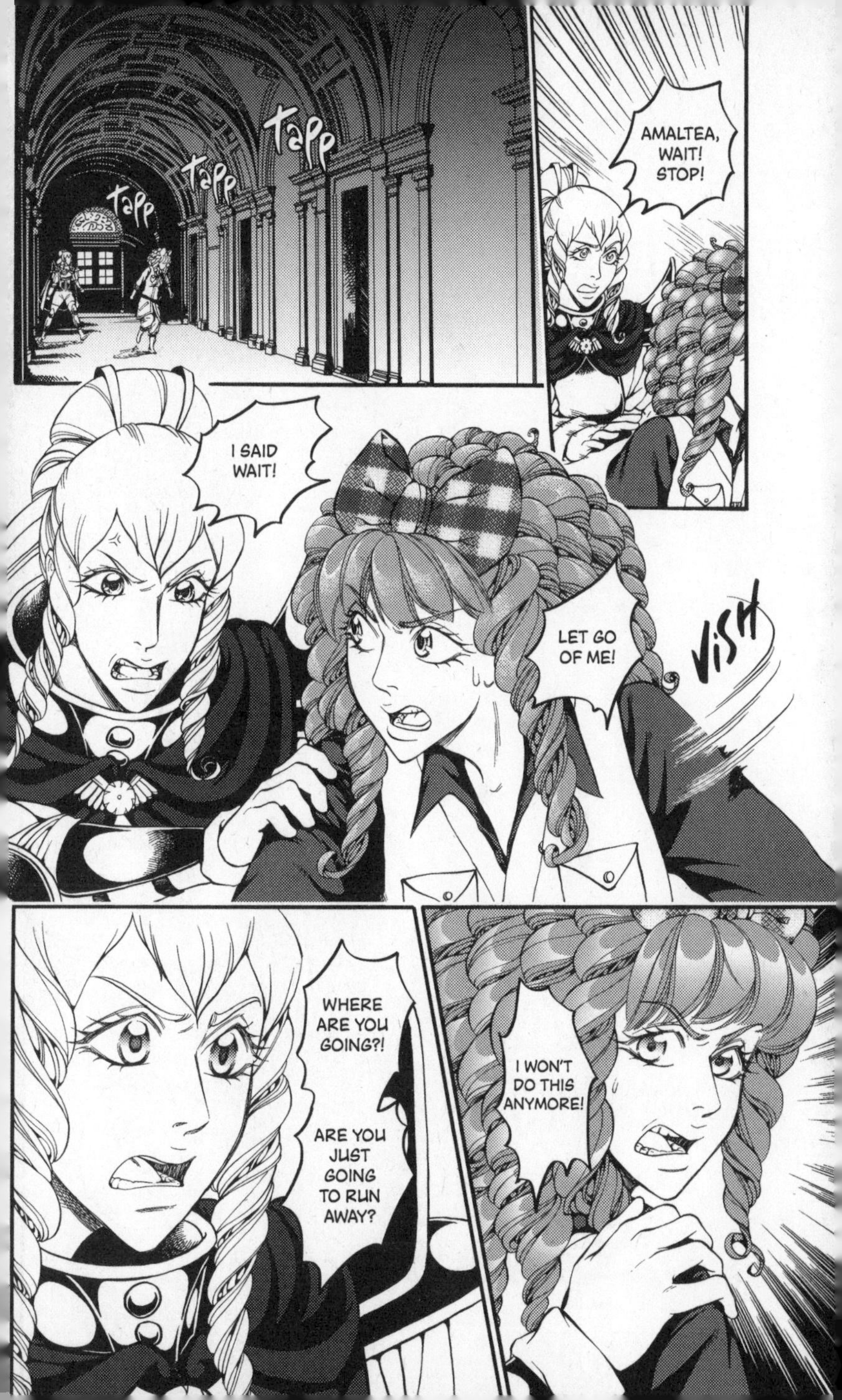
TAPP
TAPP
TAPP
AMALTEA, WAIT! STOP!
I SAID WAIT!
LET GO OF ME!
VISH
WHERE ARE YOU GOING?!
ARE YOU JUST GOING TO RUN AWAY?
I WON'T DO THIS ANYMORE!

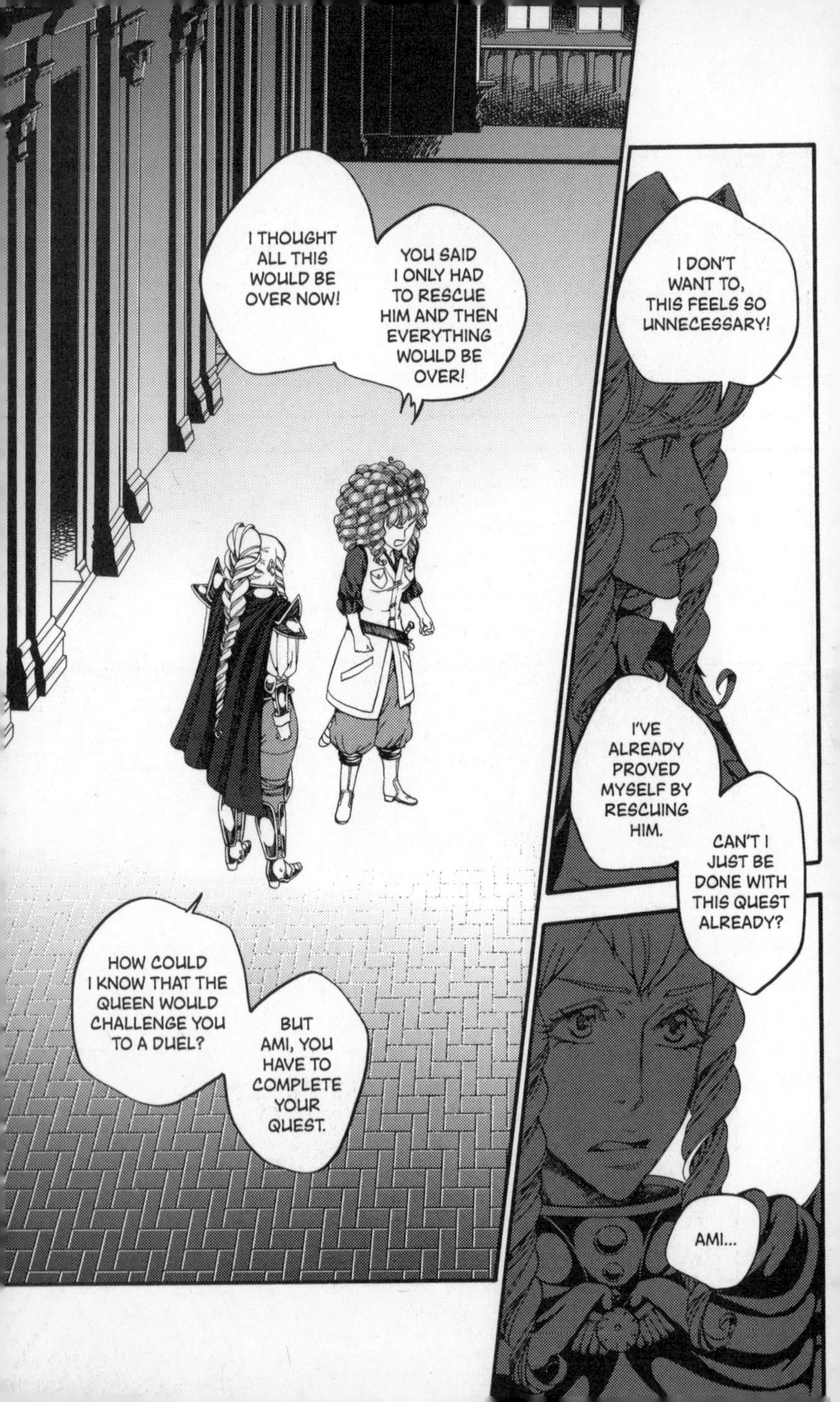
I THOUGHT ALL THIS WOULD BE OVER NOW!
YOU SAID I ONLY HAD TO RESCUE HIM AND THEN EVERYTHING WOULD BE OVER!
HOW COULD I KNOW THAT THE QUEEN WOULD CHALLENGE YOU TO A DUEL?
BUT AMI, YOU HAVE TO COMPLETE YOUR QUEST.
I DON'T WANT TO, THIS FEELS SO UNNECESSARY!
I'VE ALREADY PROVED MYSELF BY RESCUING HIM.
CAN'T I JUST BE DONE WITH THIS QUEST ALREADY?
AMI...

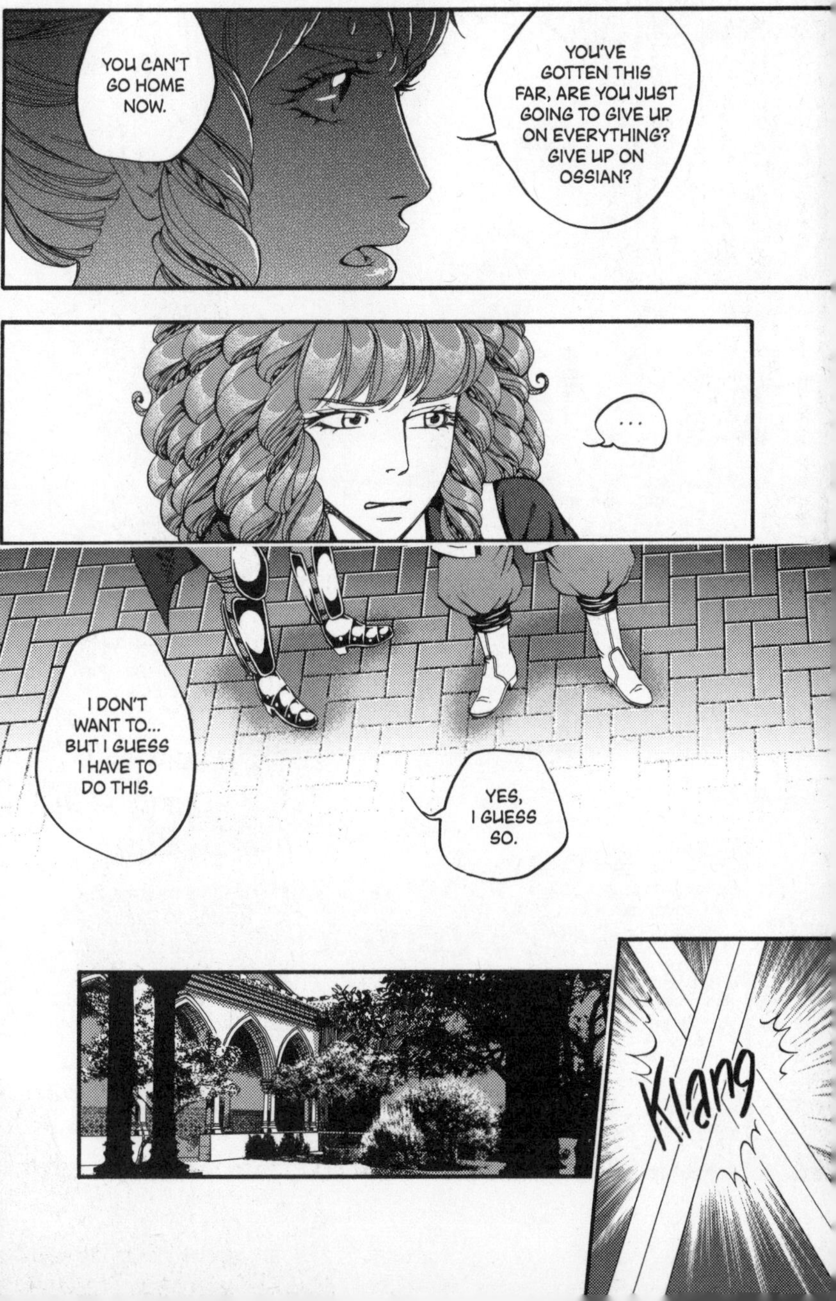
YOU'VE GOTTEN THIS FAR, ARE YOU JUST GOING TO GIVE UP ON EVERYTHING? GIVE UP ON OSSIAN?
YOU CAN'T GO HOME NOW.
...
YES, I GUESS SO.
I DON'T WANT TO... BUT I GUESS I HAVE TO DO THIS.
Klang

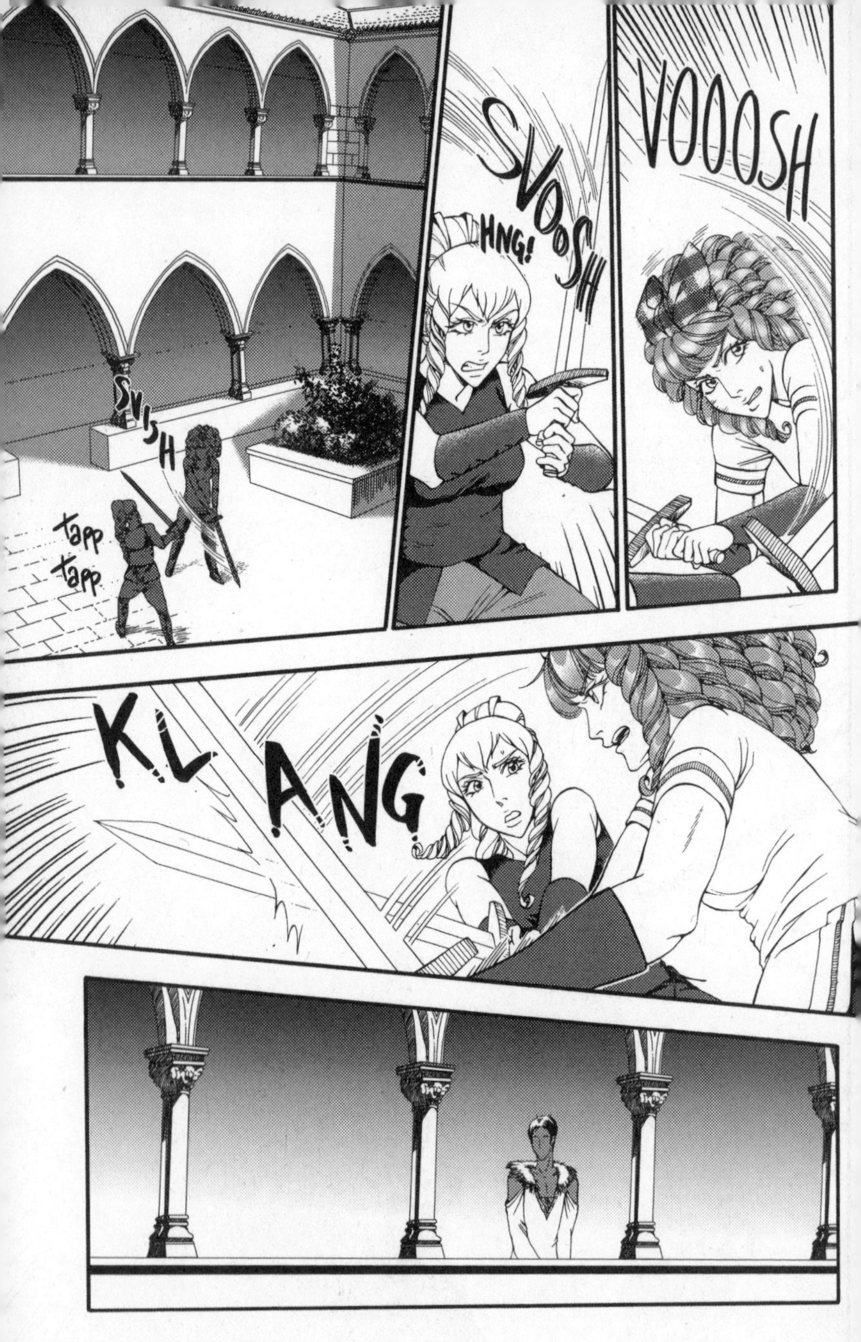
VOOOSH
SVOOSH
HNG!
SVISH
tapp
tapp
KLANG

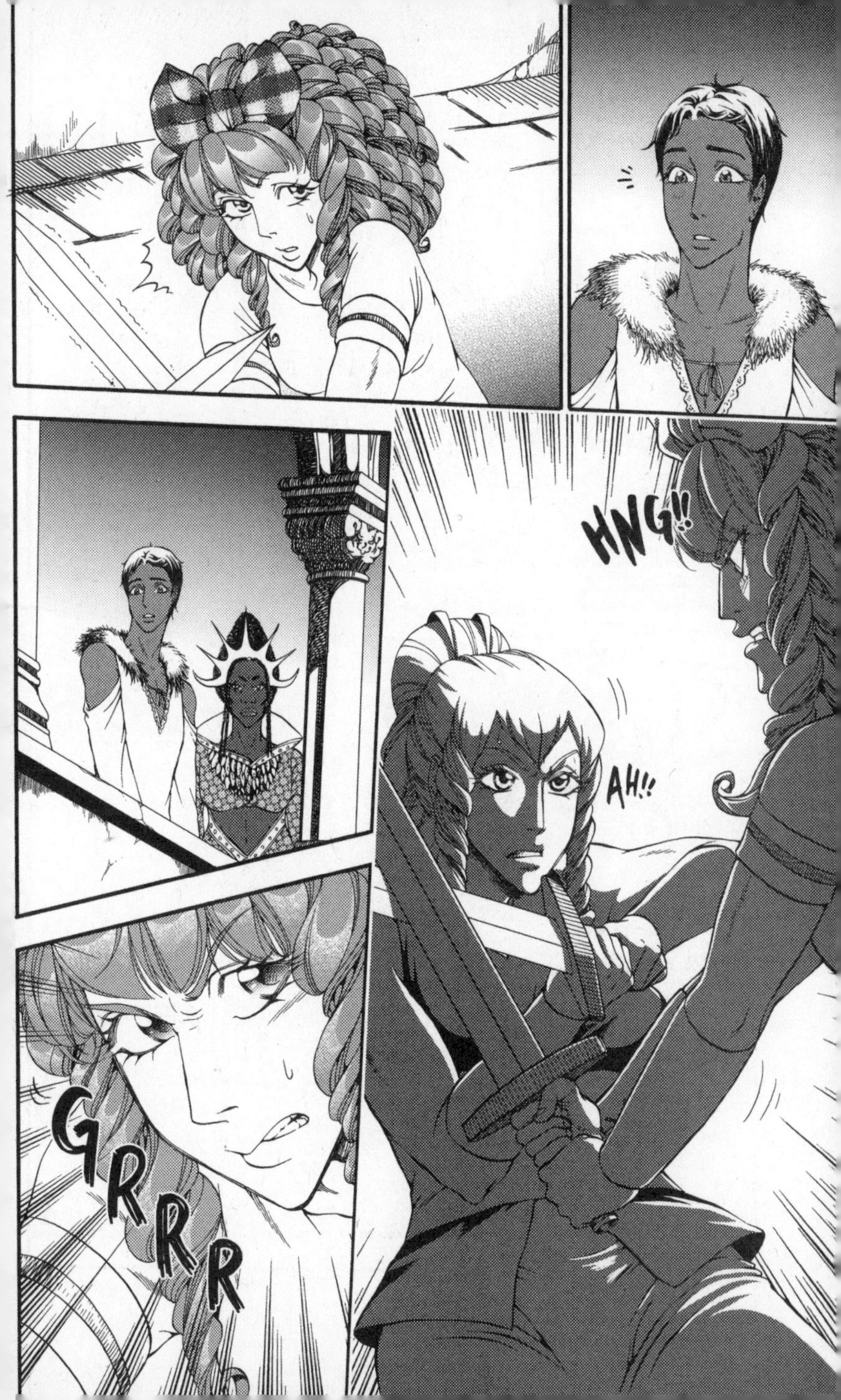
HNG!!
AH!!
GRRR

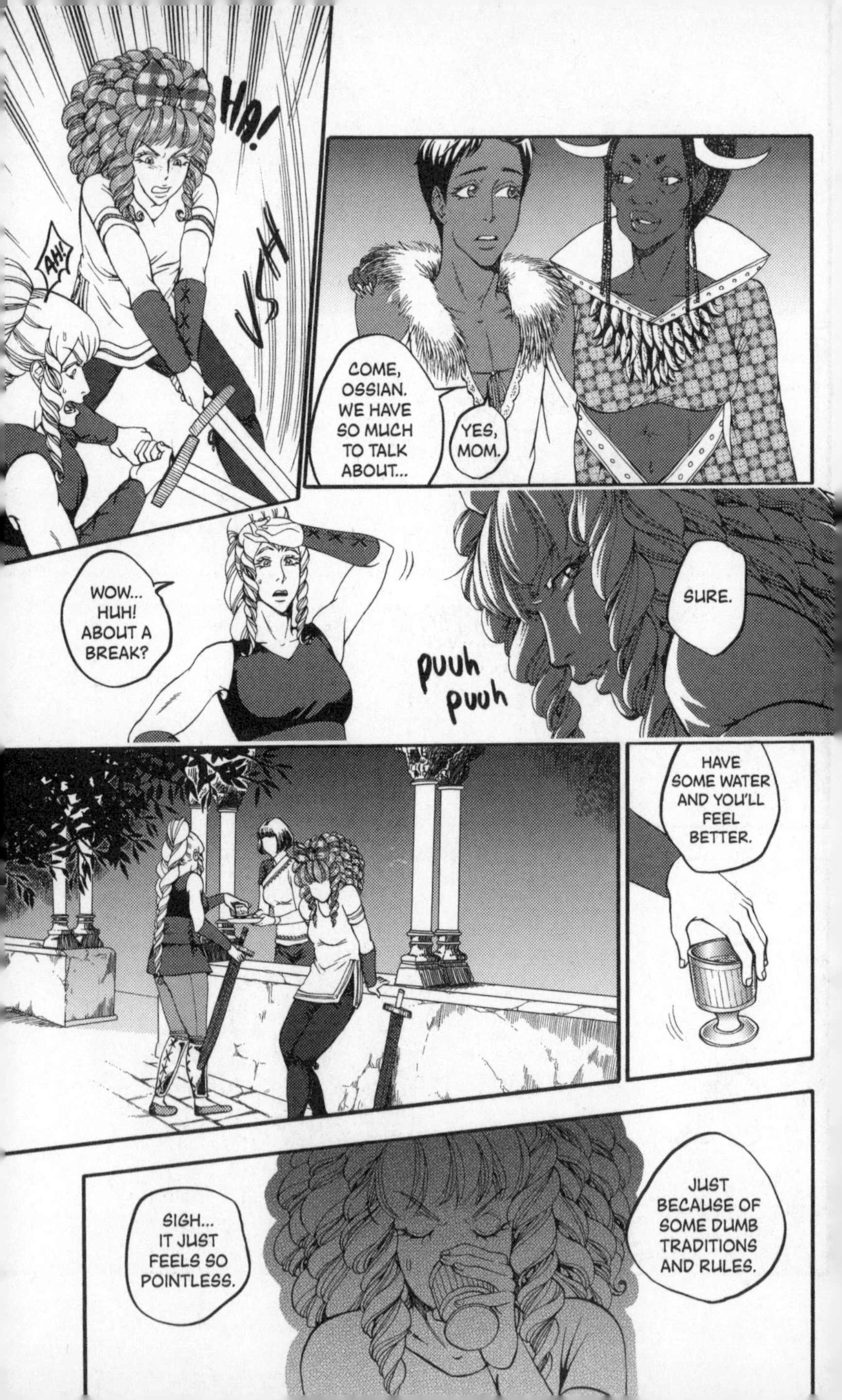
HA!
AH!
VSH
COME, OSSIAN. WE HAVE SO MUCH TO TALK ABOUT...
YES, MOM.
WOW... HUH! ABOUT A BREAK?
puuh puuh
SURE.
HAVE SOME WATER AND YOU'LL FEEL BETTER.
SIGH... IT JUST FEELS SO POINTLESS.
JUST BECAUSE OF SOME DUMB TRADITIONS AND RULES.

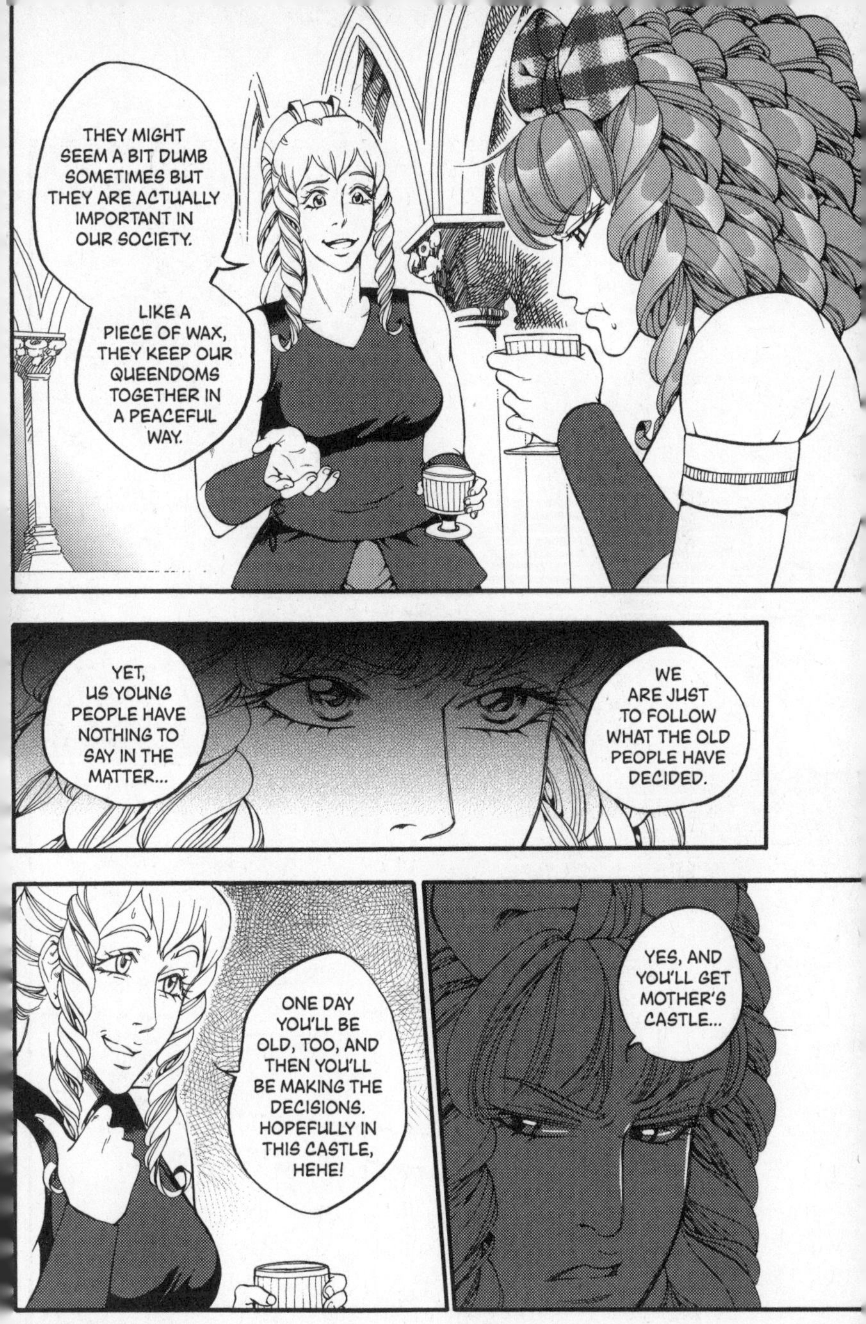

THEY MIGHT SEEM A BIT DUMB SOMETIMES BUT THEY ARE ACTUALLY IMPORTANT IN OUR SOCIETY.
LIKE A PIECE OF WAX, THEY KEEP OUR QUEENDOMS TOGETHER IN A PEACEFUL WAY.
YET, US YOUNG PEOPLE HAVE NOTHING TO SAY IN THE MATTER...
WE ARE JUST TO FOLLOW WHAT THE OLD PEOPLE HAVE DECIDED.
ONE DAY YOU'LL BE OLD, TOO, AND THEN YOU'LL BE MAKING THE DECISIONS. HOPEFULLY IN THIS CASTLE, HEHE!
YES, AND YOU'LL GET MOTHER'S CASTLE...

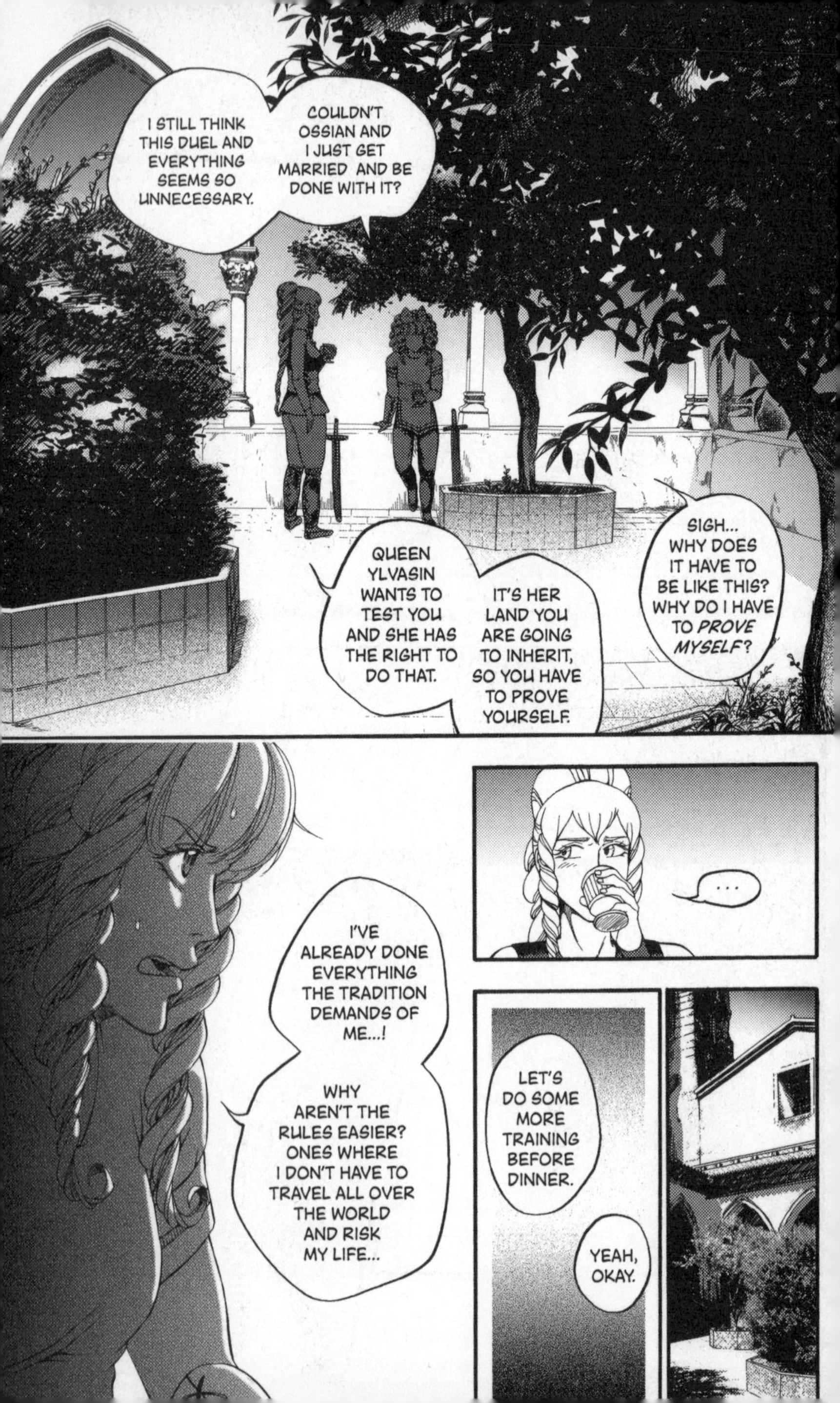
I STILL THINK THIS DUEL AND EVERYTHING SEEMS SO UNNECESSARY.
COULDN'T OSSIAN AND I JUST GET MARRIED AND BE DONE WITH IT?
QUEEN YLVASIN WANTS TO TEST YOU AND SHE HAS THE RIGHT TO DO THAT.
IT'S HER LAND YOU ARE GOING TO INHERIT, SO YOU HAVE TO PROVE YOURSELF.
SIGH... WHY DOES IT HAVE TO BE LIKE THIS? WHY DO I HAVE TO *PROVE MYSELF*?
I'VE ALREADY DONE EVERYTHING THE TRADITION DEMANDS OF ME...!
WHY AREN'T THE RULES EASIER? ONES WHERE I DON'T HAVE TO TRAVEL ALL OVER THE WORLD AND RISK MY LIFE...
...
LET'S DO SOME MORE TRAINING BEFORE DINNER.
YEAH, OKAY.

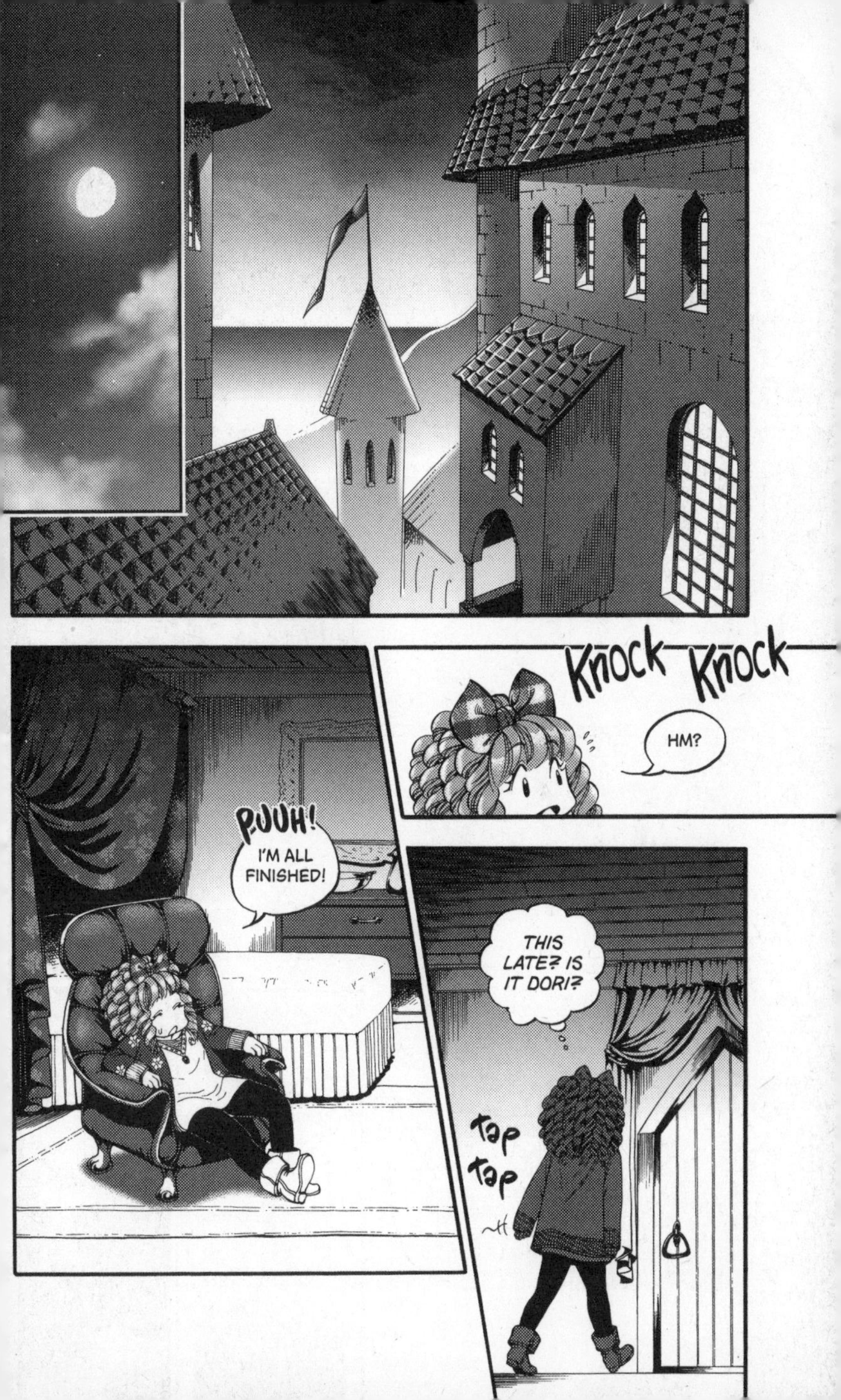
PUUH!
I'M ALL FINISHED!
Knock Knock
HM?
THIS LATE? IS IT DORI?
tap tap

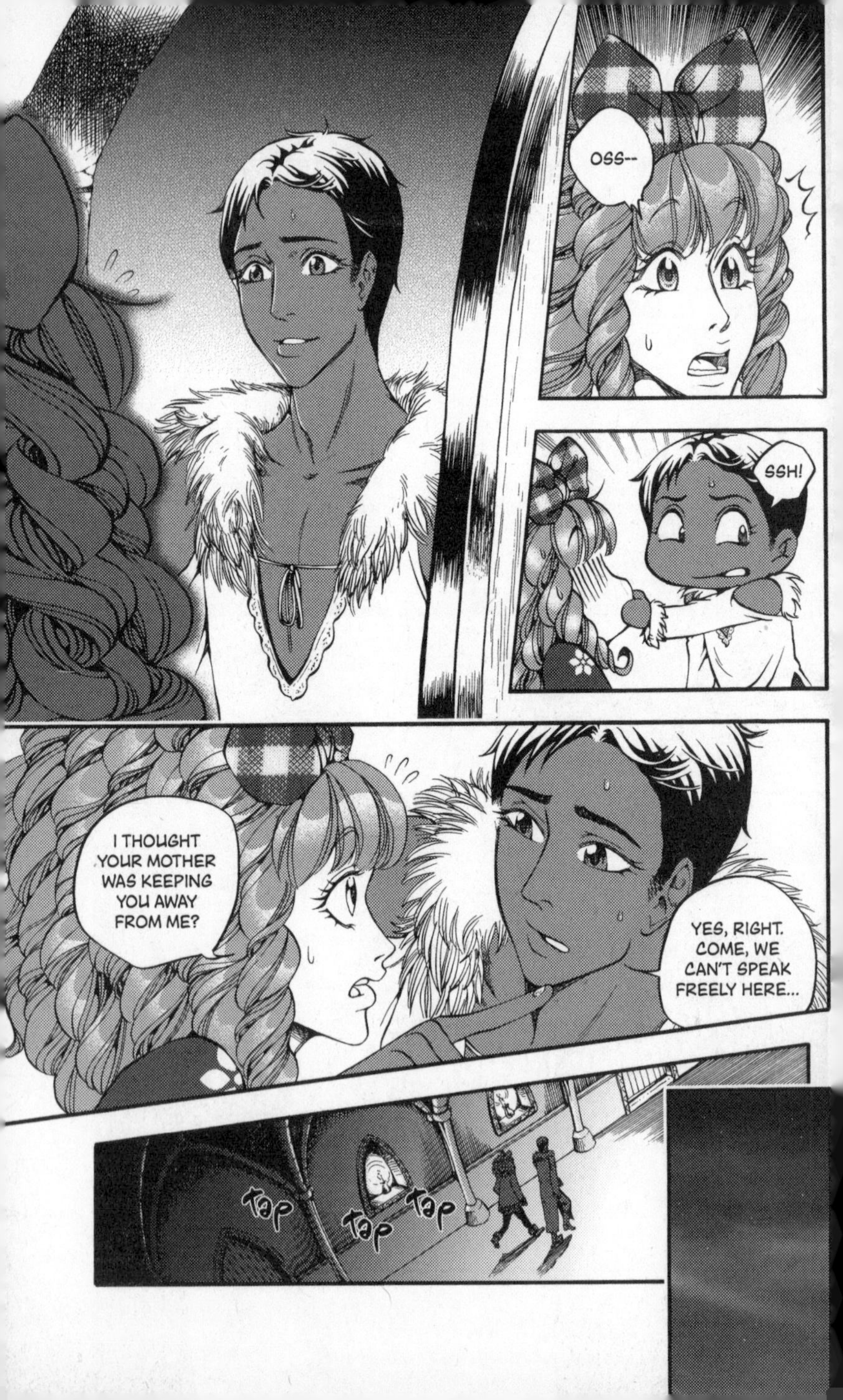
OSS--
SSH!
I THOUGHT YOUR MOTHER WAS KEEPING YOU AWAY FROM ME?
YES, RIGHT. COME, WE CAN'T SPEAK FREELY HERE...
TAP TAP TAP

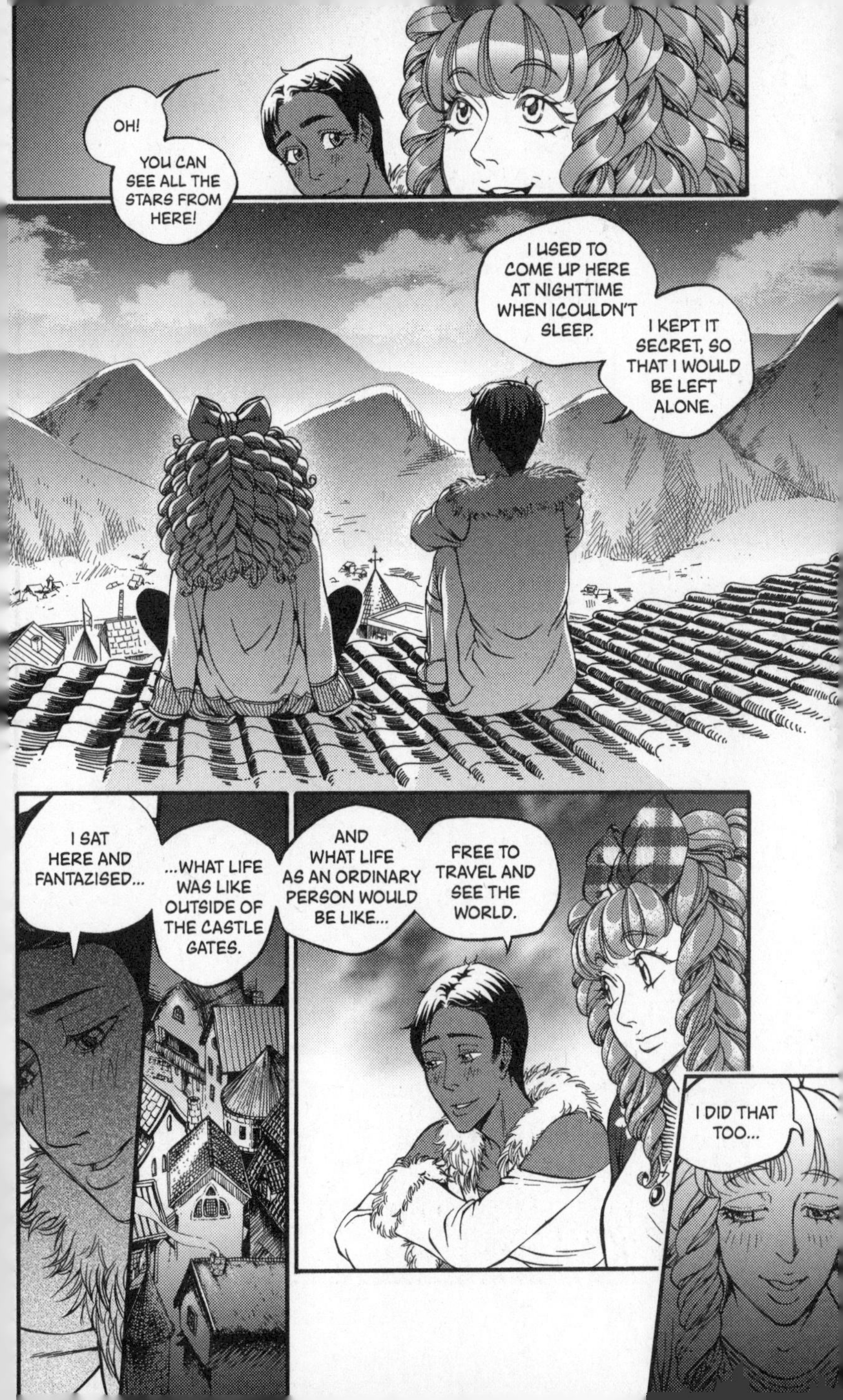
OH! YOU CAN SEE ALL THE STARS FROM HERE!
I USED TO COME UP HERE AT NIGHTTIME WHEN ICOULDN'T SLEEP.
I KEPT IT SECRET, SO THAT I WOULD BE LEFT ALONE.
I SAT HERE AND FANTAZISED...
...WHAT LIFE WAS LIKE OUTSIDE OF THE CASTLE GATES.
AND WHAT LIFE AS AN ORDINARY PERSON WOULD BE LIKE...
FREE TO TRAVEL AND SEE THE WORLD.
I DID THAT TOO...

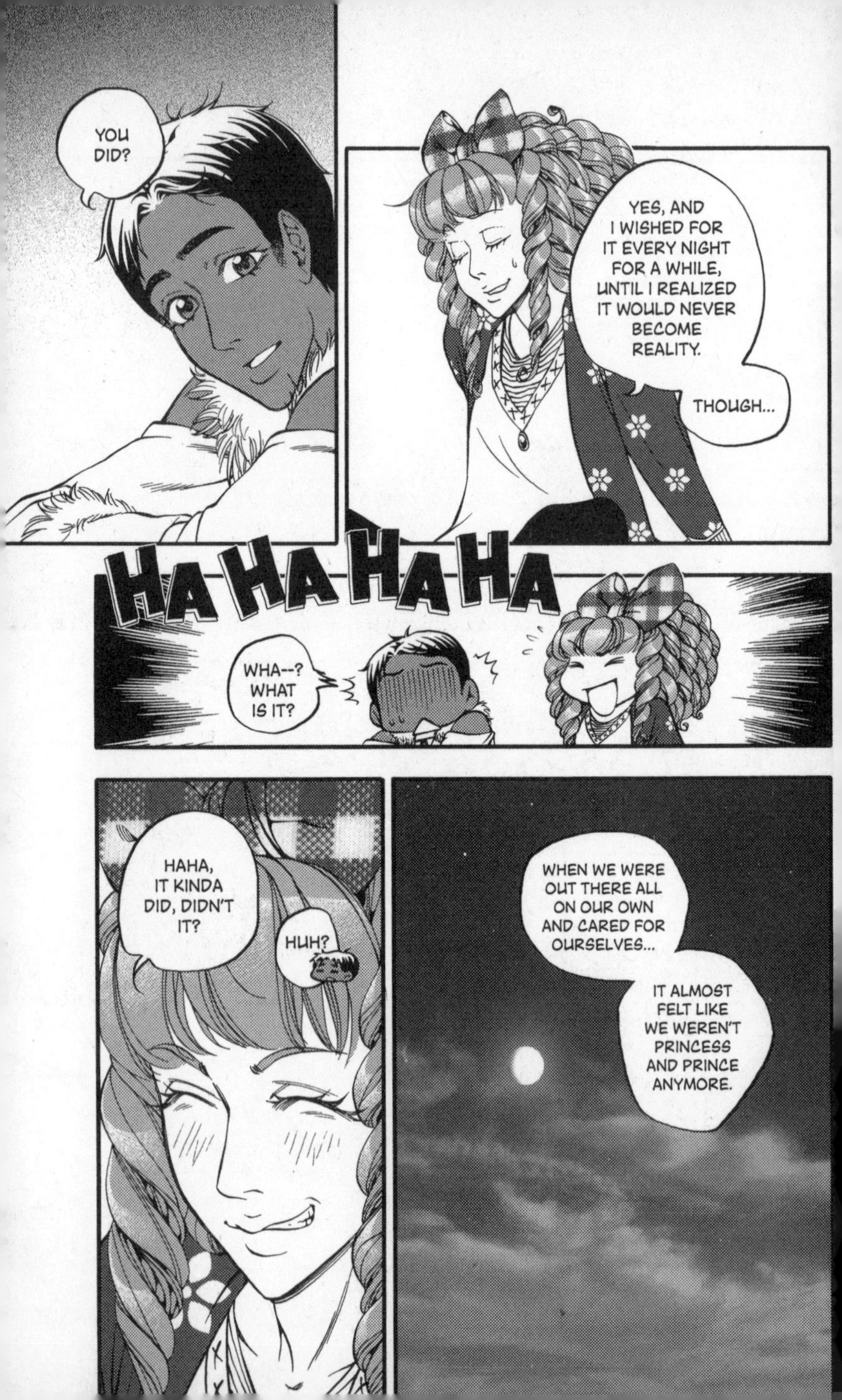
YOU DID?
YES, AND I WISHED FOR IT EVERY NIGHT FOR A WHILE, UNTIL I REALIZED IT WOULD NEVER BECOME REALITY.
THOUGH...
HA HA HA HA HA
WHA--? WHAT IS IT?
HAHA, IT KINDA DID, DIDN'T IT?
HUH?
WHEN WE WERE OUT THERE ALL ON OUR OWN AND CARED FOR OURSELVES...
IT ALMOST FELT LIKE WE WEREN'T PRINCESS AND PRINCE ANYMORE.

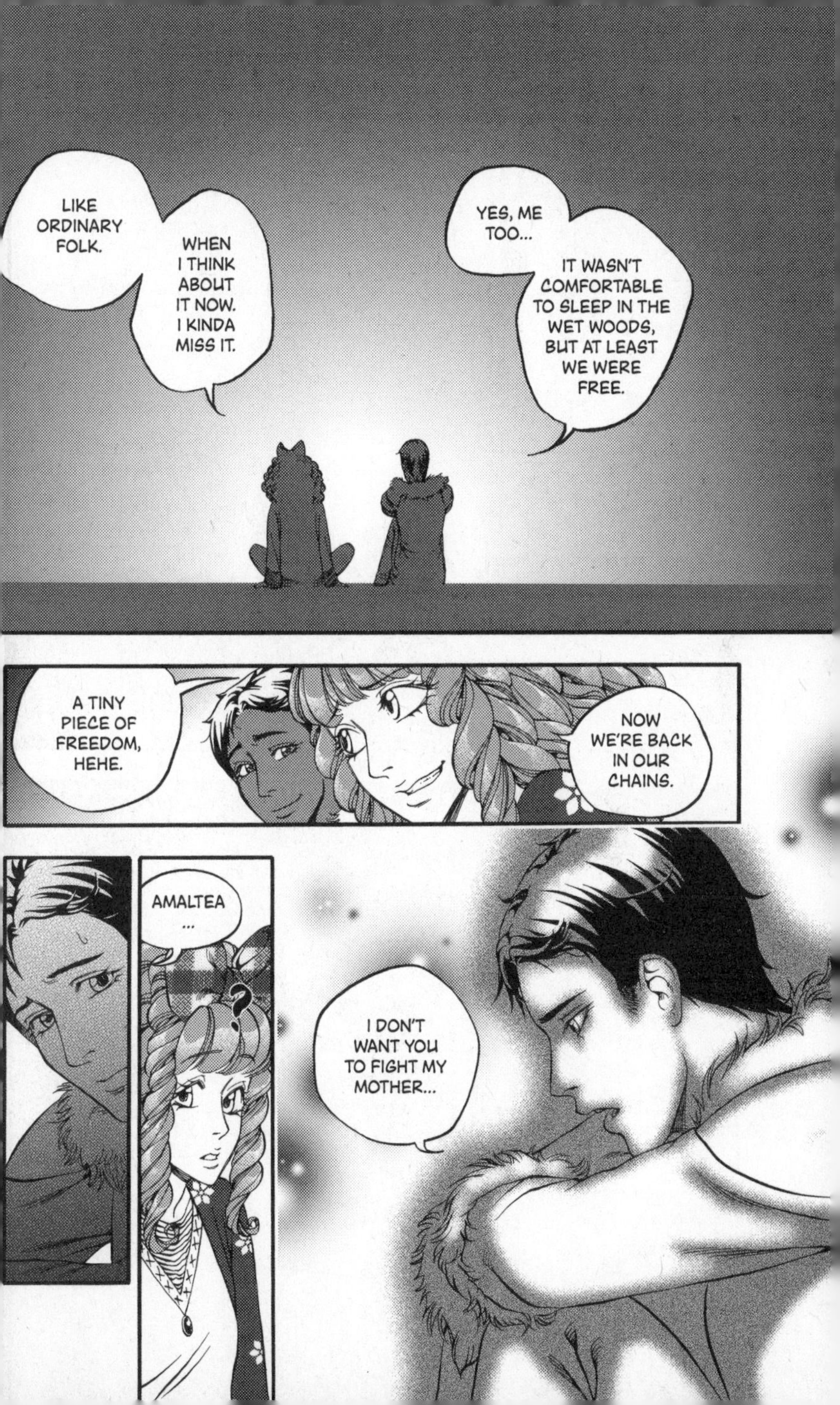
LIKE ORDINARY FOLK.
WHEN I THINK ABOUT IT NOW. I KINDA MISS IT.
YES, ME TOO...
IT WASN'T COMFORTABLE TO SLEEP IN THE WET WOODS, BUT AT LEAST WE WERE FREE.
A TINY PIECE OF FREEDOM, HEHE.
NOW WE'RE BACK IN OUR CHAINS.
AMALTEA ...
?
I DON'T WANT YOU TO FIGHT MY MOTHER...

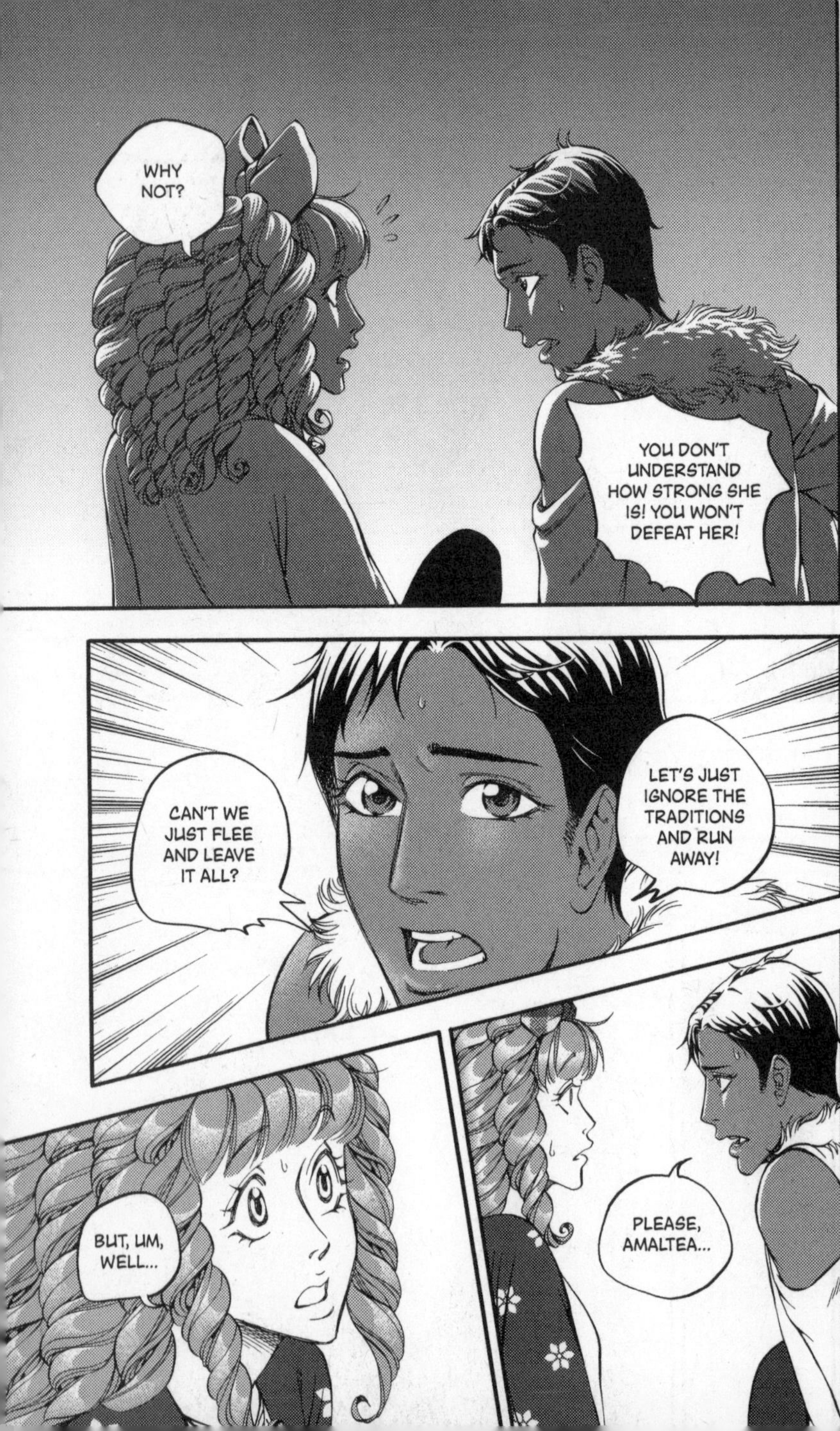
WHY NOT?
YOU DON'T UNDERSTAND HOW STRONG SHE IS! YOU WON'T DEFEAT HER!
LET'S JUST IGNORE THE TRADITIONS AND RUN AWAY!
CAN'T WE JUST FLEE AND LEAVE IT ALL?
PLEASE, AMALTEA...
BUT, UM, WELL...

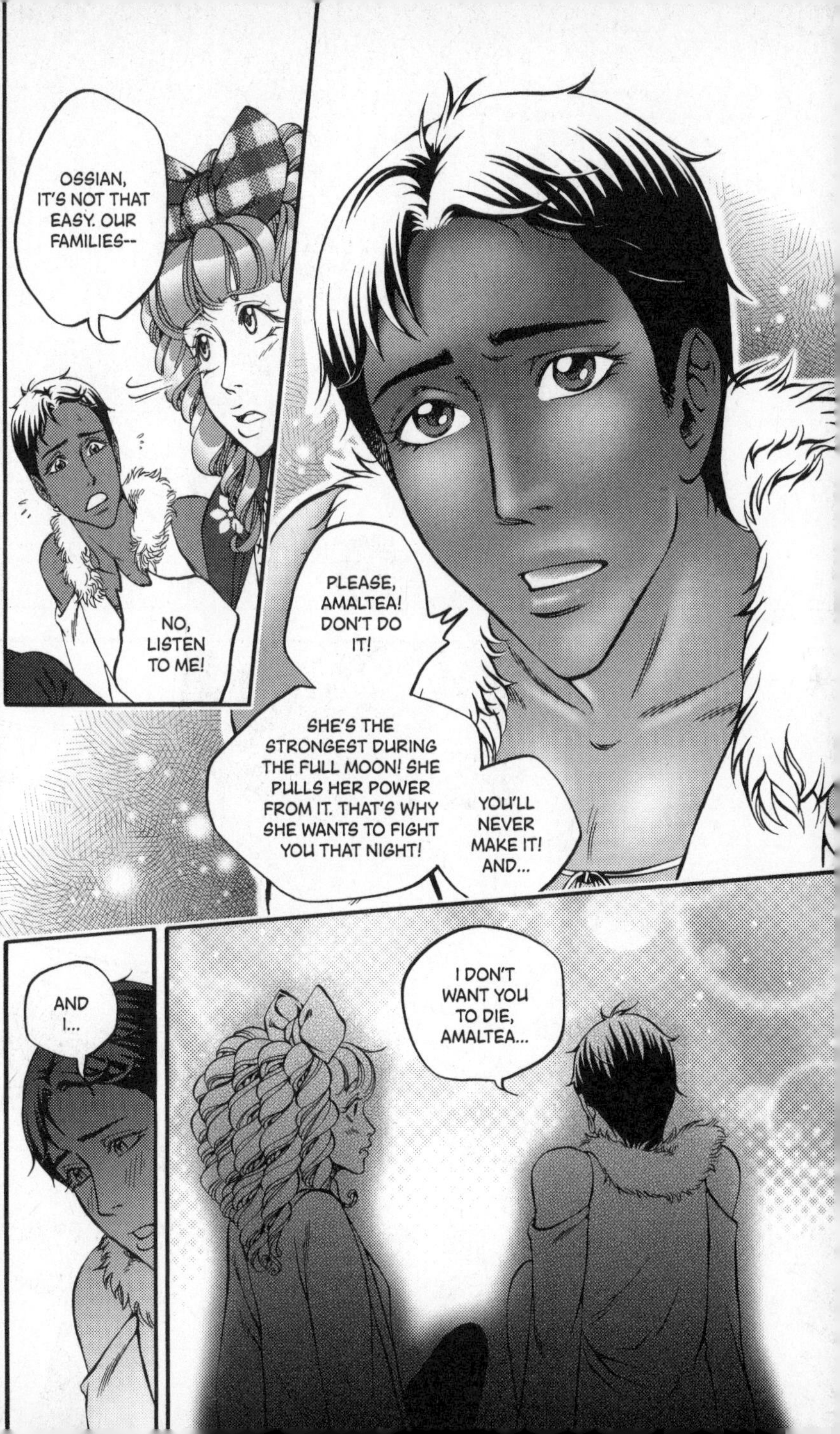
OSSIAN, IT'S NOT THAT EASY. OUR FAMILIES--
NO, LISTEN TO ME!
PLEASE, AMALTEA! DON'T DO IT!
SHE'S THE STRONGEST DURING THE FULL MOON! SHE PULLS HER POWER FROM IT. THAT'S WHY SHE WANTS TO FIGHT YOU THAT NIGHT!
YOU'LL NEVER MAKE IT! AND...
AND I...
I DON'T WANT YOU TO DIE, AMALTEA...

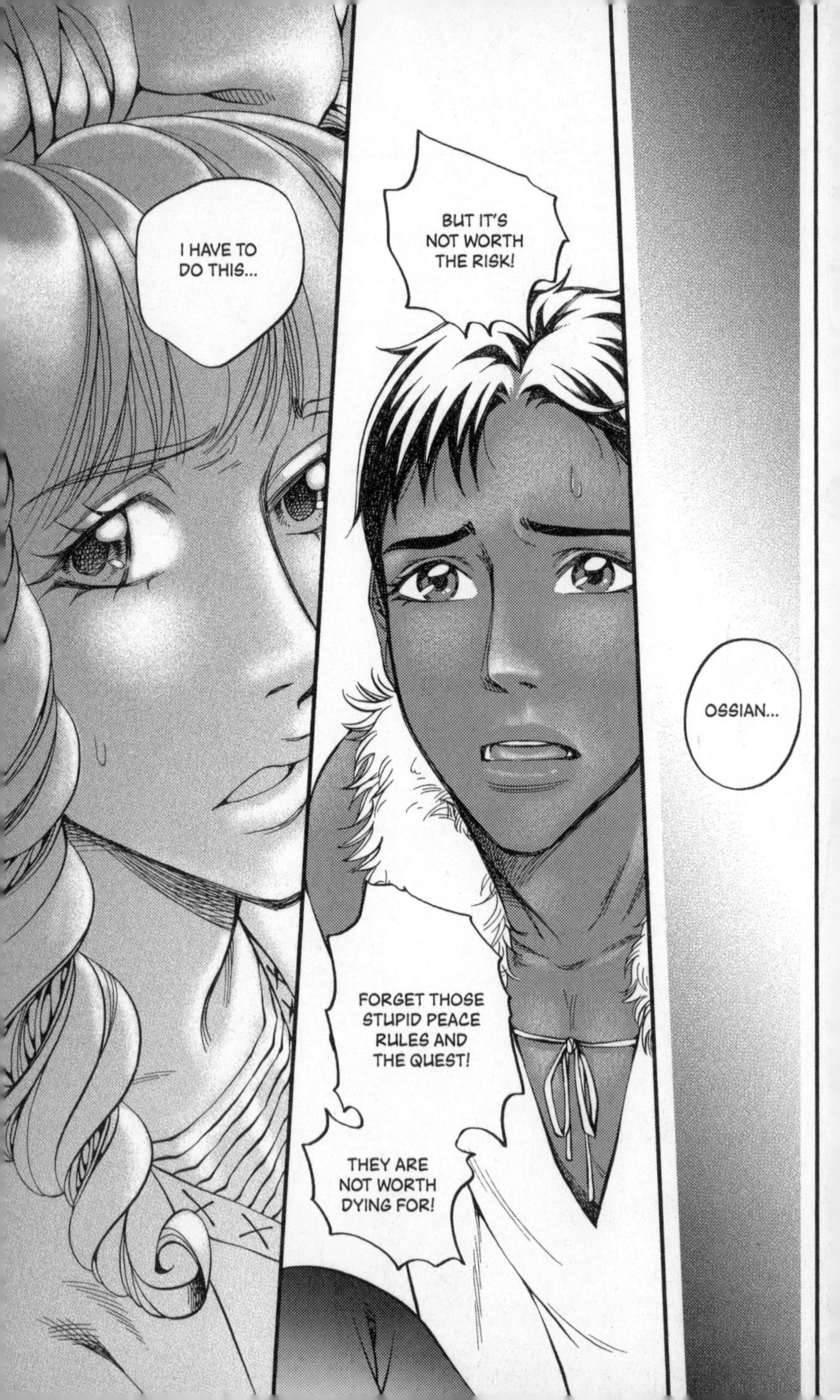
OSSIAN...
BUT IT'S NOT WORTH THE RISK!
FORGET THOSE STUPID PEACE RULES AND THE QUEST!
THEY ARE NOT WORTH DYING FOR!
I HAVE TO DO THIS...

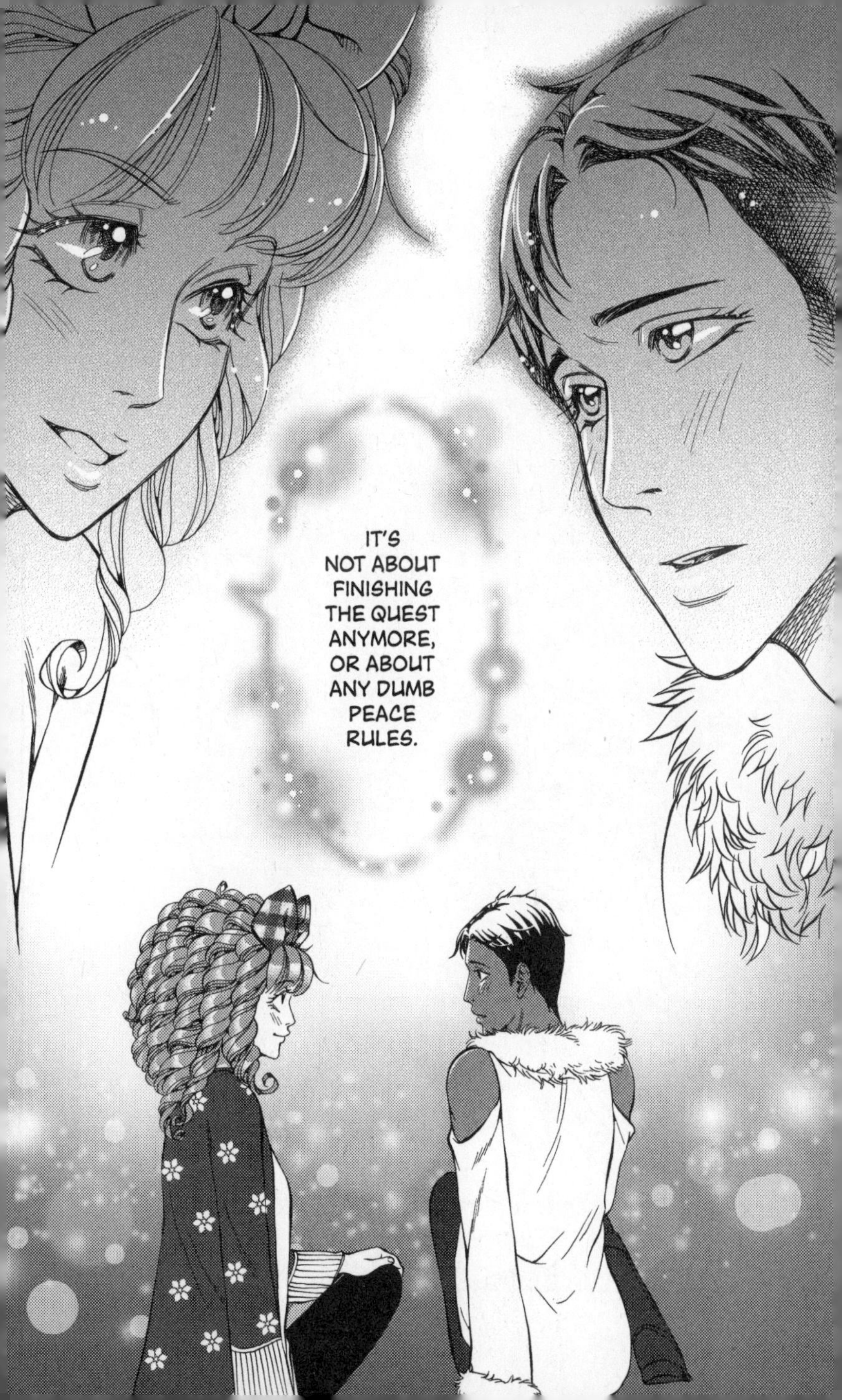
IT'S NOT ABOUT FINISHING THE QUEST ANYMORE, OR ABOUT ANY DUMB PEACE RULES.

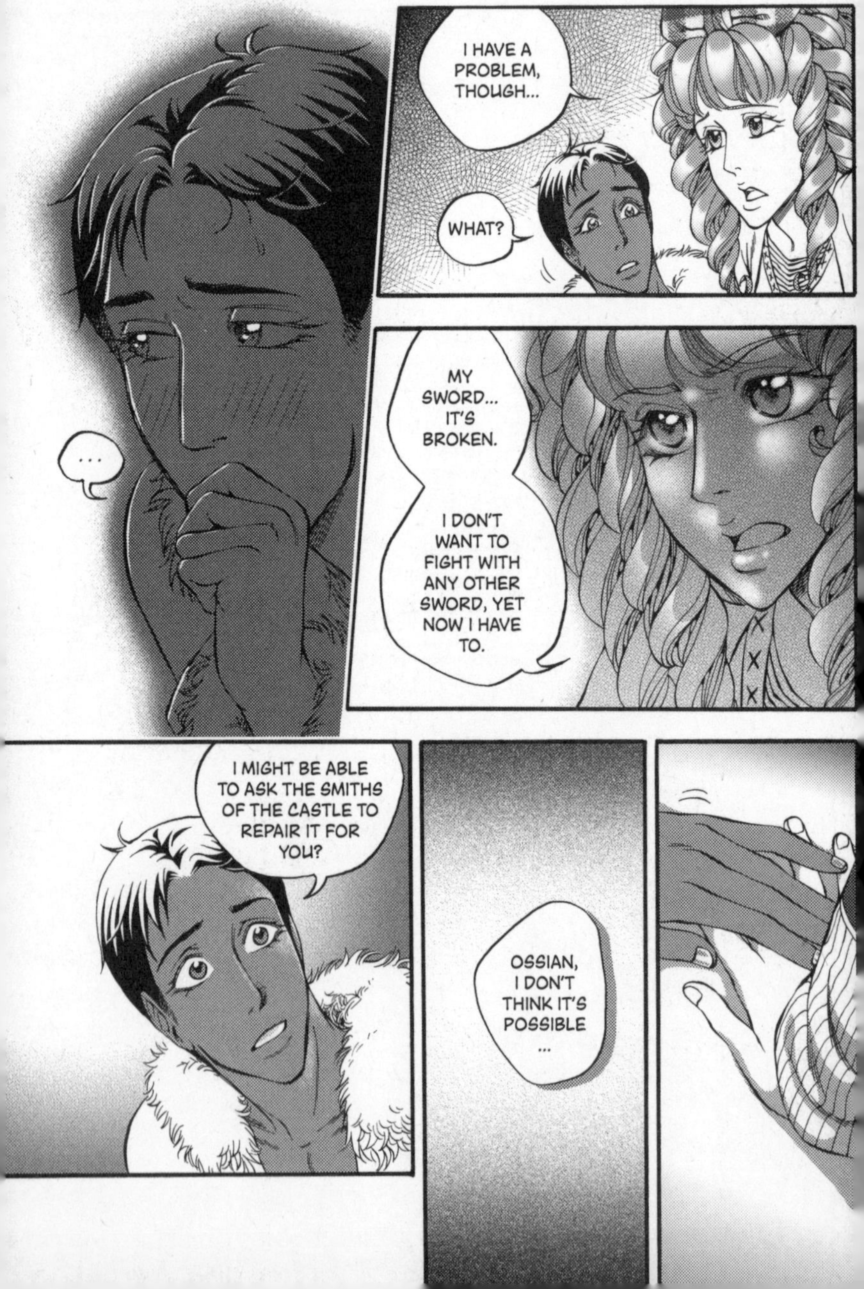
...
I HAVE A PROBLEM, THOUGH...
WHAT?
MY SWORD... IT'S BROKEN.
I DON'T WANT TO FIGHT WITH ANY OTHER SWORD, YET NOW I HAVE TO.
I MIGHT BE ABLE TO ASK THE SMITHS OF THE CASTLE TO REPAIR IT FOR YOU?
OSSIAN, I DON'T THINK IT'S POSSIBLE ...

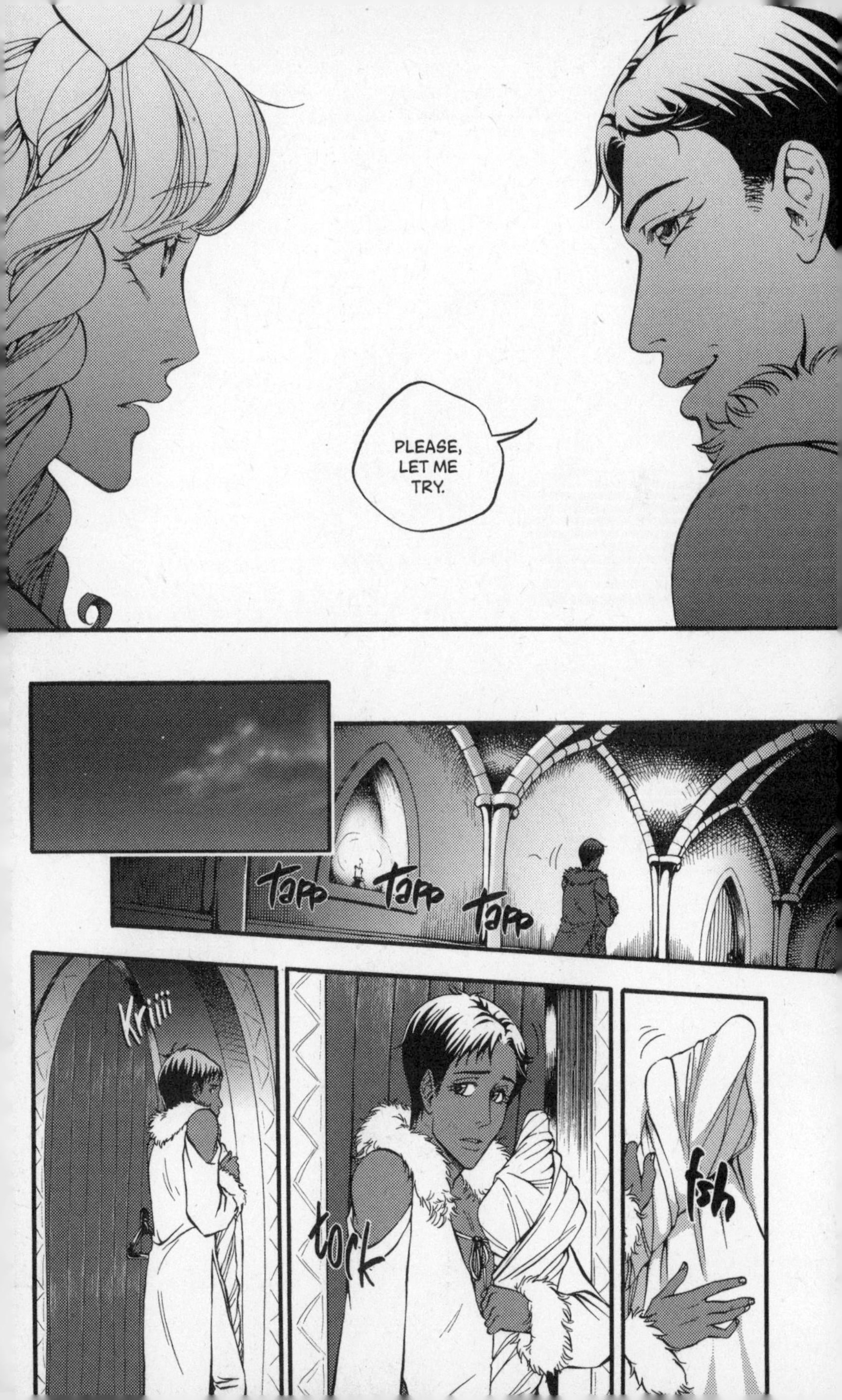
PLEASE, LET ME TRY.
Tapp Tapp Tapp
fsh
tock
Kriiii

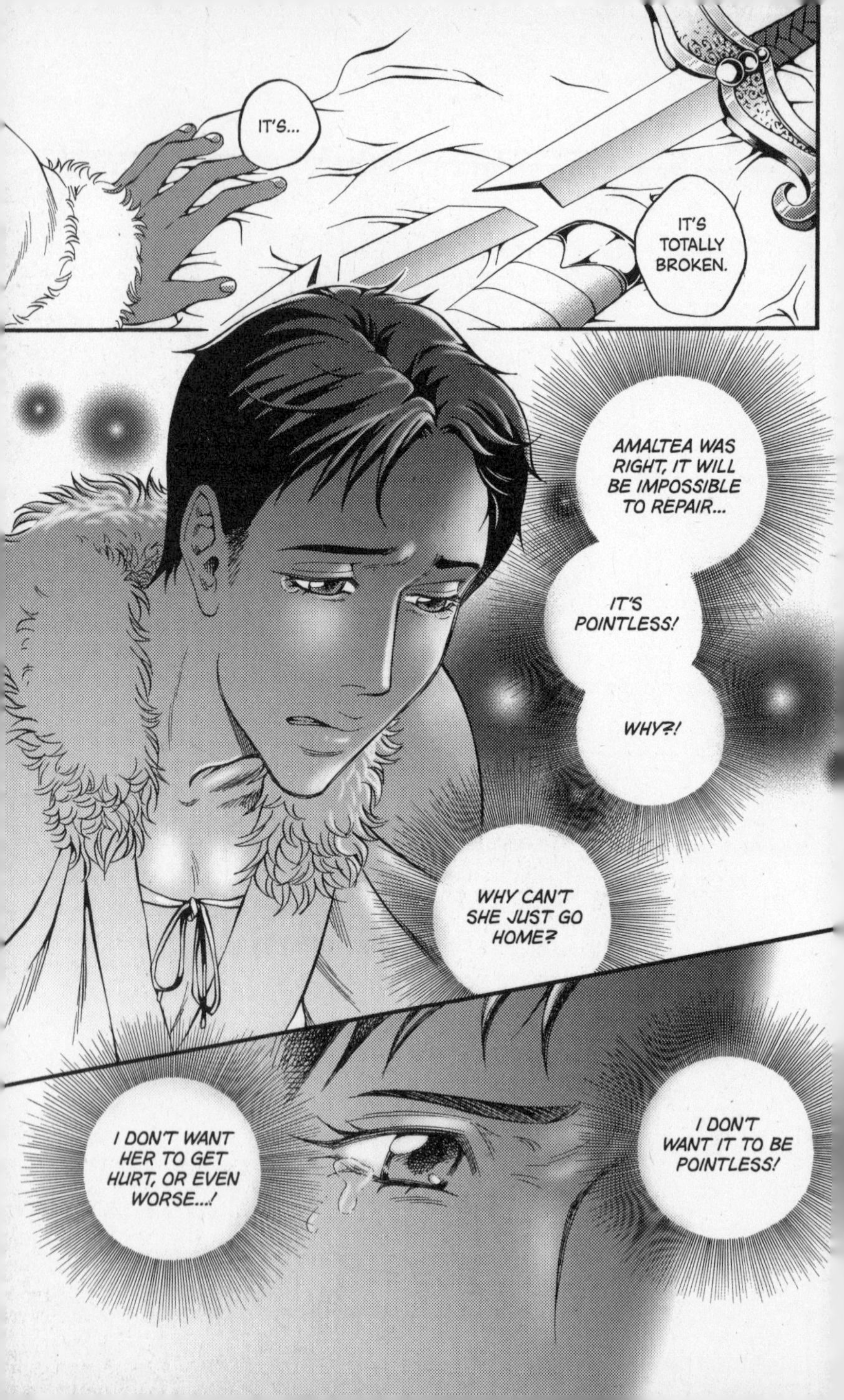
IT'S...
IT'S TOTALLY BROKEN.
AMALTEA WAS RIGHT, IT WILL BE IMPOSSIBLE TO REPAIR...
IT'S POINTLESS!
WHY?!
WHY CAN'T SHE JUST GO HOME?
I DON'T WANT IT TO BE POINTLESS!
I DON'T WANT HER TO GET HURT, OR EVEN WORSE...!

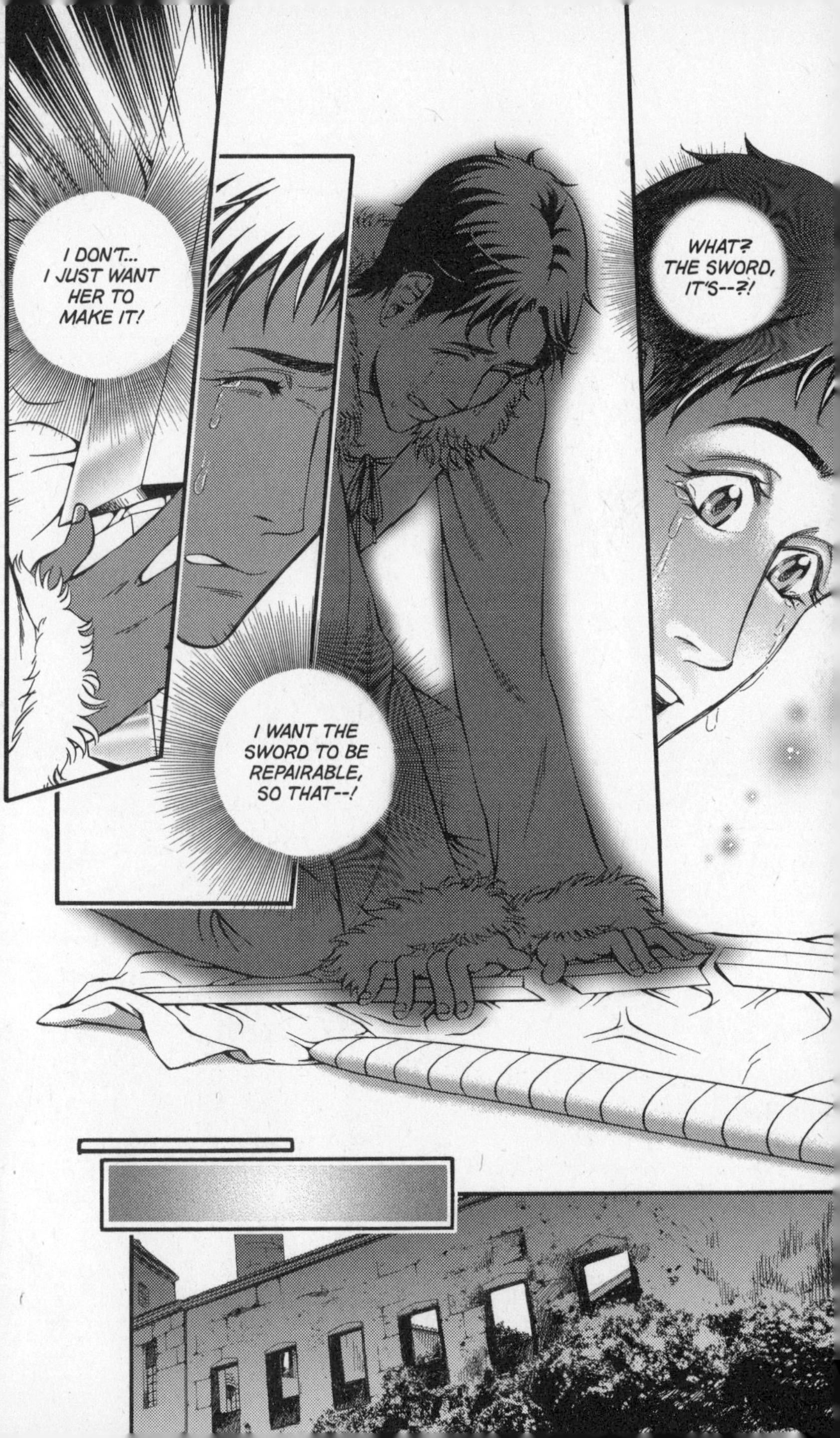
WHAT? THE SWORD, IT'S--?!
I DON'T... I JUST WANT HER TO MAKE IT!
I WANT THE SWORD TO BE REPAIRABLE, SO THAT--!

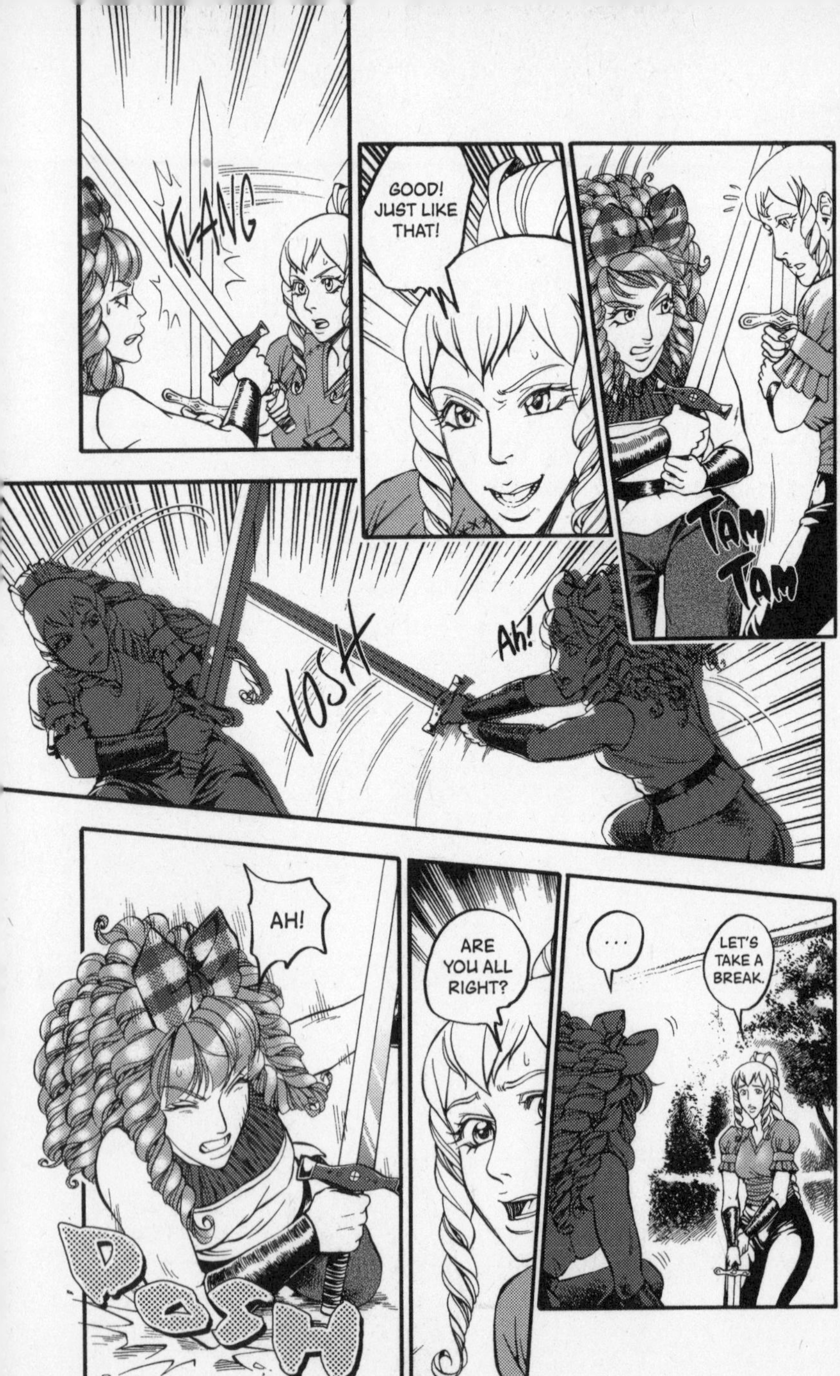
KLANG
GOOD! JUST LIKE THAT!
TAM TAM
VOSH
Ah!
AH!
DOSH
ARE YOU ALL RIGHT?
...
LET'S TAKE A BREAK.

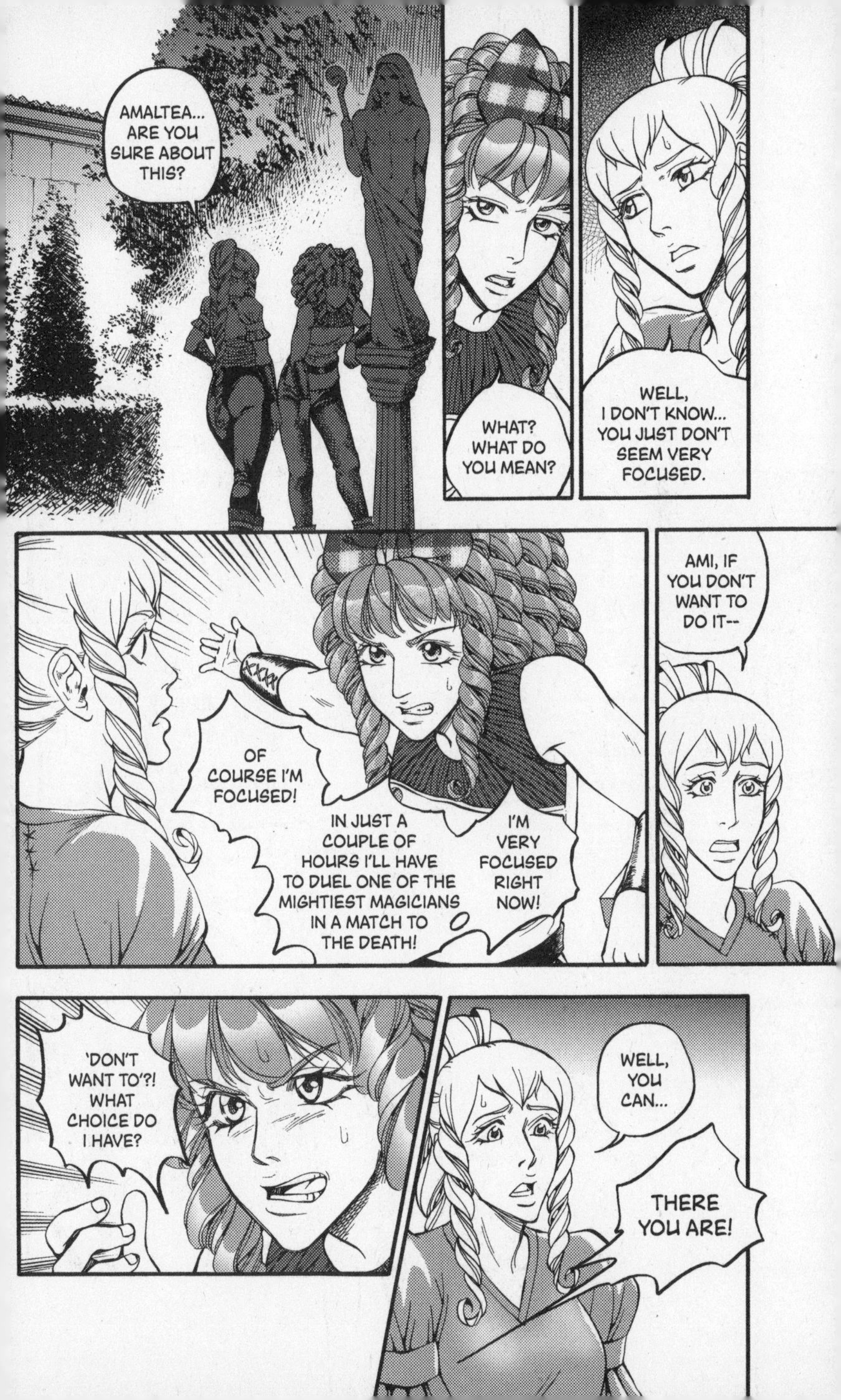
AMALTEA... ARE YOU SURE ABOUT THIS?
WHAT? WHAT DO YOU MEAN?
WELL, I DON'T KNOW... YOU JUST DON'T SEEM VERY FOCUSED.
OF COURSE I'M FOCUSED!
IN JUST A COUPLE OF HOURS I'LL HAVE TO DUEL ONE OF THE MIGHTIEST MAGICIANS IN A MATCH TO THE DEATH!
I'M VERY FOCUSED RIGHT NOW!
AMI, IF YOU DON'T WANT TO DO IT--
'DON'T WANT TO'?! WHAT CHOICE DO I HAVE?
WELL, YOU CAN...
THERE YOU ARE!

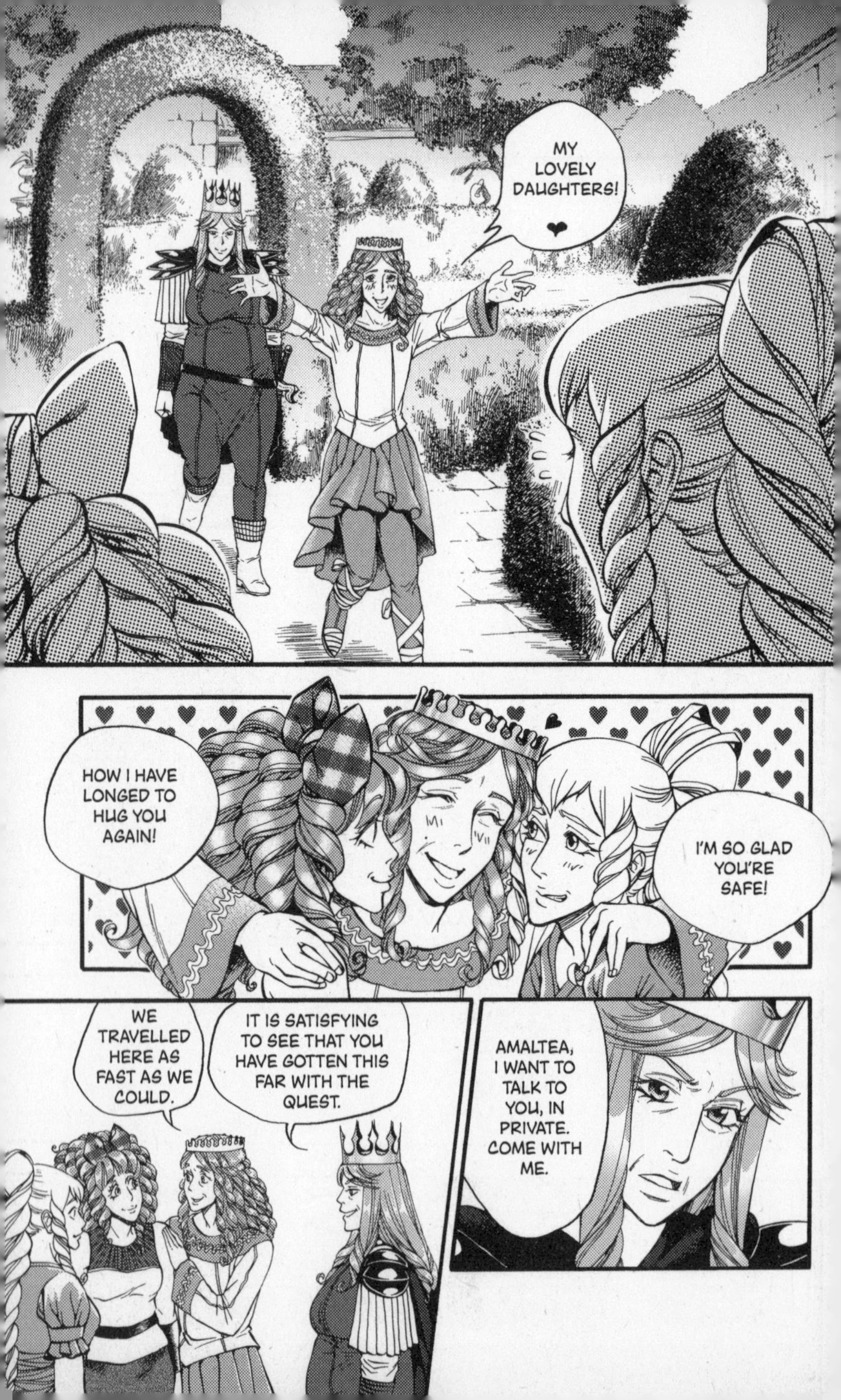
MY LOVELY DAUGHTERS! ❤
HOW I HAVE LONGED TO HUG YOU AGAIN!
I'M SO GLAD YOU'RE SAFE!
WE TRAVELLED HERE AS FAST AS WE COULD.
IT IS SATISFYING TO SEE THAT YOU HAVE GOTTEN THIS FAR WITH THE QUEST.
AMALTEA, I WANT TO TALK TO YOU, IN PRIVATE. COME WITH ME.

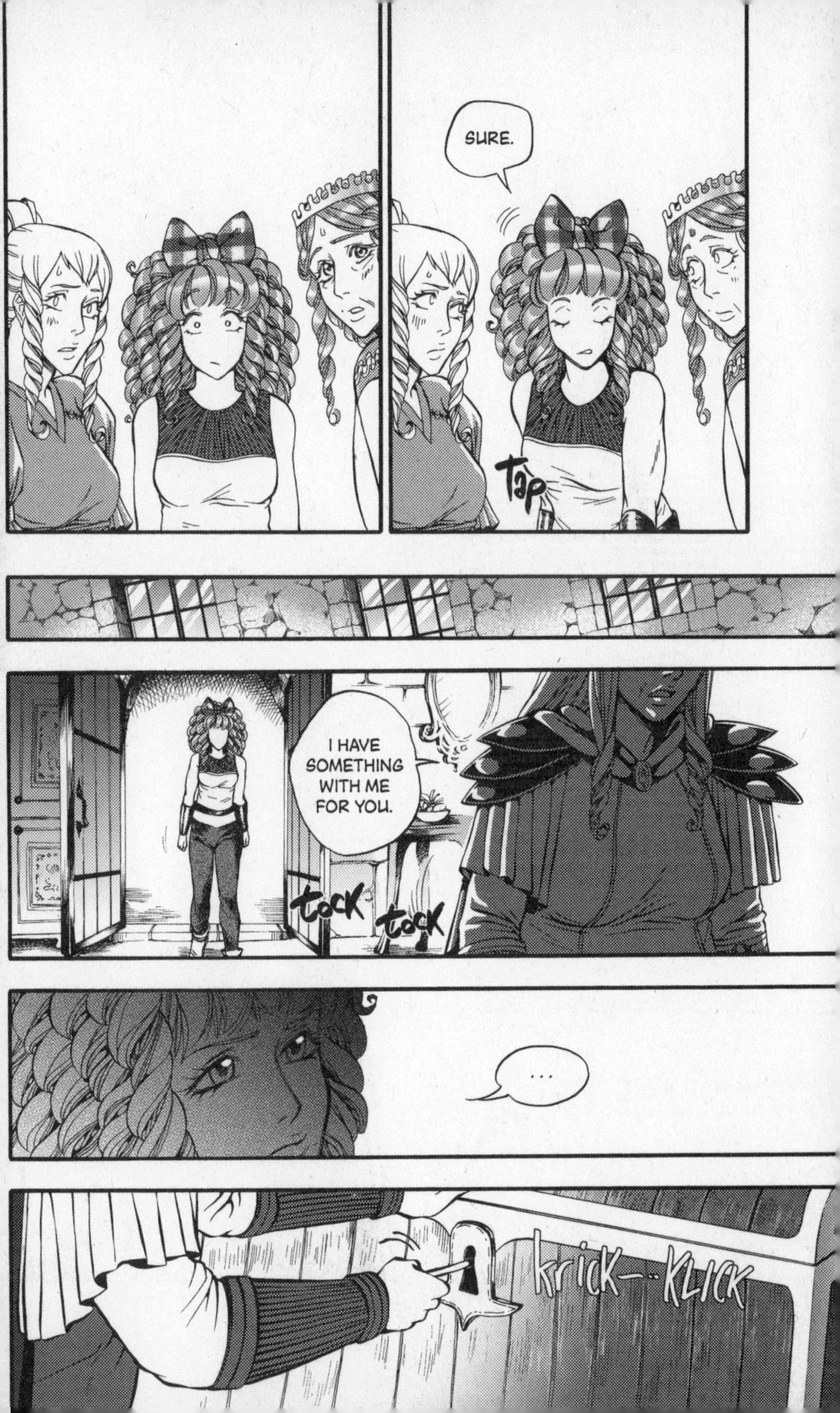
SURE.
TAP
I HAVE SOMETHING WITH ME FOR YOU.
TOCK
TOCK
...
KRICK-KLICK

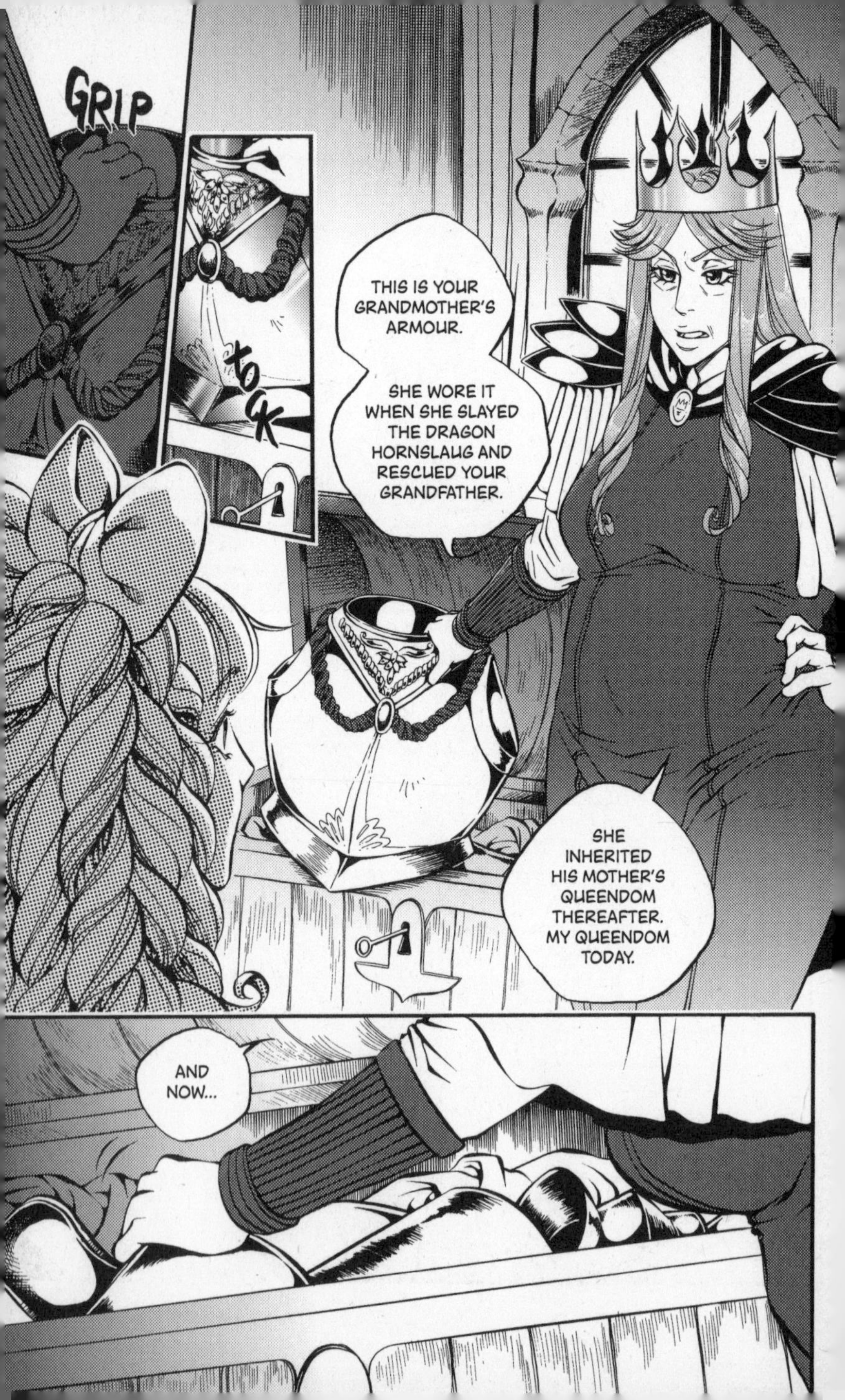
GRIP
TOCK
THIS IS YOUR GRANDMOTHER'S ARMOUR.
SHE WORE IT WHEN SHE SLAYED THE DRAGON HORNSLAUG AND RESCUED YOUR GRANDFATHER.
SHE INHERITED HIS MOTHER'S QUEENDOM THEREAFTER. MY QUEENDOM TODAY.
AND NOW...

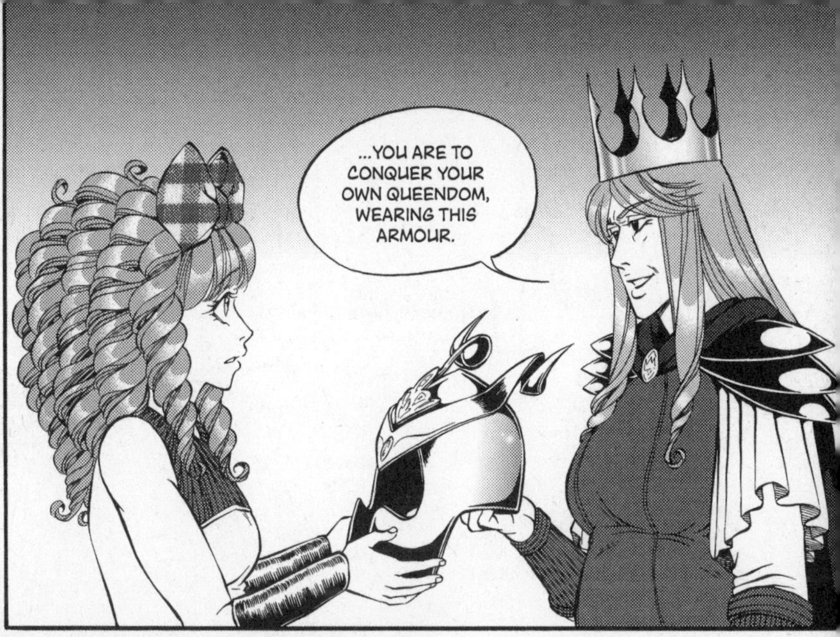
...YOU ARE TO CONQUER YOUR OWN QUEENDOM, WEARING THIS ARMOUR.
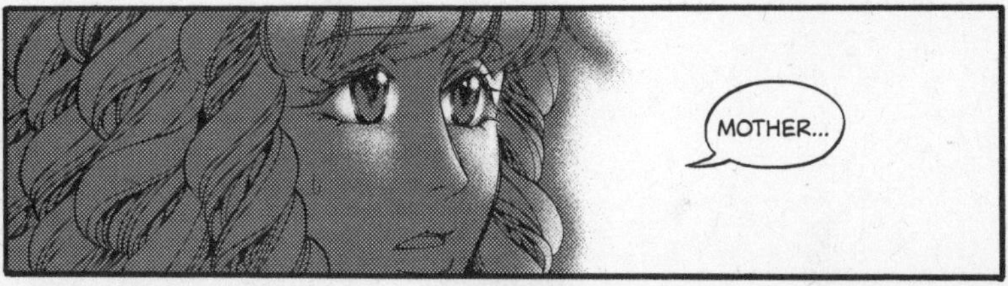
MOTHER...
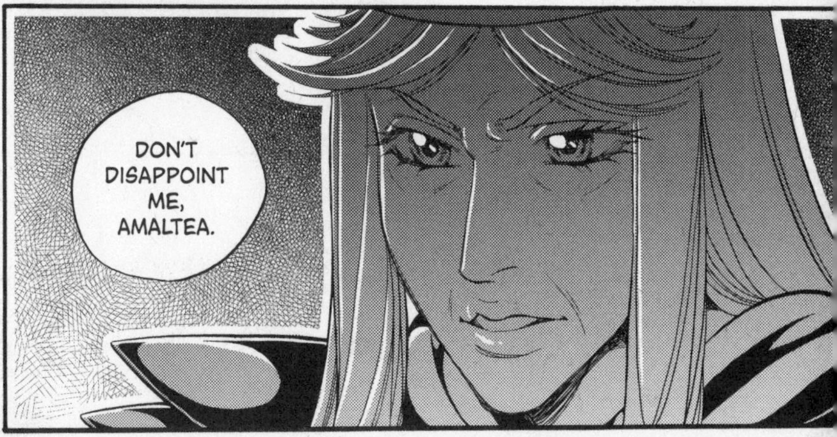
DON'T DISAPPOINT ME, AMALTEA.

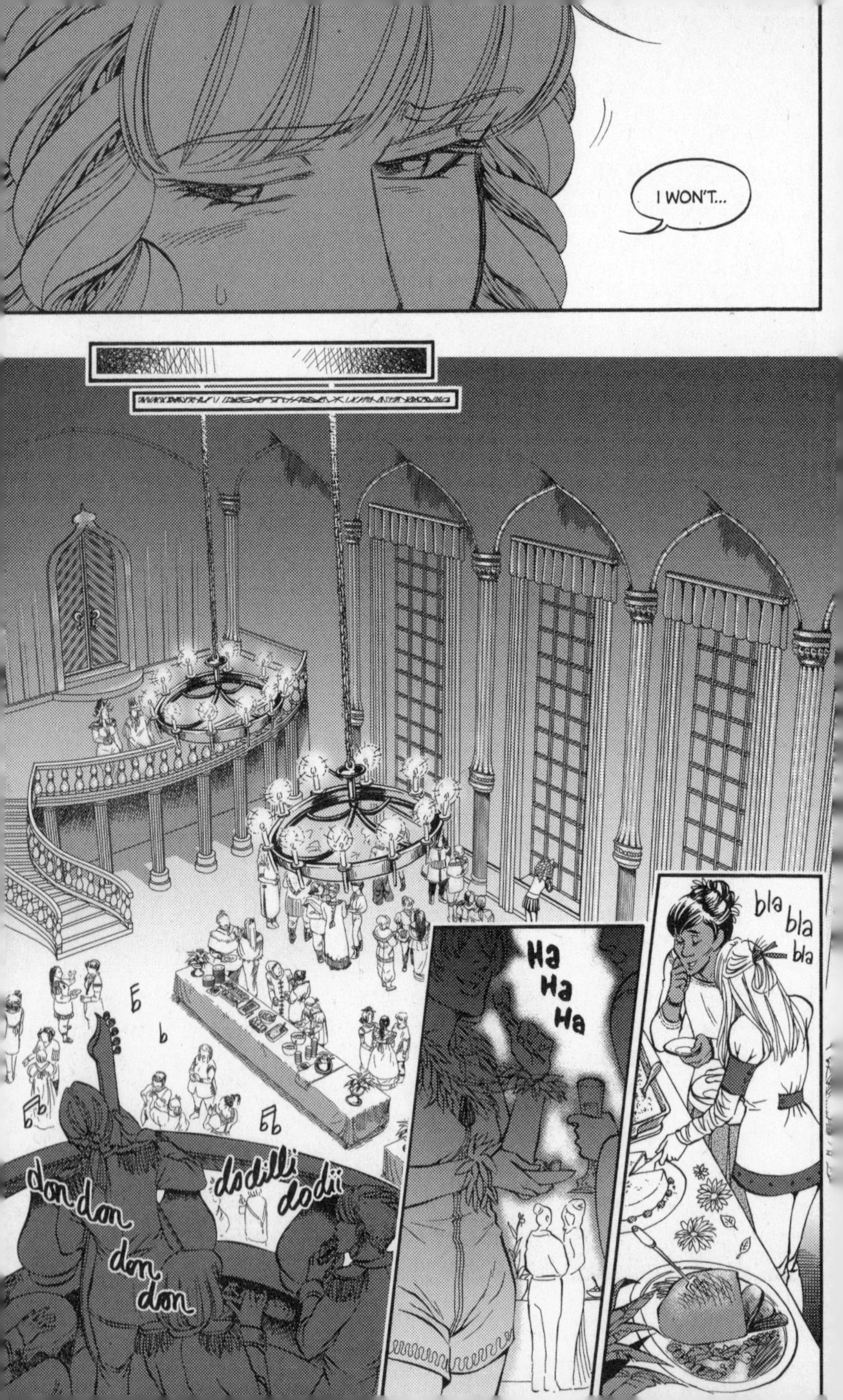
I WON'T...
bla bla bla
Ha Ha Ha
dodilli dodii
don don don don don

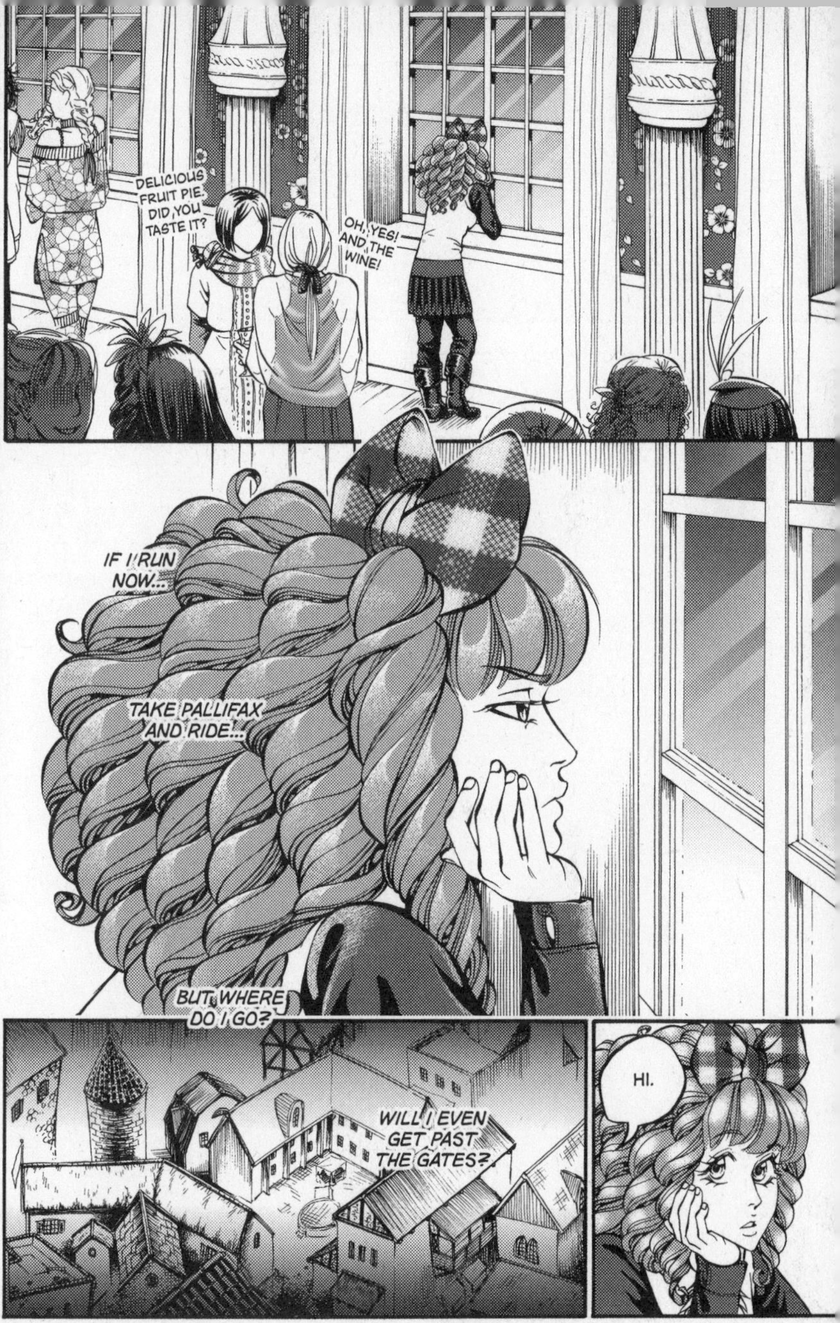
DELICIOUS FRUIT PIE. DID YOU TASTE IT?
OH, YES! AND THE WINE!
IF I RUN NOW...
TAKE PALLIFAX AND RIDE...
BUT WHERE DO I GO?
WILL I EVEN GET PAST THE GATES?
HI.

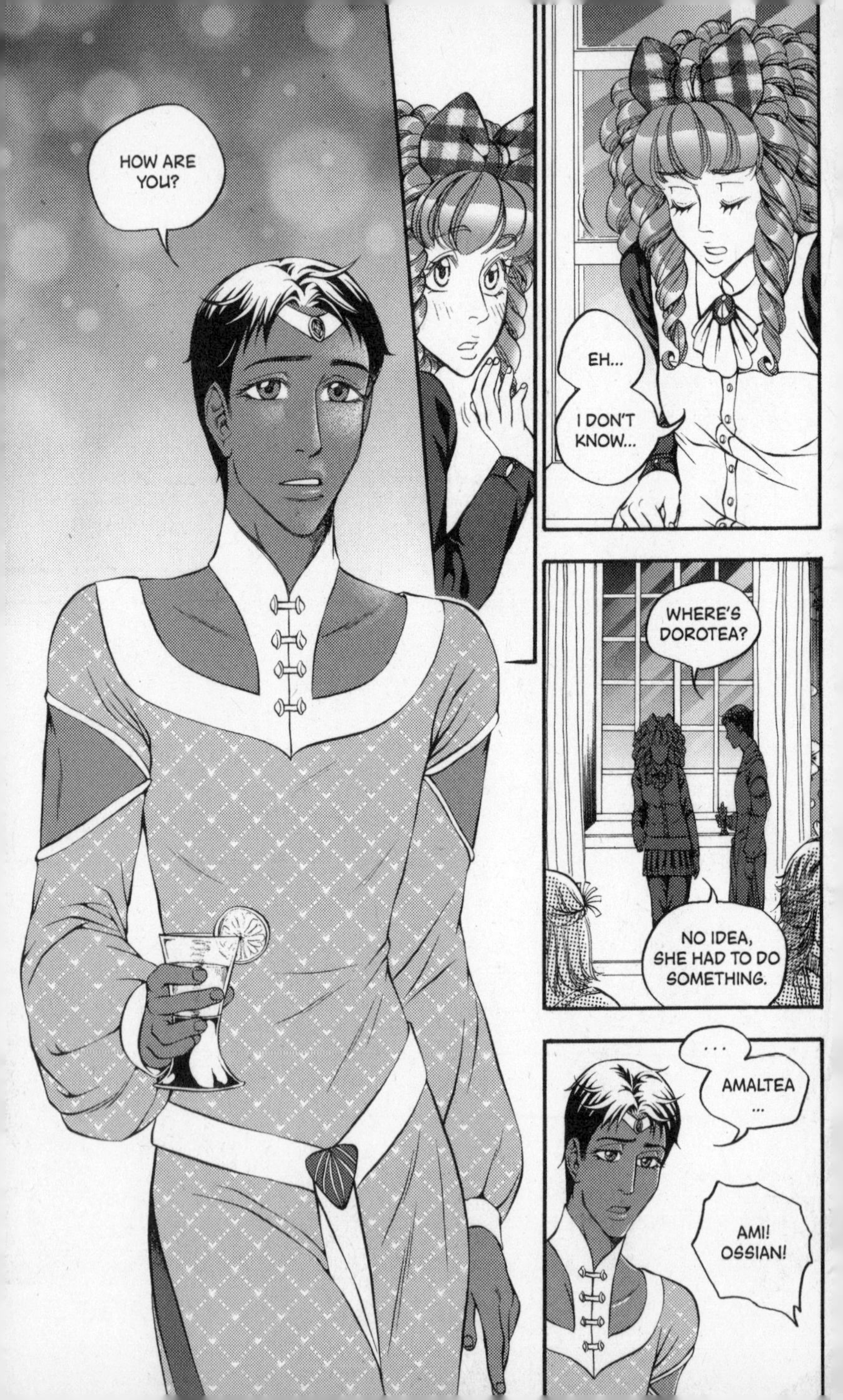
HOW ARE YOU?
EH...
I DON'T KNOW...
WHERE'S DOROTEA?
NO IDEA, SHE HAD TO DO SOMETHING.
...
AMALTEA ...
AMI! OSSIAN!

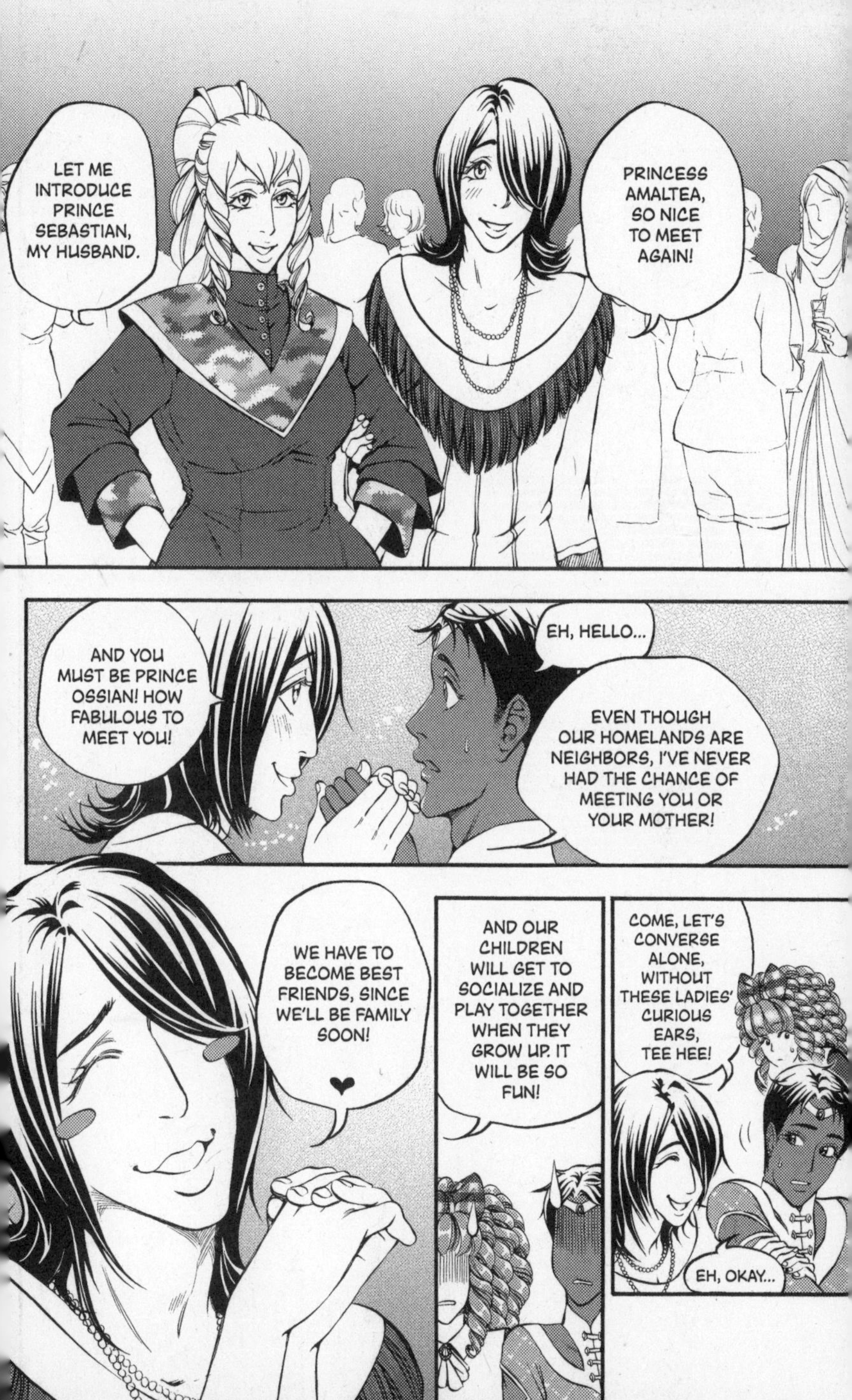
LET ME INTRODUCE PRINCE SEBASTIAN, MY HUSBAND.
PRINCESS AMALTEA, SO NICE TO MEET AGAIN!
AND YOU MUST BE PRINCE OSSIAN! HOW FABULOUS TO MEET YOU!
EH, HELLO...
EVEN THOUGH OUR HOMELANDS ARE NEIGHBORS, I'VE NEVER HAD THE CHANCE OF MEETING YOU OR YOUR MOTHER!
WE HAVE TO BECOME BEST FRIENDS, SINCE WE'LL BE FAMILY SOON!
AND OUR CHILDREN WILL GET TO SOCIALIZE AND PLAY TOGETHER WHEN THEY GROW UP. IT WILL BE SO FUN!
COME, LET'S CONVERSE ALONE, WITHOUT THESE LADIES' CURIOUS EARS, TEE HEE!
EH, OKAY...

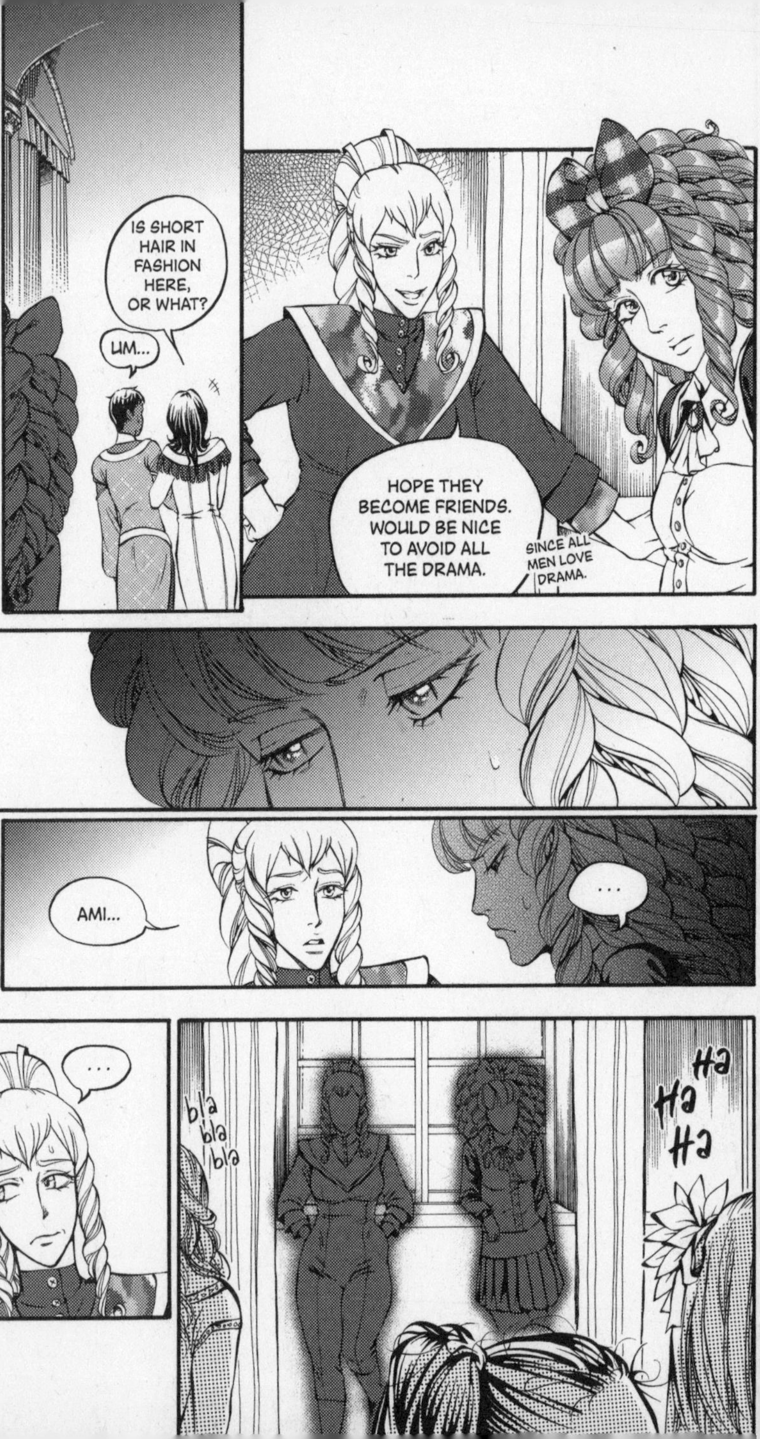
HOPE THEY BECOME FRIENDS. WOULD BE NICE TO AVOID ALL THE DRAMA.
SINCE ALL MEN LOVE DRAMA.
IS SHORT HAIR IN FASHION HERE, OR WHAT?
UM...
...
AMI...
Ha Ha Ha
bla bla bla
...

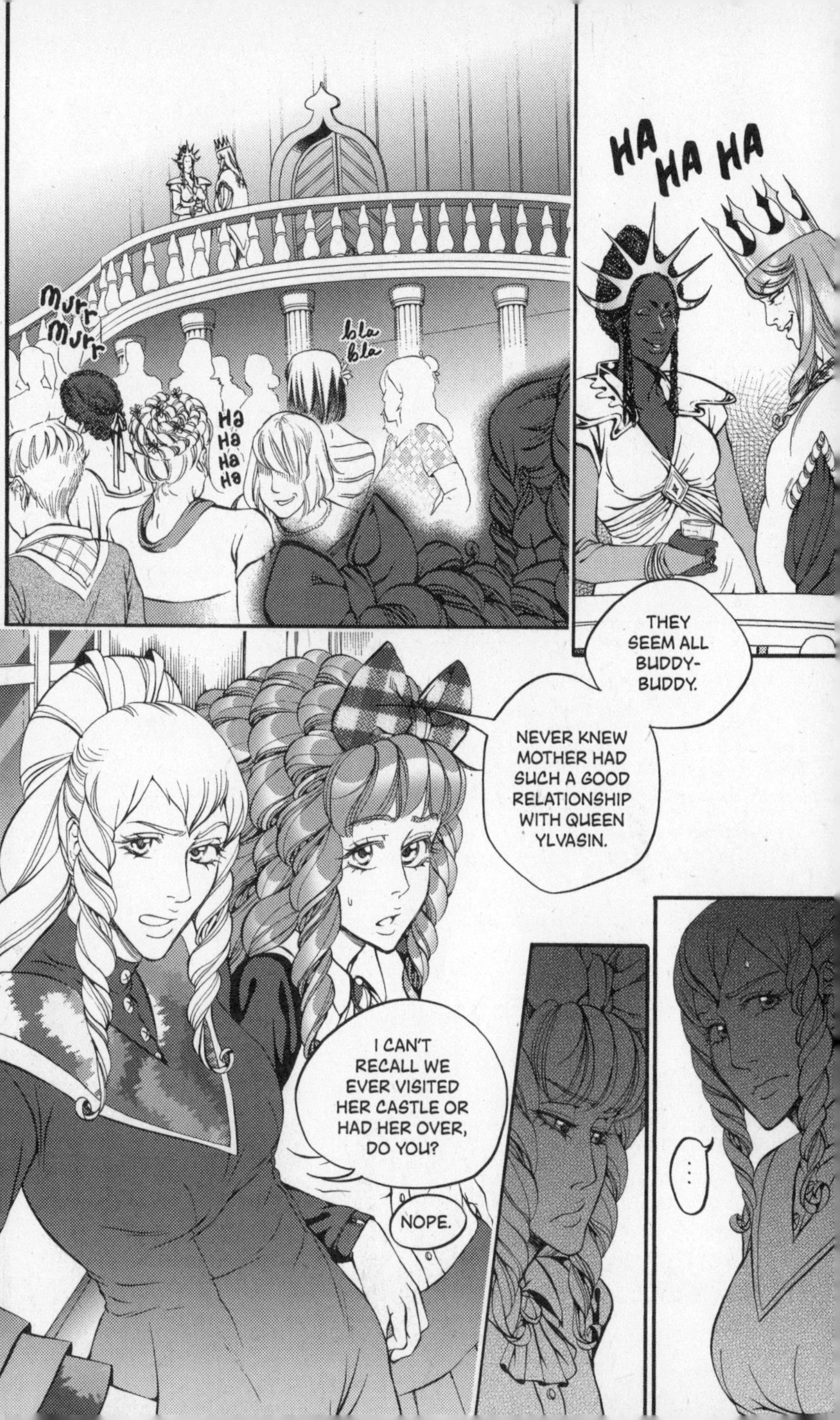
murr murr
bla bla
Ha Ha Ha Ha
HA HA HA
THEY SEEM ALL BUDDY-BUDDY.
NEVER KNEW MOTHER HAD SUCH A GOOD RELATIONSHIP WITH QUEEN YLVASIN.
I CAN'T RECALL WE EVER VISITED HER CASTLE OR HAD HER OVER, DO YOU?
NOPE.
...

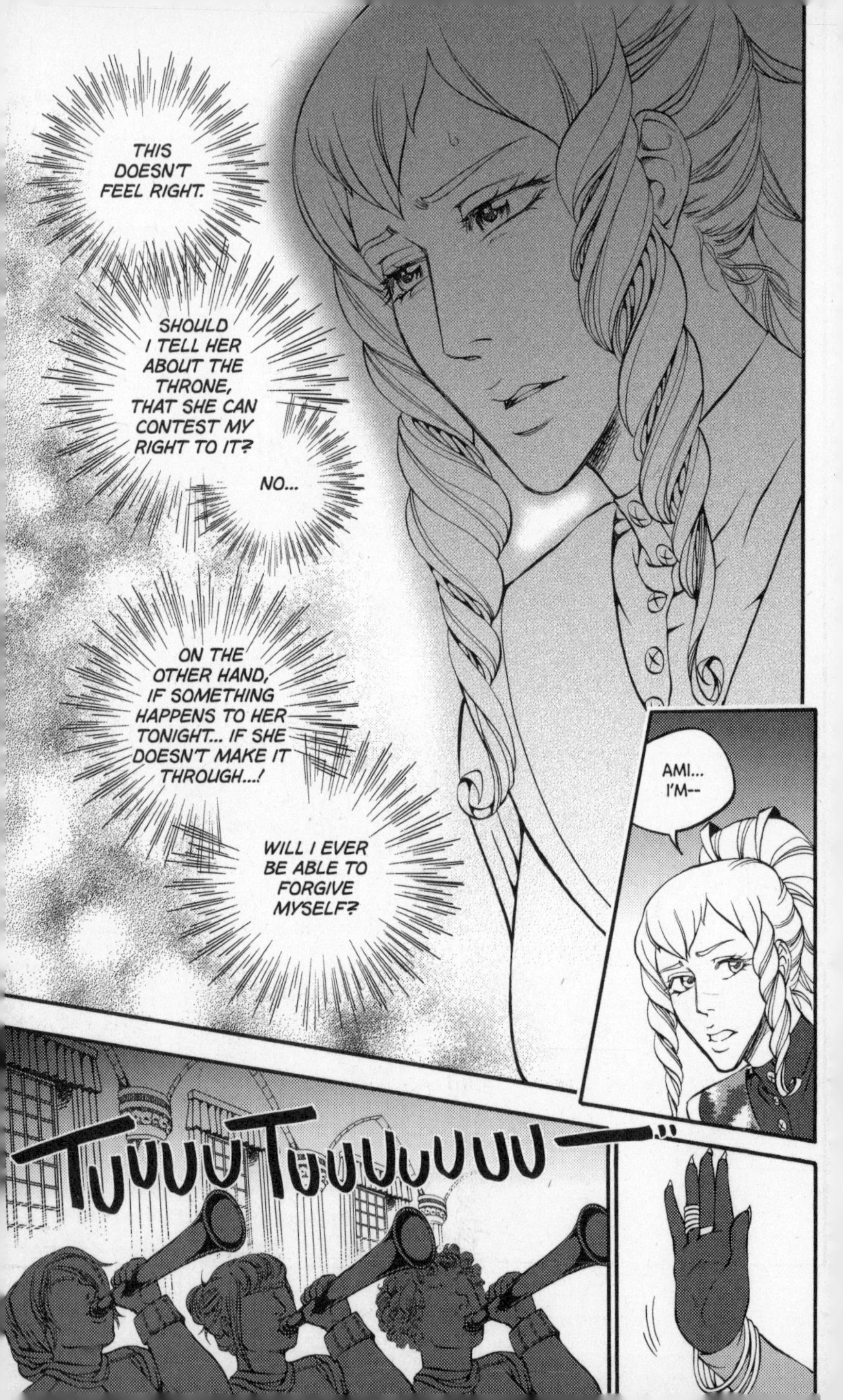
THIS DOESN'T FEEL RIGHT.
SHOULD I TELL HER ABOUT THE THRONE, THAT SHE CAN CONTEST MY RIGHT TO IT?
NO...
ON THE OTHER HAND, IF SOMETHING HAPPENS TO HER TONIGHT... IF SHE DOESN'T MAKE IT THROUGH...!
WILL I EVER BE ABLE TO FORGIVE MYSELF?
AMI... I'M--
TUUUUTUUUUUUU—

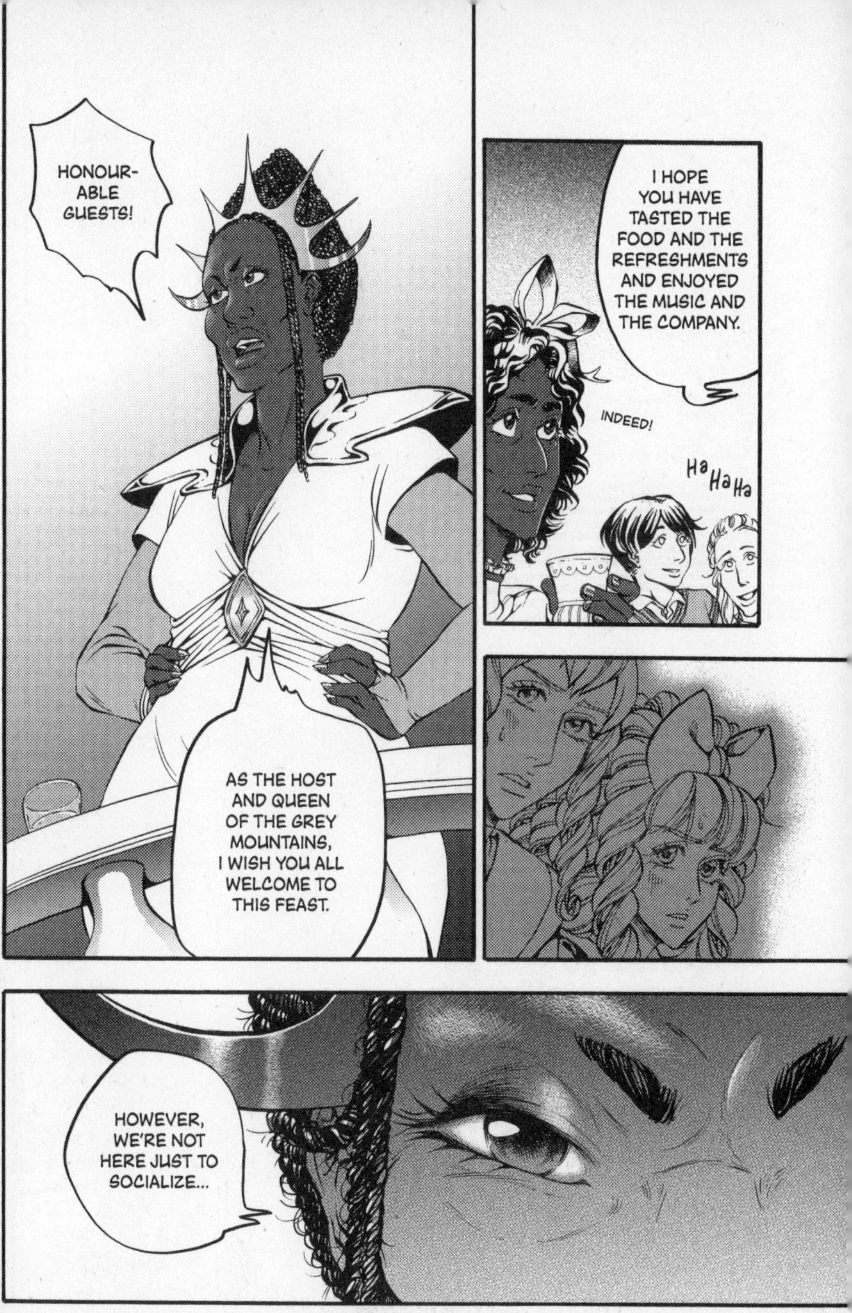
HONOUR-ABLE GUESTS!
AS THE HOST AND QUEEN OF THE GREY MOUNTAINS, I WISH YOU ALL WELCOME TO THIS FEAST.
I HOPE YOU HAVE TASTED THE FOOD AND THE REFRESHMENTS AND ENJOYED THE MUSIC AND THE COMPANY.
INDEED!
Ha Ha Ha
HOWEVER, WE'RE NOT HERE JUST TO SOCIALIZE...

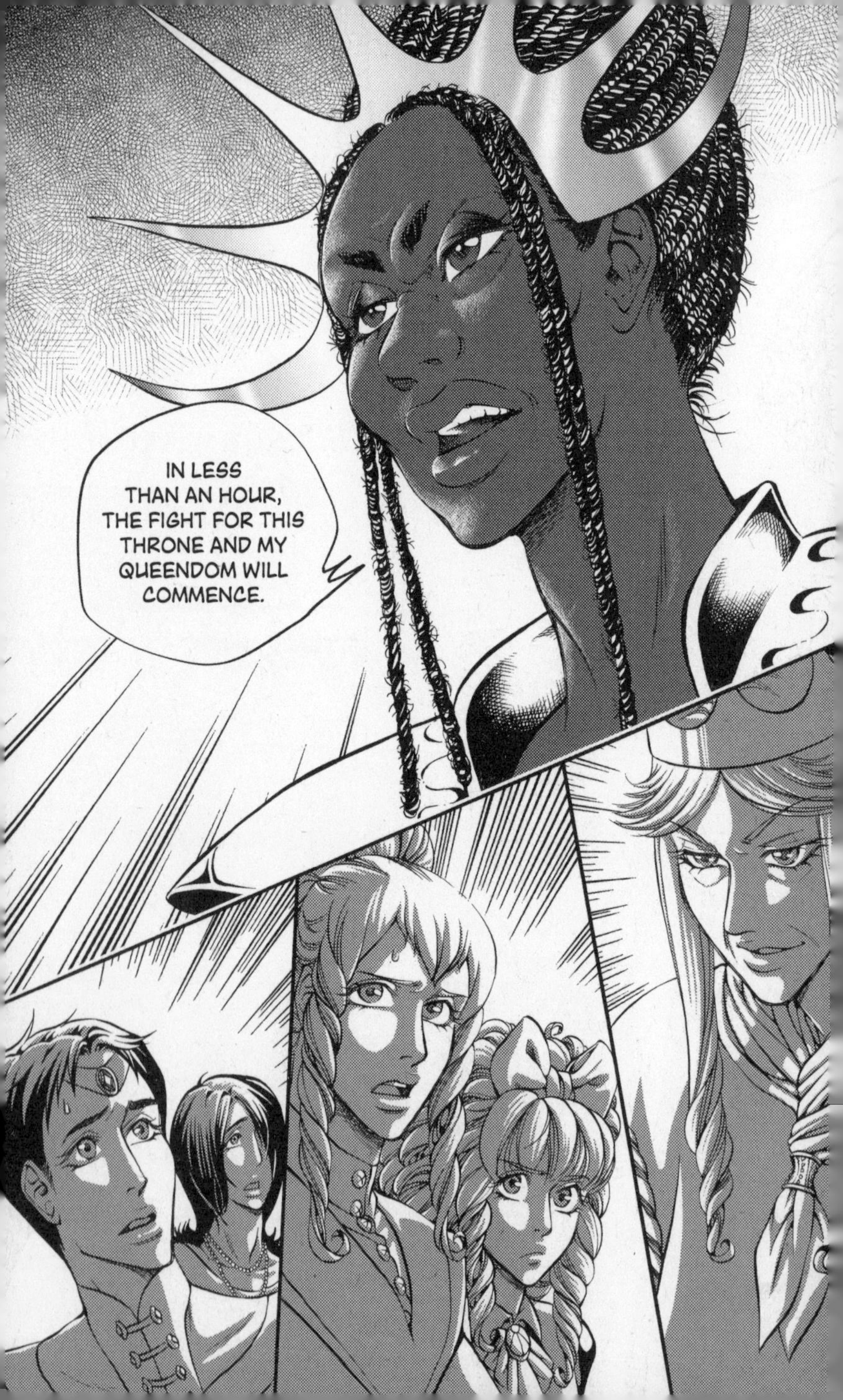
IN LESS THAN AN HOUR, THE FIGHT FOR THIS THRONE AND MY QUEENDOM WILL COMMENCE.

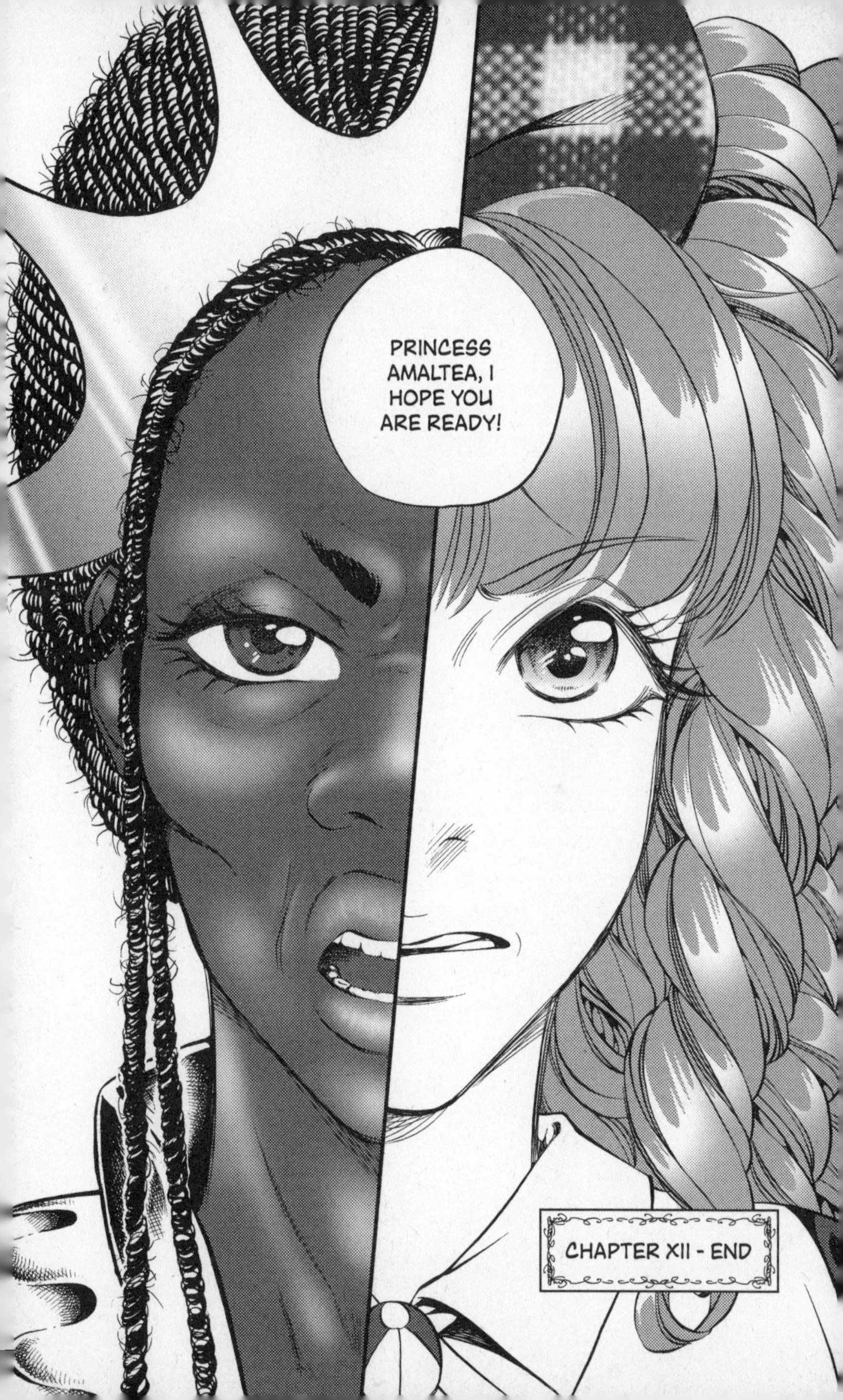
PRINCESS AMALTEA, I HOPE YOU ARE READY!
CHAPTER XII - END

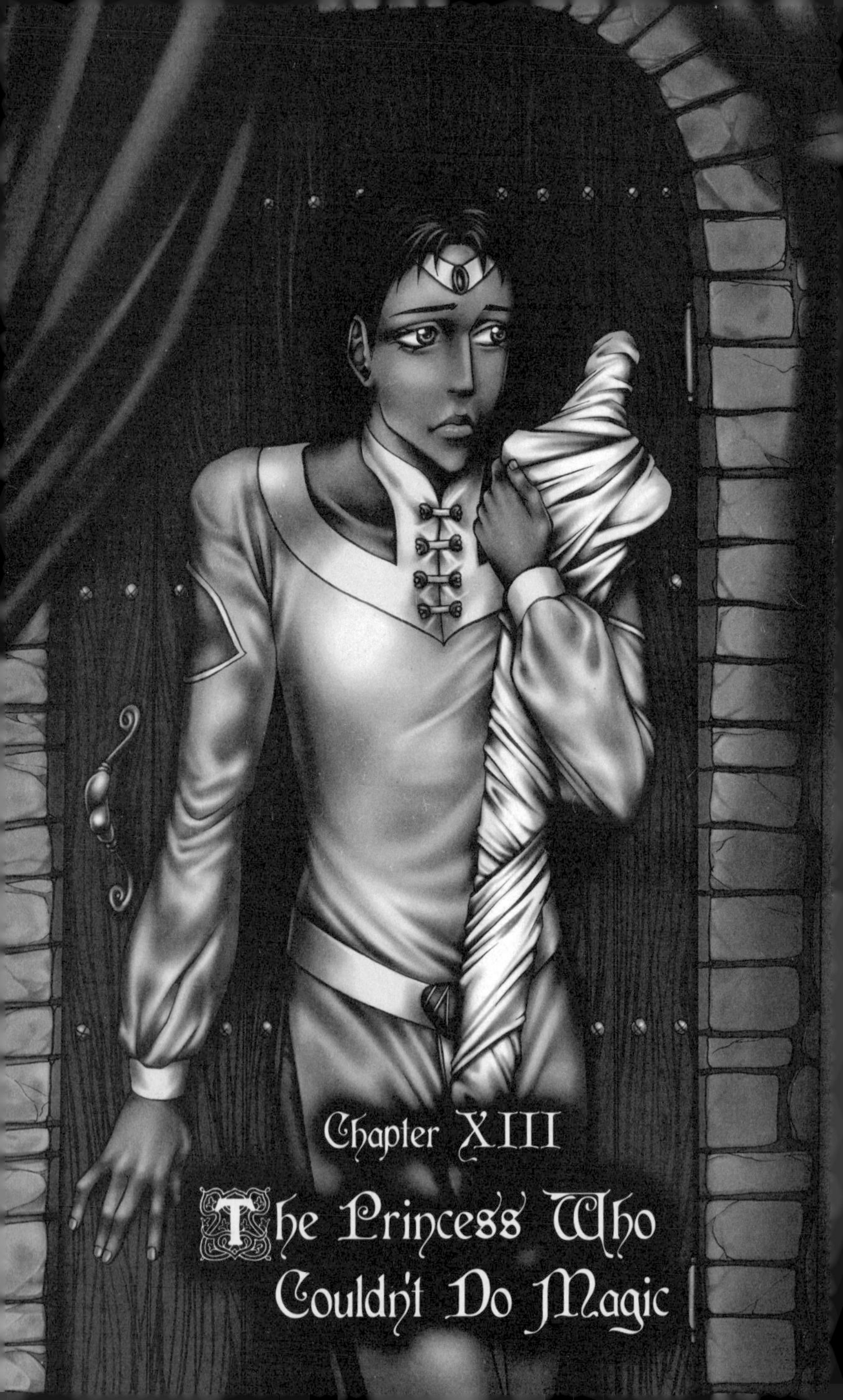
Chapter XIII
The Princess Who Couldn't Do Magic

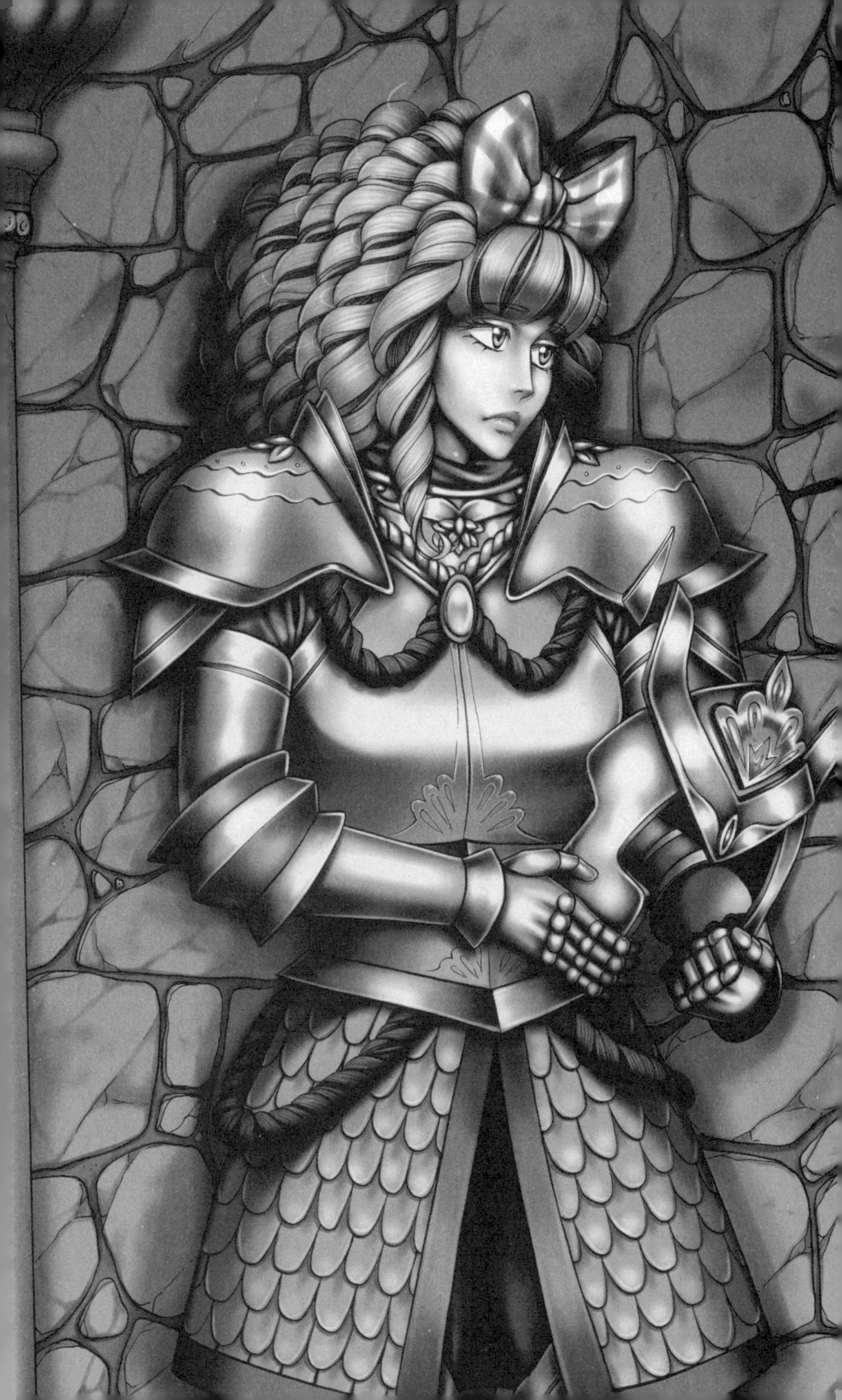

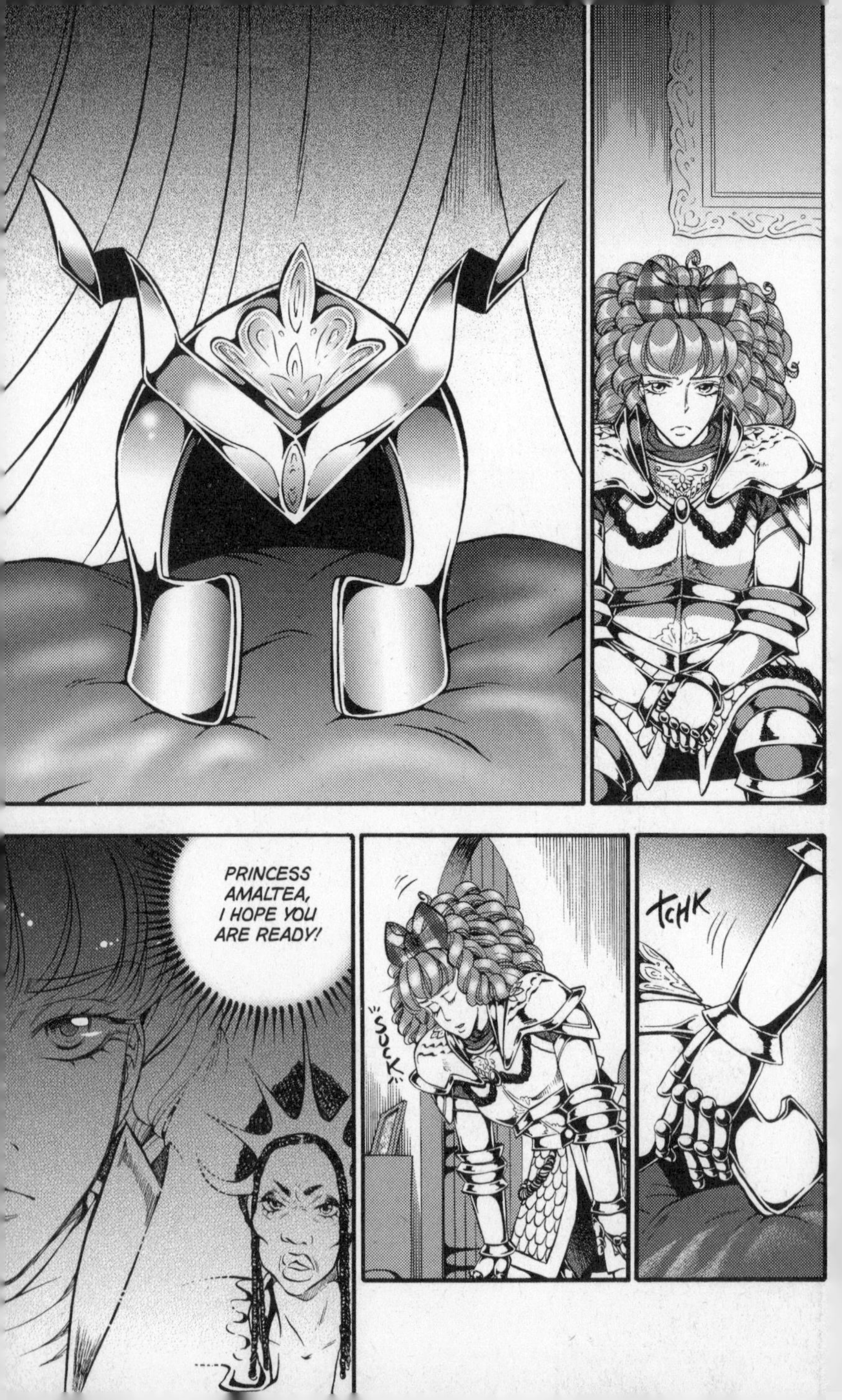
PRINCESS AMALTEA, I HOPE YOU ARE READY!
SUCK
TCHK

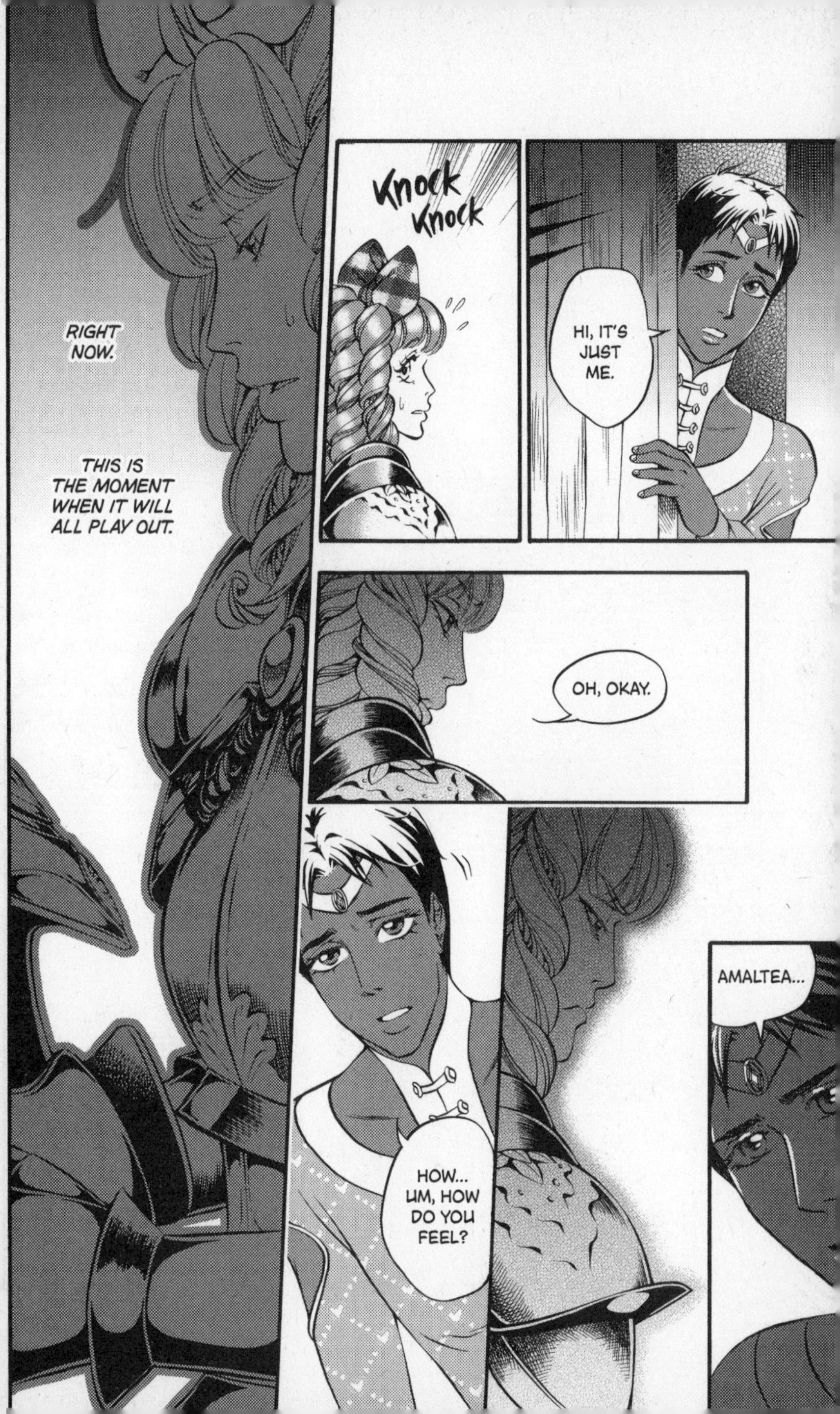
RIGHT NOW.
THIS IS THE MOMENT WHEN IT WILL ALL PLAY OUT.
Knock Knock
HI, IT'S JUST ME.
OH, OKAY.
HOW... UM, HOW DO YOU FEEL?
AMALTEA...

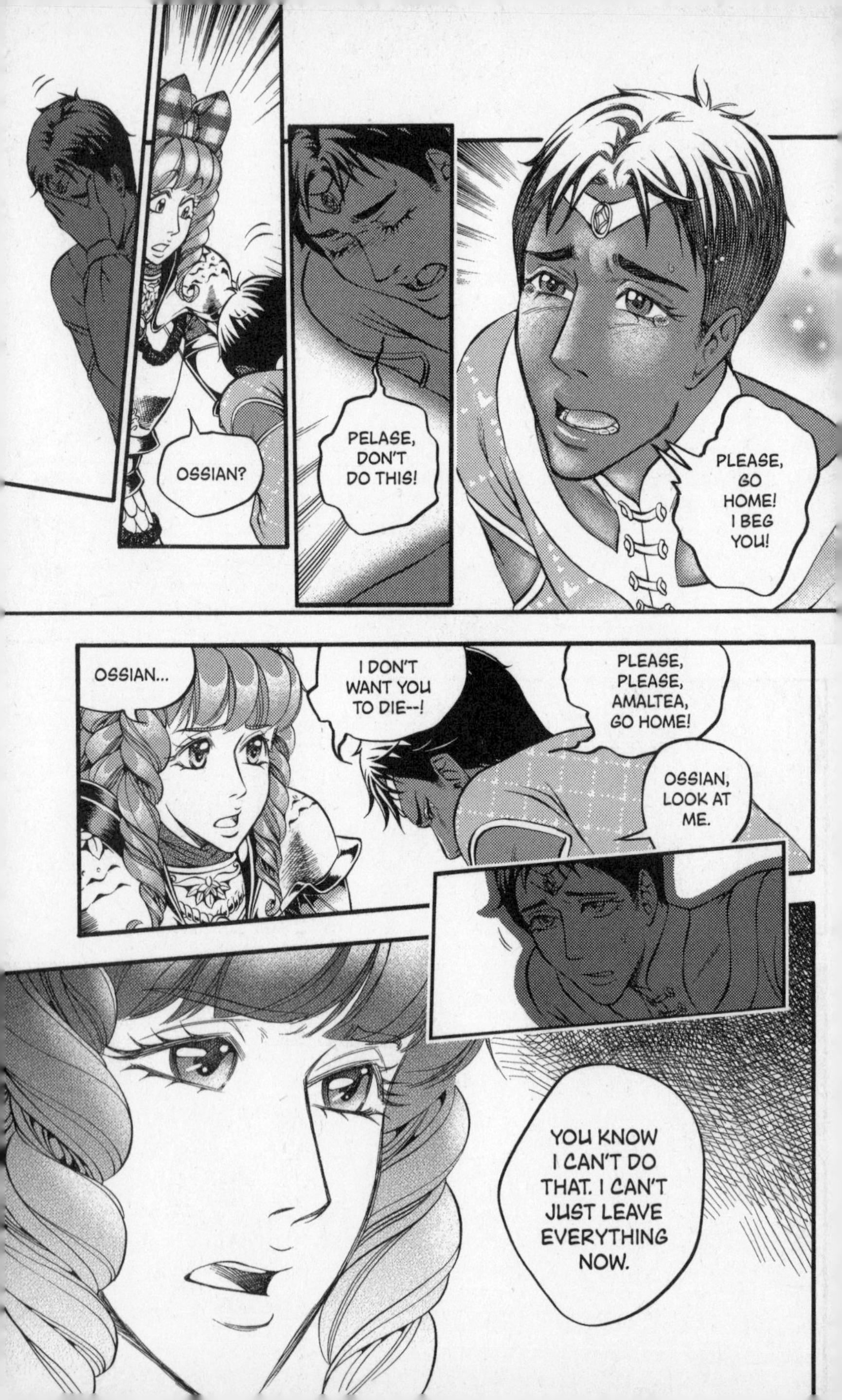
OSSIAN?
PELASE, DON'T DO THIS!
PLEASE, GO HOME! I BEG YOU!
OSSIAN...
I DON'T WANT YOU TO DIE--!
PLEASE, PLEASE, AMALTEA, GO HOME!
OSSIAN, LOOK AT ME.
YOU KNOW I CAN'T DO THAT. I CAN'T JUST LEAVE EVERYTHING NOW.

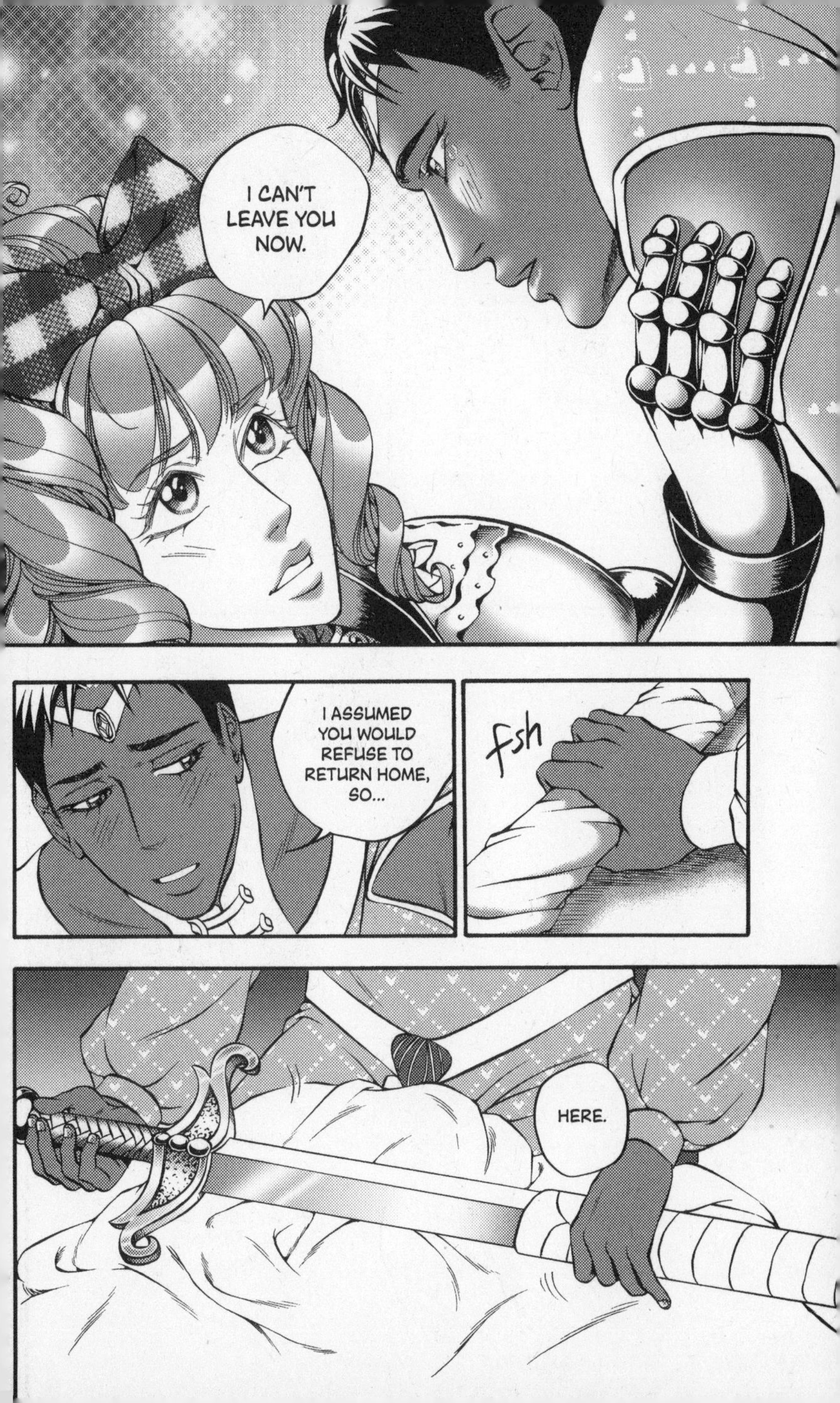
I CAN'T LEAVE YOU NOW.
fsh
I ASSUMED YOU WOULD REFUSE TO RETURN HOME, SO...
HERE.

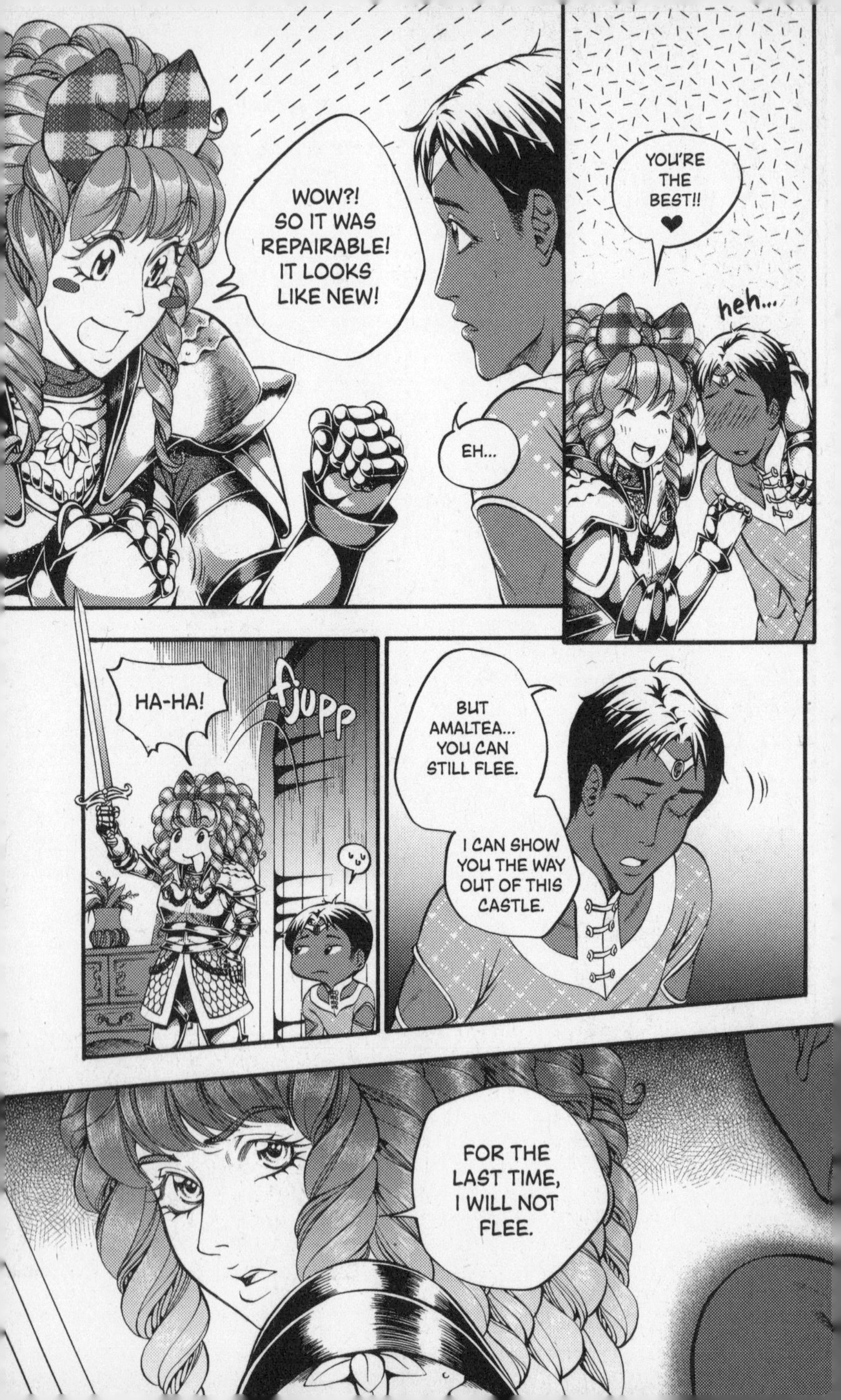
WOW?! SO IT WAS REPAIRABLE! IT LOOKS LIKE NEW!
EH...
YOU'RE THE BEST!! ❤
heh...
HA-HA!
fjupp
BUT AMALTEA... YOU CAN STILL FLEE.
I CAN SHOW YOU THE WAY OUT OF THIS CASTLE.
FOR THE LAST TIME, I WILL NOT FLEE.

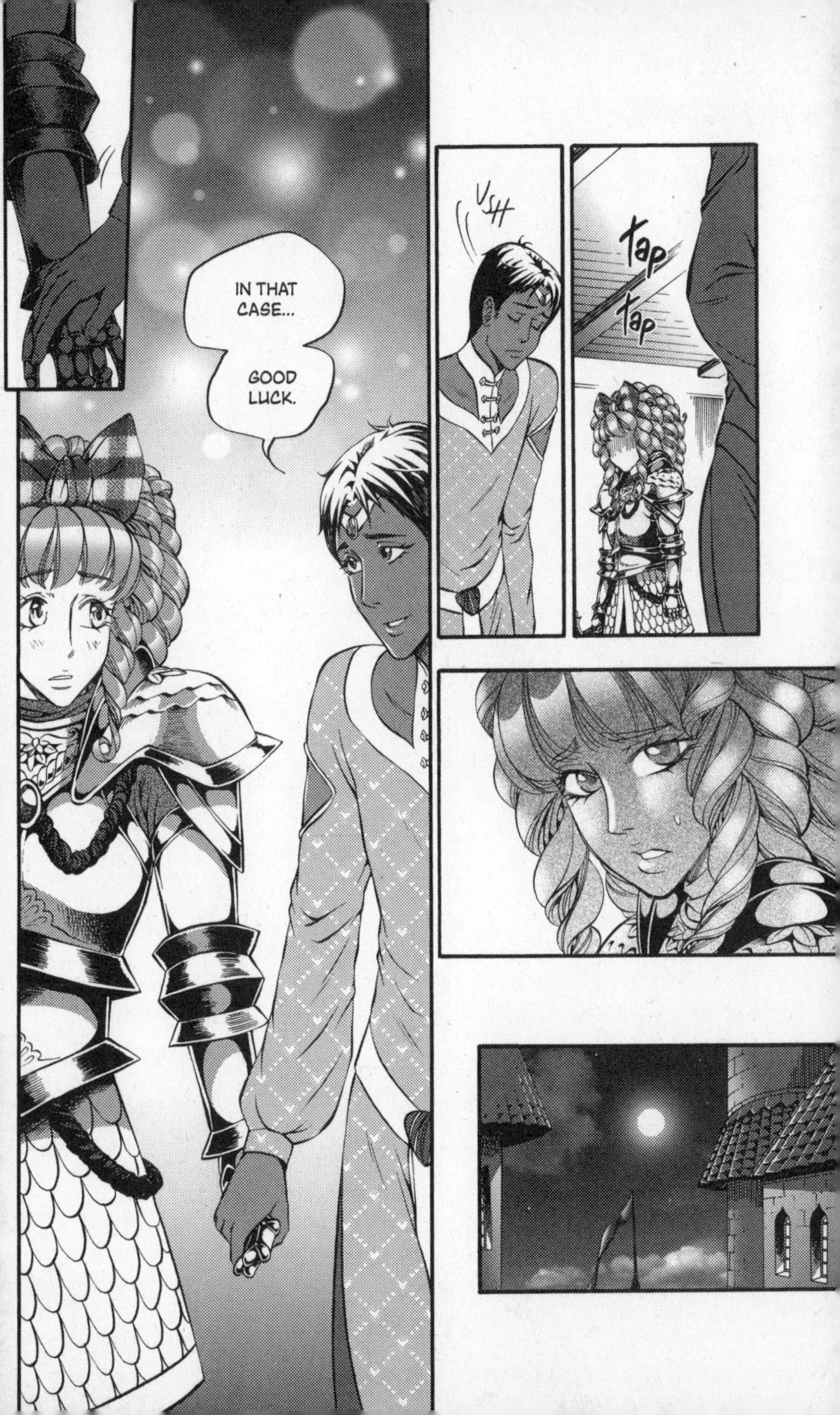
TAP
TAP
VSH
IN THAT CASE...
GOOD LUCK.

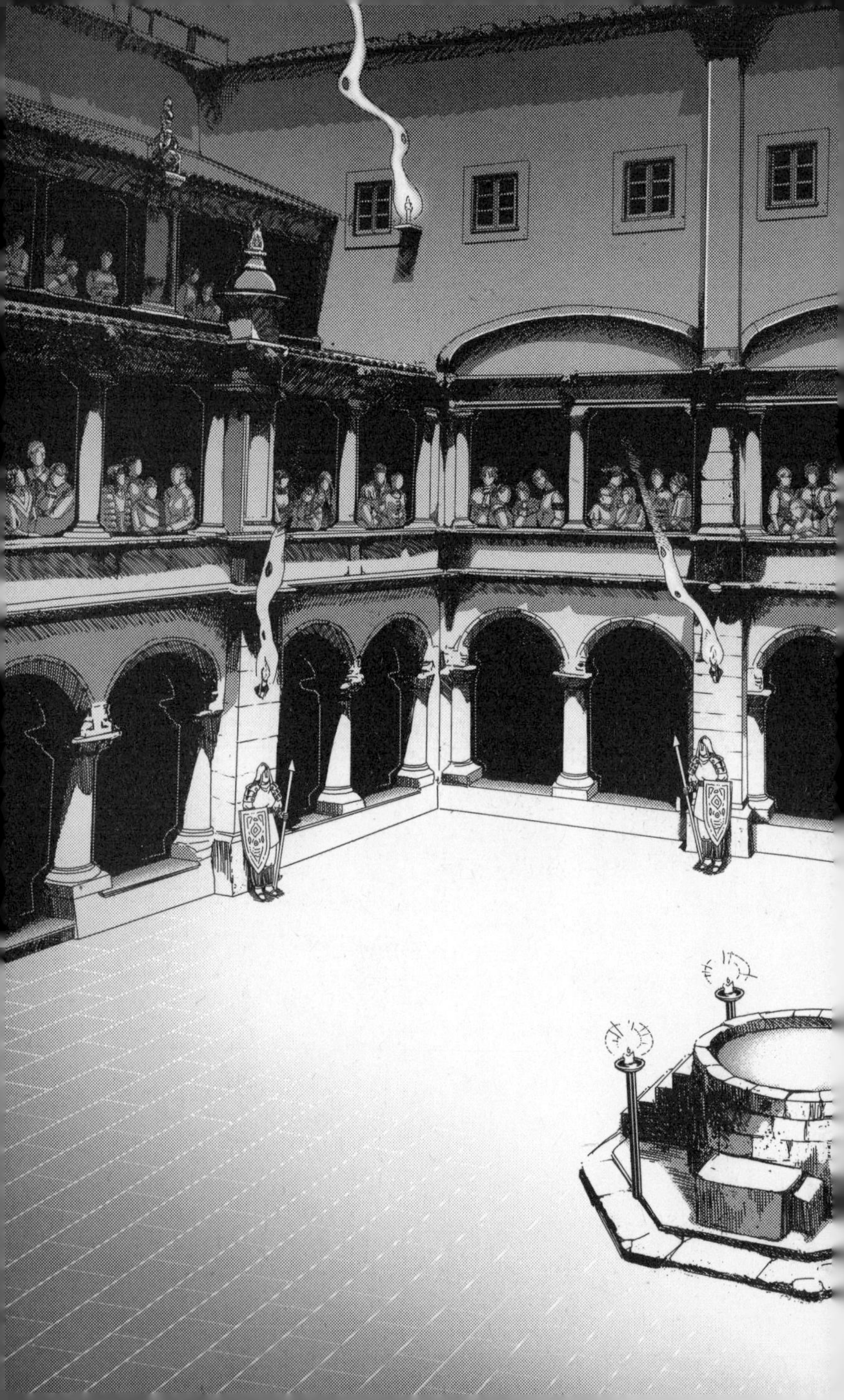

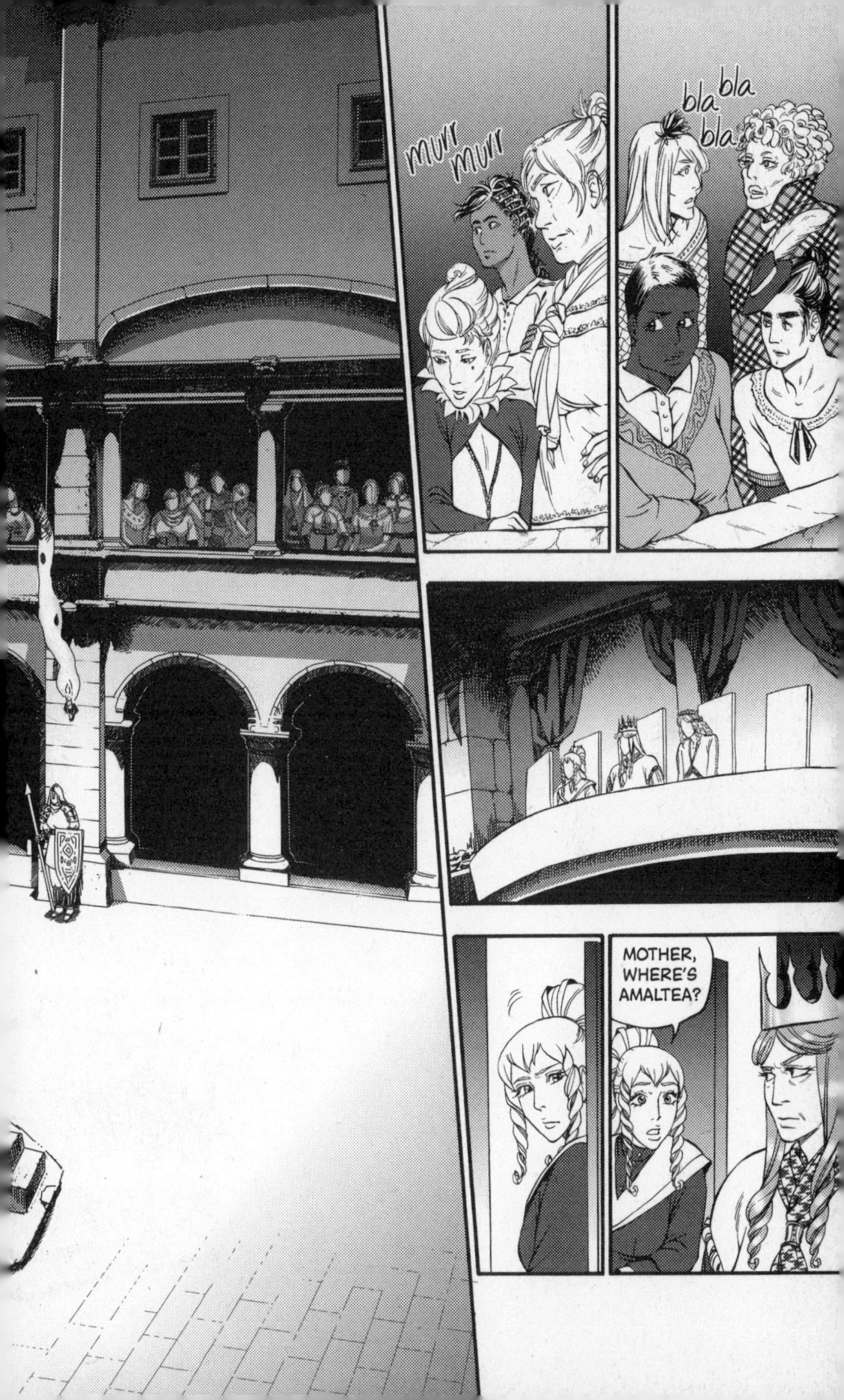
bla bla bla
murr murr
MOTHER, WHERE'S AMALTEA?

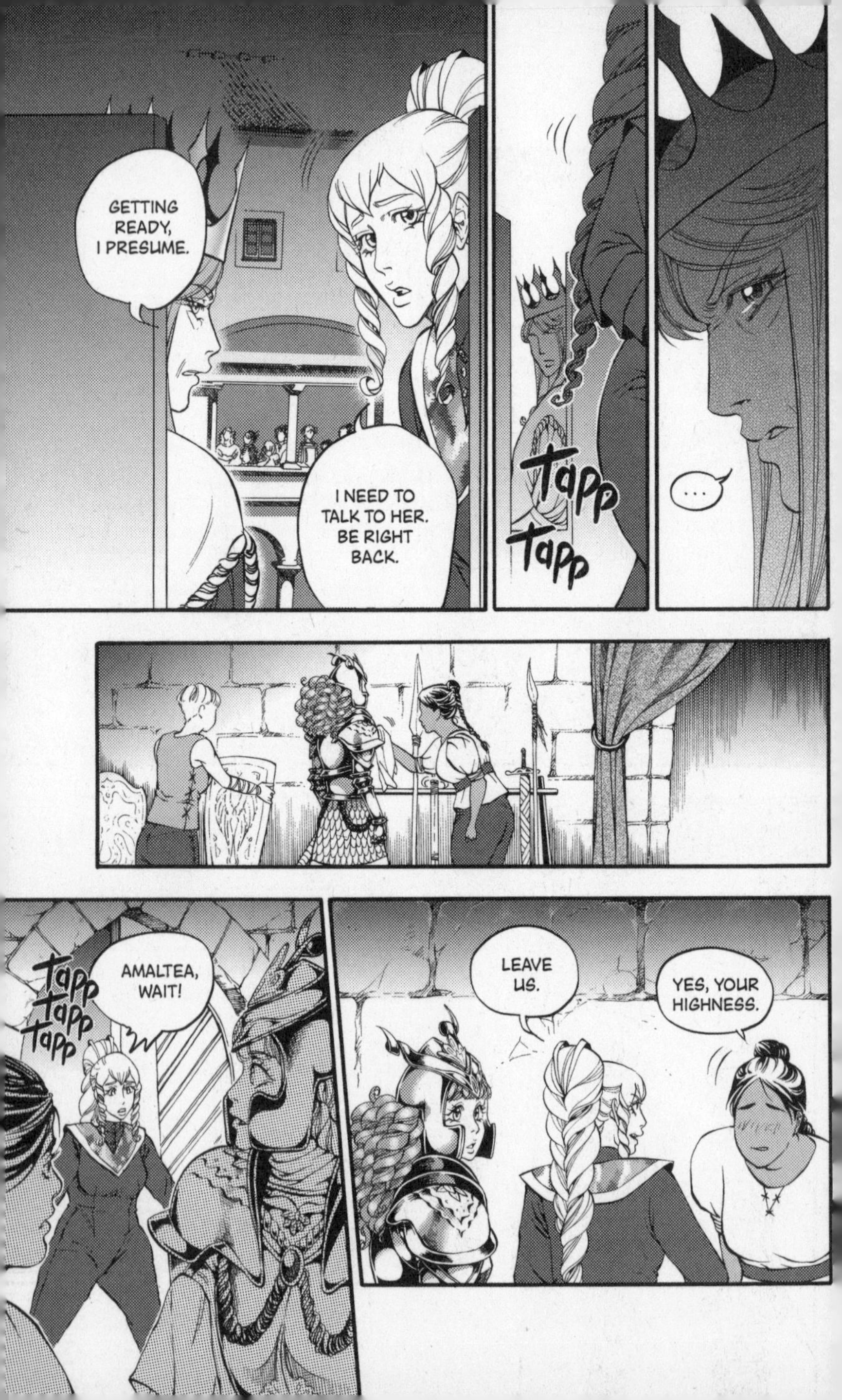
GETTING READY, I PRESUME.
I NEED TO TALK TO HER. BE RIGHT BACK.
TAPP
TAPP
...
TAPP TAPP TAPP
AMALTEA, WAIT!
LEAVE US.
YES, YOUR HIGHNESS.

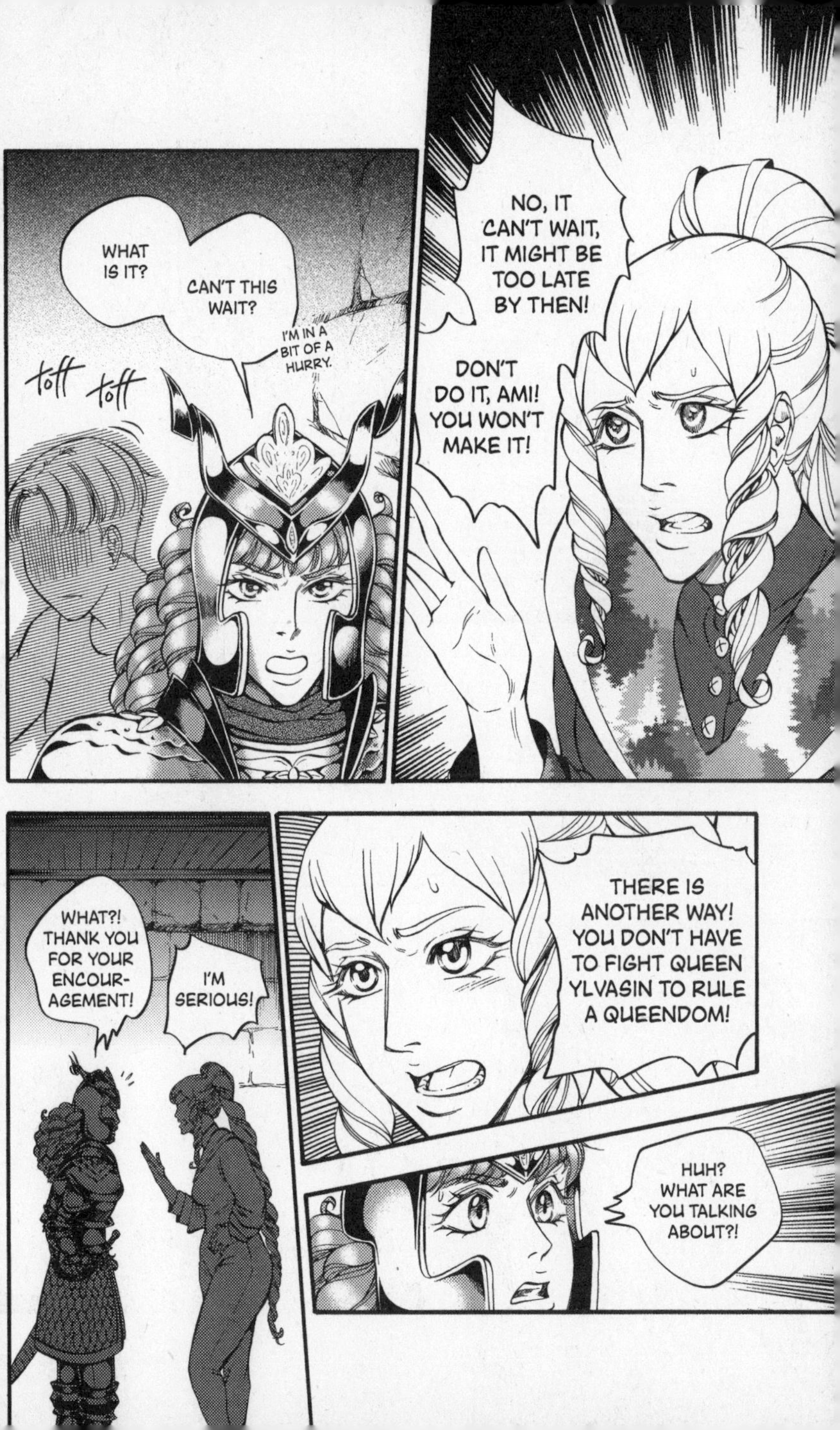
WHAT IS IT?
CAN'T THIS WAIT?
I'M IN A BIT OF A HURRY.
toff toff
NO, IT CAN'T WAIT, IT MIGHT BE TOO LATE BY THEN!
DON'T DO IT, AMI! YOU WON'T MAKE IT!
WHAT?! THANK YOU FOR YOUR ENCOUR- AGEMENT!
I'M SERIOUS!
THERE IS ANOTHER WAY! YOU DON'T HAVE TO FIGHT QUEEN YLVASIN TO RULE A QUEENDOM!
HUH? WHAT ARE YOU TALKING ABOUT?!

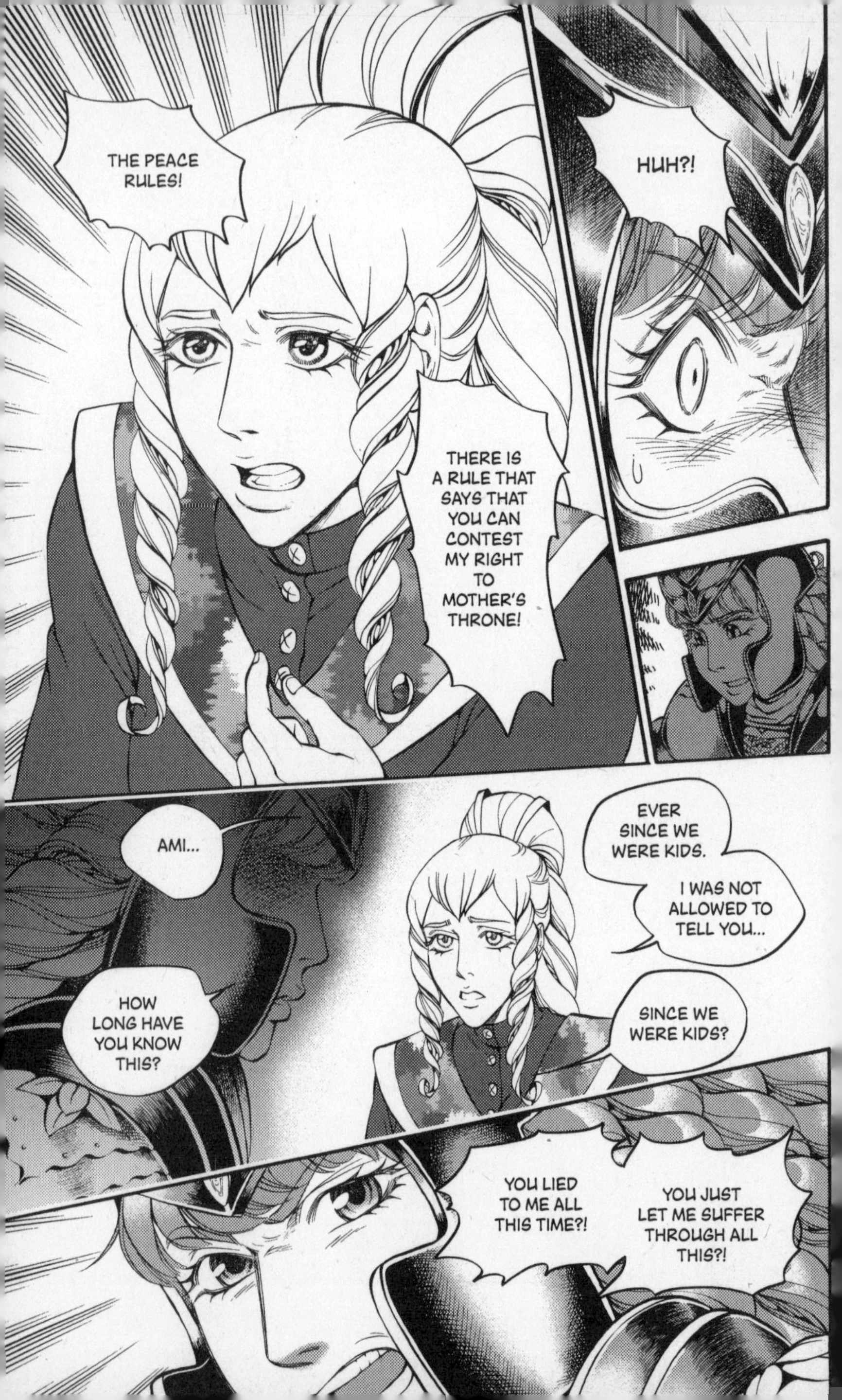
THE PEACE RULES!
THERE IS A RULE THAT SAYS THAT YOU CAN CONTEST MY RIGHT TO MOTHER'S THRONE!
HUH?!
AMI...
HOW LONG HAVE YOU KNOW THIS?
EVER SINCE WE WERE KIDS.
I WAS NOT ALLOWED TO TELL YOU...
SINCE WE WERE KIDS?
YOU LIED TO ME ALL THIS TIME?!
YOU JUST LET ME SUFFER THROUGH ALL THIS?!

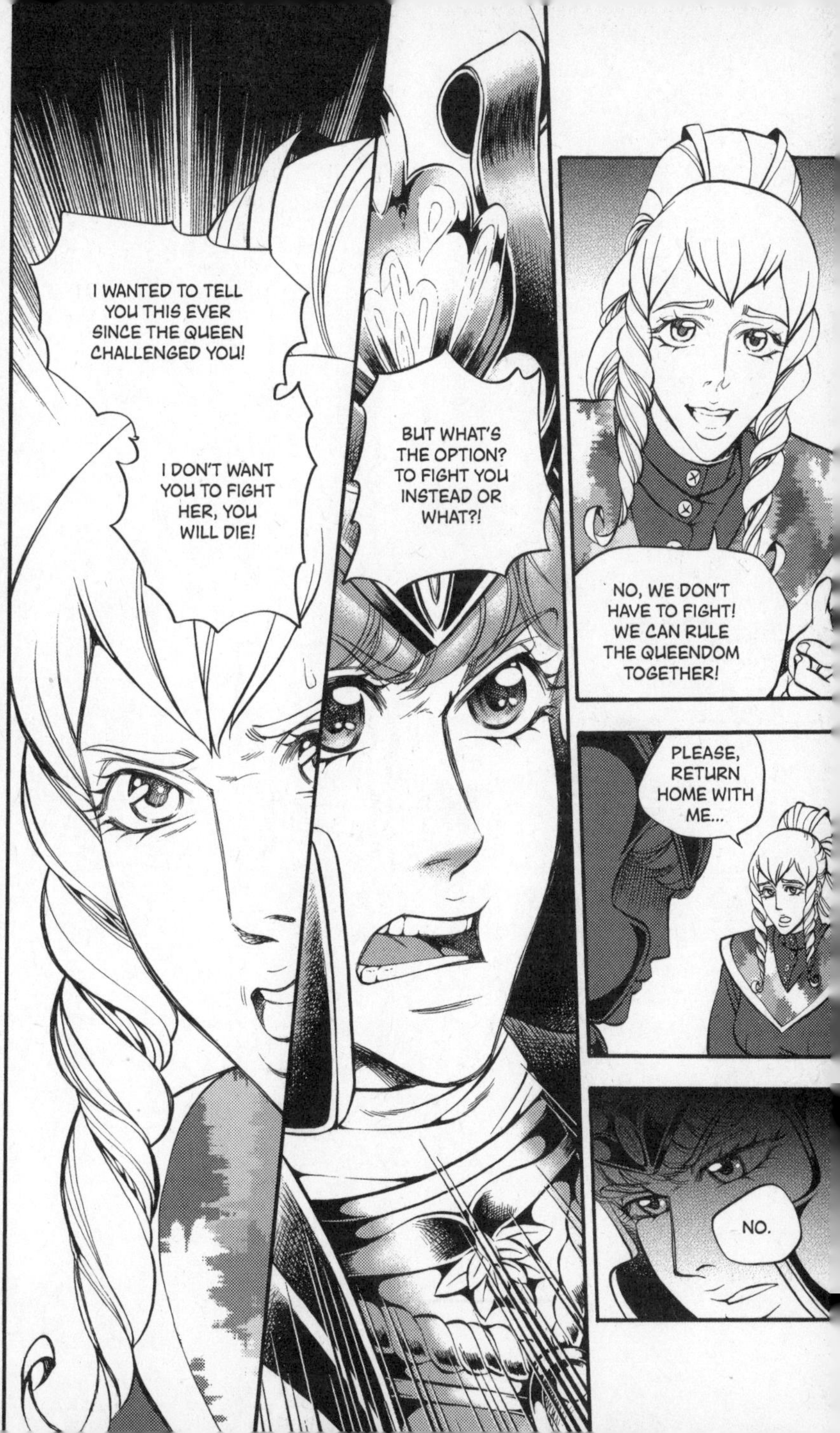
I WANTED TO TELL YOU THIS EVER SINCE THE QUEEN CHALLENGED YOU!
I DON'T WANT YOU TO FIGHT HER, YOU WILL DIE!
BUT WHAT'S THE OPTION? TO FIGHT YOU INSTEAD OR WHAT?!
NO, WE DON'T HAVE TO FIGHT! WE CAN RULE THE QUEENDOM TOGETHER!
PLEASE, RETURN HOME WITH ME...
NO.

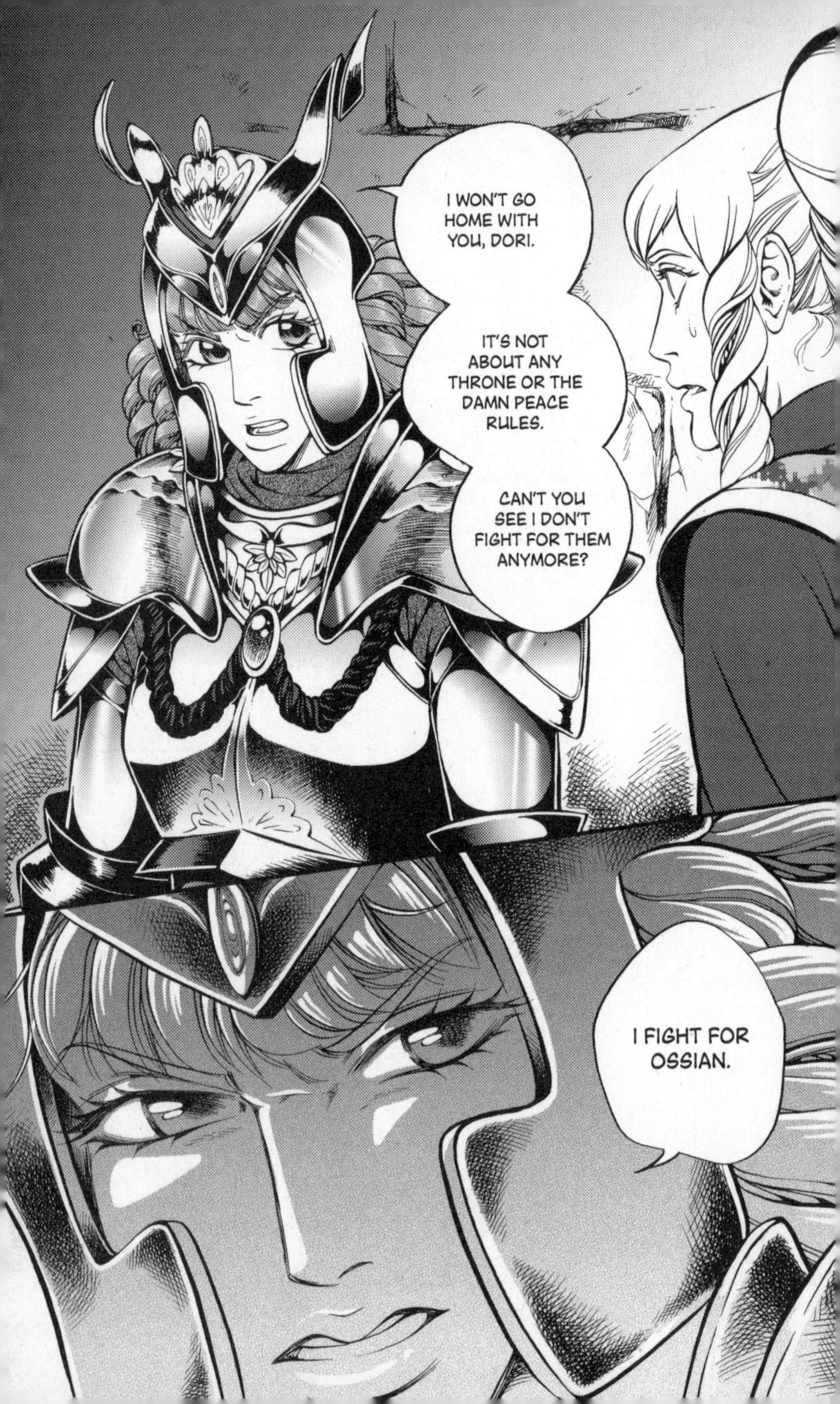
I WON'T GO HOME WITH YOU, DORI.
IT'S NOT ABOUT ANY THRONE OR THE DAMN PEACE RULES.
CAN'T YOU SEE I DON'T FIGHT FOR THEM ANYMORE?
I FIGHT FOR OSSIAN.

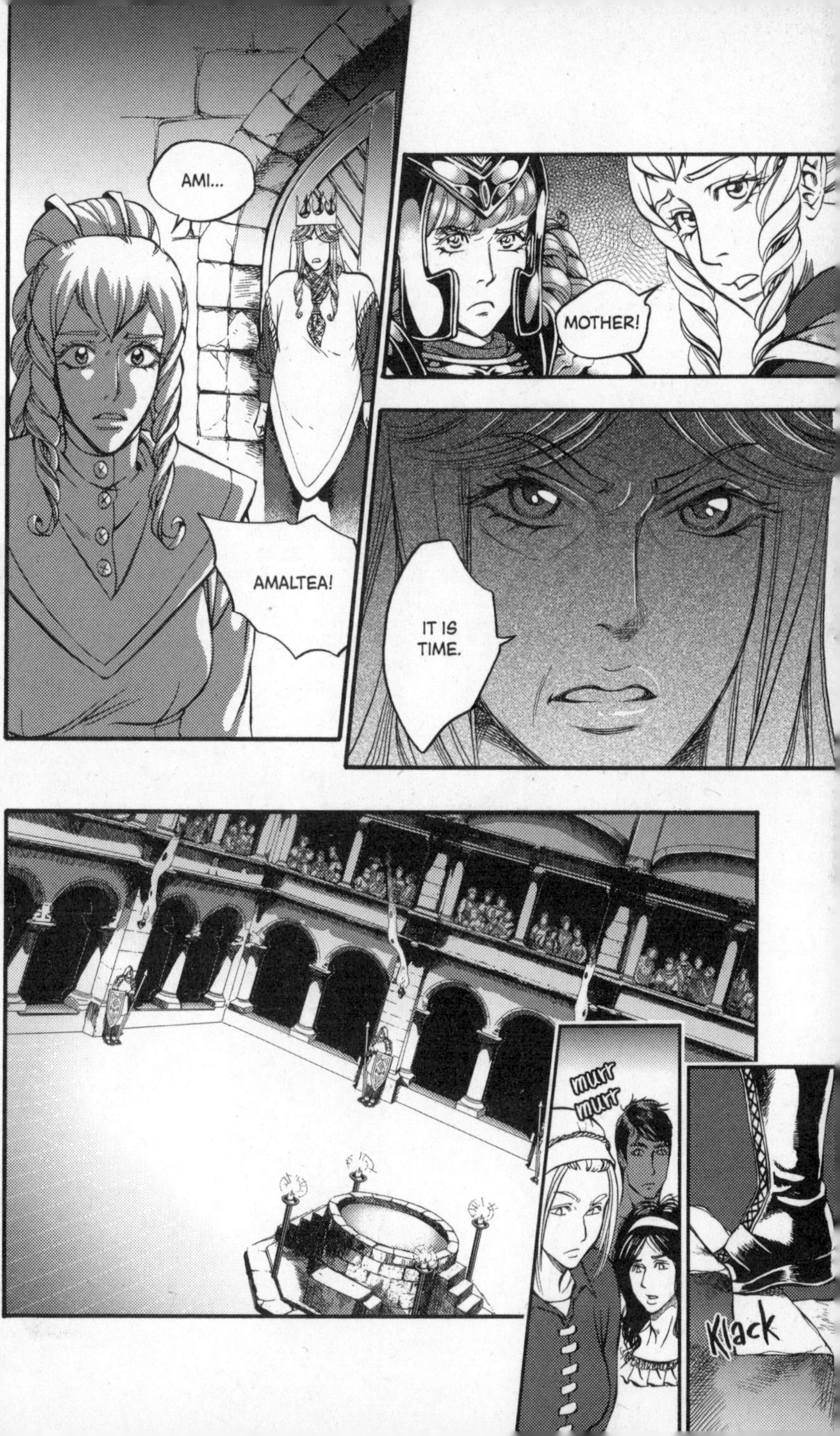
AMI...
AMALTEA!
MOTHER!
IT IS TIME.
murr murr
Klack

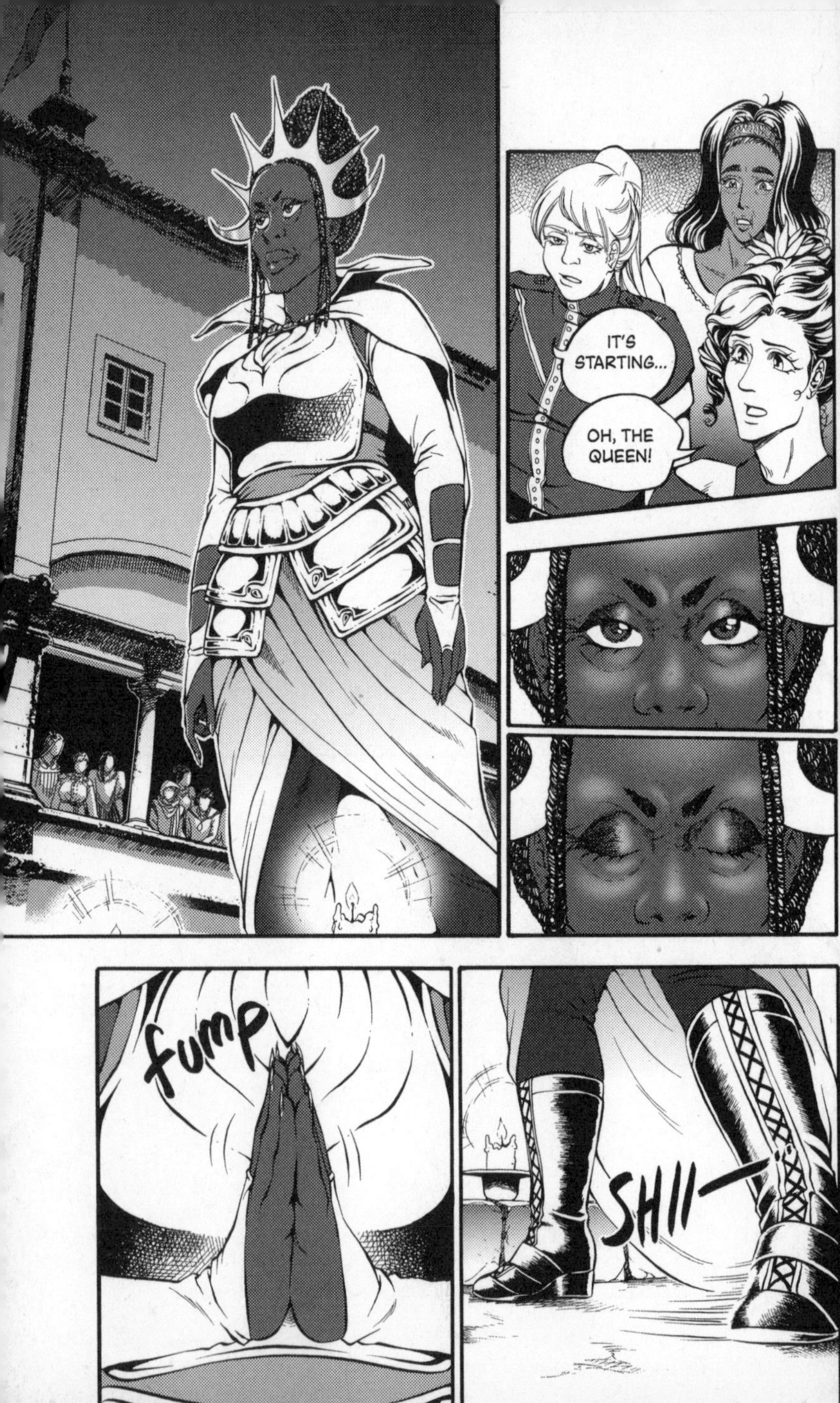
IT'S STARTING...
OH, THE QUEEN!
SHII—
fump

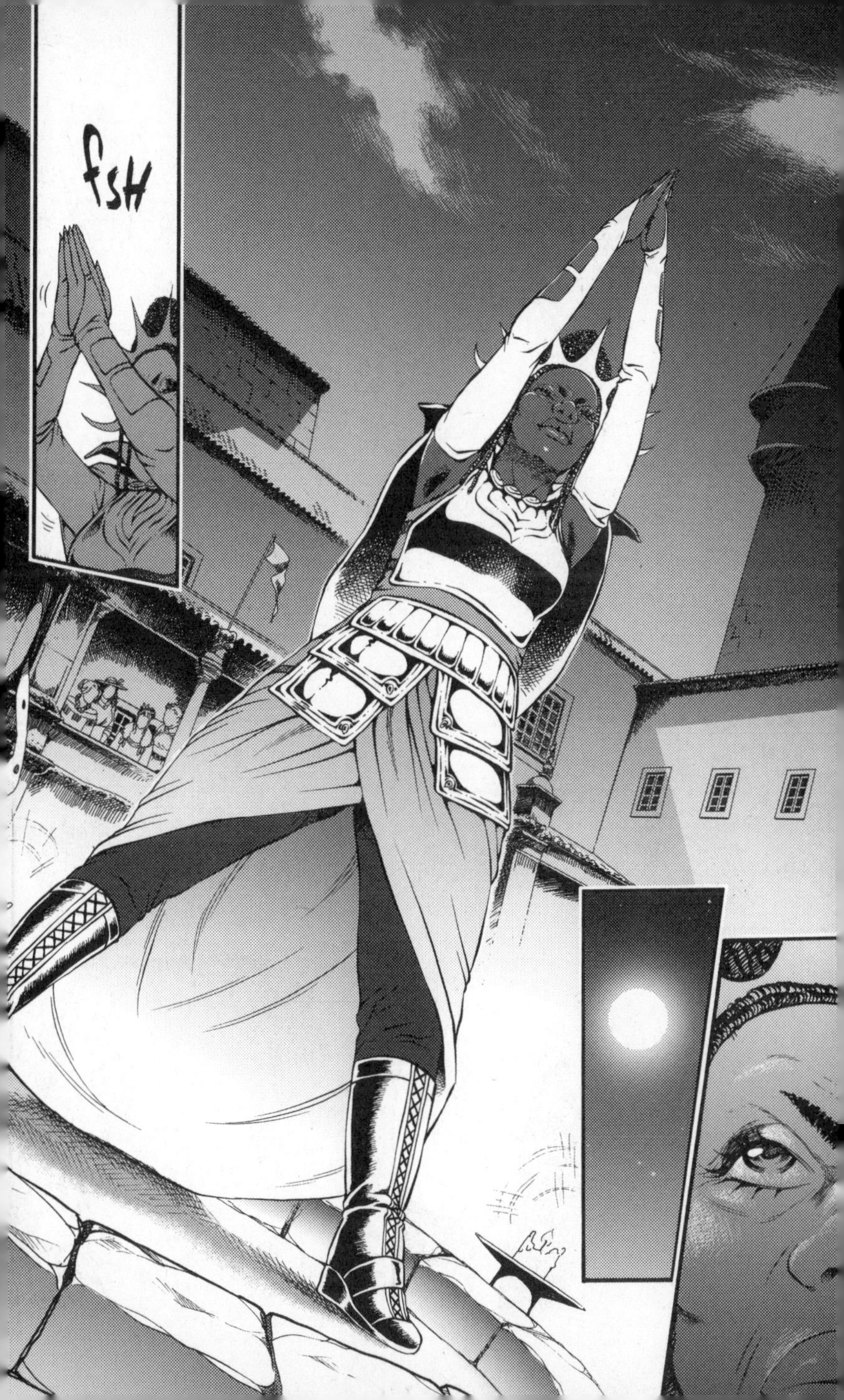
fsH

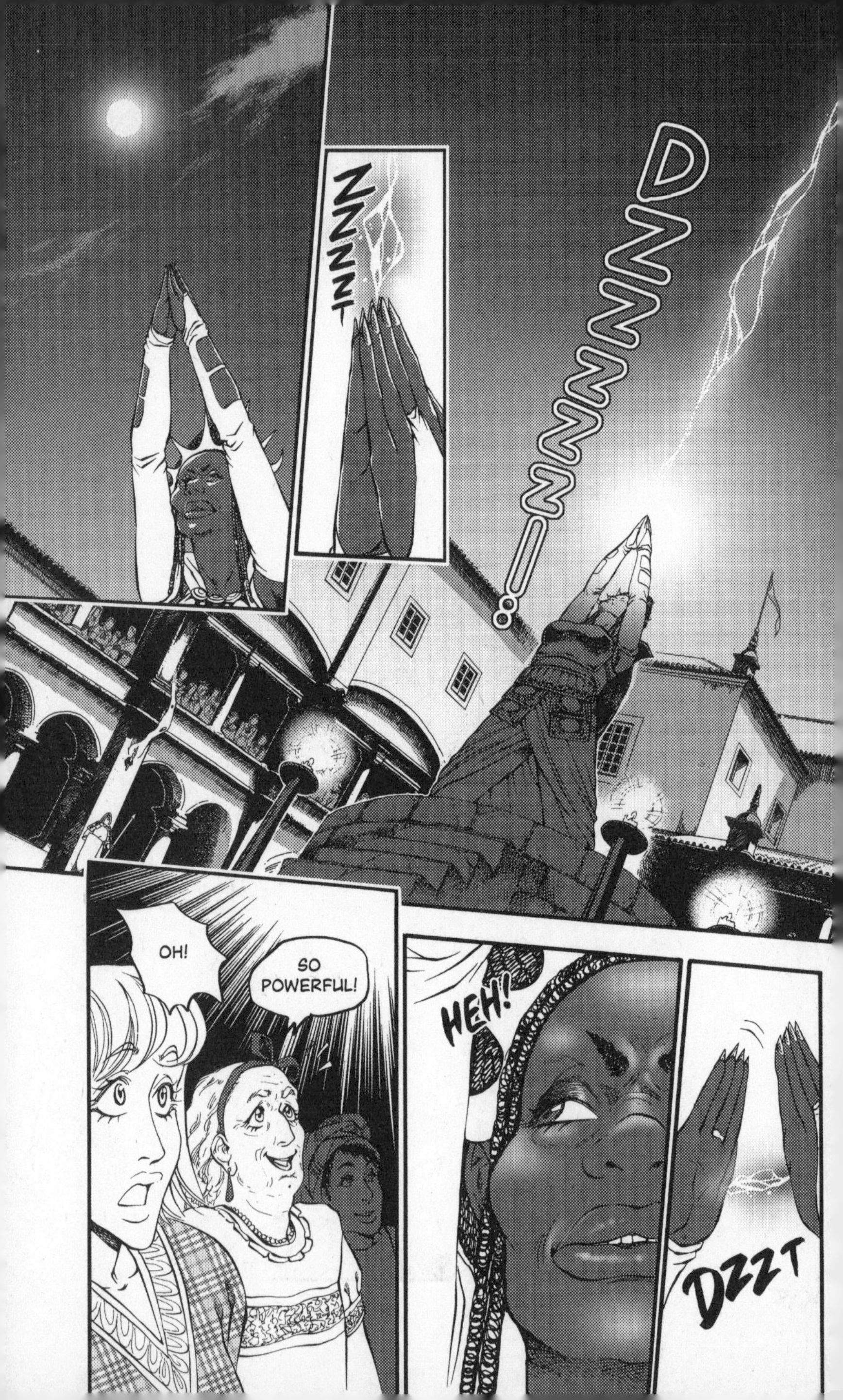
DZZZZZZZ—!!
ZZZZZT
DZZT
HEH!
OH!
SO POWERFUL!

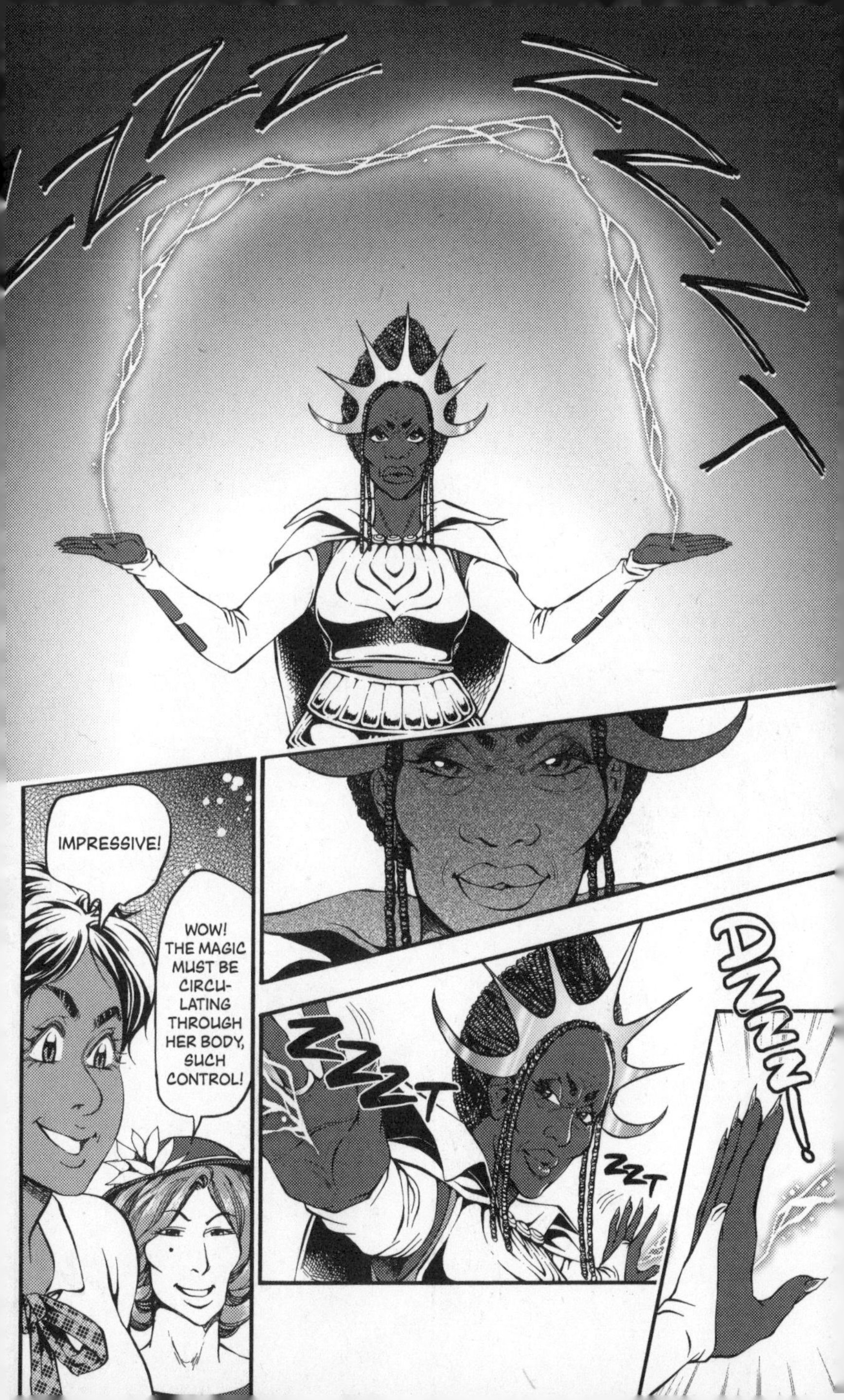
ZZZZZZNNNT
ZZZZ-T
ZZT
ANNN!
IMPRESSIVE!
WOW! THE MAGIC MUST BE CIRCU-LATING THROUGH HER BODY, SUCH CONTROL!

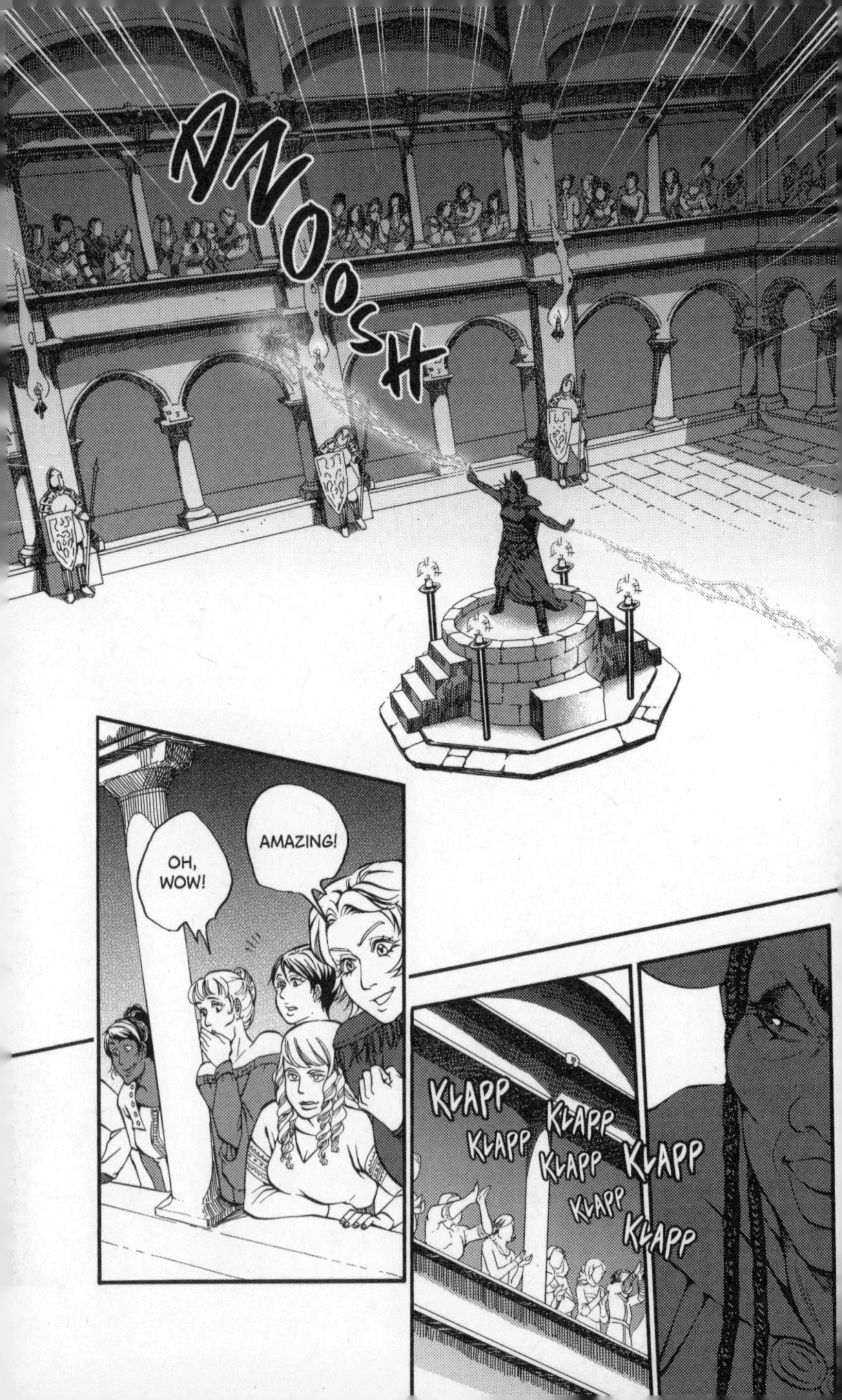
WOOOSH
AMAZING!
OH, WOW!
KLAPP
KLAPP
KLAPP
KLAPP
KLAPP
KLAPP
KLAPP

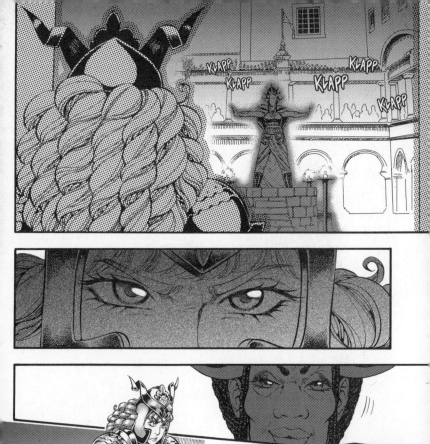

KLAPP
KLAPP
KLAPP
KLAPP
KLAPP

TCK
TCK

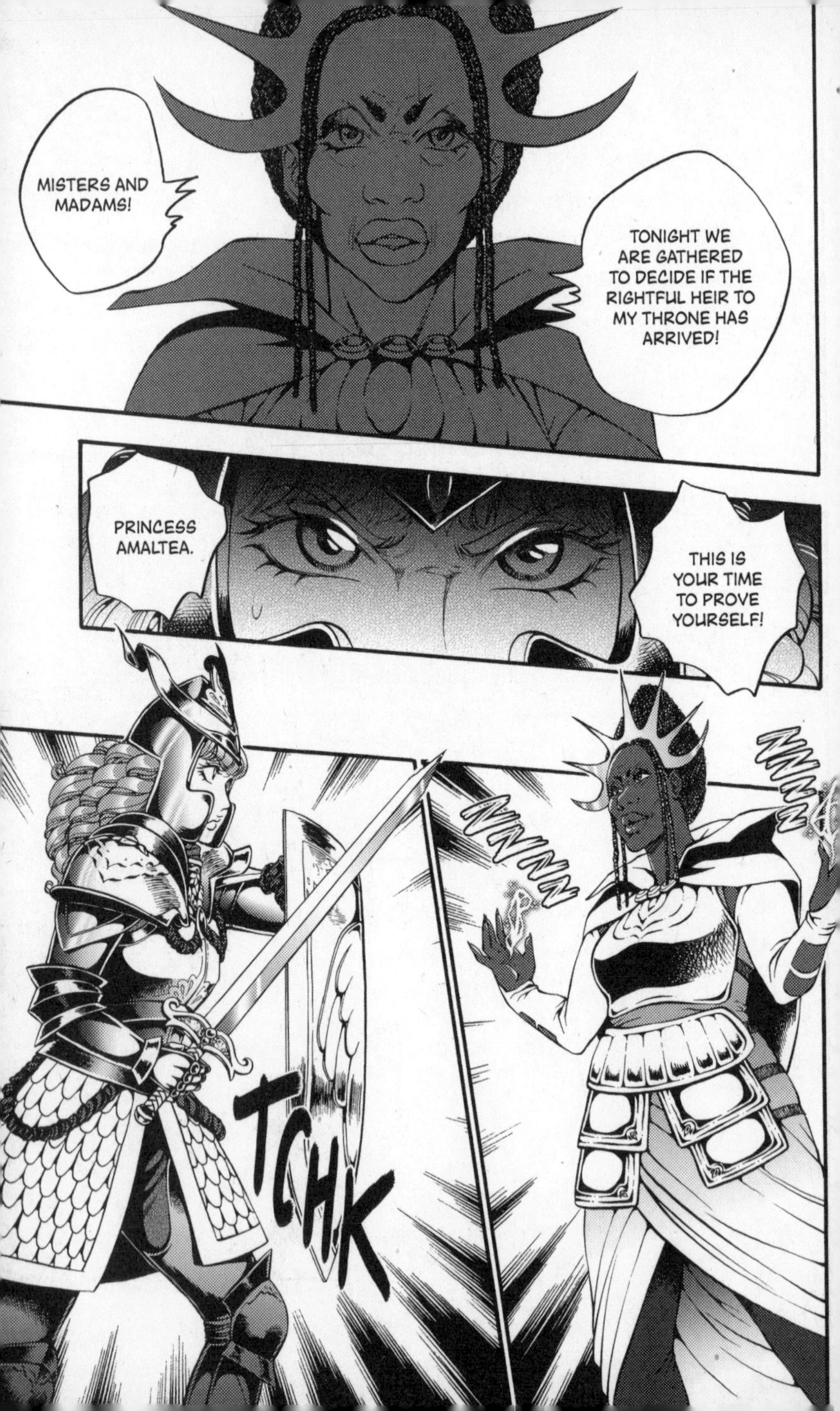
MISTERS AND MADAMS!
TONIGHT WE ARE GATHERED TO DECIDE IF THE RIGHTFUL HEIR TO MY THRONE HAS ARRIVED!
PRINCESS AMALTEA.
THIS IS YOUR TIME TO PROVE YOURSELF!
NNNNNN
NNNNN
TCHK

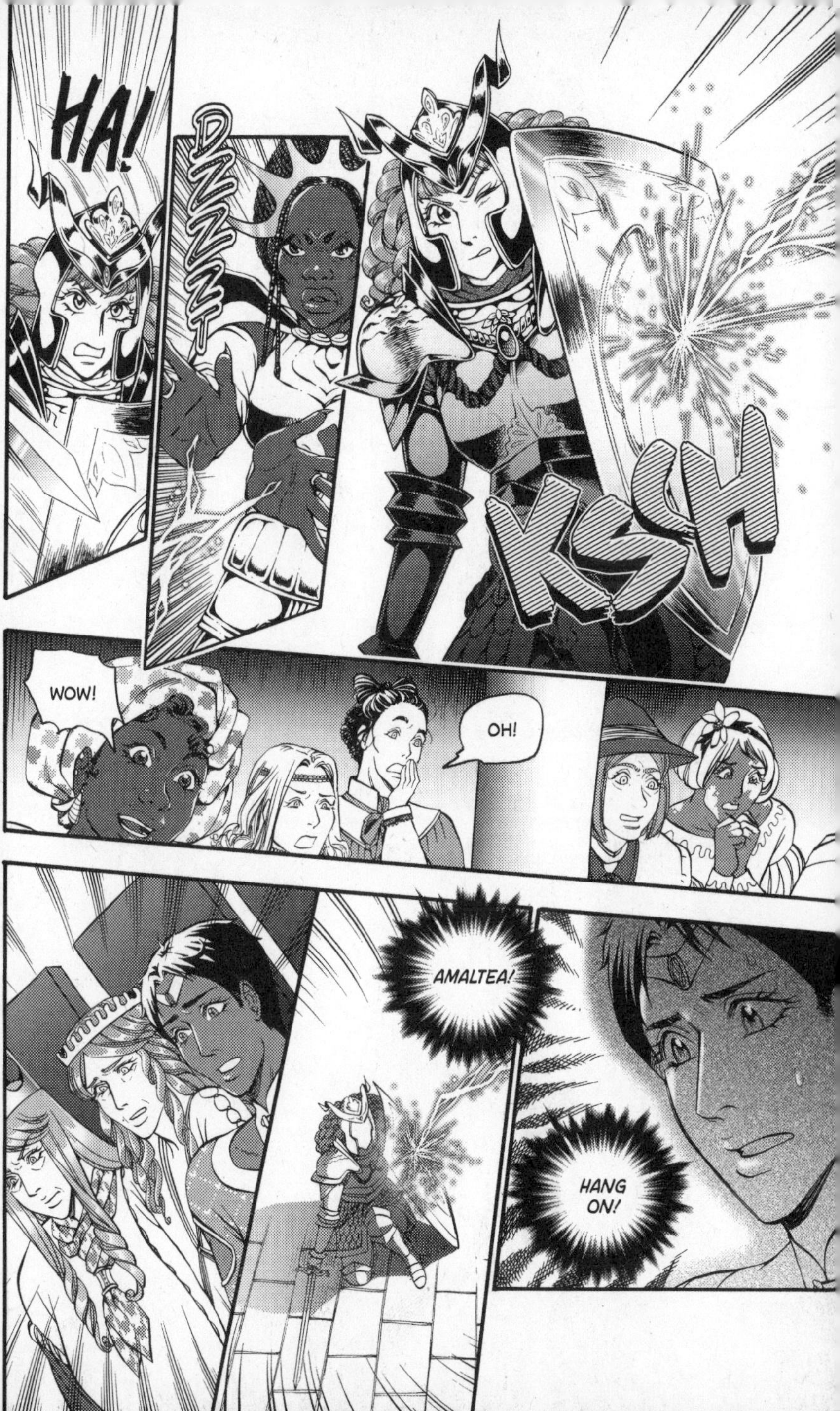
KSSH
DZZZT
HA!
OH!
WOW!
AMALTEA!
HANG ON!

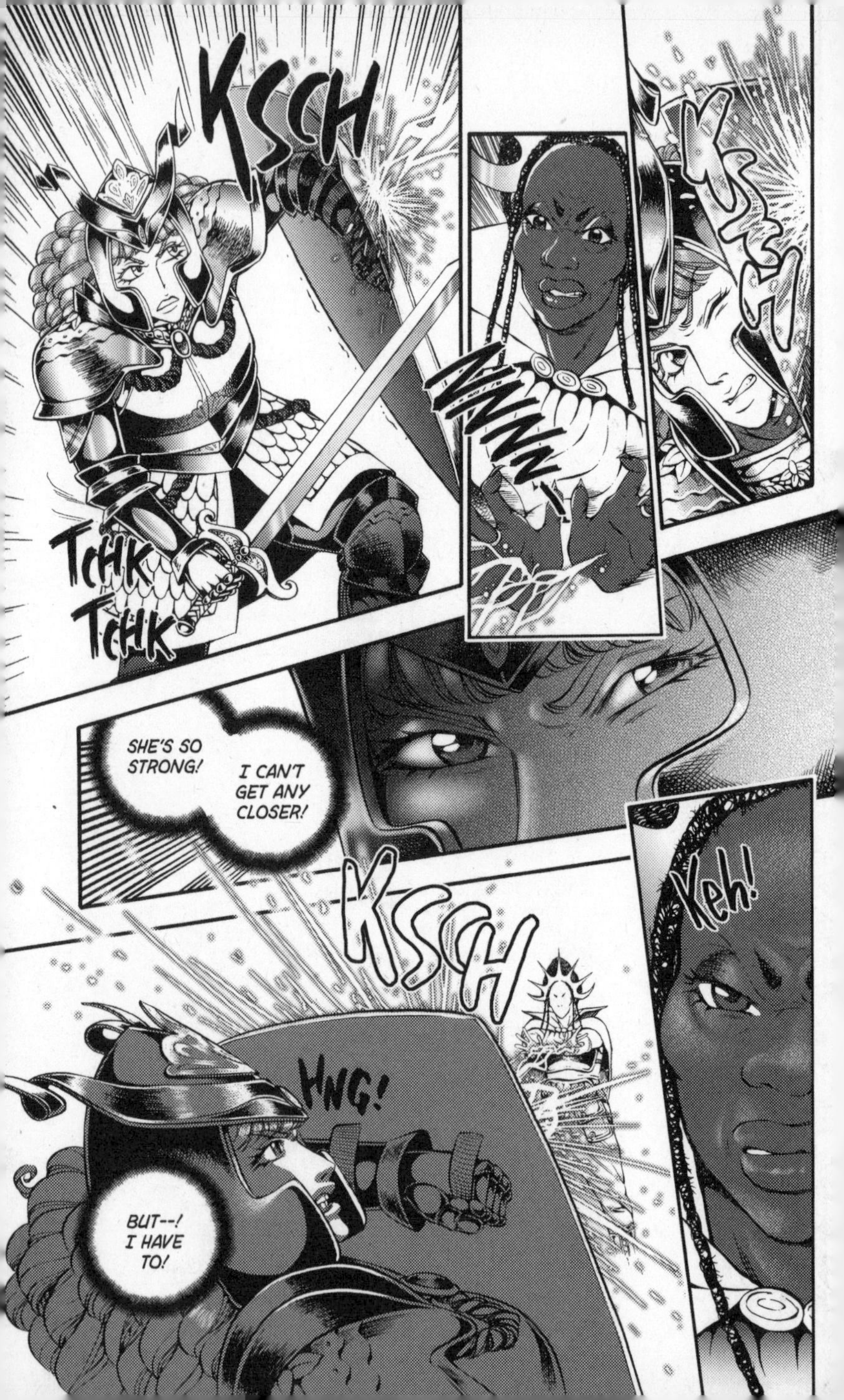
KSCH
TCHK
TCHK
SHE'S SO STRONG!
I CAN'T GET ANY CLOSER!
Keh!
KSCH
HNG!
BUT--! I HAVE TO!

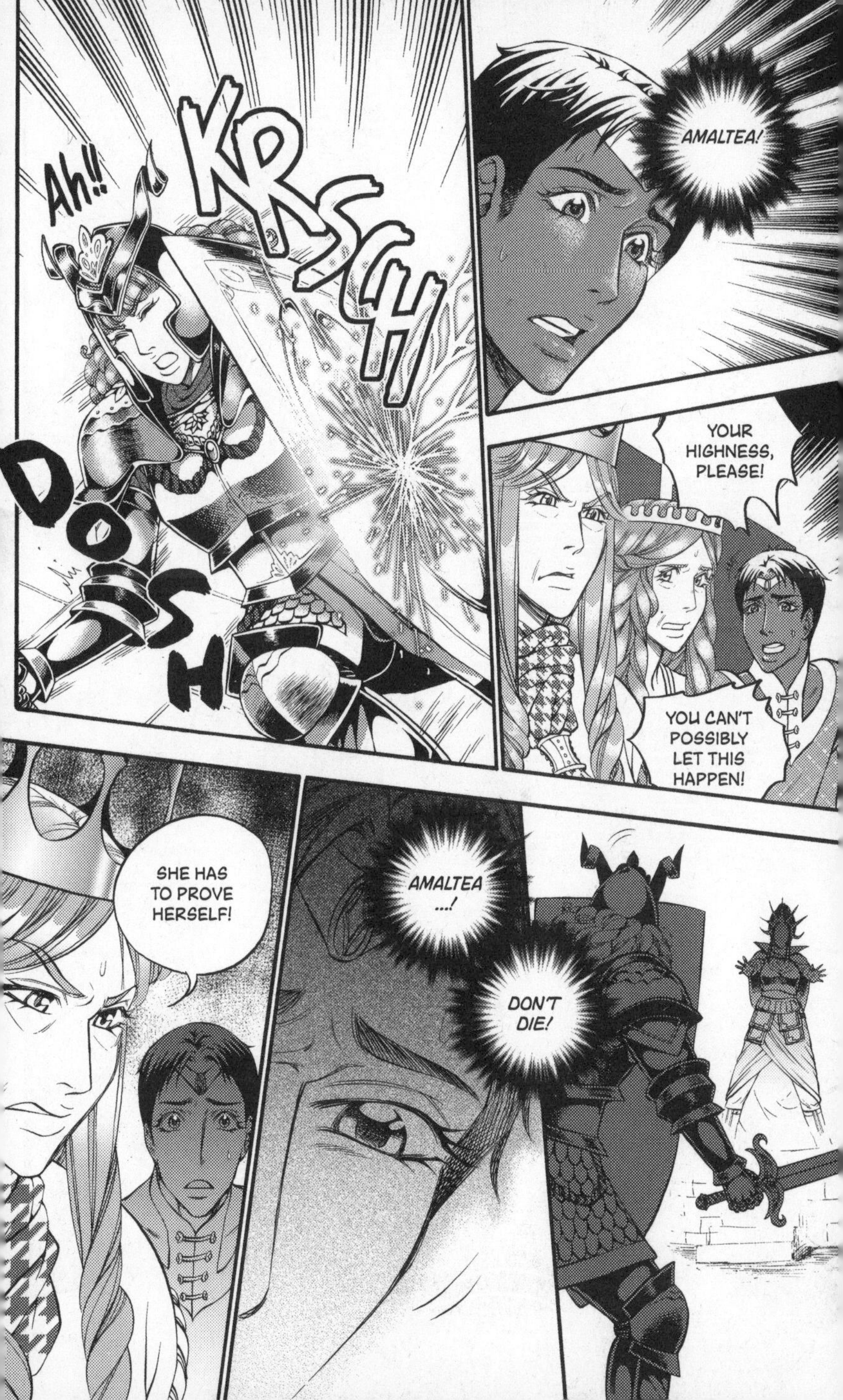
AMALTEA!
YOUR HIGHNESS, PLEASE!
YOU CAN'T POSSIBLY LET THIS HAPPEN!
Ah!!
KRSCH
DOSH
AMALTEA ...!
DON'T DIE!
SHE HAS TO PROVE HERSELF!

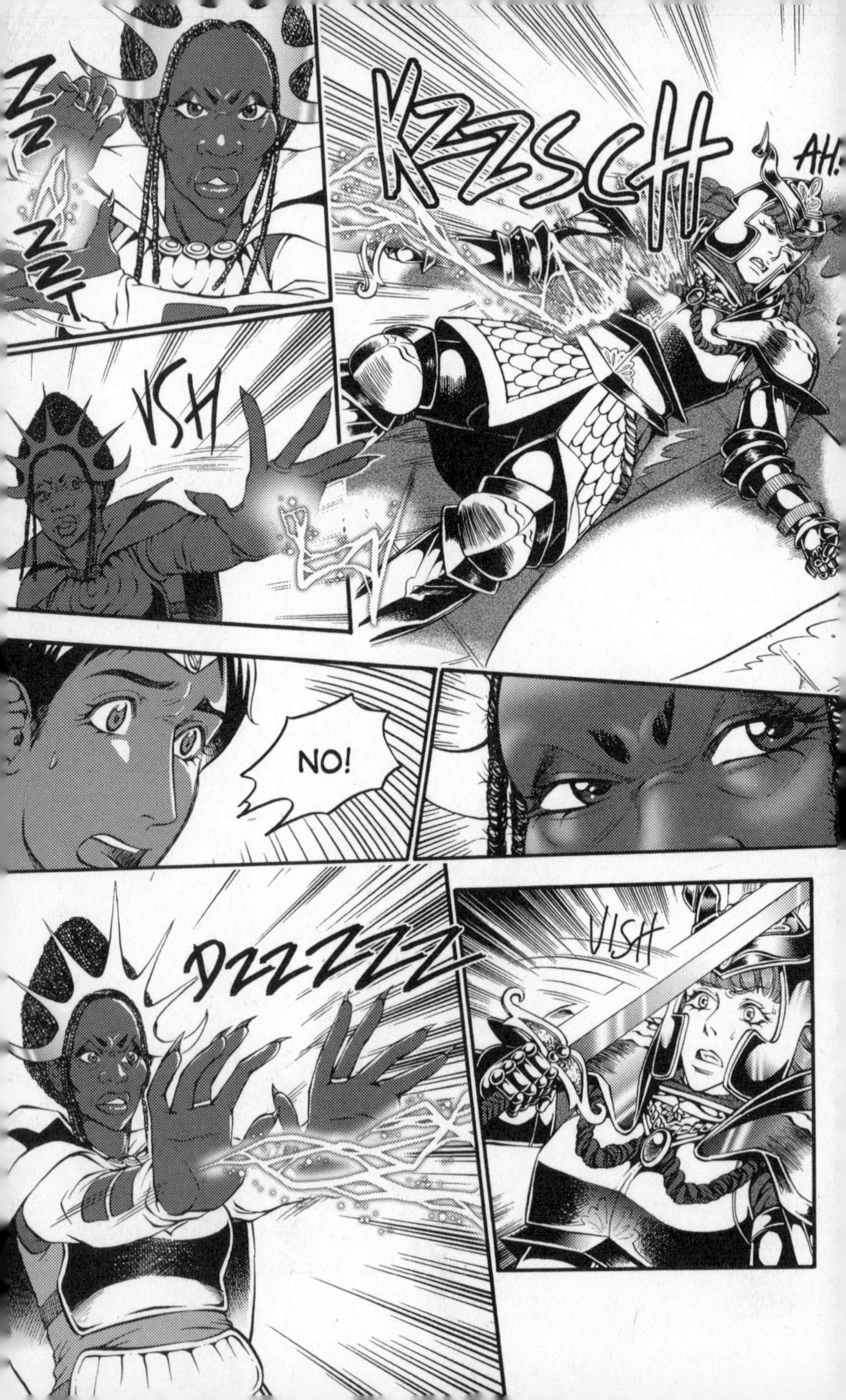
KRZSCH
AH!
ZZZ
ZZZT
VSH
NO!
VISH
DZZZZZZ

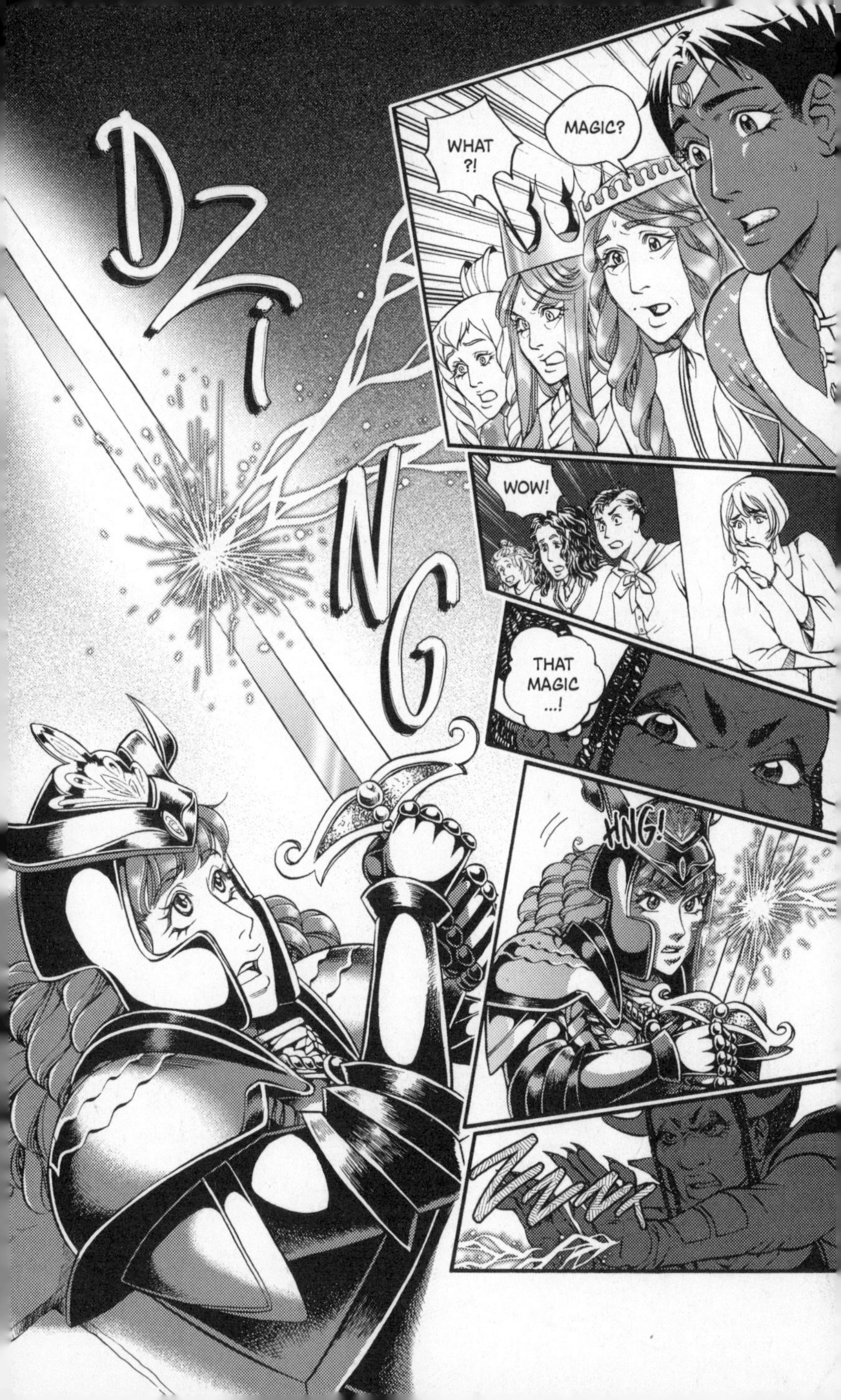
MAGIC?
WHAT ?!
WOW!
THAT MAGIC ...!
HNG!
DZING

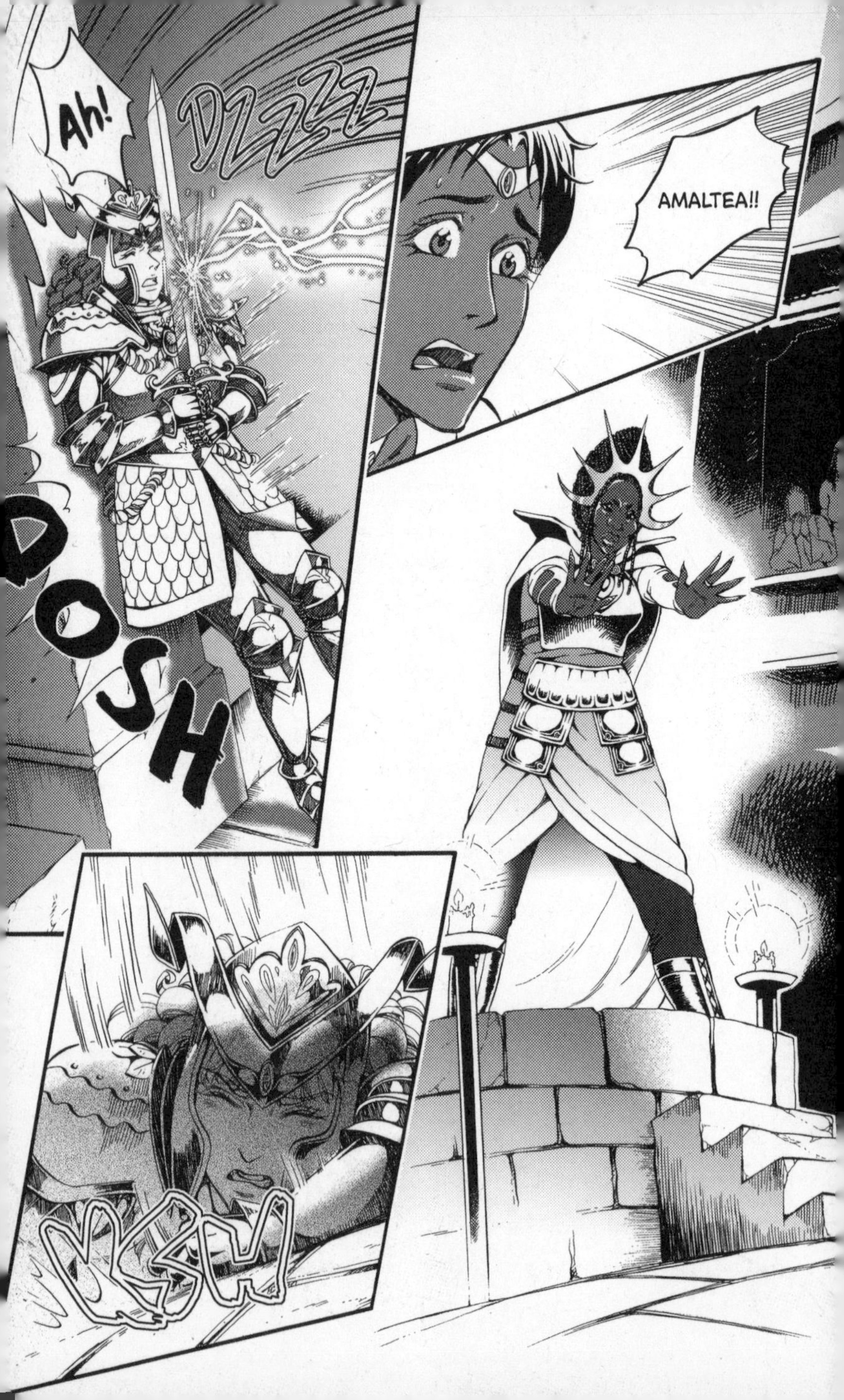
AMALTEA!!
Ah!
DZZZZZ
DOSH
KSH

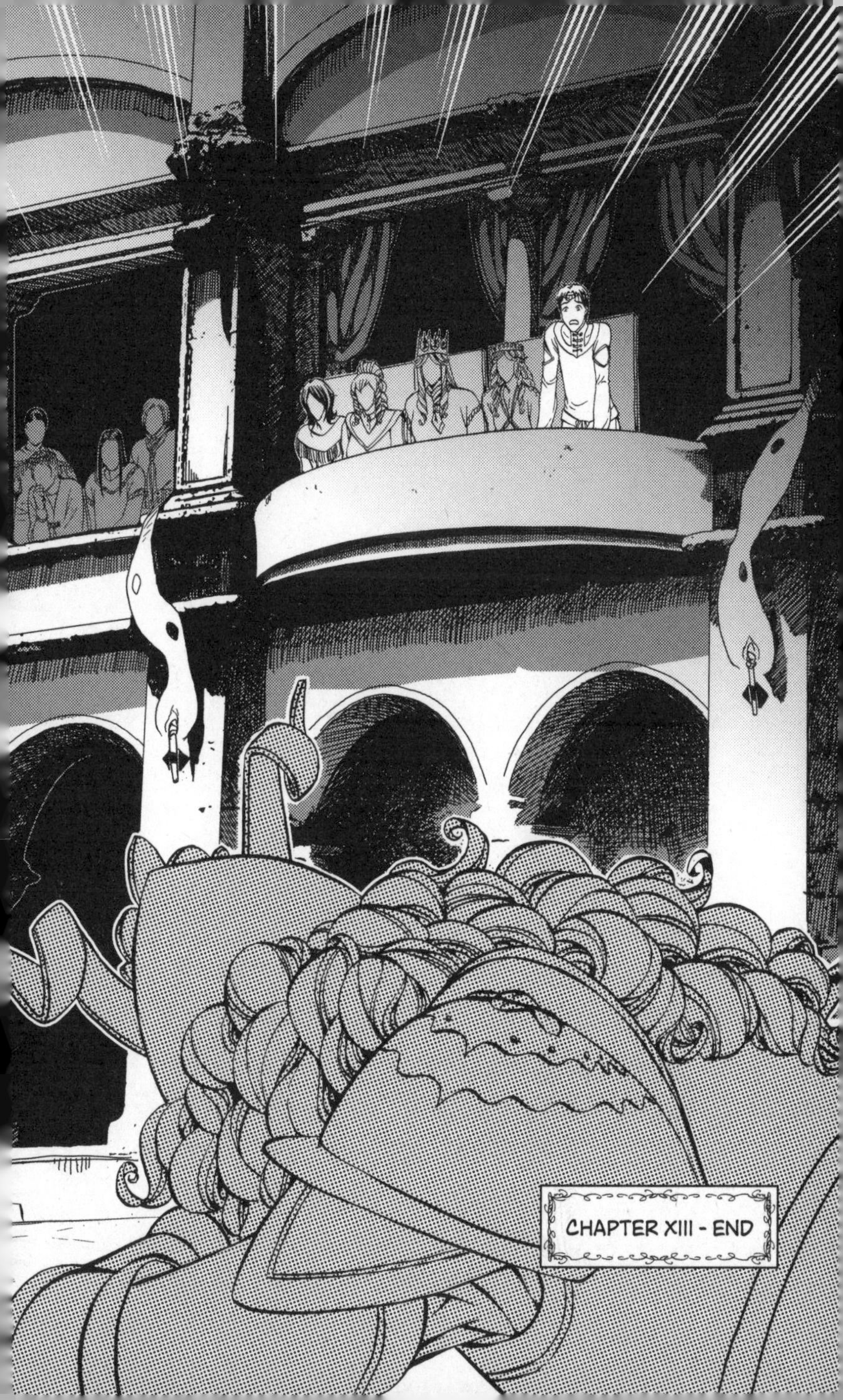
CHAPTER XIII - END

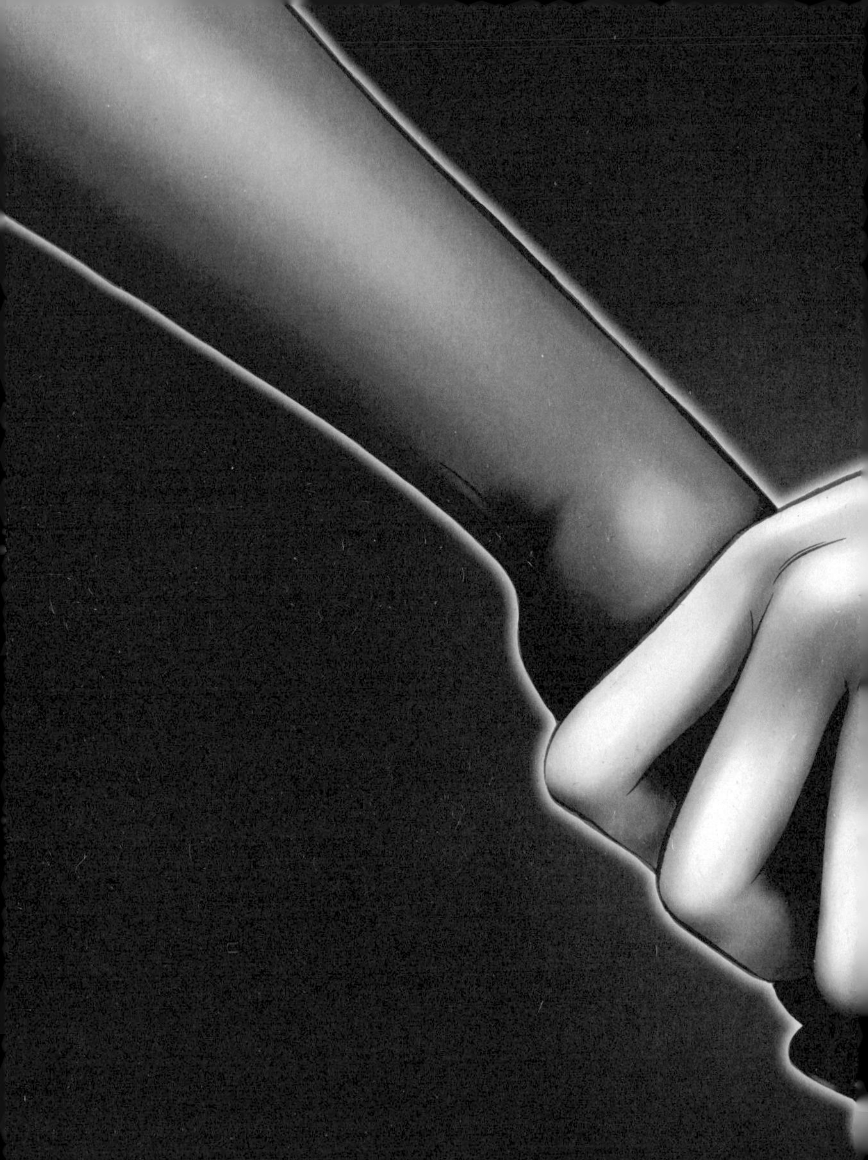

Chapter XIV

The Princess And The Prince

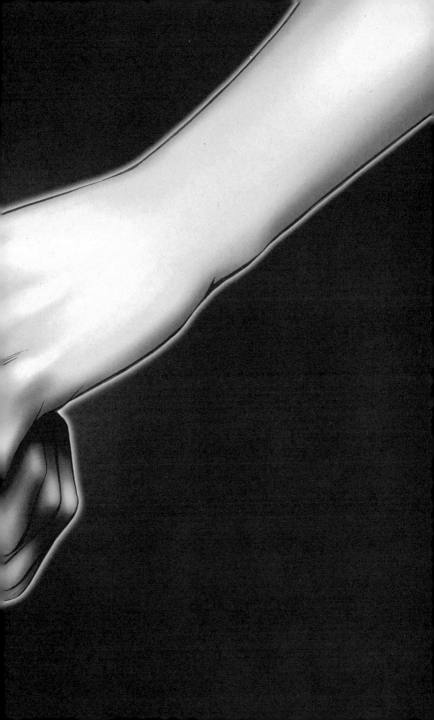

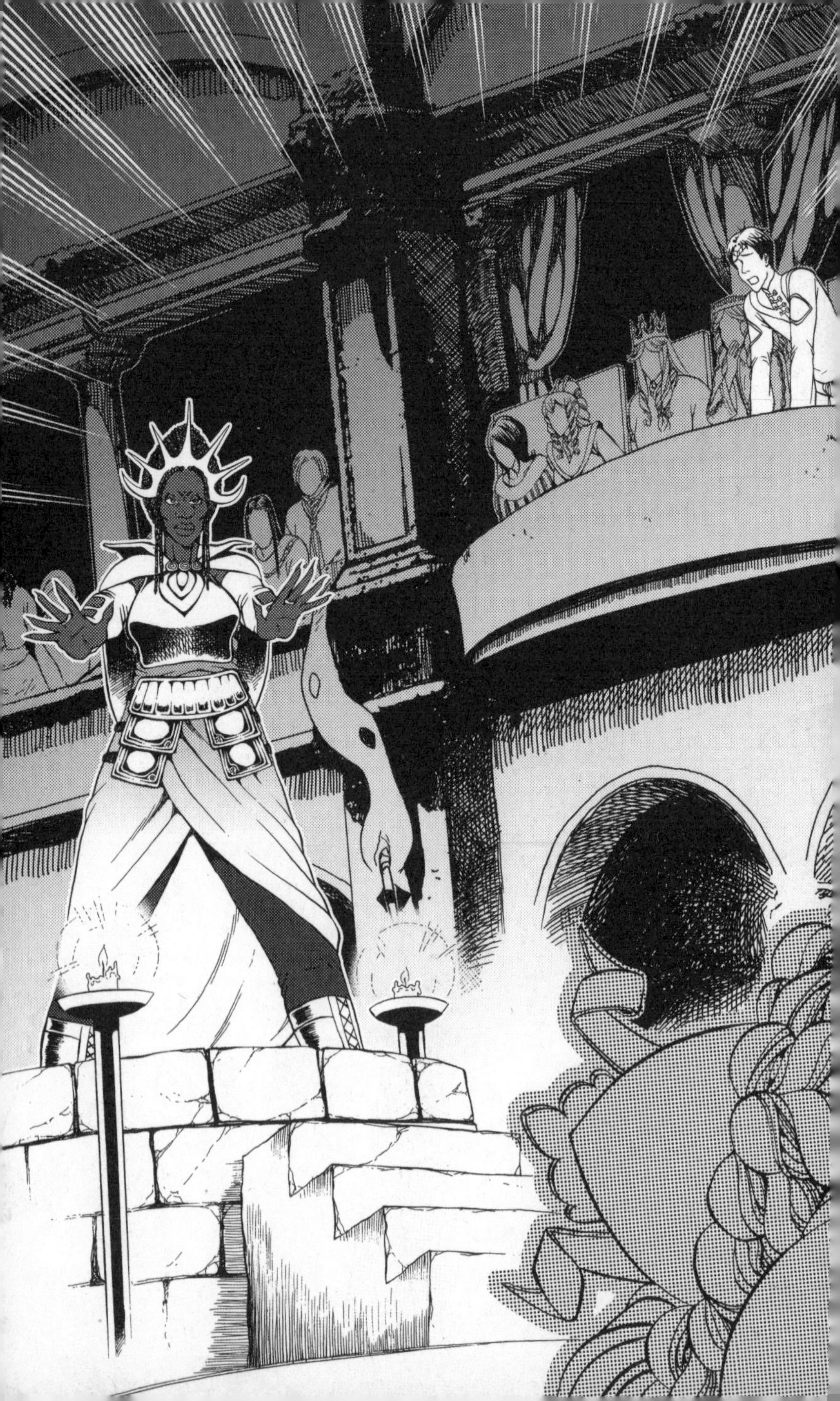

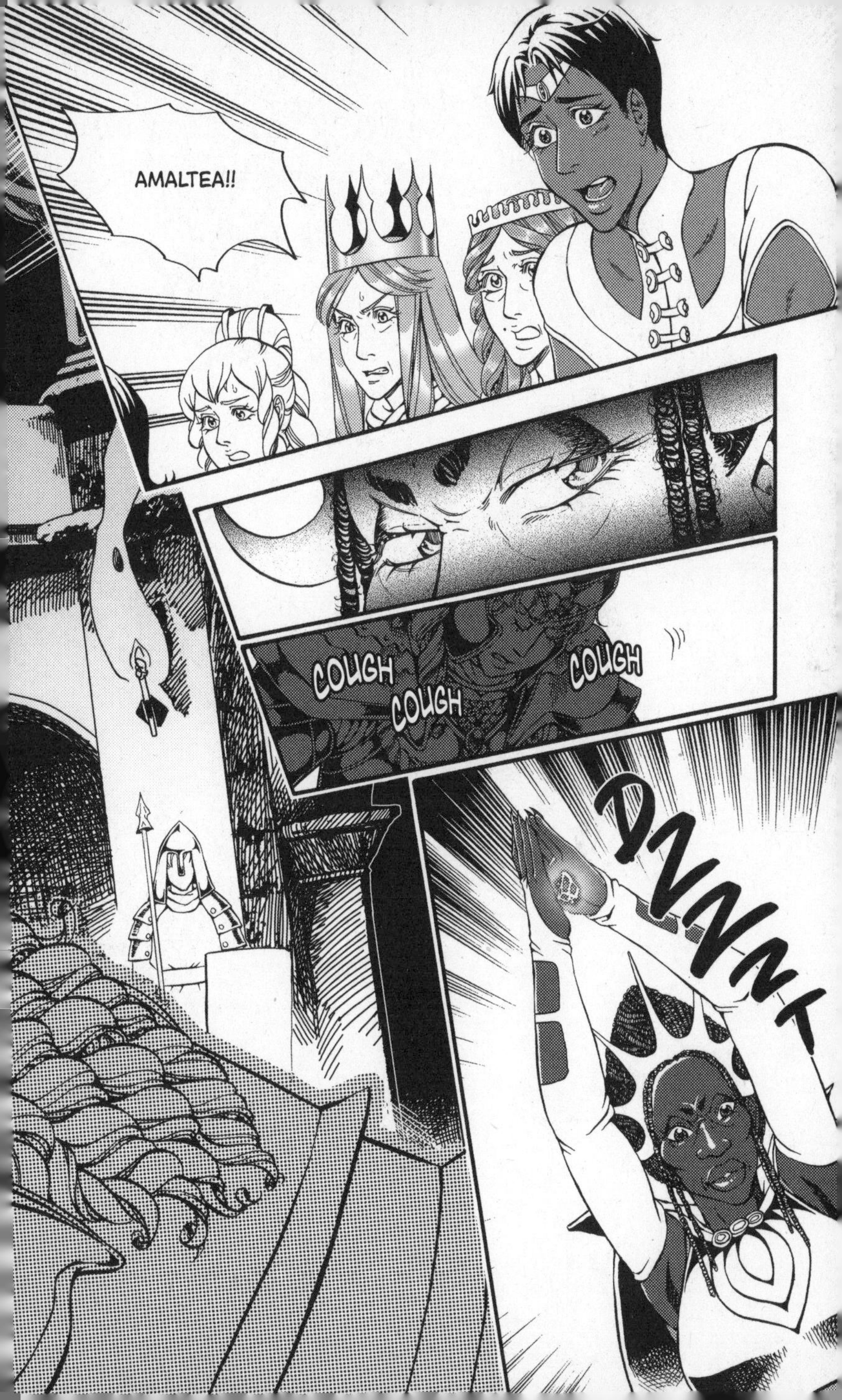
AMALTEA!!
COUGH
COUGH
COUGH
DZZZNNK

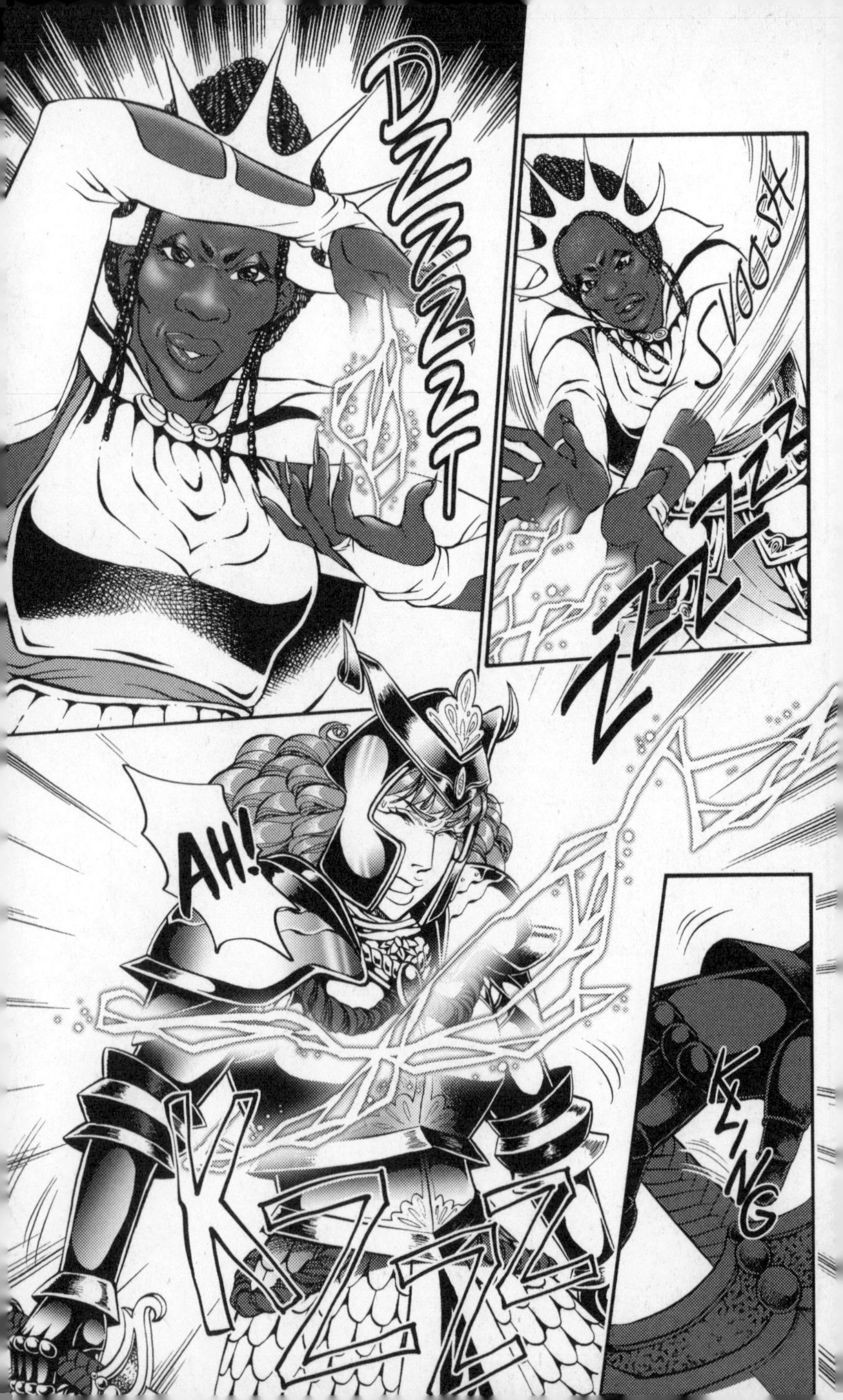
SWOOSH
ZZZZZ
DZZZZT
KLING
AH!
KZZZ

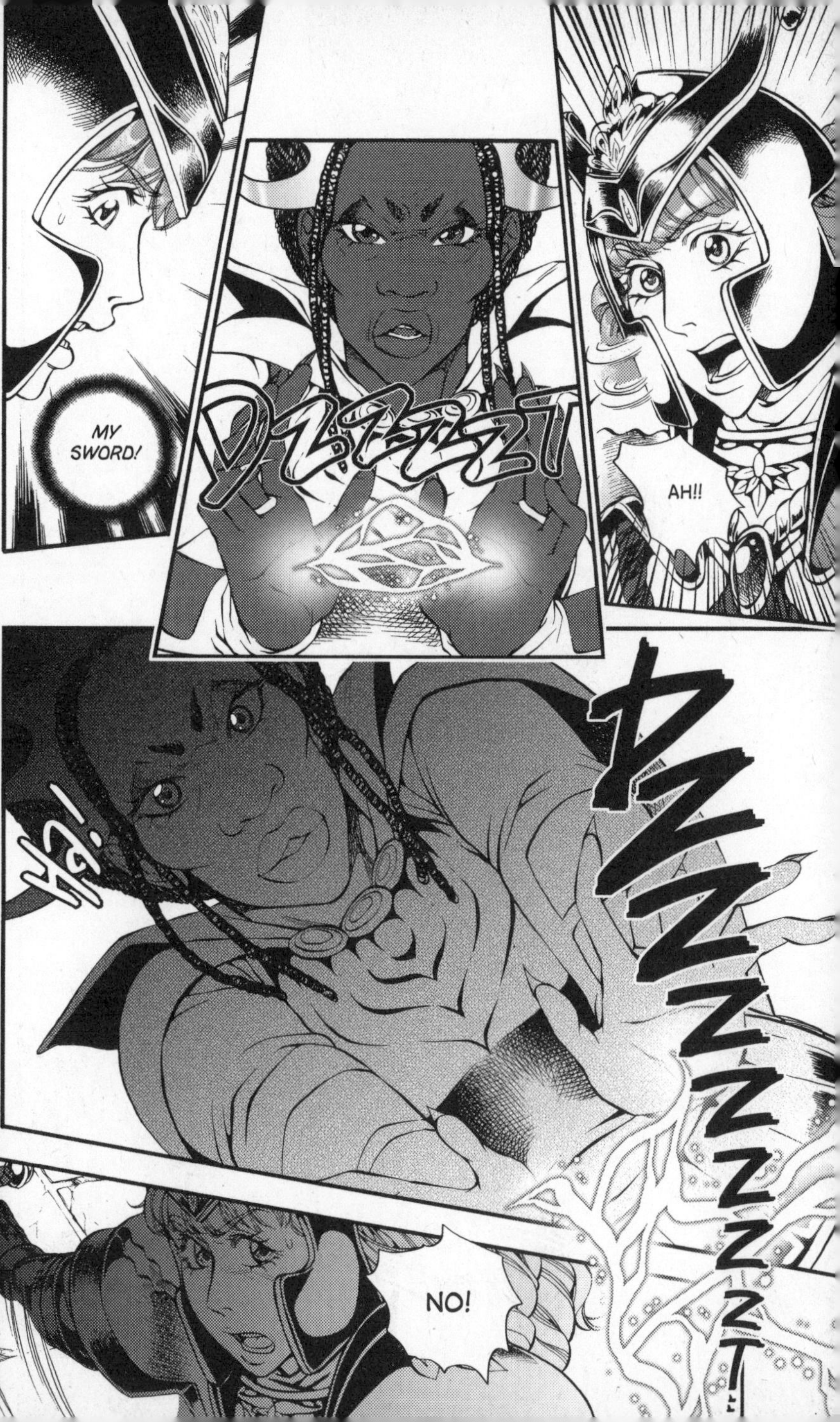
AH!!
DZZZZZT
MY SWORD!
NO!

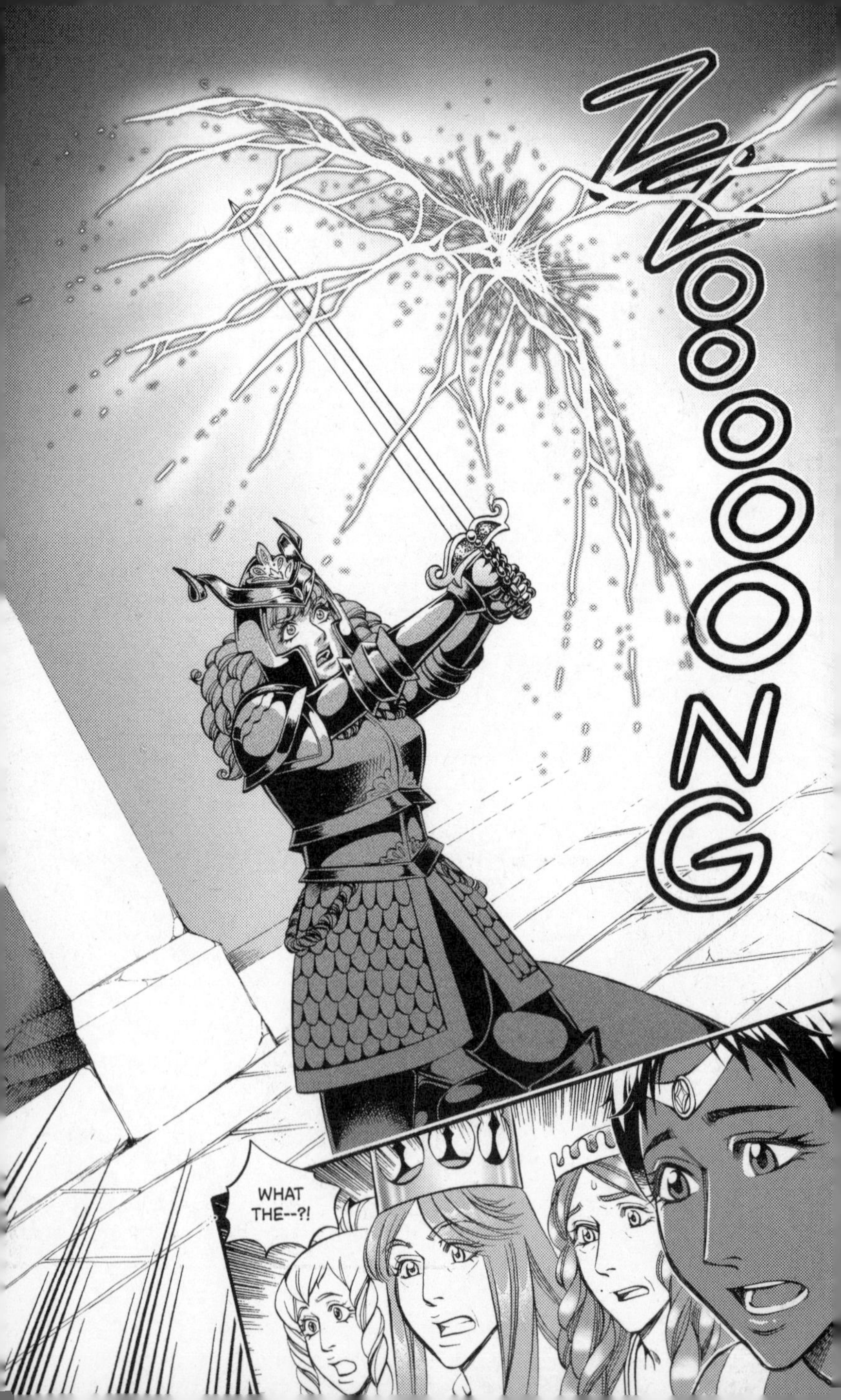
ZWOOOOONG
WHAT THE--?!

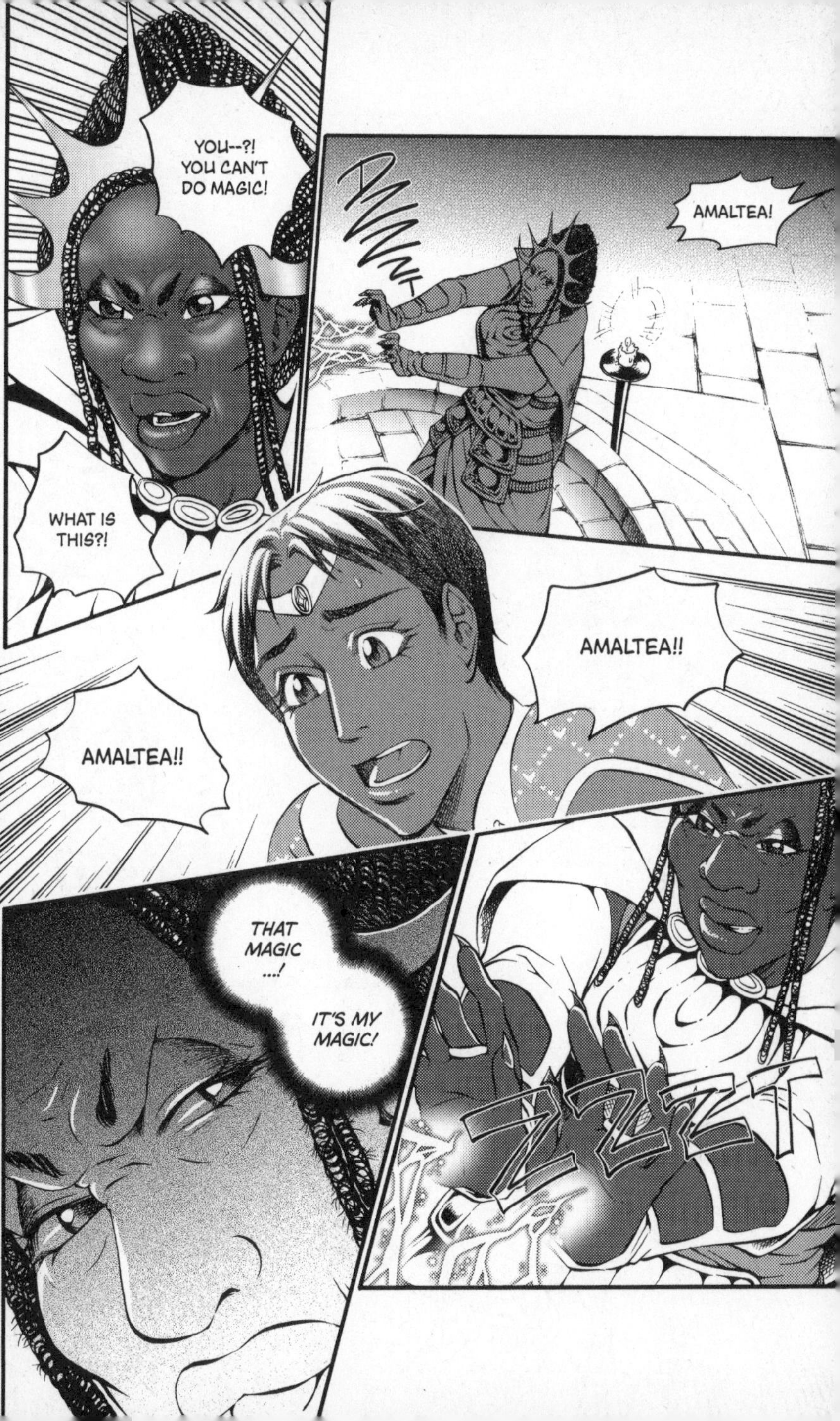
YOU--?! YOU CAN'T DO MAGIC!
WHAT IS THIS?!
AMALTEA!
AMALTEA!!
AMALTEA!!
THAT MAGIC ...!
IT'S MY MAGIC!
ZZZT

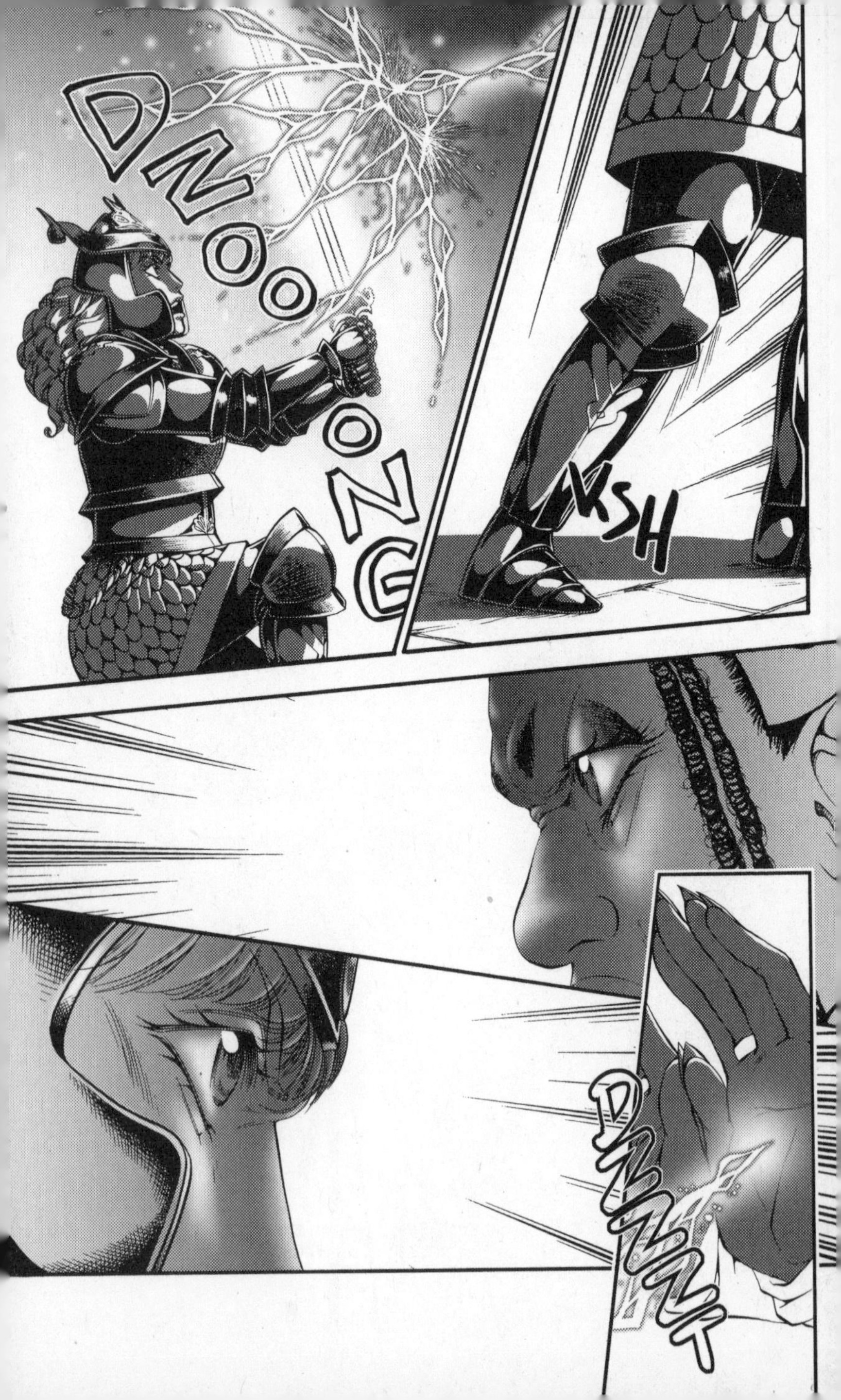
KSH
DNOOOONG
DINNNK

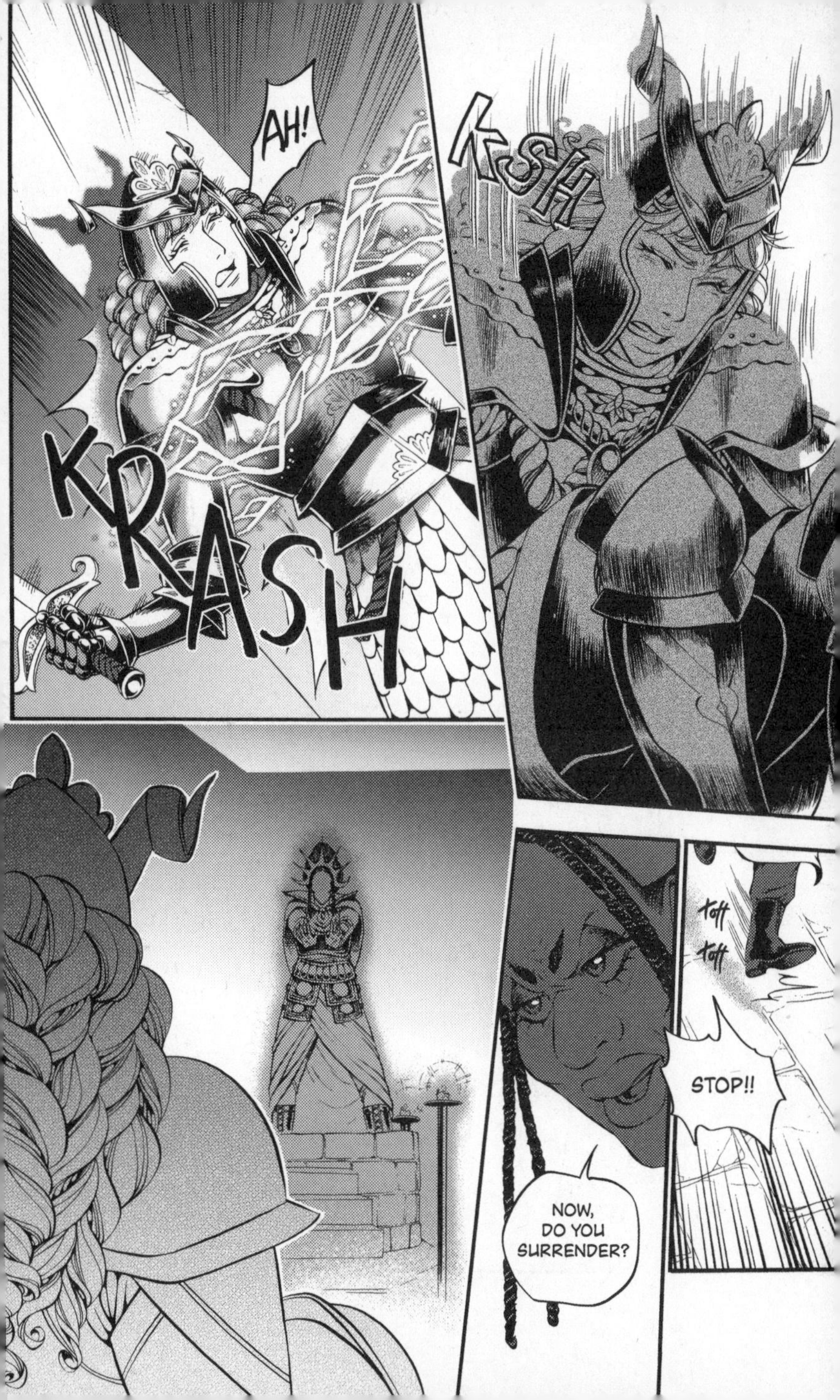
KSH
AH!
KRASH
toff toff
STOP!!
NOW, DO YOU SURRENDER?

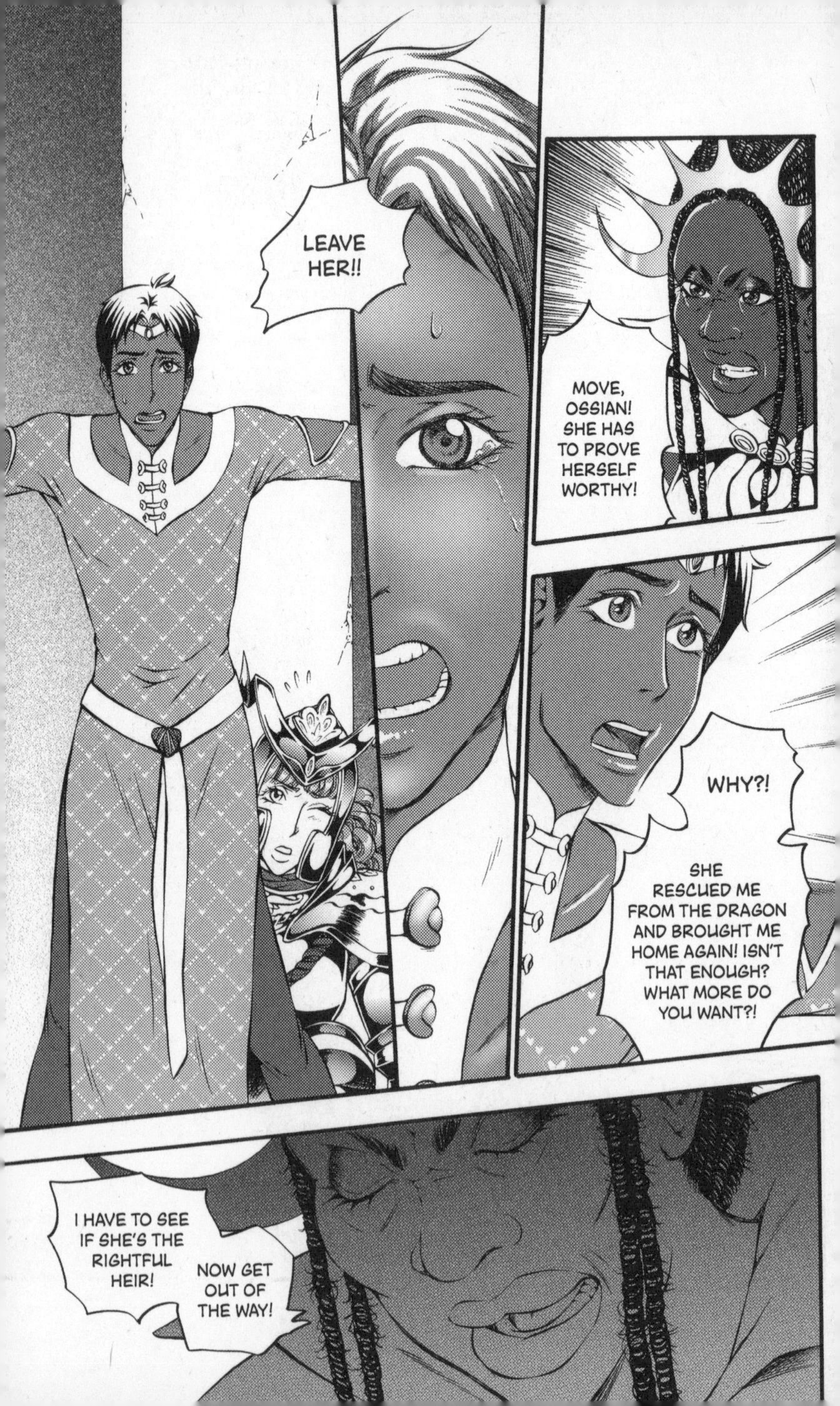
LEAVE HER!!
MOVE, OSSIAN! SHE HAS TO PROVE HERSELF WORTHY!
WHY?!
SHE RESCUED ME FROM THE DRAGON AND BROUGHT ME HOME AGAIN! ISN'T THAT ENOUGH? WHAT MORE DO YOU WANT?!
I HAVE TO SEE IF SHE'S THE RIGHTFUL HEIR!
NOW GET OUT OF THE WAY!

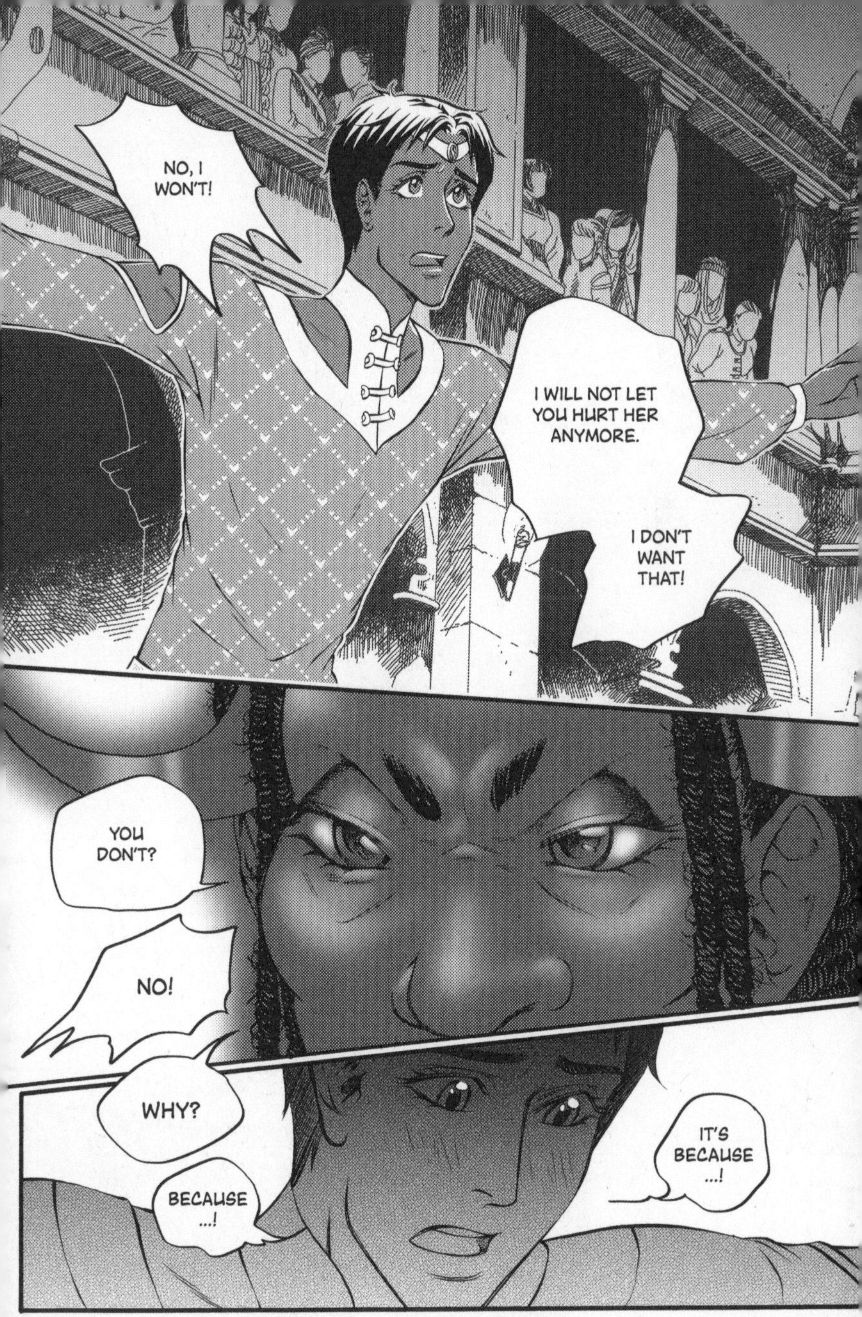
NO, I WON'T!
I WILL NOT LET YOU HURT HER ANYMORE.
I DON'T WANT THAT!
YOU DON'T?
NO!
WHY?
BECAUSE ...!
IT'S BECAUSE ...!

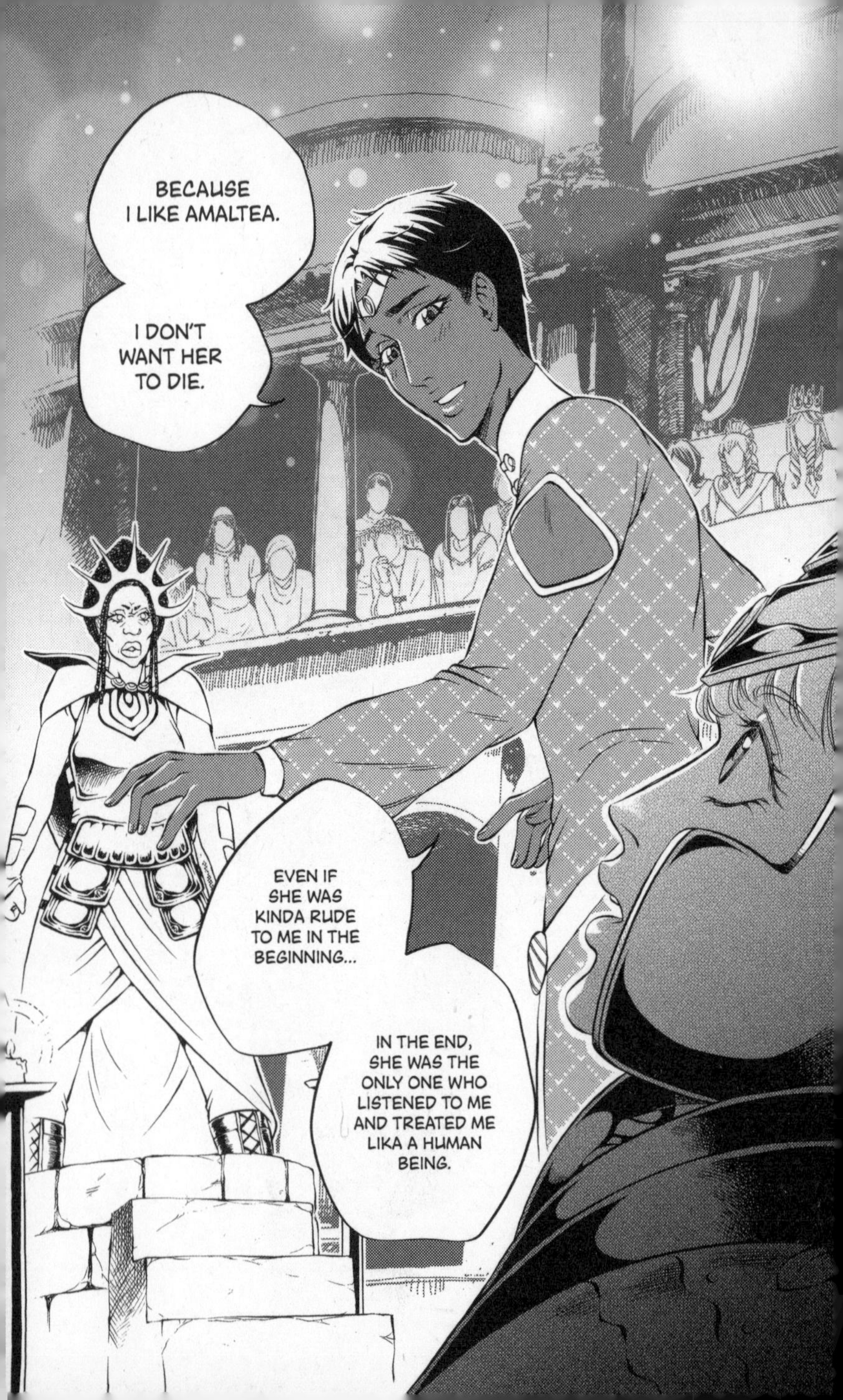
BECAUSE I LIKE AMALTEA.
I DON'T WANT HER TO DIE.
EVEN IF SHE WAS KINDA RUDE TO ME IN THE BEGINNING...
IN THE END, SHE WAS THE ONLY ONE WHO LISTENED TO ME AND TREATED ME LIKA A HUMAN BEING.

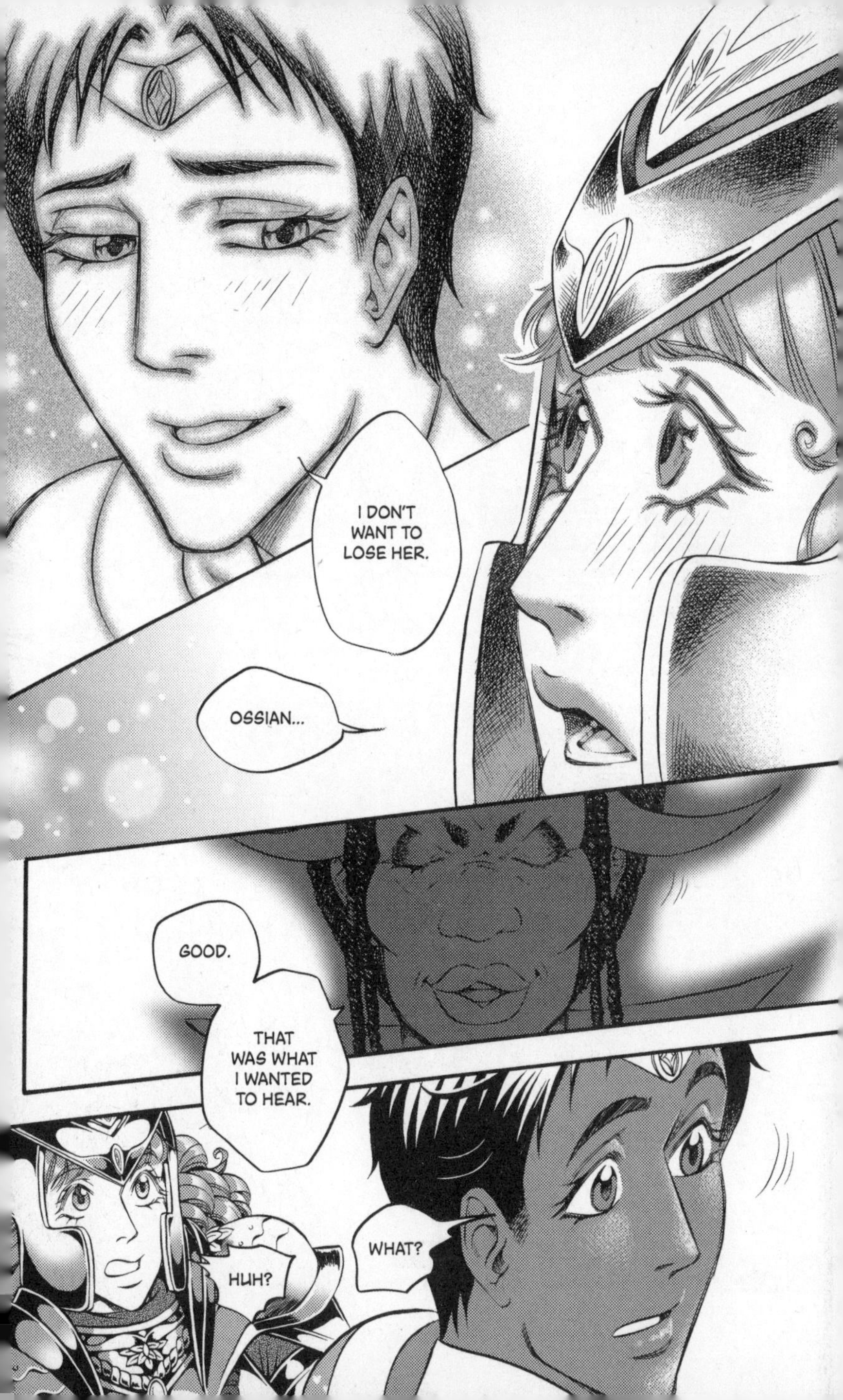
I DON'T WANT TO LOSE HER.
OSSIAN...
GOOD.
THAT WAS WHAT I WANTED TO HEAR.
WHAT?
HUH?

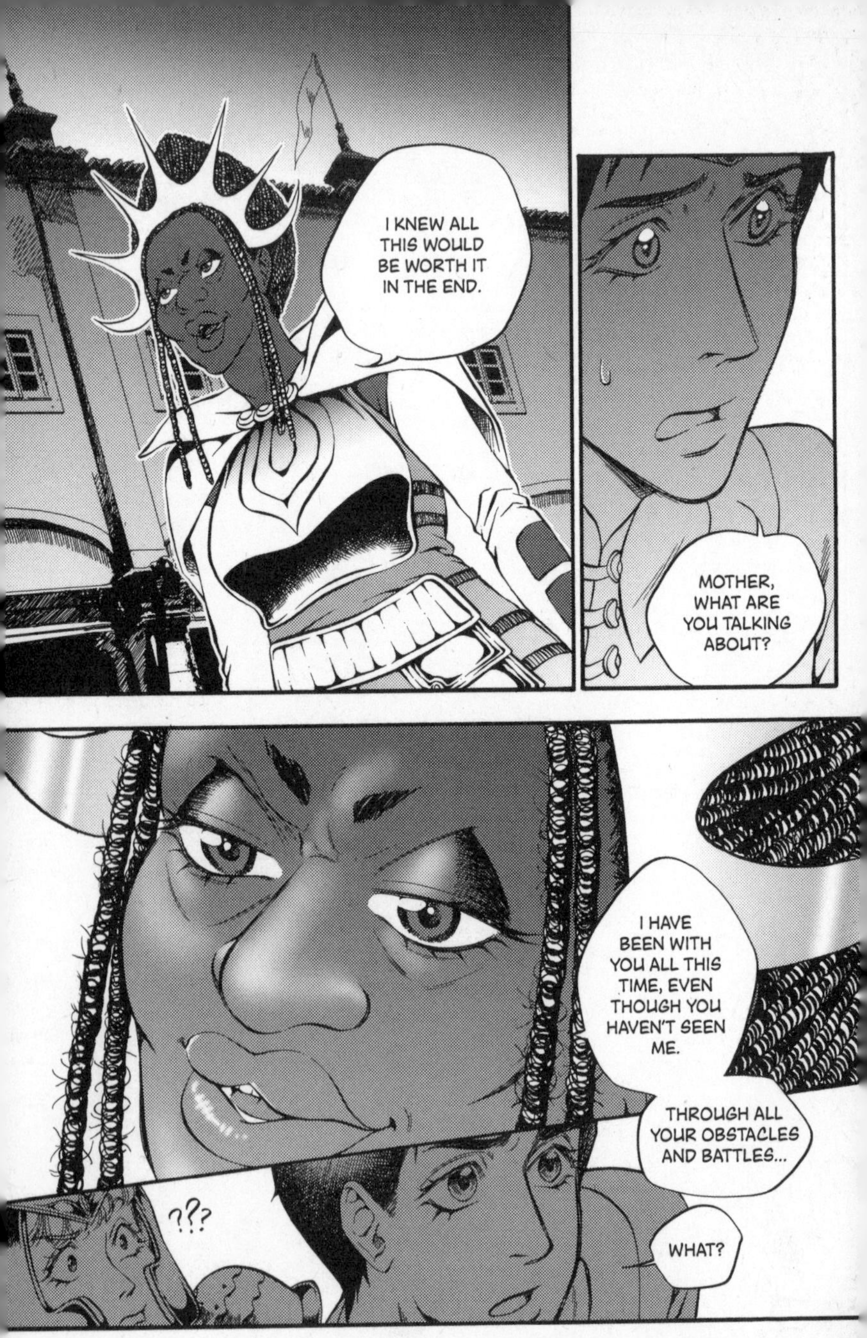
I KNEW ALL THIS WOULD BE WORTH IT IN THE END.
MOTHER, WHAT ARE YOU TALKING ABOUT?
I HAVE BEEN WITH YOU ALL THIS TIME, EVEN THOUGH YOU HAVEN'T SEEN ME.
THROUGH ALL YOUR OBSTACLES AND BATTLES...
???
WHAT?

AMALTEA, DO YOU REMEMBER THE OLD LADY YOU MET?

EH... THE GUIDE?

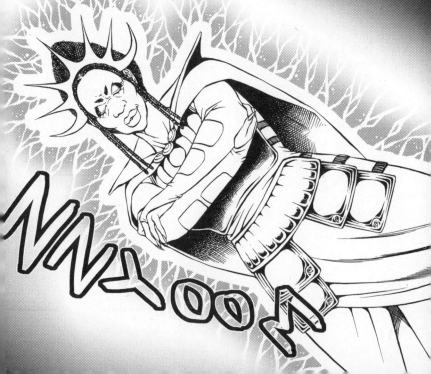

NNYOOM

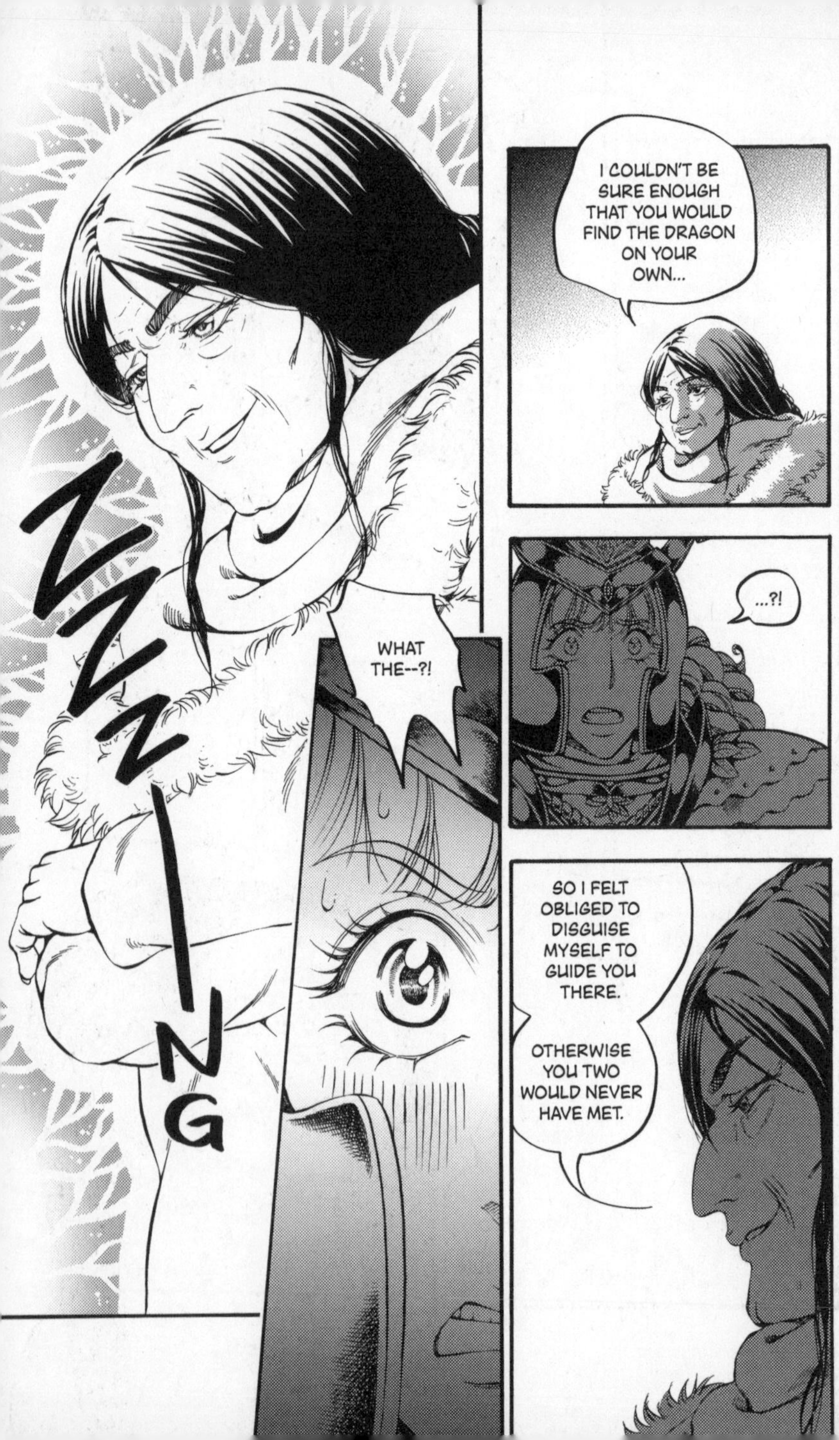
I COULDN'T BE SURE ENOUGH THAT YOU WOULD FIND THE DRAGON ON YOUR OWN...
...?!
SO I FELT OBLIGED TO DISGUISE MYSELF TO GUIDE YOU THERE.
OTHERWISE YOU TWO WOULD NEVER HAVE MET.
NNNNING
WHAT THE--?!

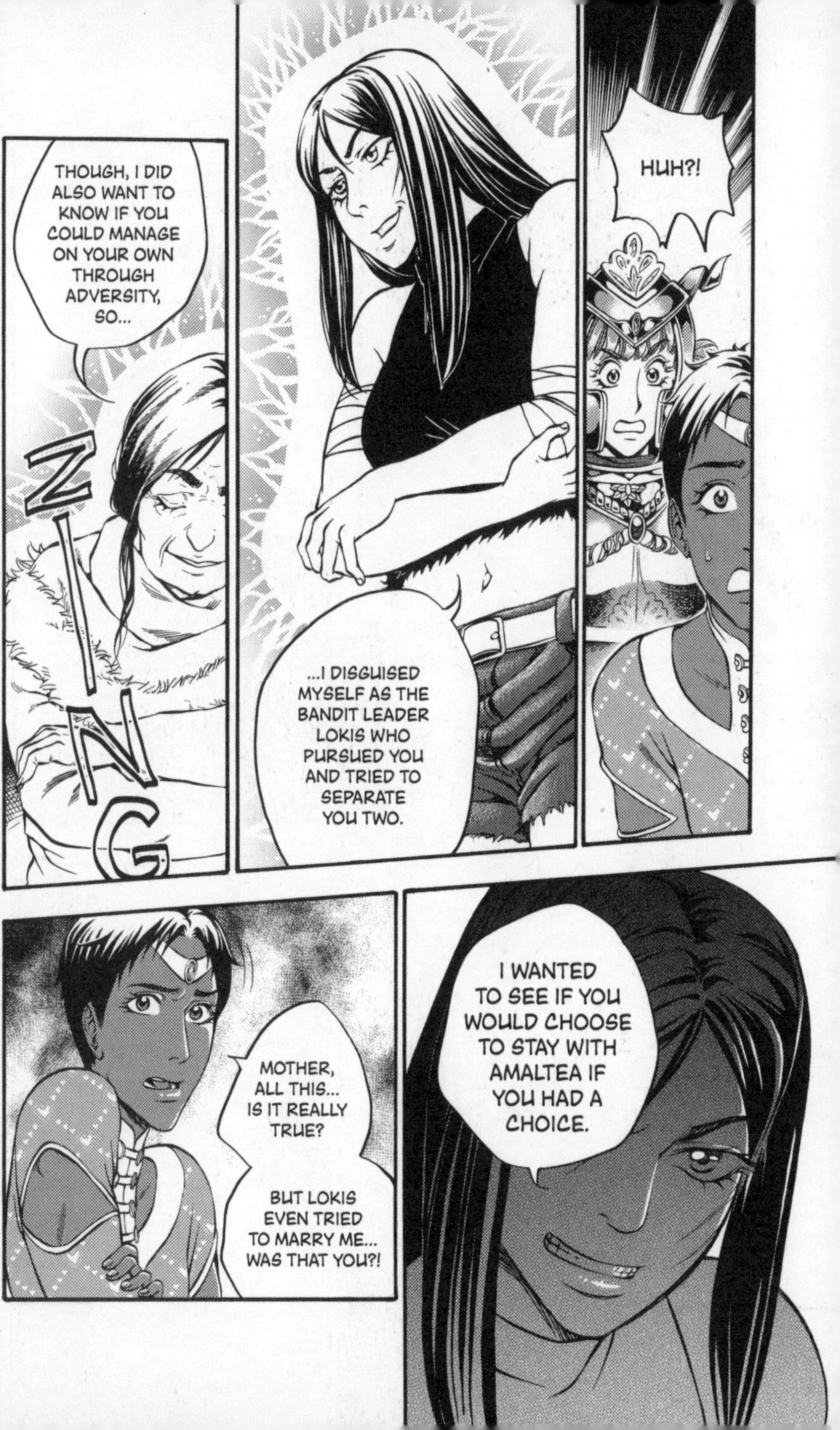
THOUGH, I DID ALSO WANT TO KNOW IF YOU COULD MANAGE ON YOUR OWN THROUGH ADVERSITY, SO...
ZING
...I DISGUISED MYSELF AS THE BANDIT LEADER LOKIS WHO PURSUED YOU AND TRIED TO SEPARATE YOU TWO.
HUH?!
MOTHER, ALL THIS... IS IT REALLY TRUE?
BUT LOKIS EVEN TRIED TO MARRY ME... WAS THAT YOU?!
I WANTED TO SEE IF YOU WOULD CHOOSE TO STAY WITH AMALTEA IF YOU HAD A CHOICE.

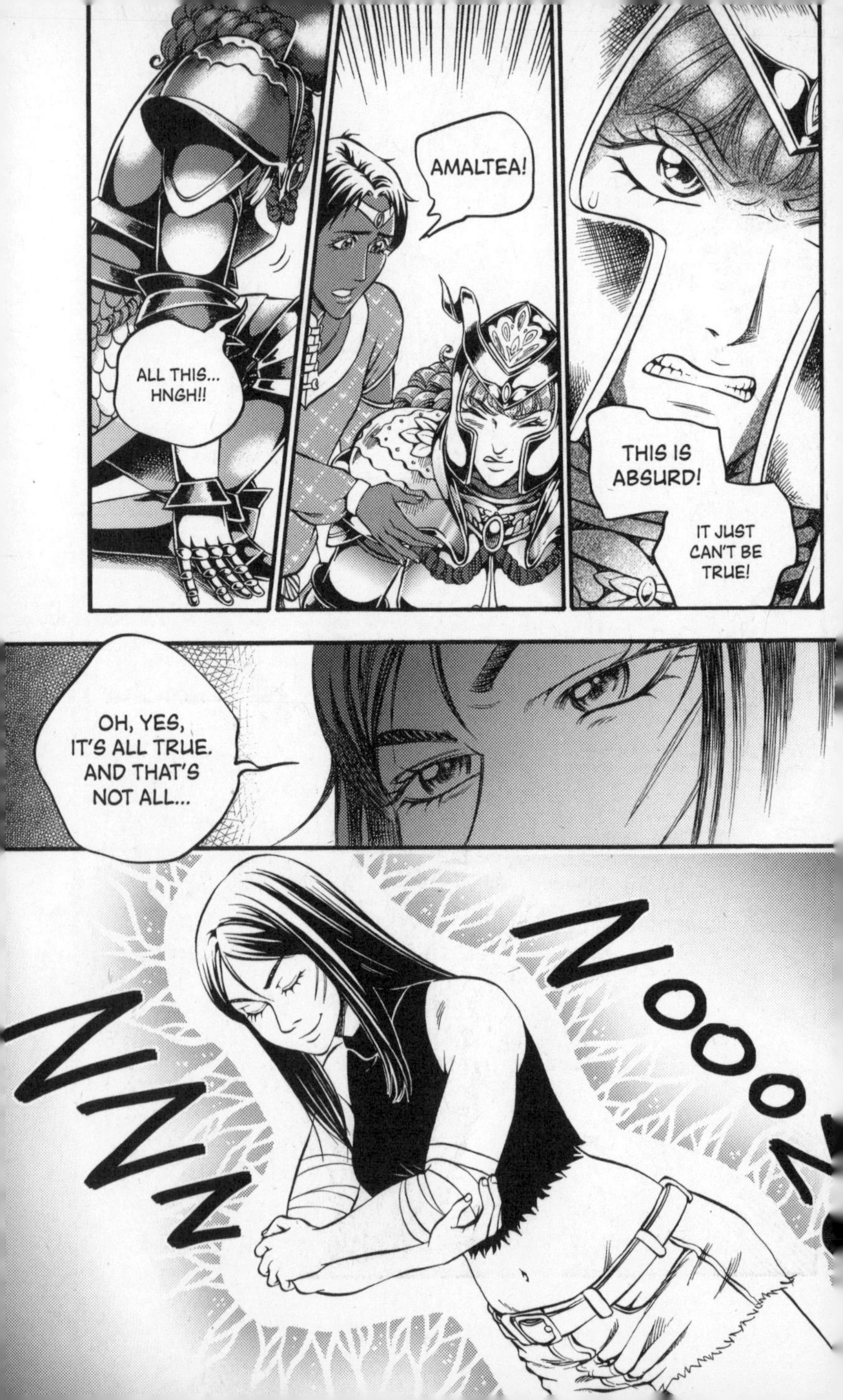
THIS IS ABSURD!
IT JUST CAN'T BE TRUE!
AMALTEA!
ALL THIS... HNGH!!
OH, YES, IT'S ALL TRUE. AND THAT'S NOT ALL...
NOOOO
NNN

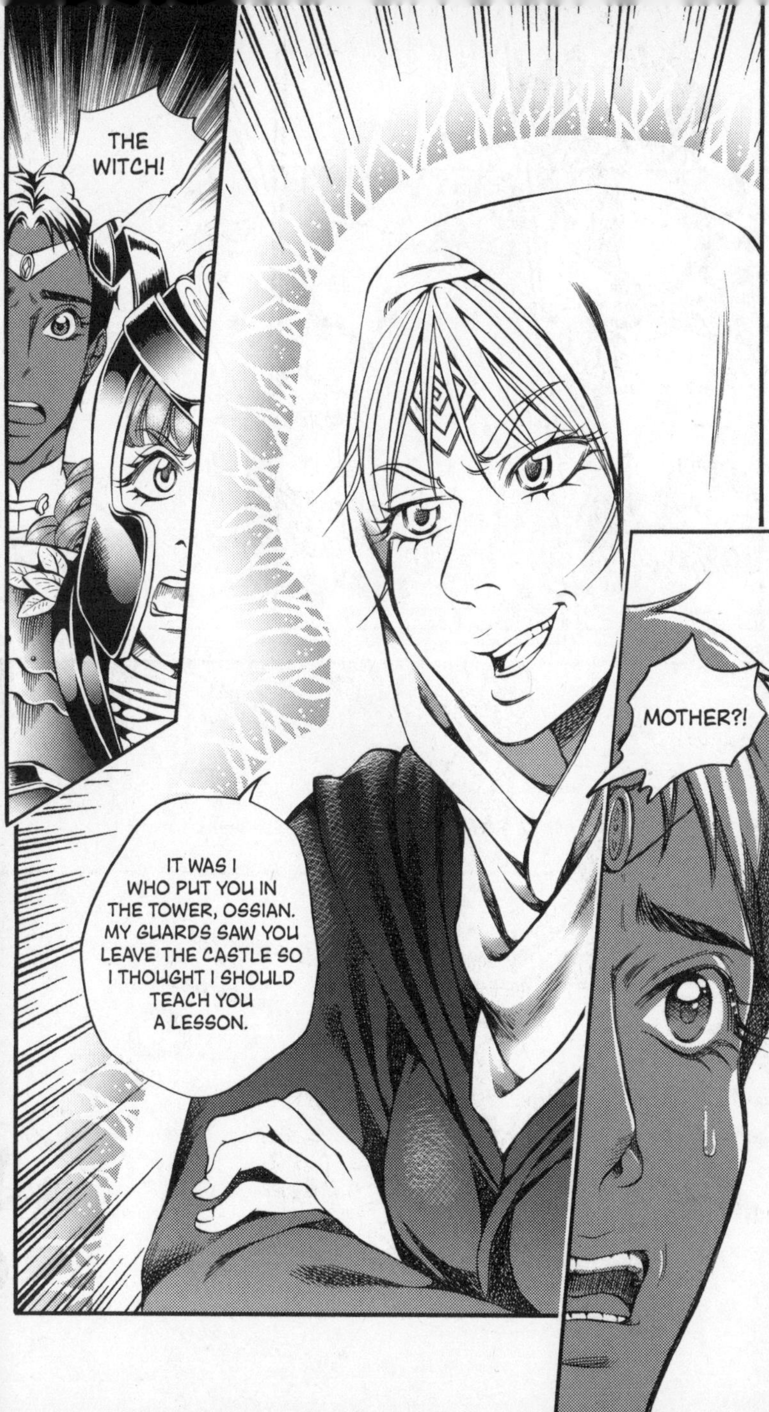
MOTHER?!
IT WAS I WHO PUT YOU IN THE TOWER, OSSIAN. MY GUARDS SAW YOU LEAVE THE CASTLE SO I THOUGHT I SHOULD TEACH YOU A LESSON.
THE WITCH!

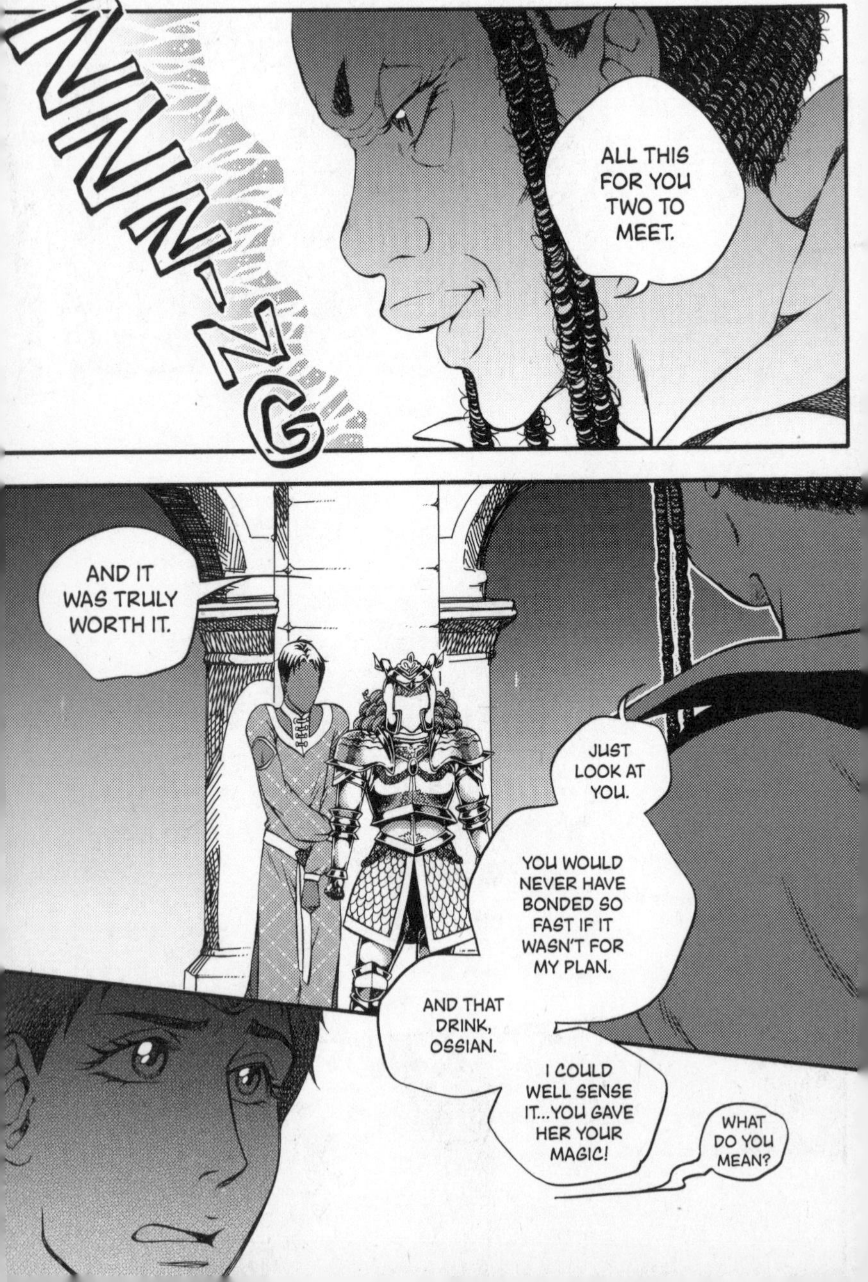
NNN-NG
ALL THIS FOR YOU TWO TO MEET.
AND IT WAS TRULY WORTH IT.
JUST LOOK AT YOU.
YOU WOULD NEVER HAVE BONDED SO FAST IF IT WASN'T FOR MY PLAN.
AND THAT DRINK, OSSIAN.
I COULD WELL SENSE IT...YOU GAVE HER YOUR MAGIC!
WHAT DO YOU MEAN?

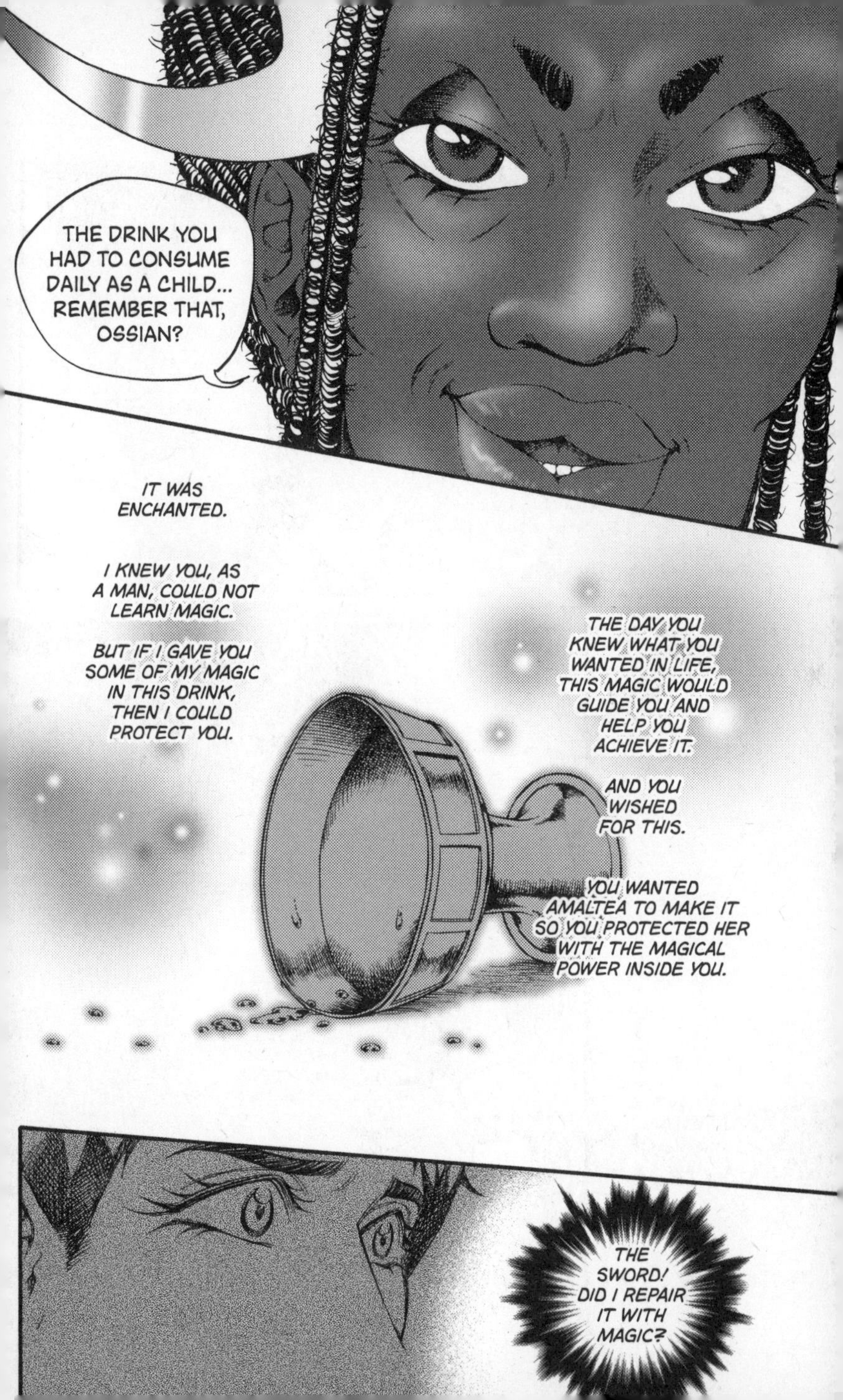
THE DRINK YOU HAD TO CONSUME DAILY AS A CHILD... REMEMBER THAT, OSSIAN?
IT WAS ENCHANTED.
I KNEW YOU, AS A MAN, COULD NOT LEARN MAGIC.
BUT IF I GAVE YOU SOME OF MY MAGIC IN THIS DRINK, THEN I COULD PROTECT YOU.
THE DAY YOU KNEW WHAT YOU WANTED IN LIFE, THIS MAGIC WOULD GUIDE YOU AND HELP YOU ACHIEVE IT.
AND YOU WISHED FOR THIS.
YOU WANTED AMALTEA TO MAKE IT SO YOU PROTECTED HER WITH THE MAGICAL POWER INSIDE YOU.
THE SWORD! DID I REPAIR IT WITH MAGIC?

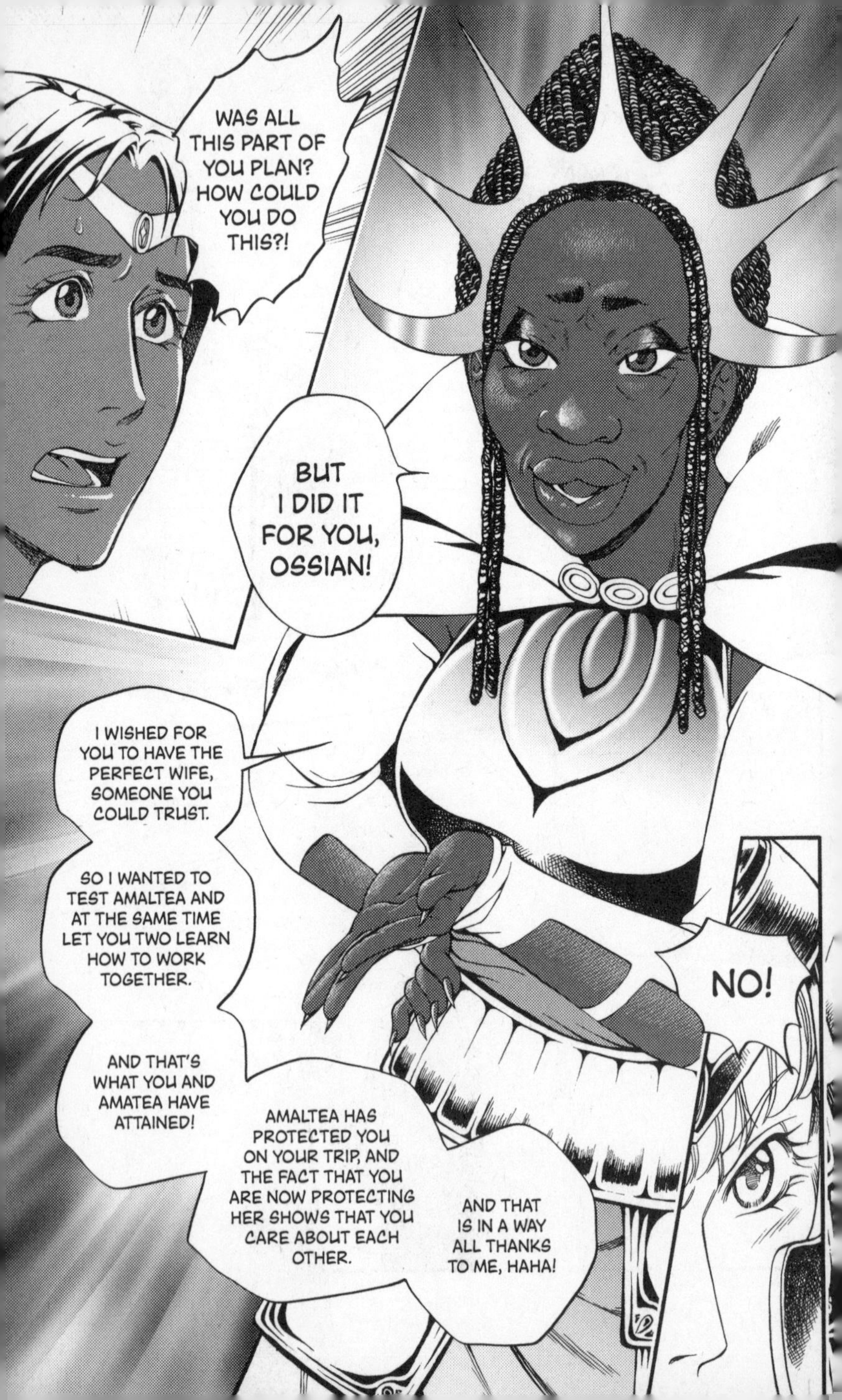
WAS ALL THIS PART OF YOU PLAN? HOW COULD YOU DO THIS?!
BUT I DID IT FOR YOU, OSSIAN!
I WISHED FOR YOU TO HAVE THE PERFECT WIFE, SOMEONE YOU COULD TRUST.
SO I WANTED TO TEST AMALTEA AND AT THE SAME TIME LET YOU TWO LEARN HOW TO WORK TOGETHER.
AND THAT'S WHAT YOU AND AMATEA HAVE ATTAINED!
AMALTEA HAS PROTECTED YOU ON YOUR TRIP, AND THE FACT THAT YOU ARE NOW PROTECTING HER SHOWS THAT YOU CARE ABOUT EACH OTHER.
AND THAT IS IN A WAY ALL THANKS TO ME, HAHA!
NO!

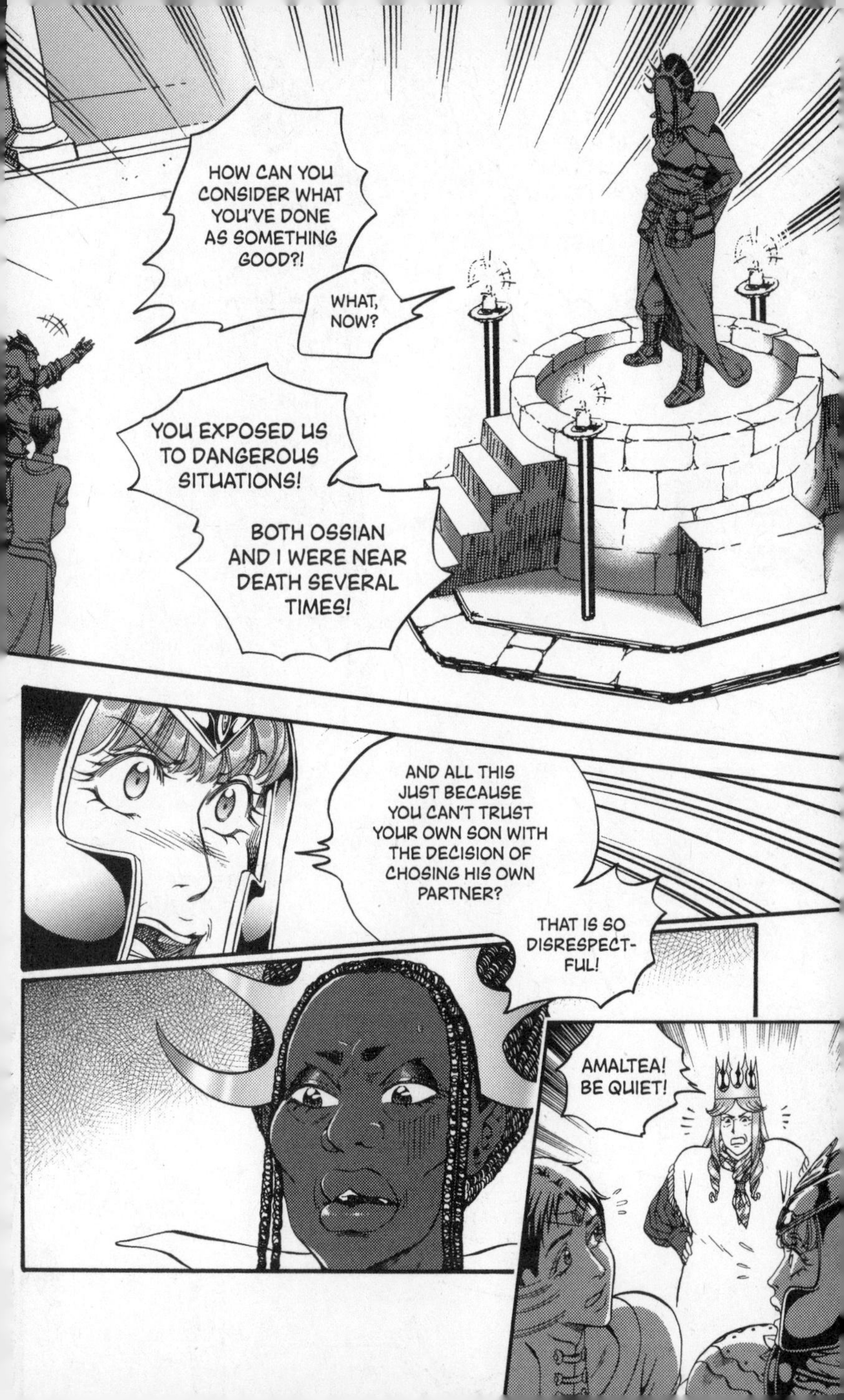
HOW CAN YOU CONSIDER WHAT YOU'VE DONE AS SOMETHING GOOD?!
WHAT, NOW?
YOU EXPOSED US TO DANGEROUS SITUATIONS!
BOTH OSSIAN AND I WERE NEAR DEATH SEVERAL TIMES!
AND ALL THIS JUST BECAUSE YOU CAN'T TRUST YOUR OWN SON WITH THE DECISION OF CHOSING HIS OWN PARTNER?
THAT IS SO DISRESPECT-FUL!
AMALTEA! BE QUIET!

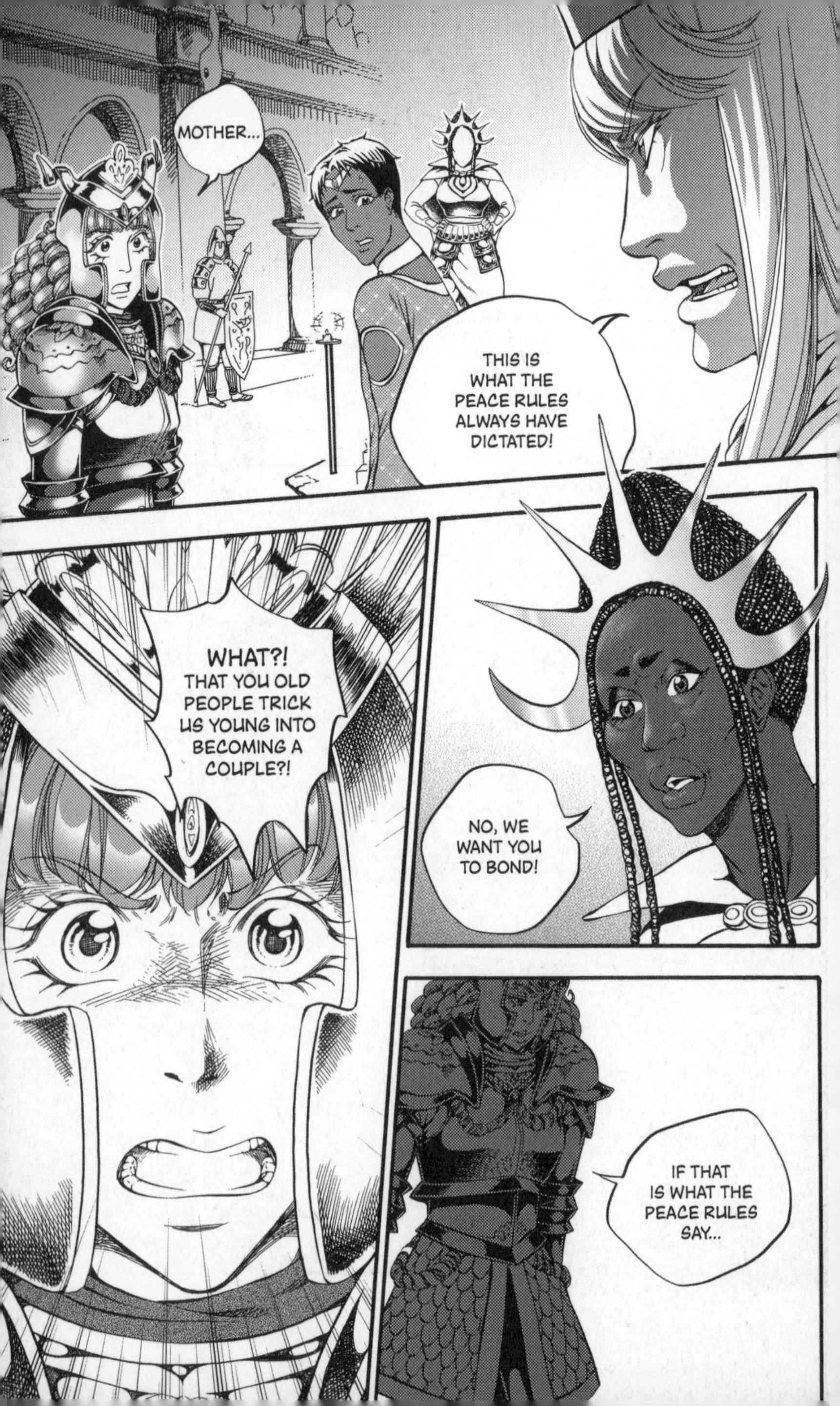
MOTHER...
THIS IS WHAT THE PEACE RULES ALWAYS HAVE DICTATED!
WHAT?! THAT YOU OLD PEOPLE TRICK US YOUNG INTO BECOMING A COUPLE?!
NO, WE WANT YOU TO BOND!
IF THAT IS WHAT THE PEACE RULES SAY...

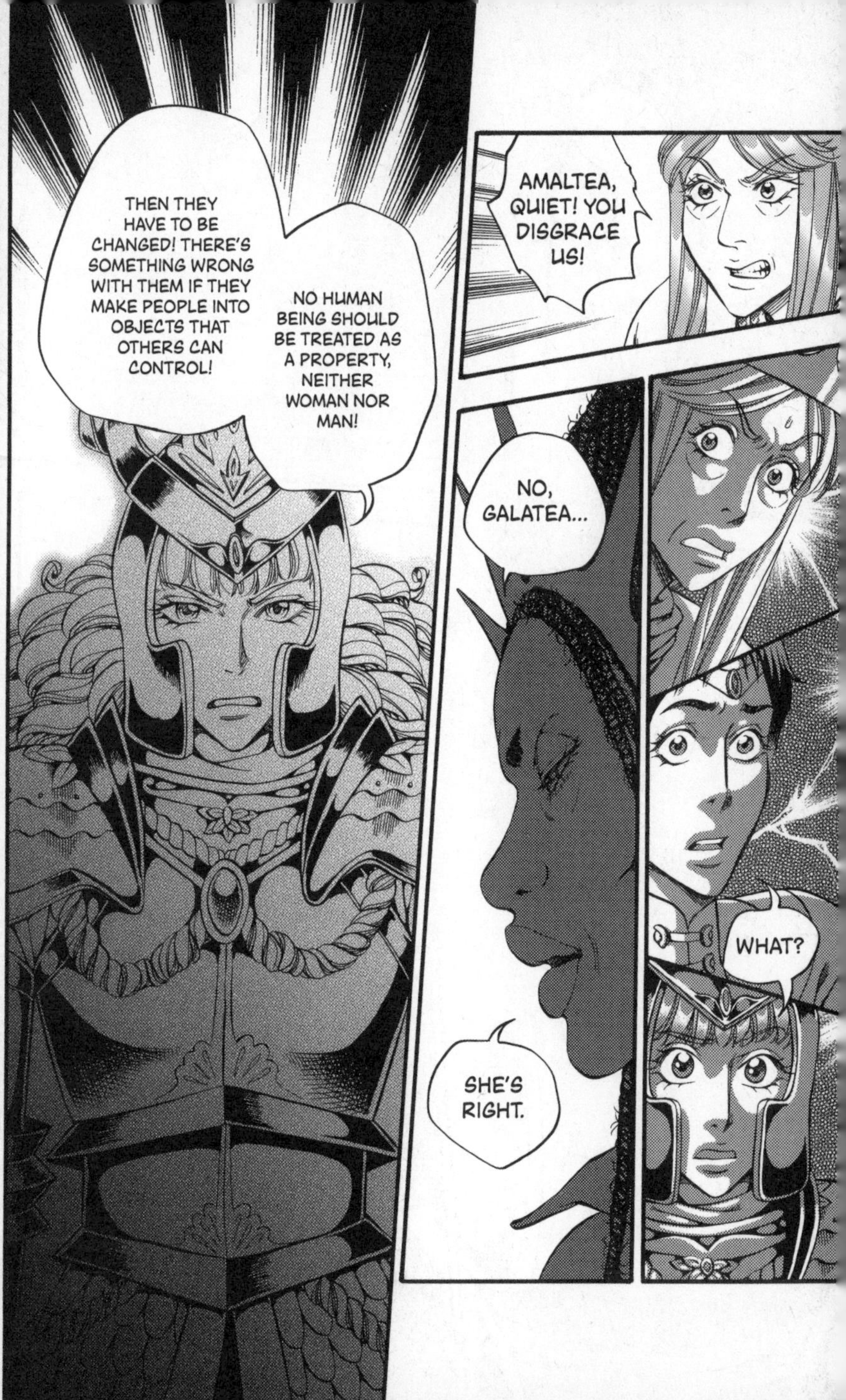
THEN THEY HAVE TO BE CHANGED! THERE'S SOMETHING WRONG WITH THEM IF THEY MAKE PEOPLE INTO OBJECTS THAT OTHERS CAN CONTROL!
NO HUMAN BEING SHOULD BE TREATED AS A PROPERTY, NEITHER WOMAN NOR MAN!
AMALTEA, QUIET! YOU DISGRACE US!
NO, GALATEA...
WHAT?
SHE'S RIGHT.

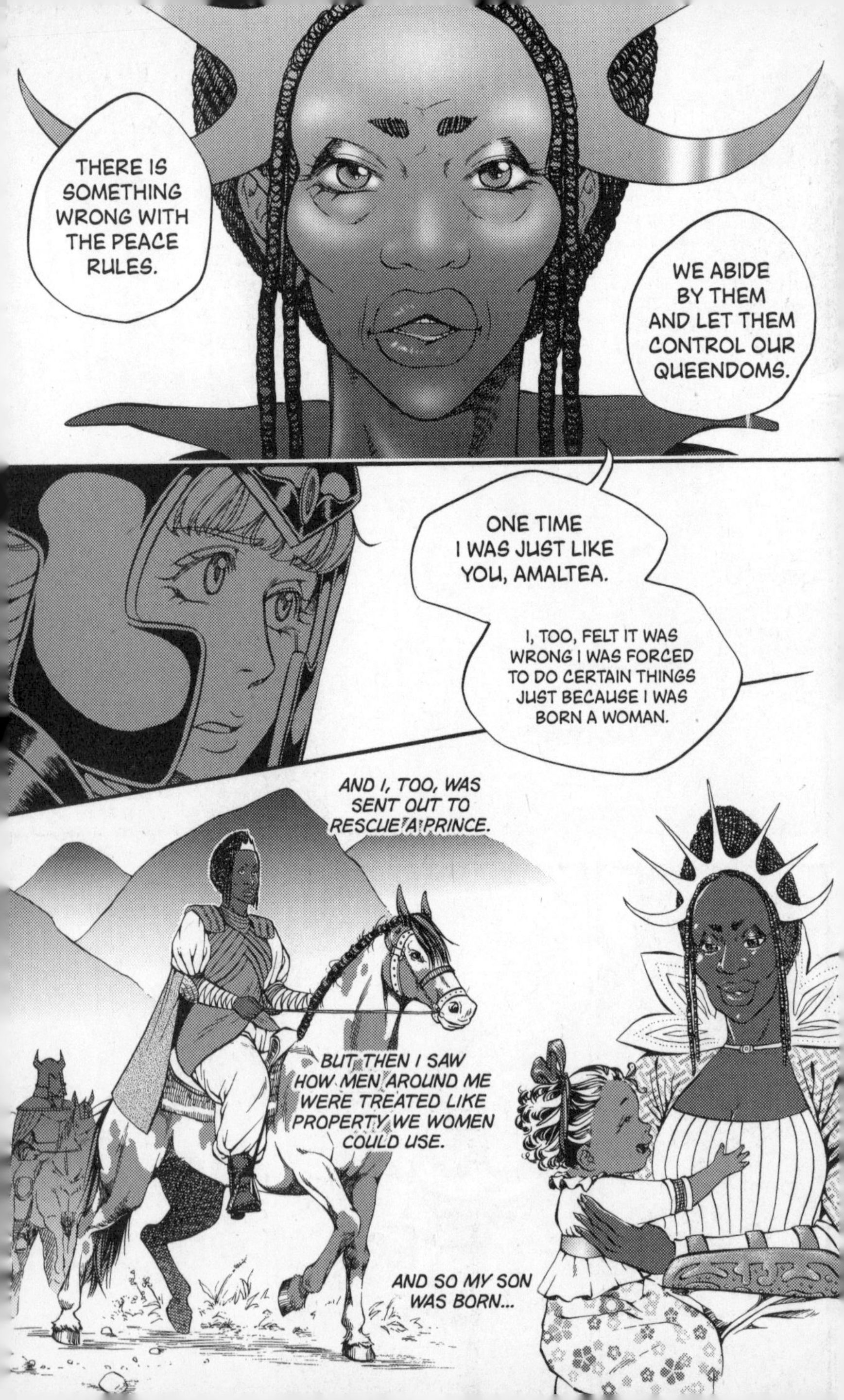
THERE IS SOMETHING WRONG WITH THE PEACE RULES.
WE ABIDE BY THEM AND LET THEM CONTROL OUR QUEENDOMS.
ONE TIME I WAS JUST LIKE YOU, AMALTEA.
I, TOO, FELT IT WAS WRONG I WAS FORCED TO DO CERTAIN THINGS JUST BECAUSE I WAS BORN A WOMAN.
AND I, TOO, WAS SENT OUT TO RESCUE A PRINCE.
BUT THEN I SAW HOW MEN AROUND ME WERE TREATED LIKE PROPERTY WE WOMEN COULD USE.
AND SO MY SON WAS BORN...

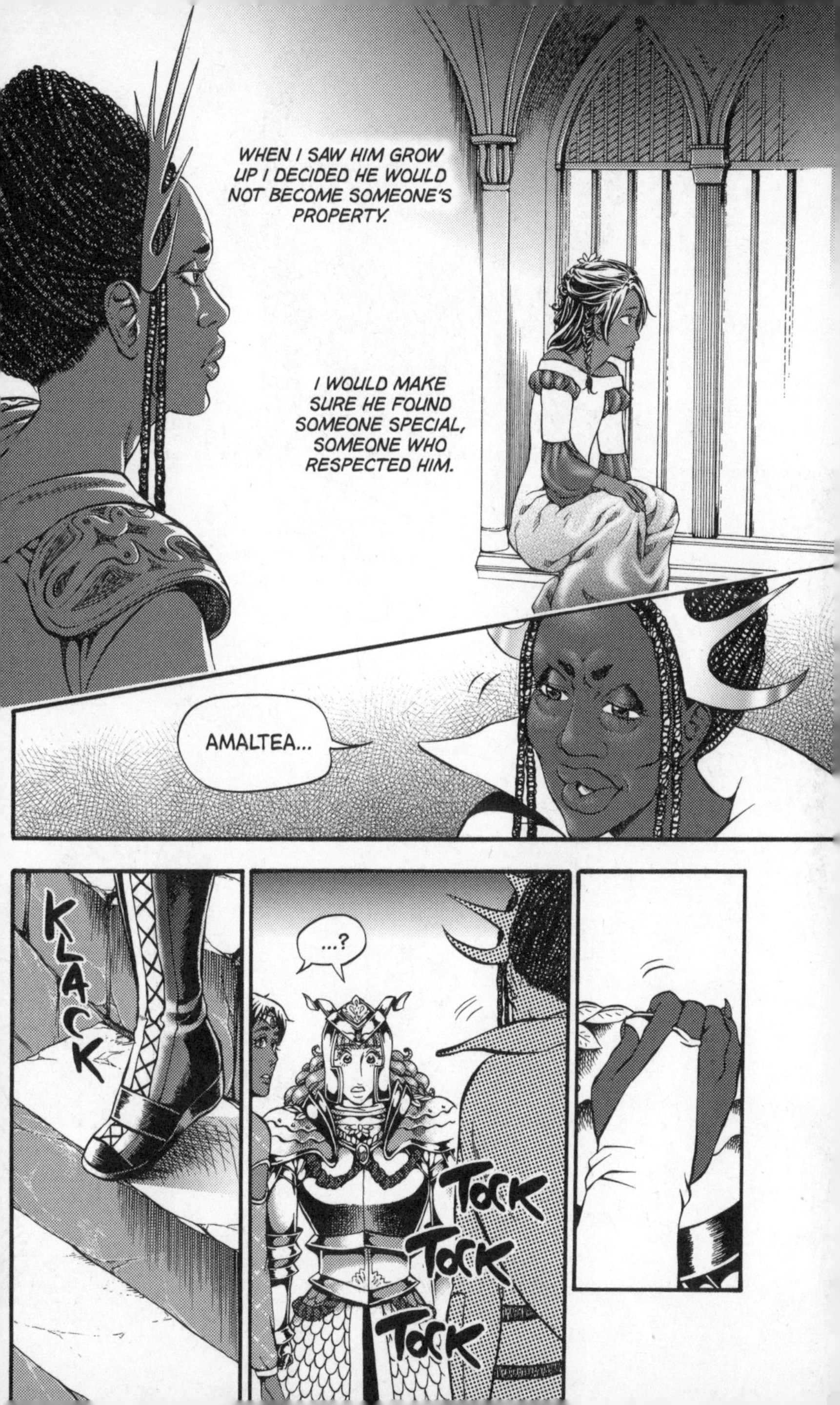
WHEN I SAW HIM GROW UP I DECIDED HE WOULD NOT BECOME SOMEONE'S PROPERTY.
I WOULD MAKE SURE HE FOUND SOMEONE SPECIAL, SOMEONE WHO RESPECTED HIM.
AMALTEA...
...?
TOCK
TOCK
TOCK
KLACK

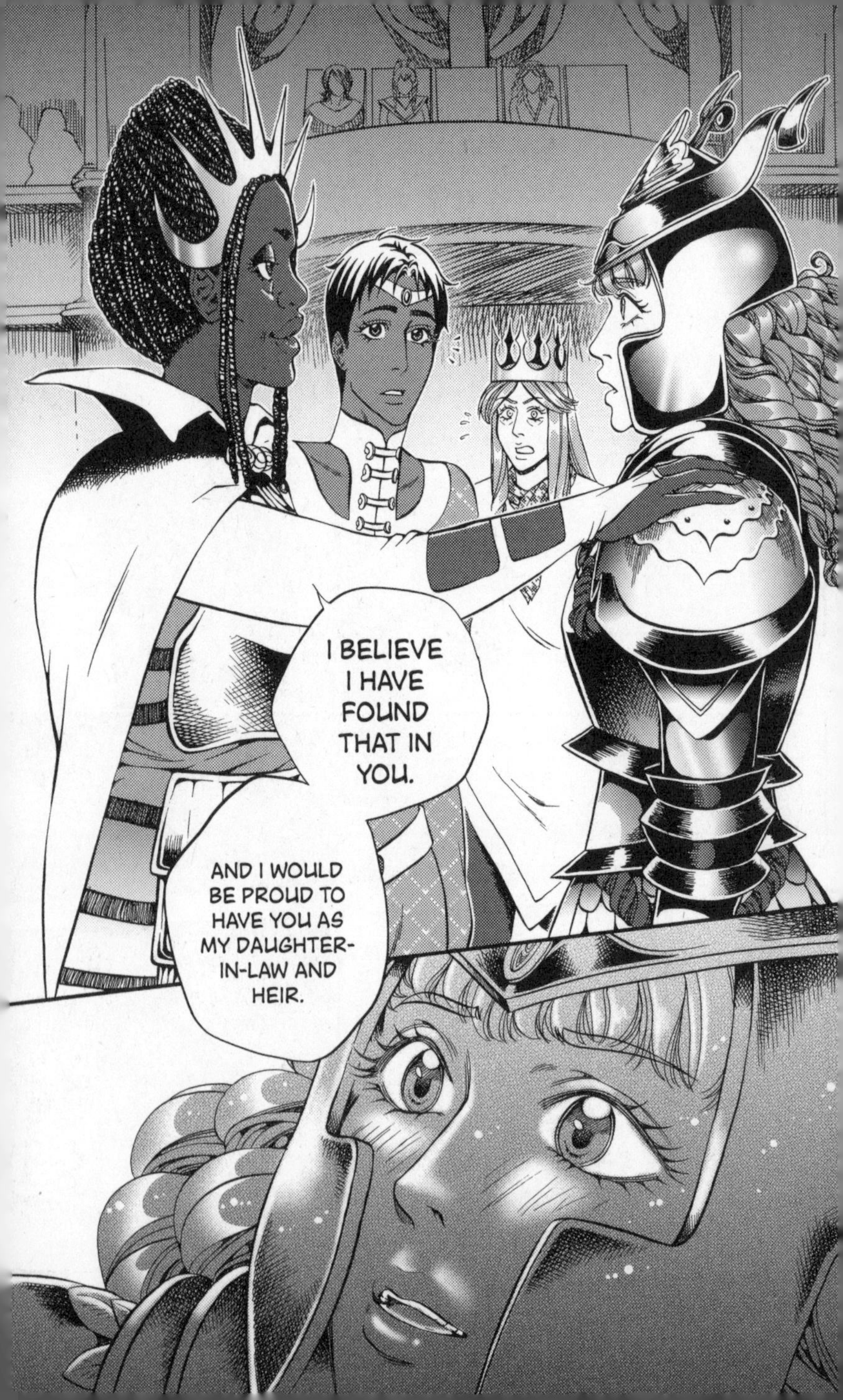
I BELIEVE I HAVE FOUND THAT IN YOU.
AND I WOULD BE PROUD TO HAVE YOU AS MY DAUGHTER-IN-LAW AND HEIR.

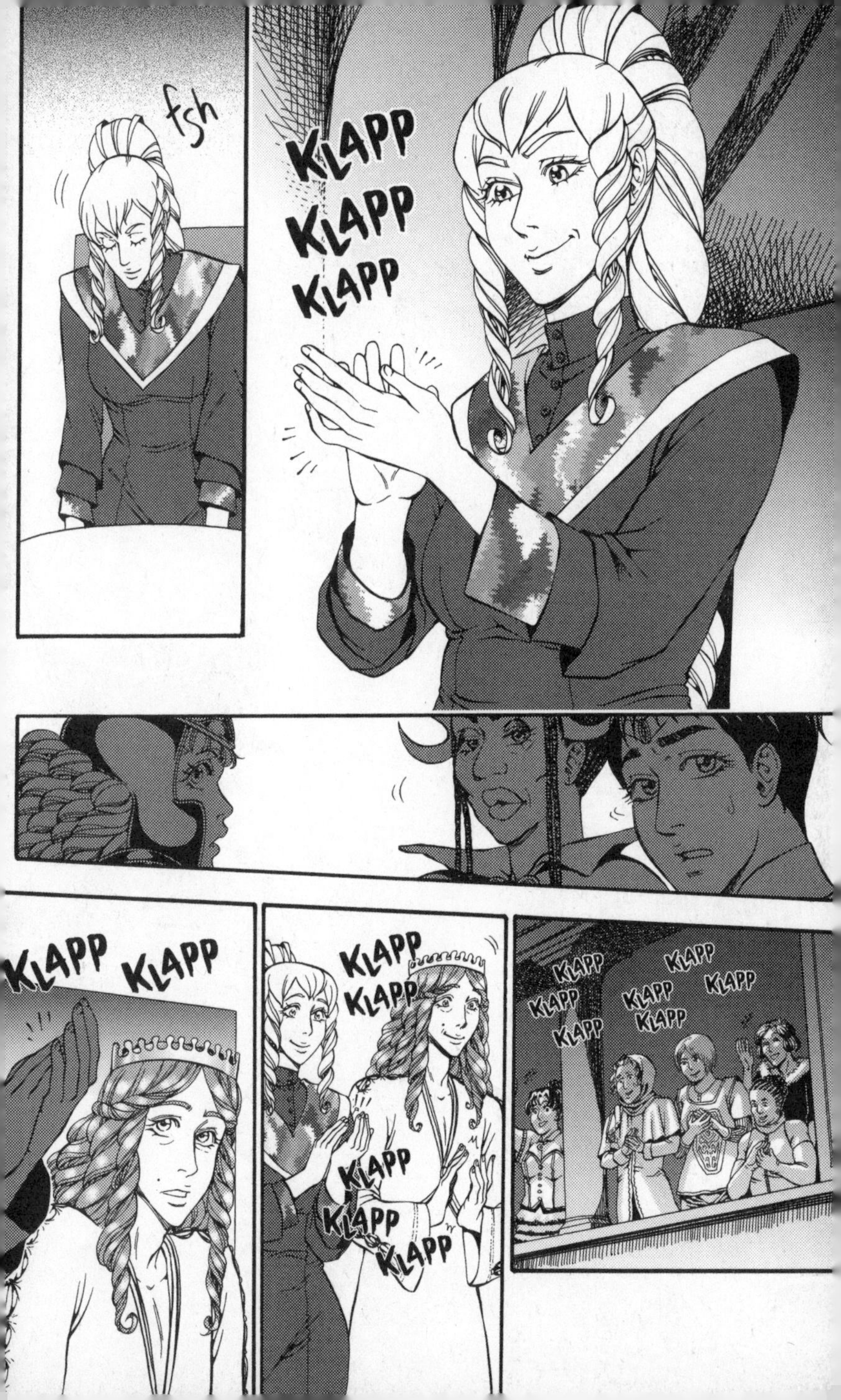
KLAPP
KLAPP
KLAPP
fsh
KLAPP
KLAPP
KLAPP
KLAPP
KLAPP
KLAPP
KLAPP
KLAPP
KLAPP
KLAPP
KLAPP
KLAPP
KLAPP
KLAPP

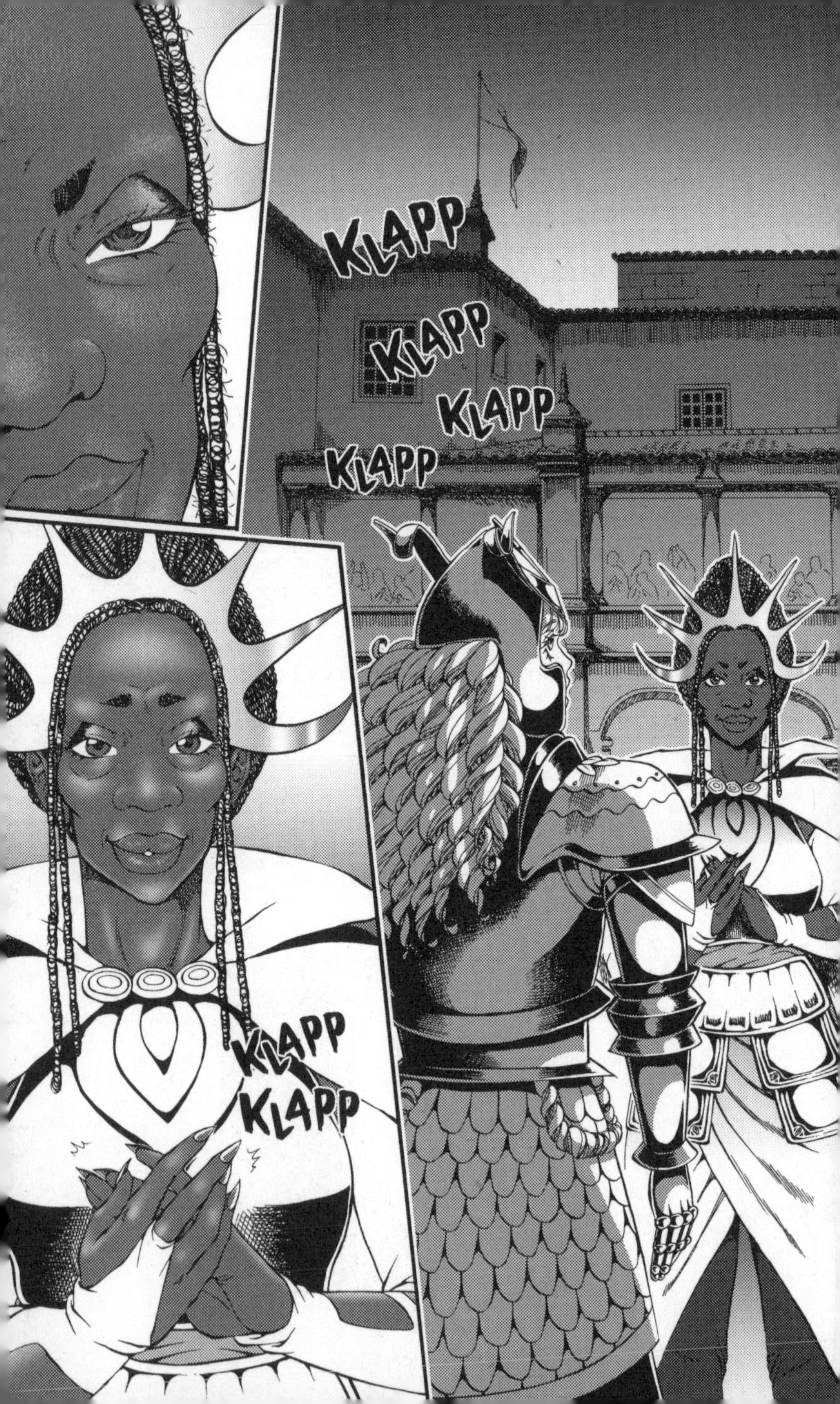
KLAPP
KLAPP
KLAPP
KLAPP
KLAPP
KLAPP

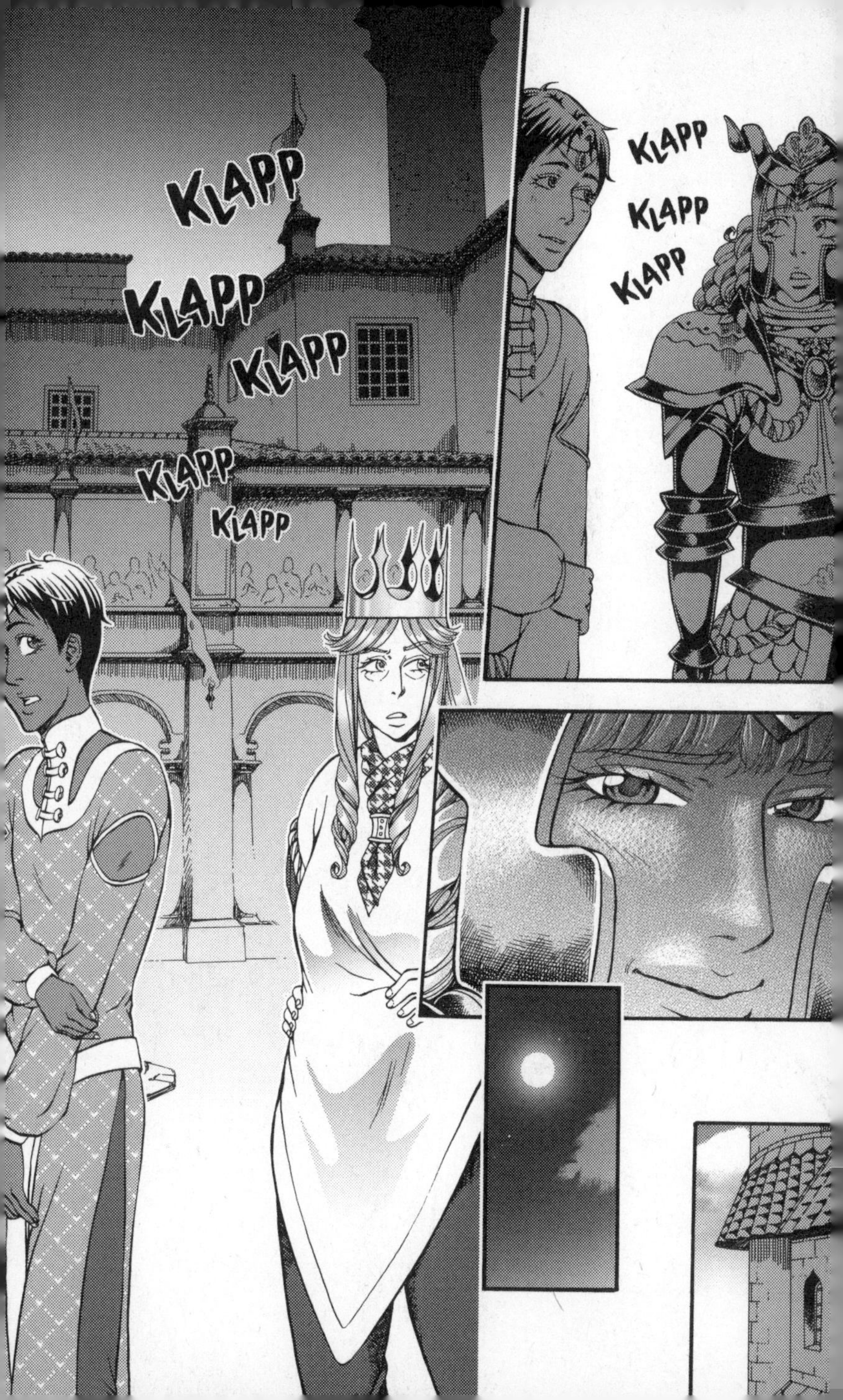
KLAPP
KLAPP
KLAPP
KLAPP
KLAPP
KLAPP
KLAPP
KLAPP

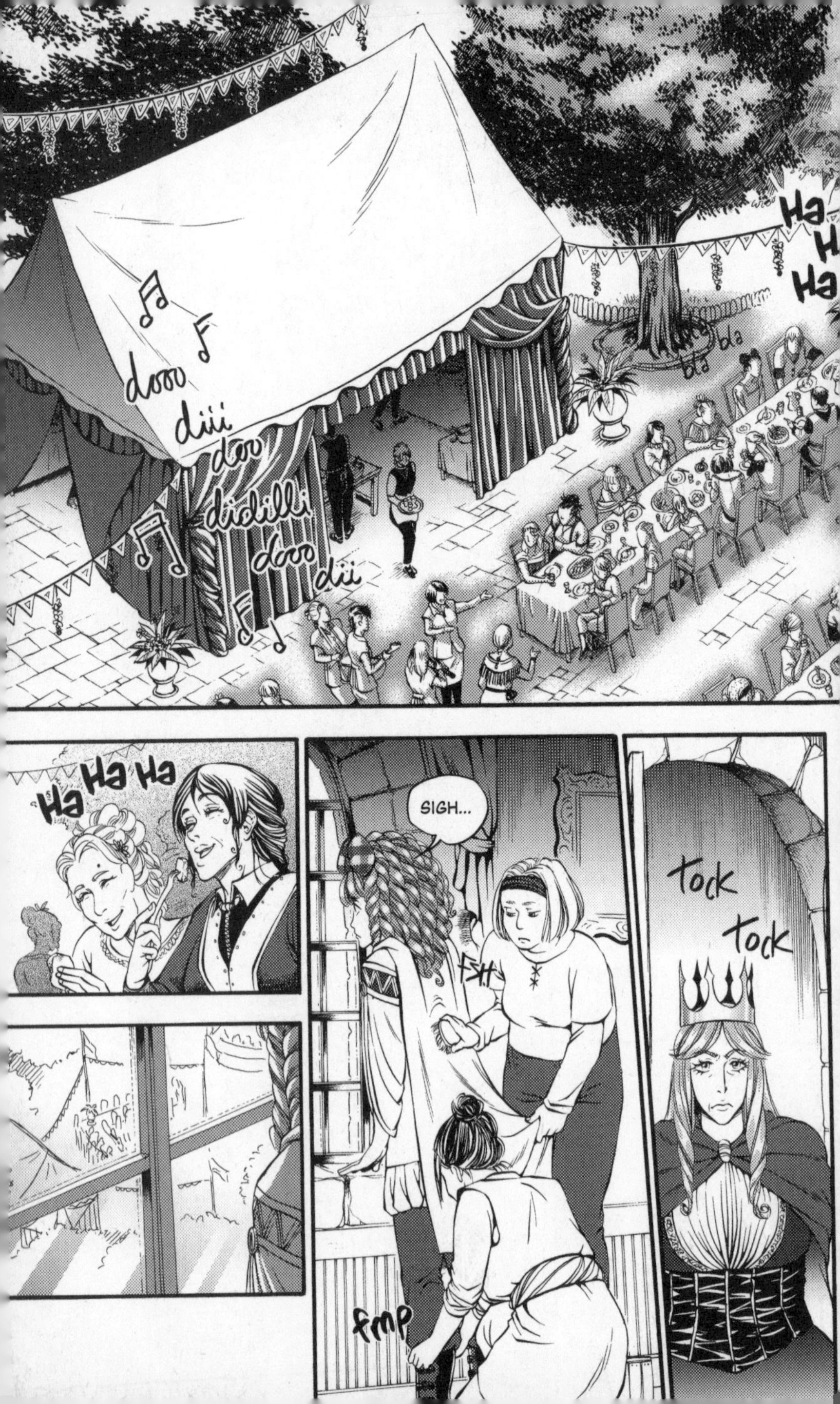
Ha Ha Ha
bla bla
dooo diii daa didilli dooo dii
Tock Tock
SIGH...
FSHT
fmp
Ha Ha Ha

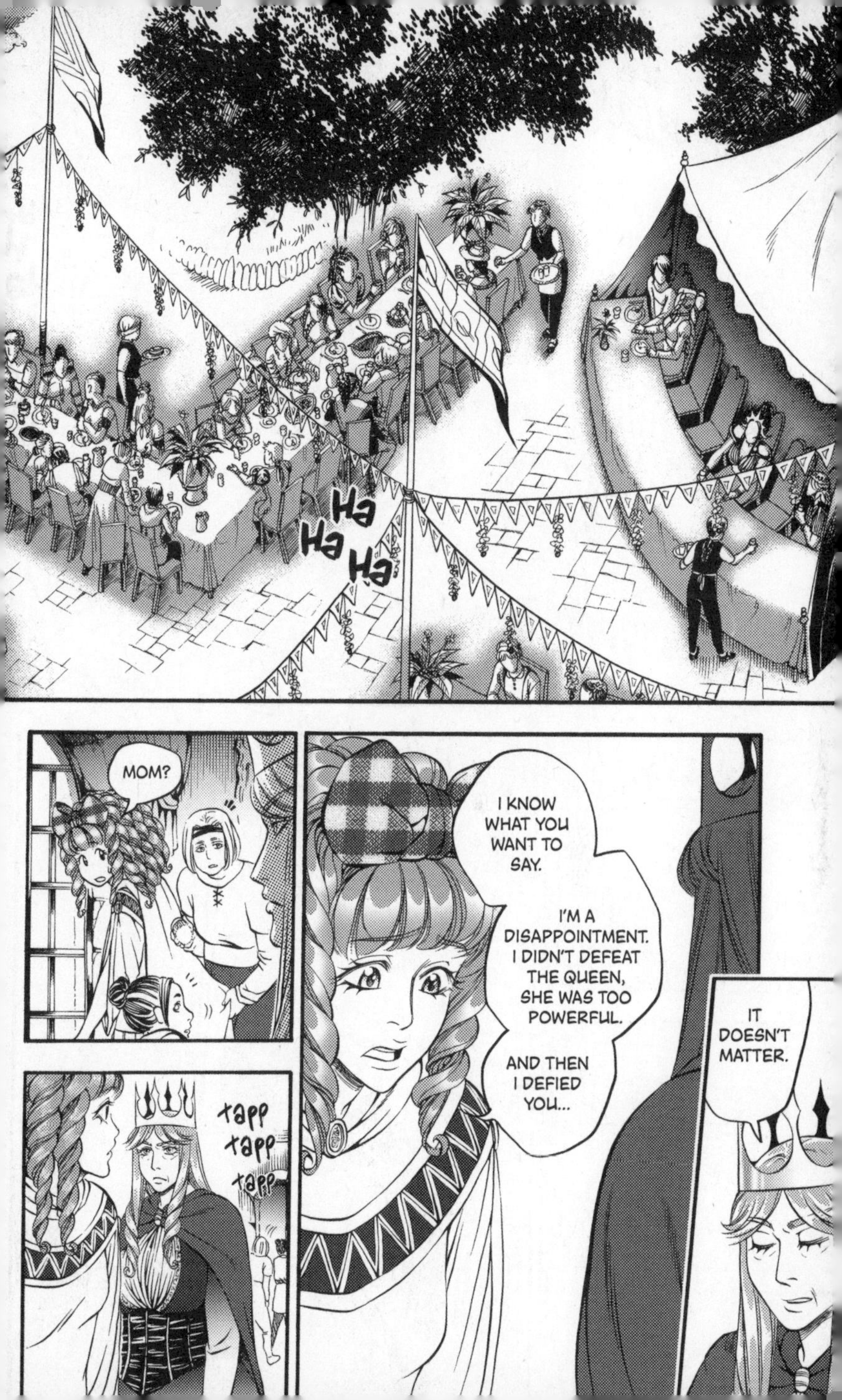
Ha
Ha
Ha
MOM?
tapp
tapp
tapp
I KNOW WHAT YOU WANT TO SAY.
I'M A DISAPPOINTMENT. I DIDN'T DEFEAT THE QUEEN, SHE WAS TOO POWERFUL.
AND THEN I DEFIED YOU...
IT DOESN'T MATTER.

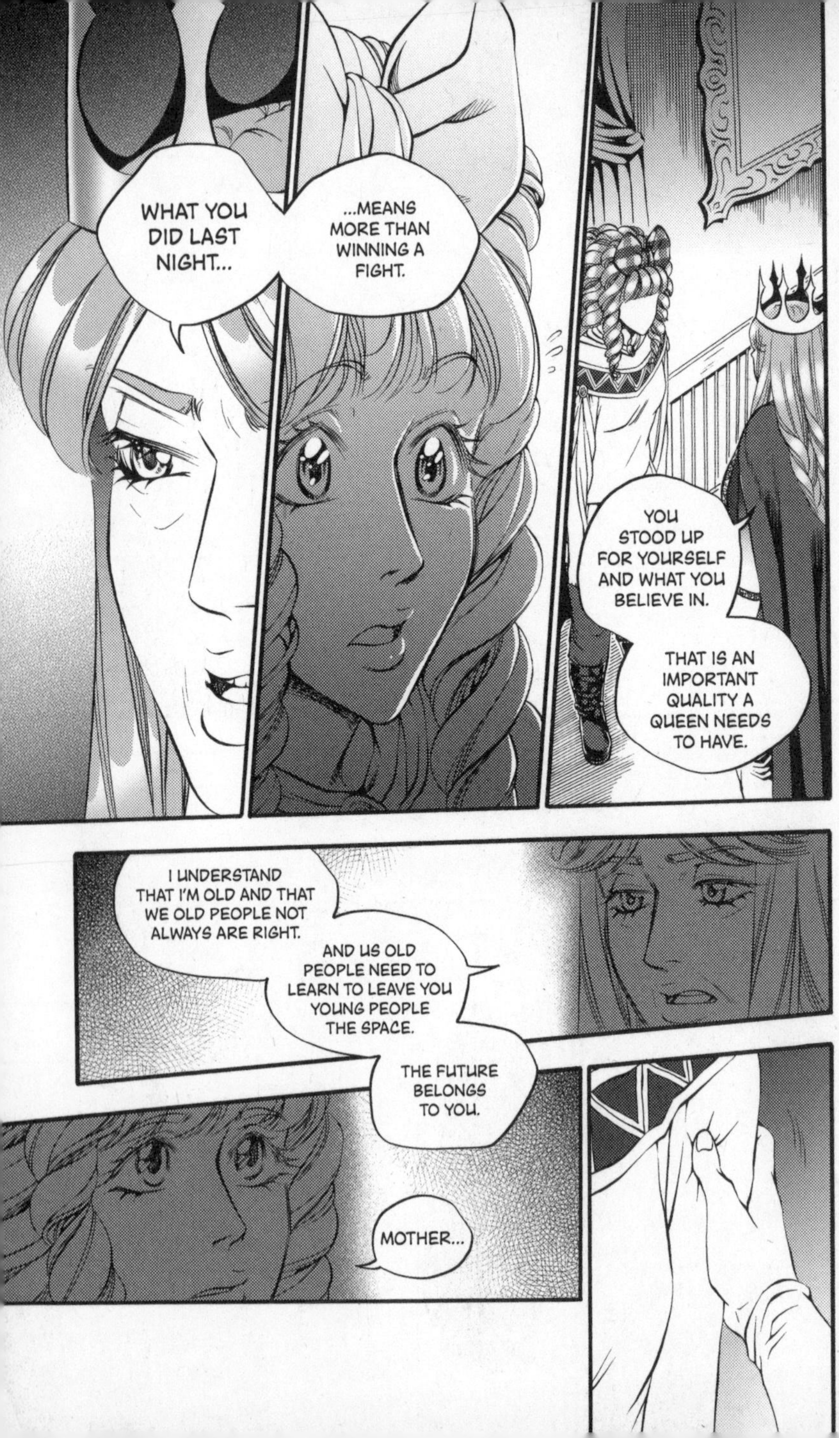
WHAT YOU DID LAST NIGHT...
...MEANS MORE THAN WINNING A FIGHT.
YOU STOOD UP FOR YOURSELF AND WHAT YOU BELIEVE IN.
THAT IS AN IMPORTANT QUALITY A QUEEN NEEDS TO HAVE.
I UNDERSTAND THAT I'M OLD AND THAT WE OLD PEOPLE NOT ALWAYS ARE RIGHT.
AND US OLD PEOPLE NEED TO LEARN TO LEAVE YOU YOUNG PEOPLE THE SPACE.
THE FUTURE BELONGS TO YOU.
MOTHER...

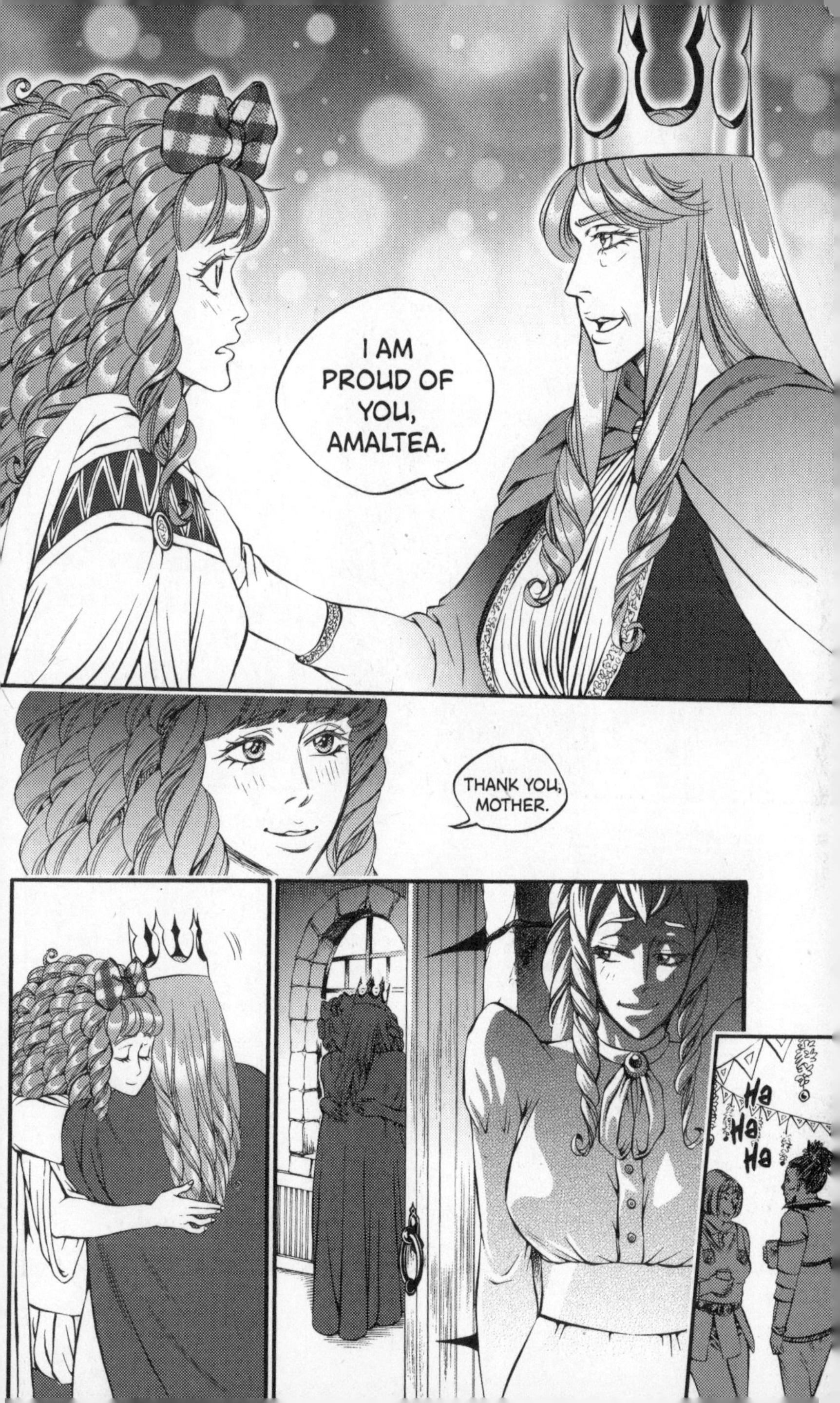
I AM PROUD OF YOU, AMALTEA.
THANK YOU, MOTHER.
Ha Ha Ha

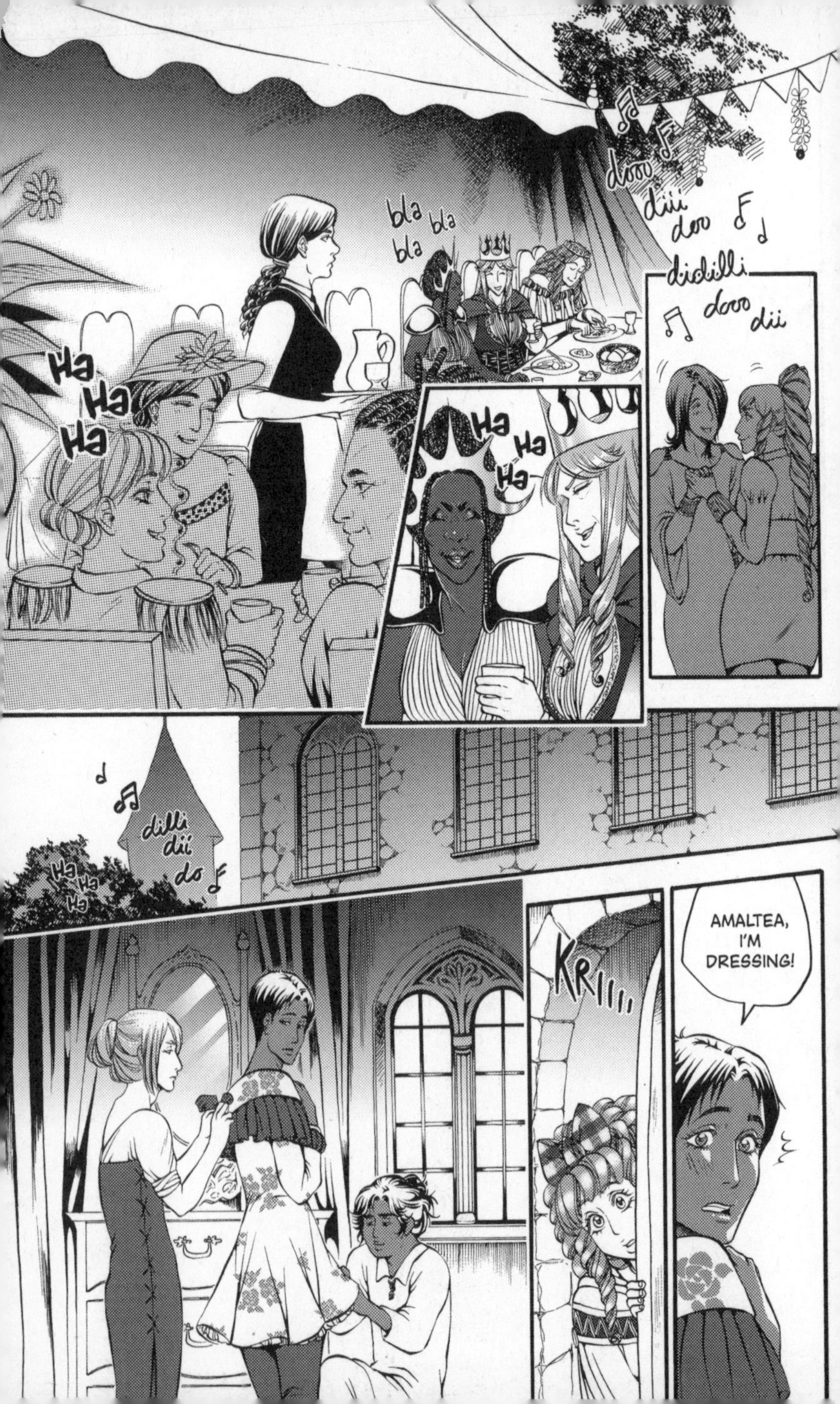
dooo
diii
doo
didilli
dooo
dii
Ha
Ha
Ha
bla
bla
bla
Ha
Ha
Ha
dilli
dii
do
Ha
ha
ha
AMALTEA, I'M DRESSING!
KRIIII

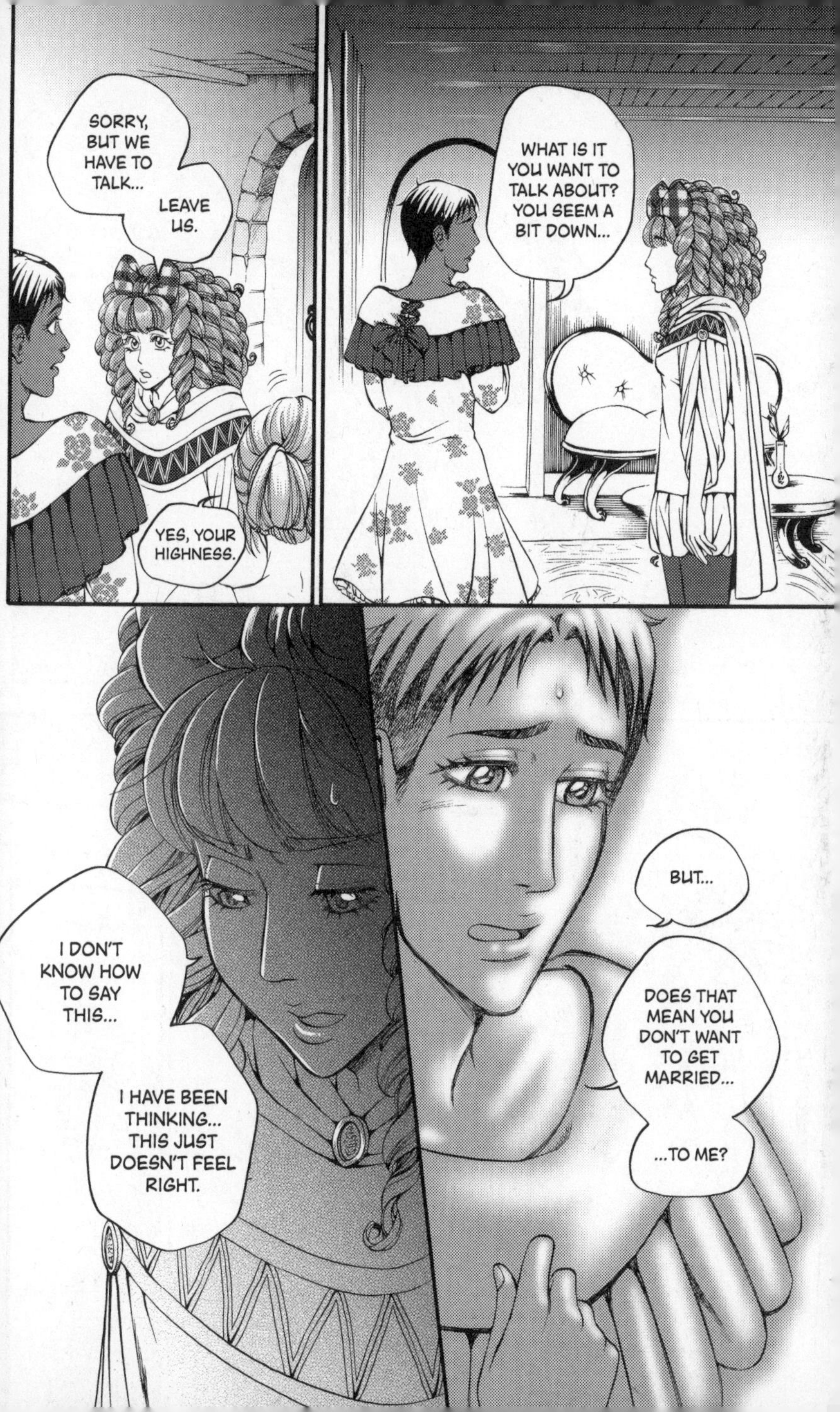
SORRY, BUT WE HAVE TO TALK...
LEAVE US.
YES, YOUR HIGHNESS.
WHAT IS IT YOU WANT TO TALK ABOUT? YOU SEEM A BIT DOWN...
I DON'T KNOW HOW TO SAY THIS...
I HAVE BEEN THINKING... THIS JUST DOESN'T FEEL RIGHT.
BUT...
DOES THAT MEAN YOU DON'T WANT TO GET MARRIED...
...TO ME?

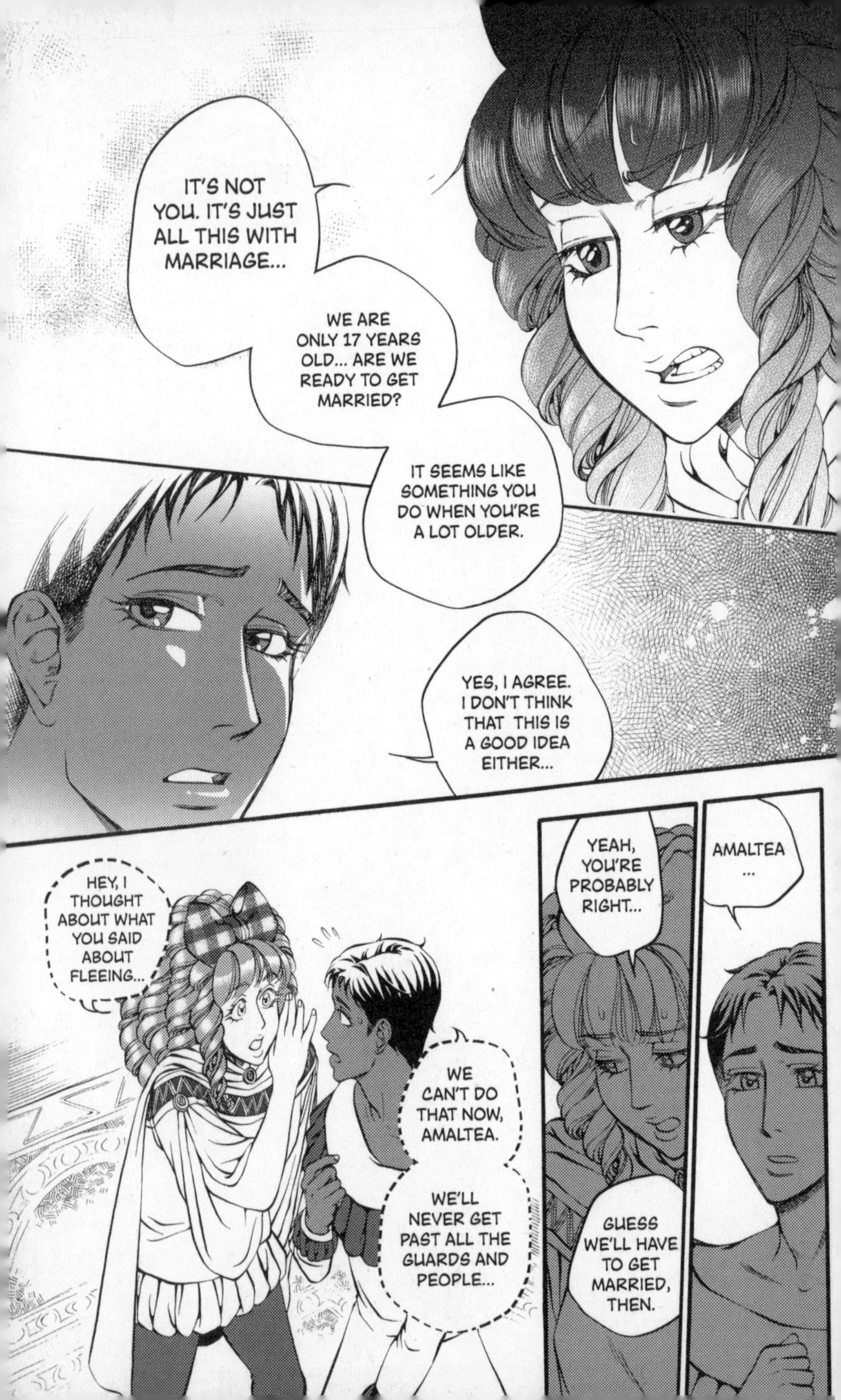
IT'S NOT YOU. IT'S JUST ALL THIS WITH MARRIAGE...
WE ARE ONLY 17 YEARS OLD... ARE WE READY TO GET MARRIED?
IT SEEMS LIKE SOMETHING YOU DO WHEN YOU'RE A LOT OLDER.
YES, I AGREE. I DON'T THINK THAT THIS IS A GOOD IDEA EITHER...
AMALTEA ...
YEAH, YOU'RE PROBABLY RIGHT...
GUESS WE'LL HAVE TO GET MARRIED, THEN.
HEY, I THOUGHT ABOUT WHAT YOU SAID ABOUT FLEEING...
WE CAN'T DO THAT NOW, AMALTEA.
WE'LL NEVER GET PAST ALL THE GUARDS AND PEOPLE...

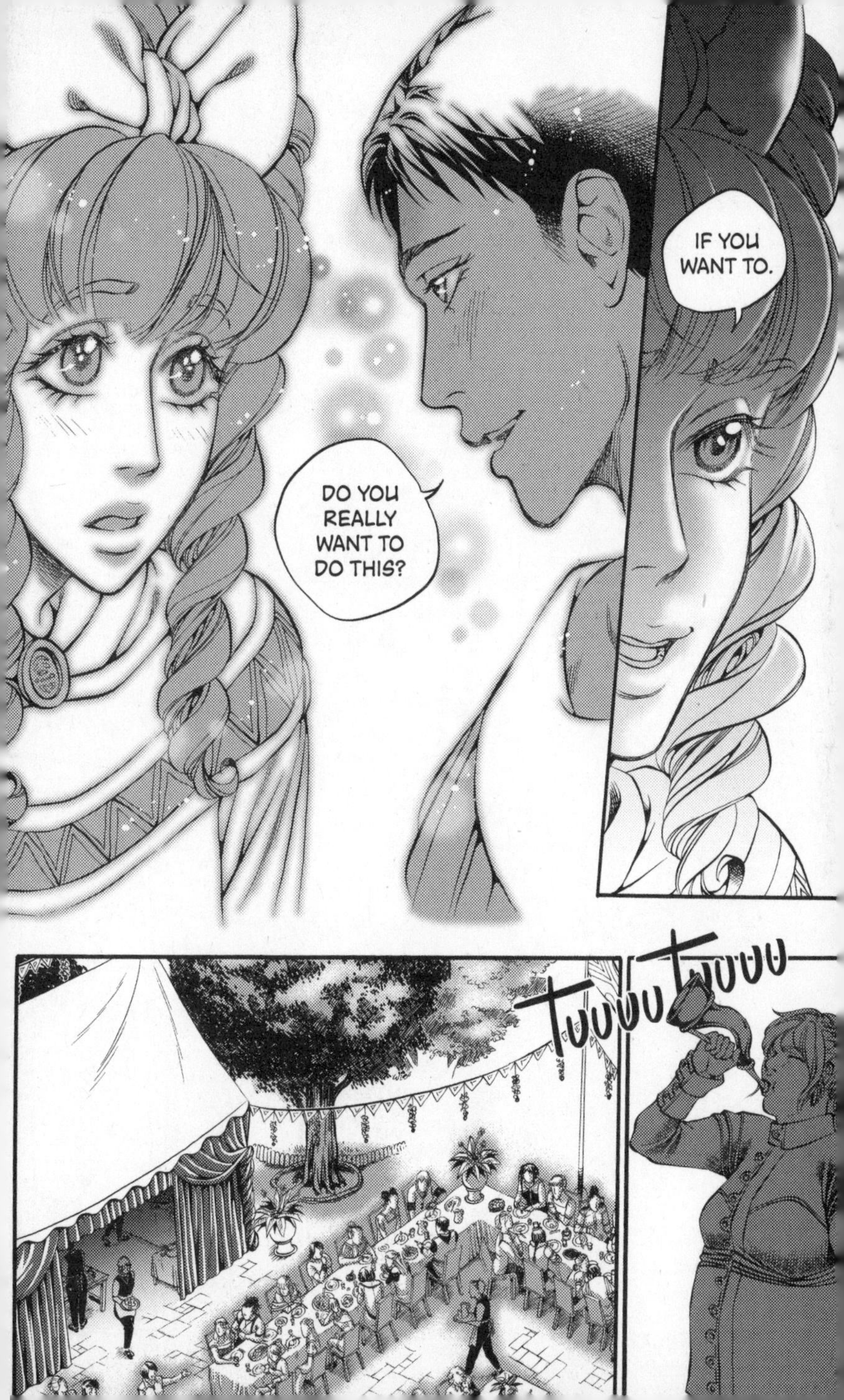
DO YOU REALLY WANT TO DO THIS?
IF YOU WANT TO.
Tuuuu tuuuu

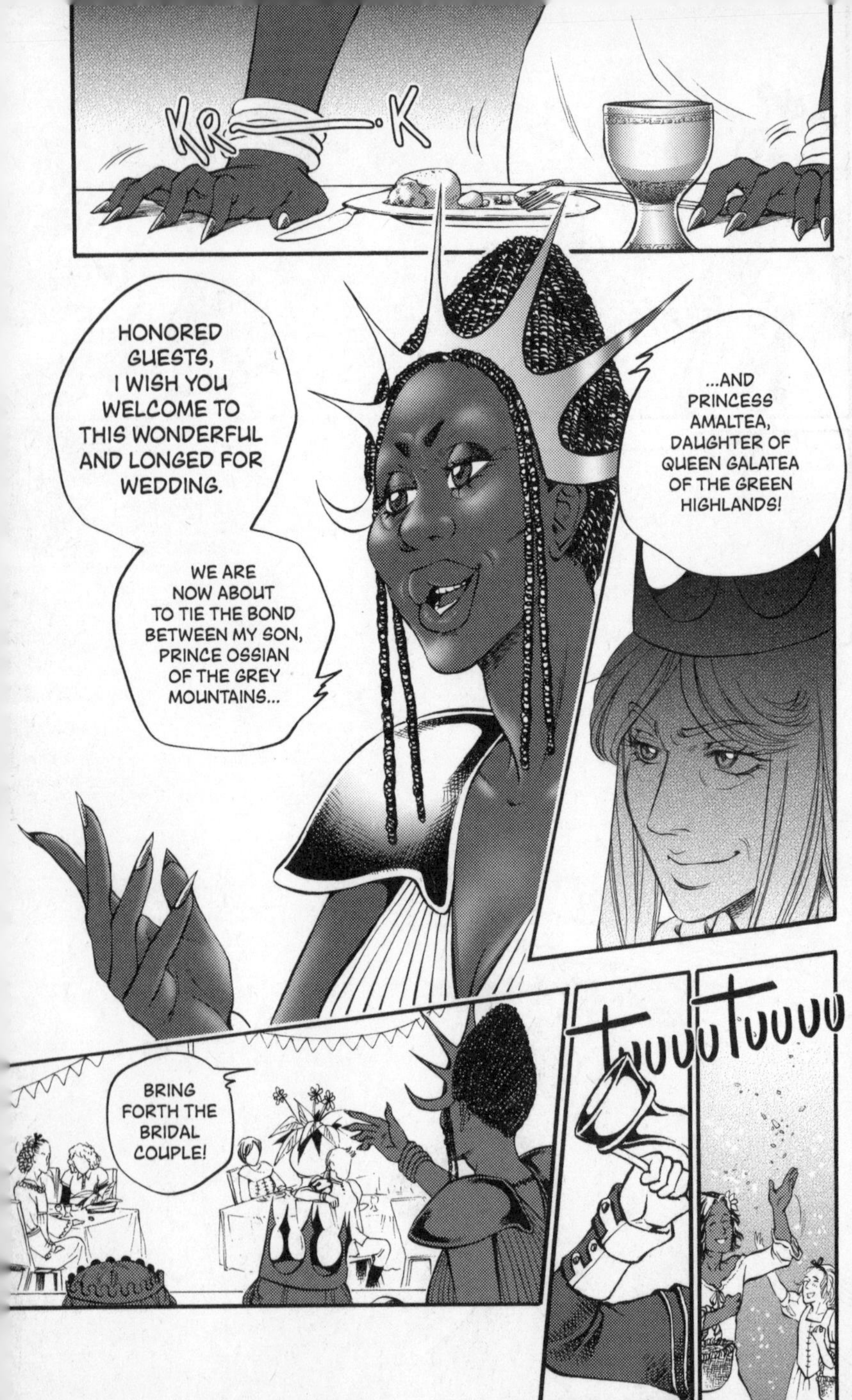
KR—K
HONORED GUESTS, I WISH YOU WELCOME TO THIS WONDERFUL AND LONGED FOR WEDDING.
WE ARE NOW ABOUT TO TIE THE BOND BETWEEN MY SON, PRINCE OSSIAN OF THE GREY MOUNTAINS...
...AND PRINCESS AMALTEA, DAUGHTER OF QUEEN GALATEA OF THE GREEN HIGHLANDS!
BRING FORTH THE BRIDAL COUPLE!
TUUUUTUUUU

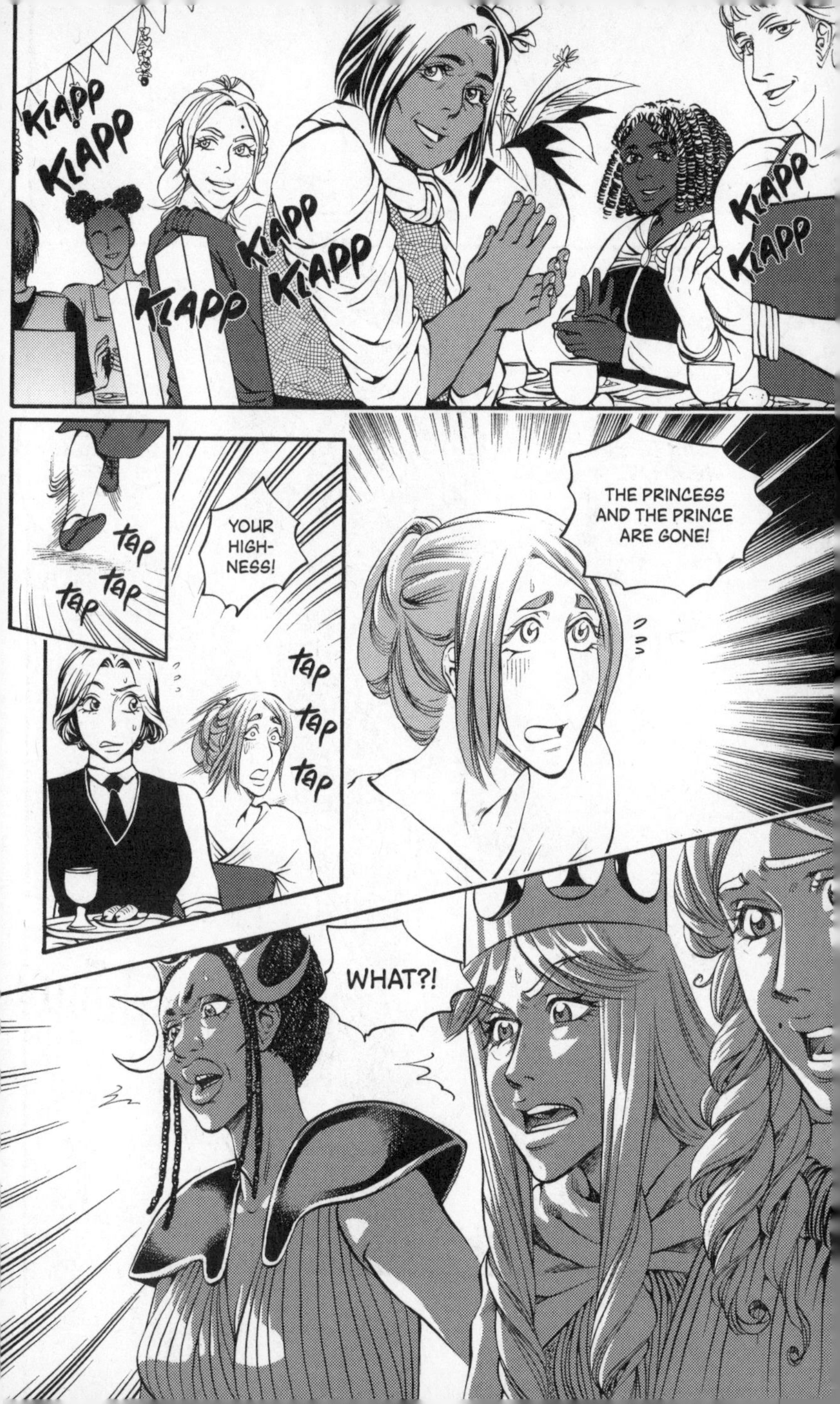

KLAPP KLAPP
KLAPP
KLAPP KLAPP
KLAPP KLAPP
tap tap tap
YOUR HIGH-NESS!
tap tap tap
THE PRINCESS AND THE PRINCE ARE GONE!
WHAT?!

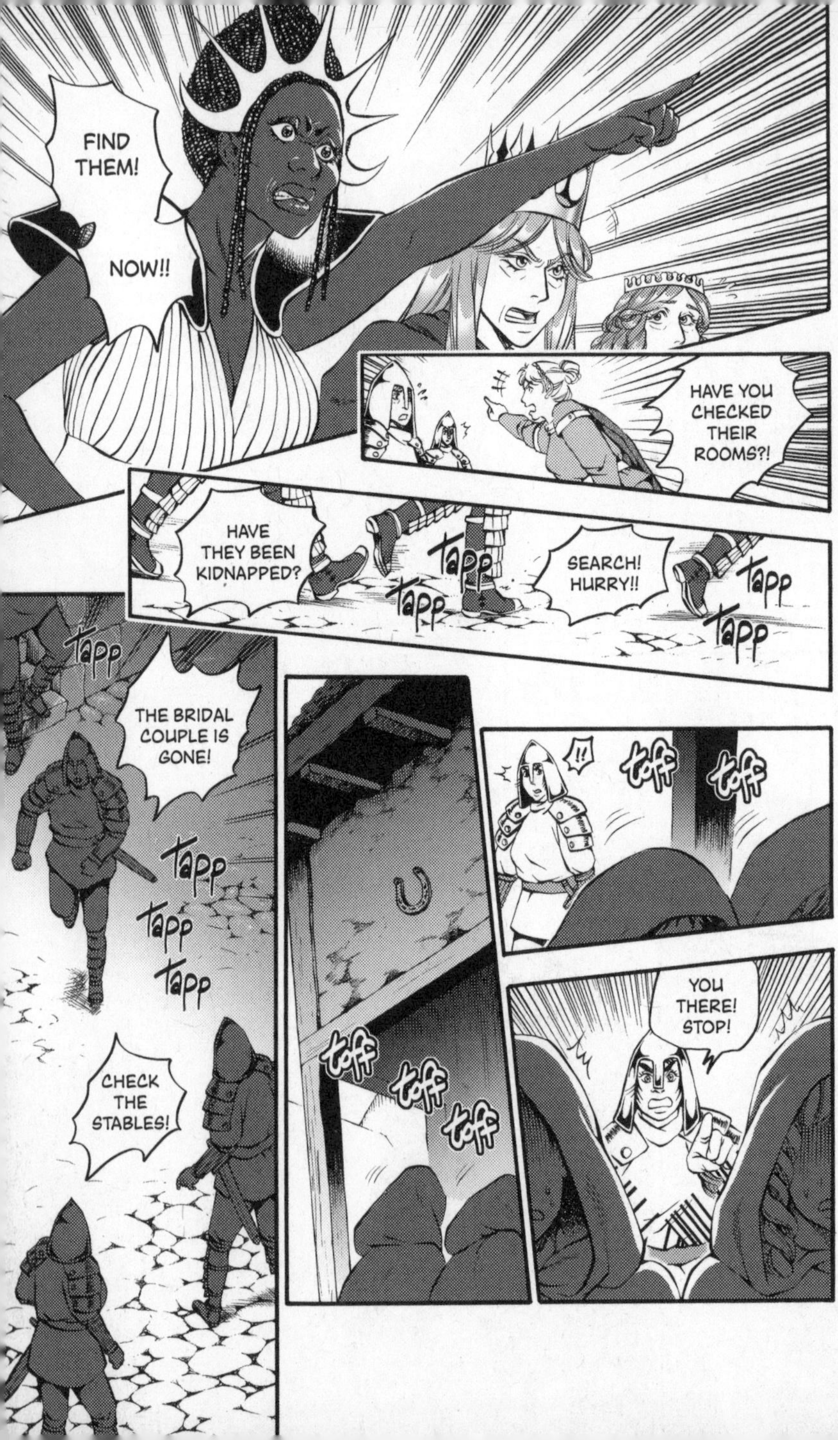
FIND THEM!
NOW!!
HAVE YOU CHECKED THEIR ROOMS?!
HAVE THEY BEEN KIDNAPPED?
TAPP TAPP
SEARCH! HURRY!!
TAPP TAPP
TAPP
THE BRIDAL COUPLE IS GONE!
TAPP TAPP TAPP
CHECK THE STABLES!
TOFF TOFF TOFF
!!
TOFF TOFF
YOU THERE! STOP!

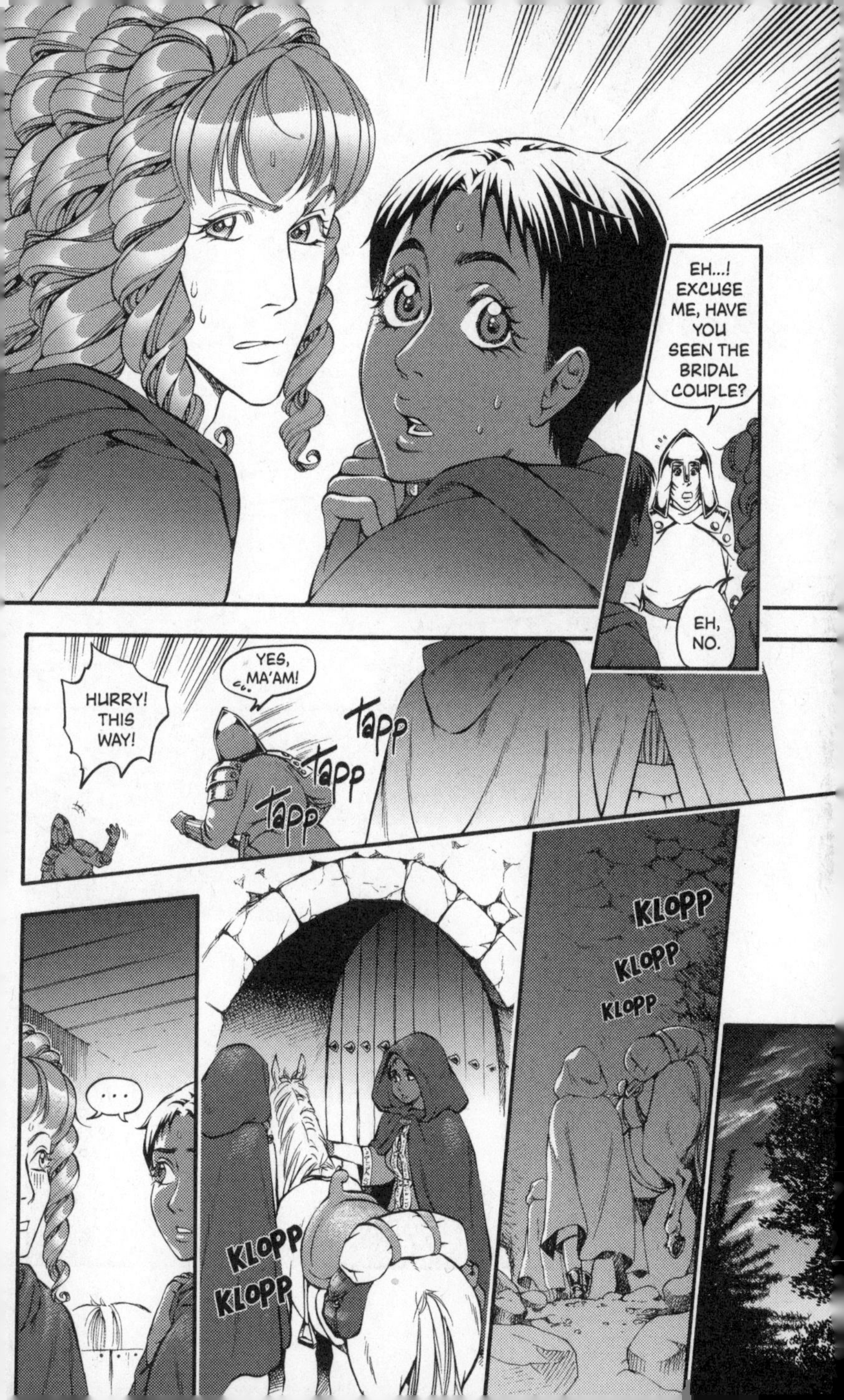
EH...! EXCUSE ME, HAVE YOU SEEN THE BRIDAL COUPLE?
EH, NO.
HURRY! THIS WAY!
YES, MA'AM!
tapp tapp tapp
...
KLOPP KLOPP
KLOPP KLOPP KLOPP

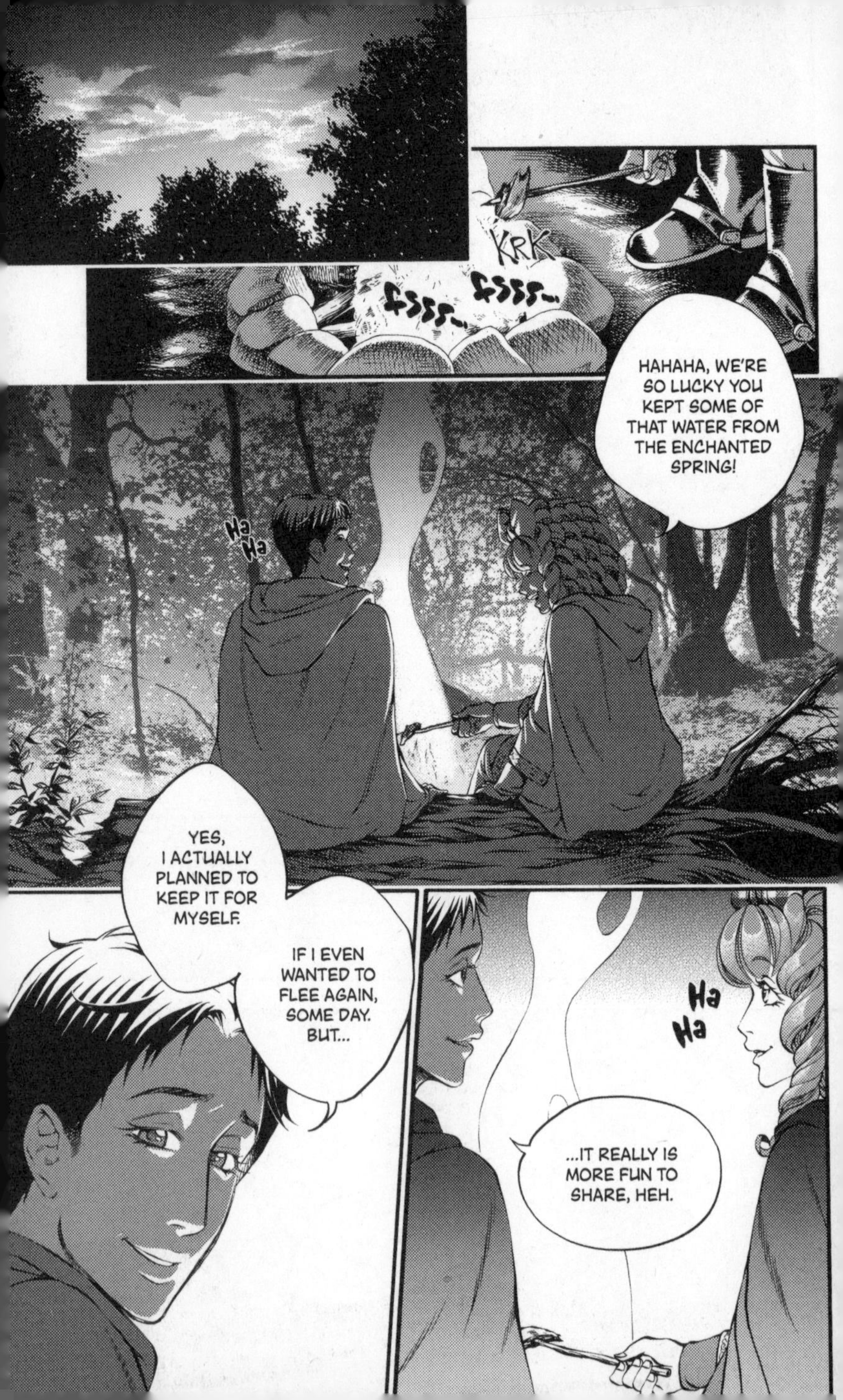
KRK
fsss-..
fsss-..
HAHAHA, WE'RE SO LUCKY YOU KEPT SOME OF THAT WATER FROM THE ENCHANTED SPRING!
Ha Ha
YES, I ACTUALLY PLANNED TO KEEP IT FOR MYSELF.
IF I EVEN WANTED TO FLEE AGAIN, SOME DAY. BUT...
Ha Ha
...IT REALLY IS MORE FUN TO SHARE, HEH.

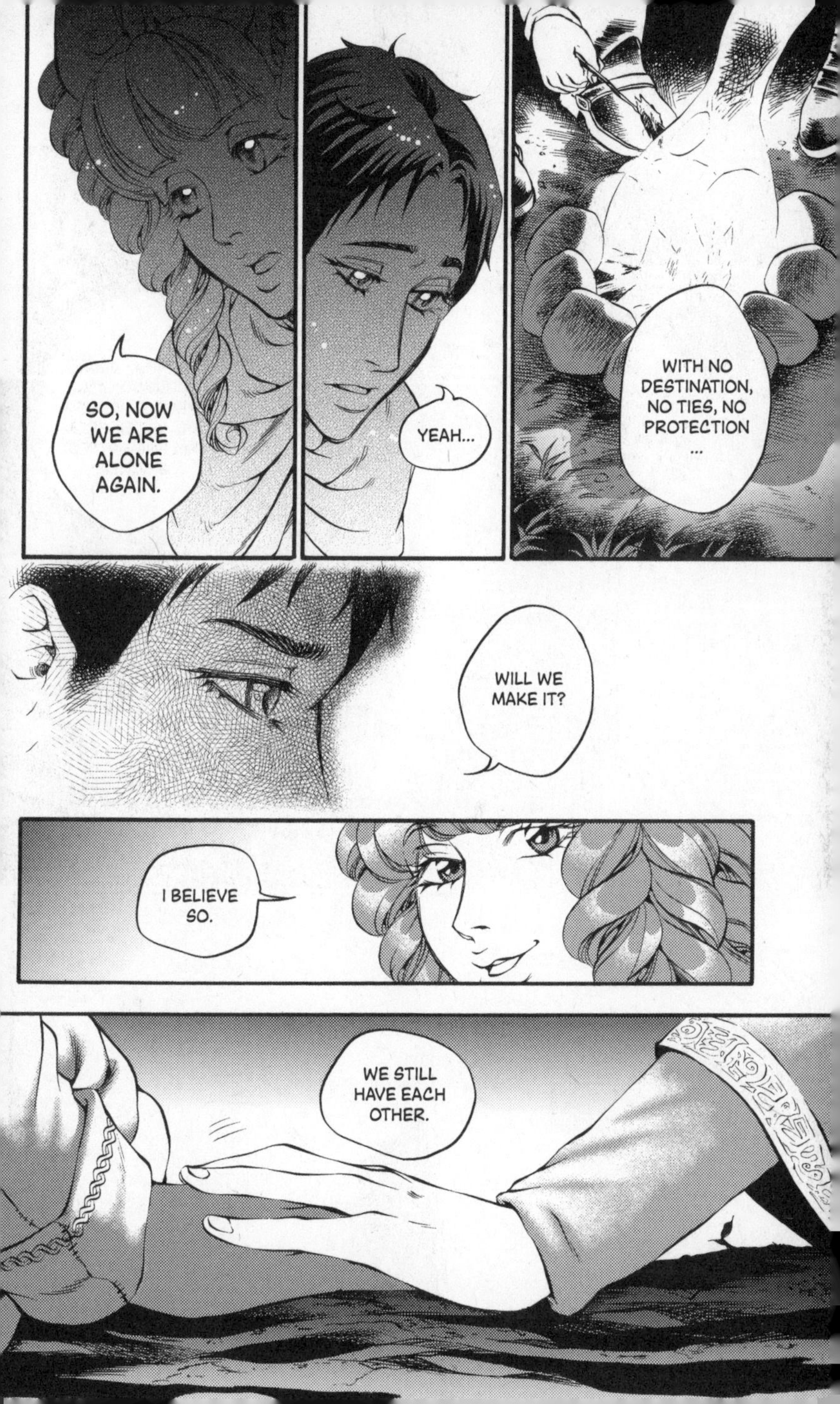
SO, NOW WE ARE ALONE AGAIN.
YEAH...
WITH NO DESTINATION, NO TIES, NO PROTECTION ...
WILL WE MAKE IT?
I BELIEVE SO.
WE STILL HAVE EACH OTHER.

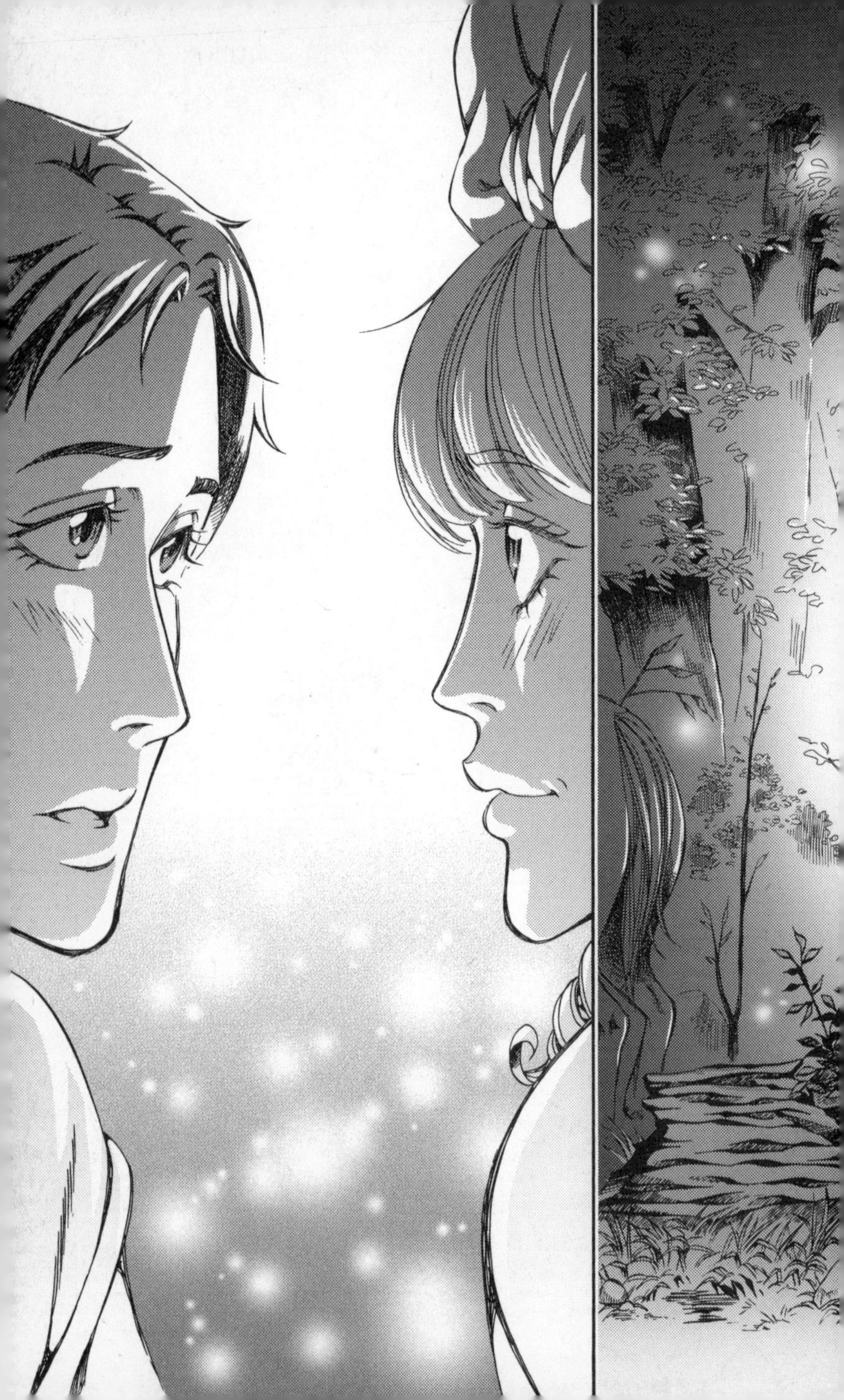

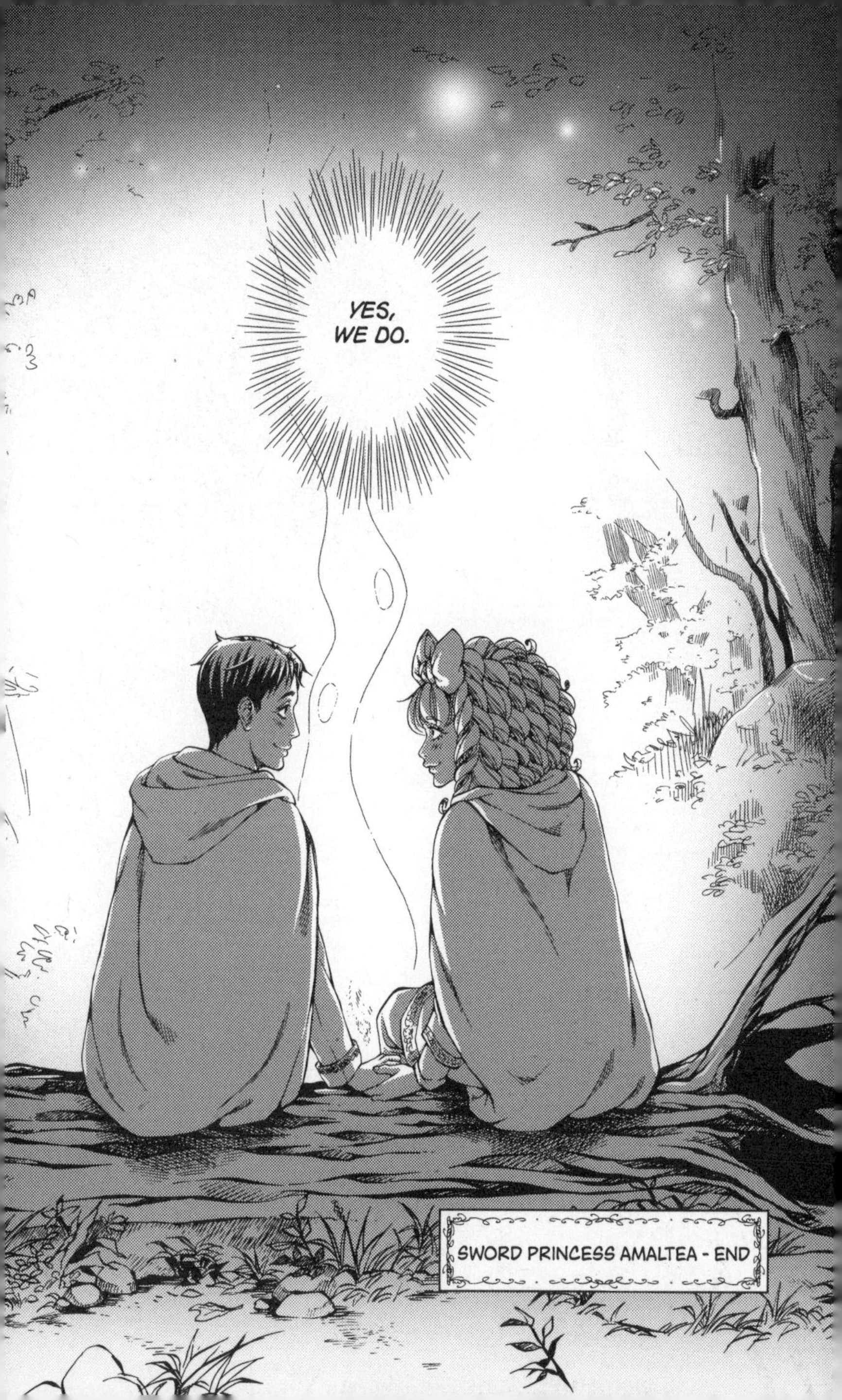
YES, WE DO.
SWORD PRINCESS AMALTEA - END

I DON'T GET IT...LOKIS JUST DISAPPEARED!

HOW WILL WE SURVIVE NOW?

GOOD QUESTION... WE CAN ALWAYS RETURN TO PICKPOCKETING LIKE WE DID BEFORE WE JOINED HER GANG.

OR...WHAT IF WE JUST START ALL OVER? TRY TO MAKE AN HONEST LIVING...?

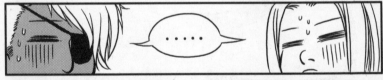

. . . . .

I'VE ALWAYS WANTED TO BECOME A GARDERNER, ACTUALLY.

. . .

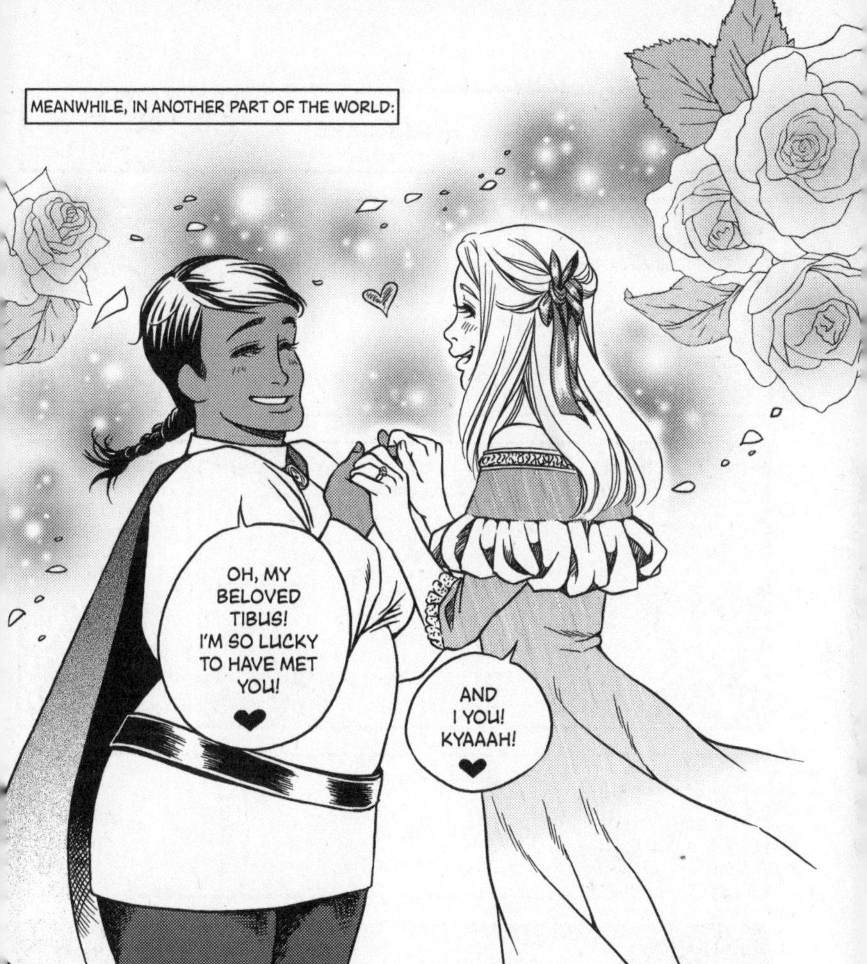
MEANWHILE, IN ANOTHER PART OF THE WORLD:
OH, MY BELOVED TIBUS! I'M SO LUCKY TO HAVE MET YOU! ❤
AND I YOU! KYAAAH! ❤

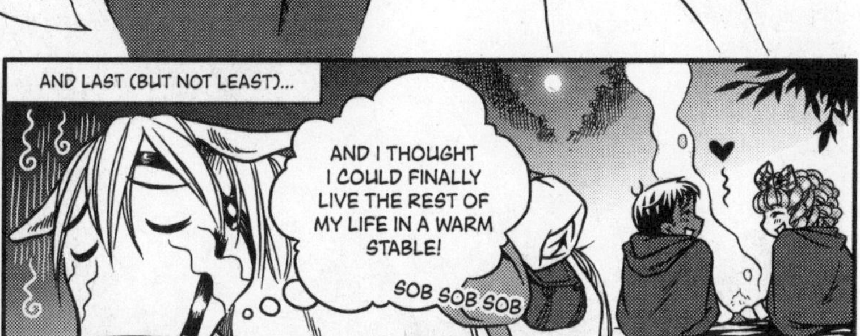
AND LAST (BUT NOT LEAST)...
AND I THOUGHT I COULD FINALLY LIVE THE REST OF MY LIFE IN A WARM STABLE!
SOB SOB SOB

SWORD PRINCESS AMALTEA

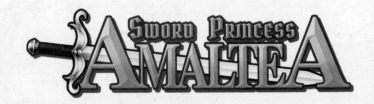

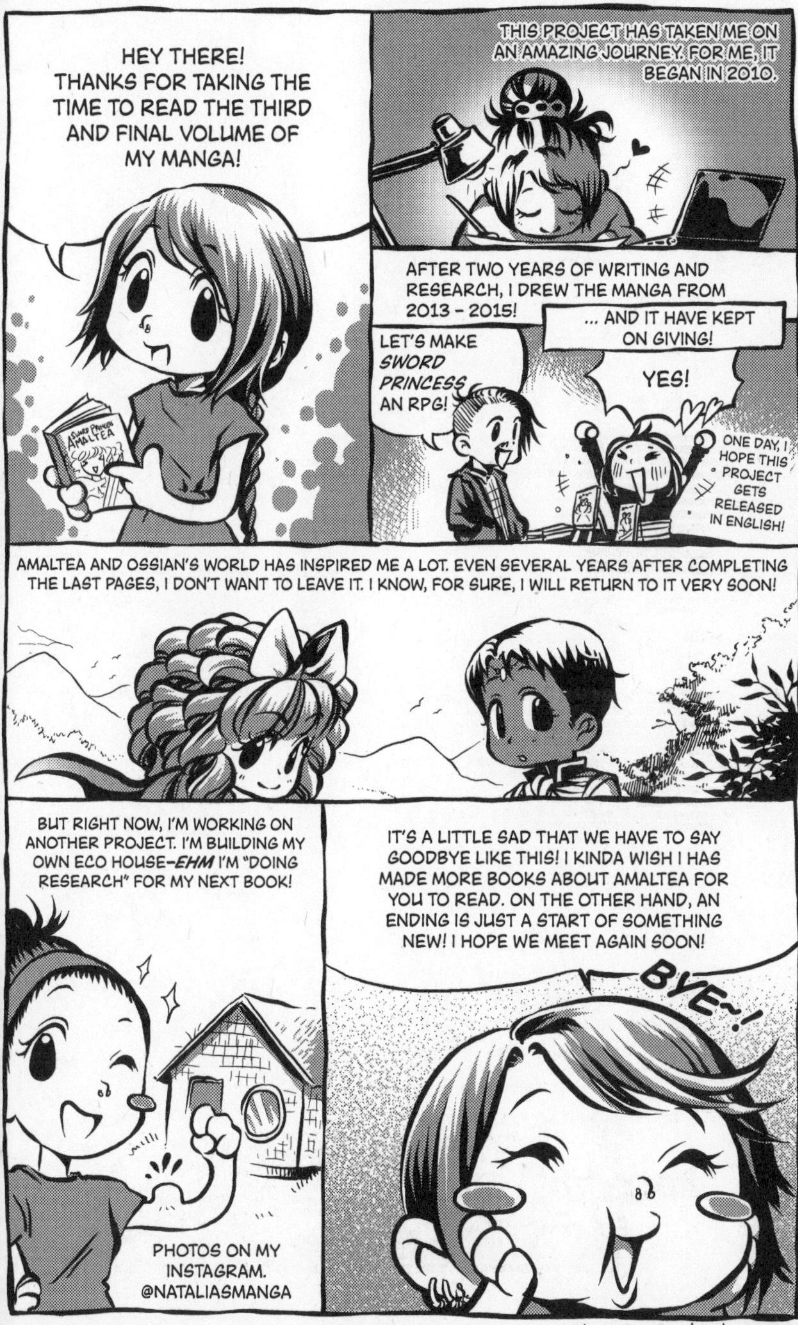
HEY THERE! THANKS FOR TAKING THE TIME TO READ THE THIRD AND FINAL VOLUME OF MY MANGA!
THIS PROJECT HAS TAKEN ME ON AN AMAZING JOURNEY. FOR ME, IT BEGAN IN 2010.
AFTER TWO YEARS OF WRITING AND RESEARCH, I DREW THE MANGA FROM 2013 - 2015!
... AND IT HAVE KEPT ON GIVING!
LET'S MAKE *SWORD PRINCESS* AN RPG!
YES!
ONE DAY, I HOPE THIS PROJECT GETS RELEASED IN ENGLISH!
AMALTEA AND OSSIAN'S WORLD HAS INSPIRED ME A LOT. EVEN SEVERAL YEARS AFTER COMPLETING THE LAST PAGES, I DON'T WANT TO LEAVE IT. I KNOW, FOR SURE, I WILL RETURN TO IT VERY SOON!
BUT RIGHT NOW, I'M WORKING ON ANOTHER PROJECT. I'M BUILDING MY OWN ECO HOUSE-*EHM* I'M "DOING RESEARCH" FOR MY NEXT BOOK!
PHOTOS ON MY INSTAGRAM. @NATALIASMANGA
IT'S A LITTLE SAD THAT WE HAVE TO SAY GOODBYE LIKE THIS! I KINDA WISH I HAS MADE MORE BOOKS ABOUT AMALTEA FOR YOU TO READ. ON THE OTHER HAND, AN ENDING IS JUST A START OF SOMETHING NEW! I HOPE WE MEET AGAIN SOON!
BYE~!

NataliaBatista★2018

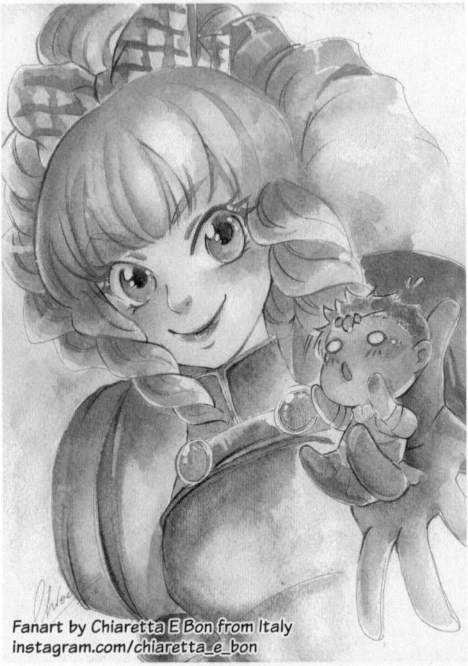

Fanart by Chiaretta E Bon from Italy
instagram.com/chiaretta_e_bon

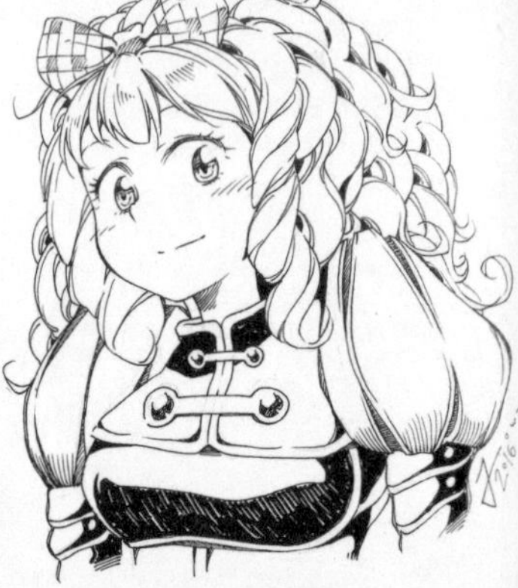

Fanart by Joakim Waller from Sweden
instagram.com/joakimwaller

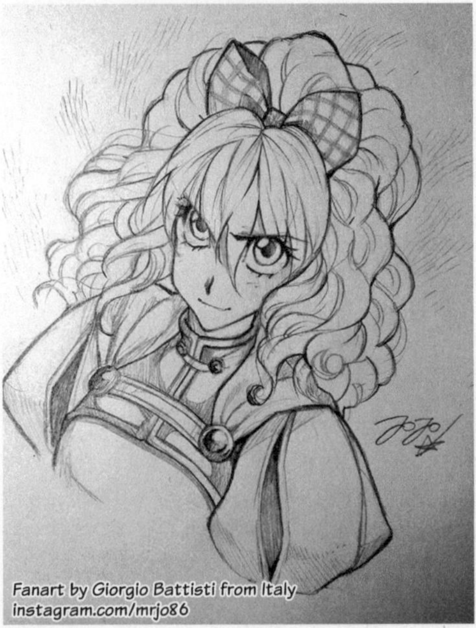

Fanart by Giorgio Battisti from Italy
instagram.com/mrjo86

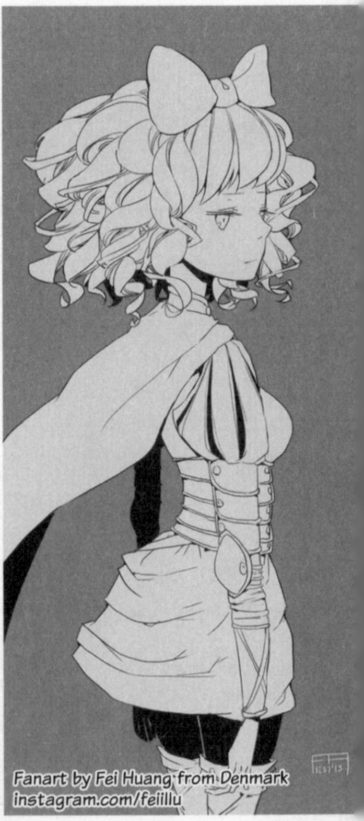

Fanart by Fei Huang from Denmark
instagram.com/feiillu

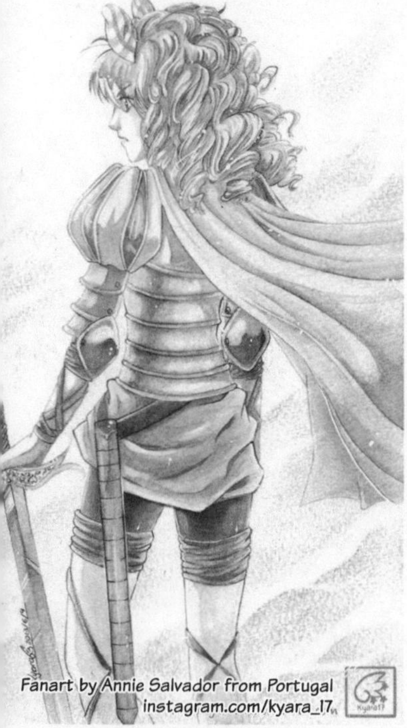

Fanart by Annie Salvador from Portugal
instagram.com/kyara_17

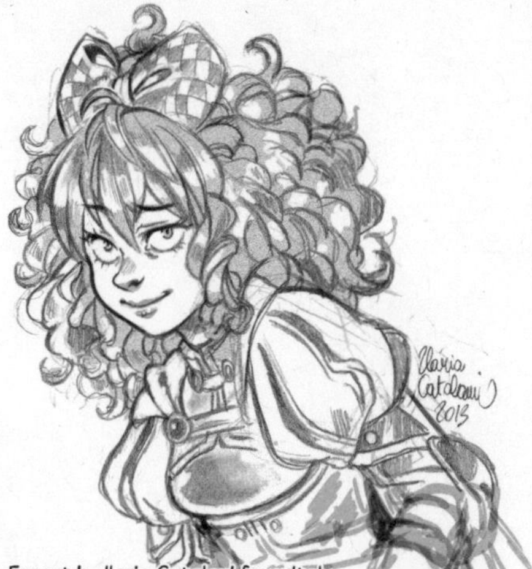

Fanart by Ilaria Catalani from Italy
instagram.com/saspieee

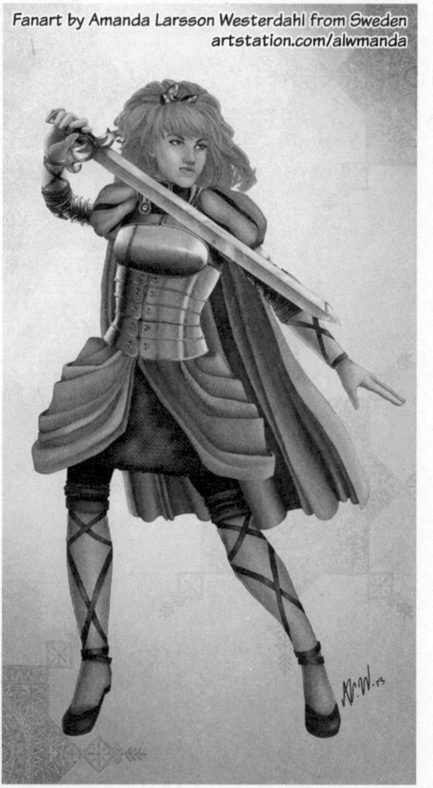

Fanart by Amanda Larsson Westerdahl from Sweden
artstation.com/alwmanda

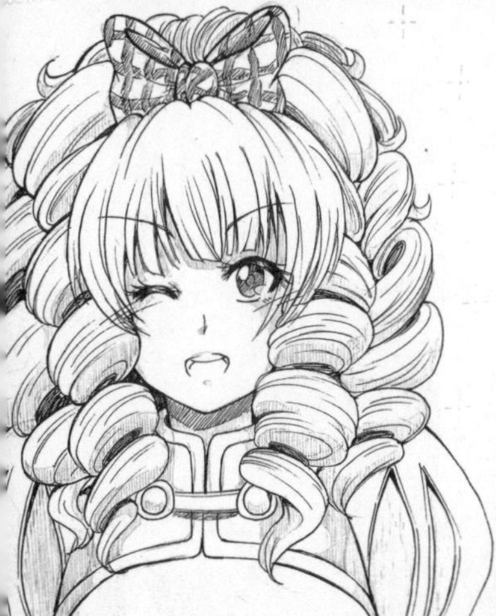

Fanart by Elena Toma from Italy
instagram.com/tonkipappero

THE AUTHOR

NATALIA BATISTA IS A SWEDISH
MANGA ARTIST, ILLUSTRATOR AND COMIC ART
TEACHER AT SERIESKOLAN IN MALMÖ, THE MOST
PROMINENT COMIC ART SCHOOL IN SWEDEN. HER
WORKS INCLUDE THE KIDS MANGA *MJAU!*, PUBLISHED
IN SWEDEN, PORTUGAL AND THE US. NATALIA WAS
A FOUNDING MEMBER OF THE SWEDISH MANGA
ARTIST COLLECTIVE AND PUBLISHER
NOSEBLEED STUDIO.

NATALIA LOVES LISTENING TO PODCASTS,
COOKING VEGAN FOOD AND FARMING HER OWN
VEGETABLES. SHE'S GOT TWO CATS WHO LIKES
HANGING OUT NEAR HER WHEN SHE DRAWS, AND
OCCASIONALLY SPILL HER WATER CUPS.

 Nosebleed Studio
www.nosebleed-studio.com

Do you want to read more manga by Swedish creators?
Nosebleed Studio is Sweden's most prominent manga artist collective
and publisher, with talented members that make books and webcomics.
Follow us on social media to get to know the Swedish manga culture!

 Like Nosebleed Studio on Facebook

 Follow @NosebleedStudio on Instagram and Twitter

TOKYOPOP
· PRESENTS ·

INTERNATIONAL
WOMEN of MANGA

Nana Yaa

GOLDFISCH

An award-winning German manga artist with a large following for her free webcomic, ***CRUSHED!!***

Sophie-Cha─

Ocean of Secrets

A self-taught manga artist from ┤ Middle East, with a huge YouTu─ following!

Ban Zarbo

KAMO
PACT WITH THE SPIRIT WORLD

A lifelong manga fan from Switzerland, she and her twin sister take inspiration from their Dominican roots!

Gin Zarbo

UNDEAD MESSIAH

An aspiring manga artist since she w─ a child, along with her twin sister sł─ releasing her debut title!

Natalia Batista

Sword Princess Amaltea
Natalia Batista

A Swedish creator whose popular manga has already been published in Sweden, Italy and the Czech Republic!

www.TOKYOPOP.com

KYOPOP GmbH / *Goldfisch* - NANA YAA / *Kamo* - BAN ZARBO / *Undead Messiah* - GIN ZARBO / *Ocean of Secrets* - SOPHIE-CHAN / *d Princess Amaltea* - NATALIA BATISTA

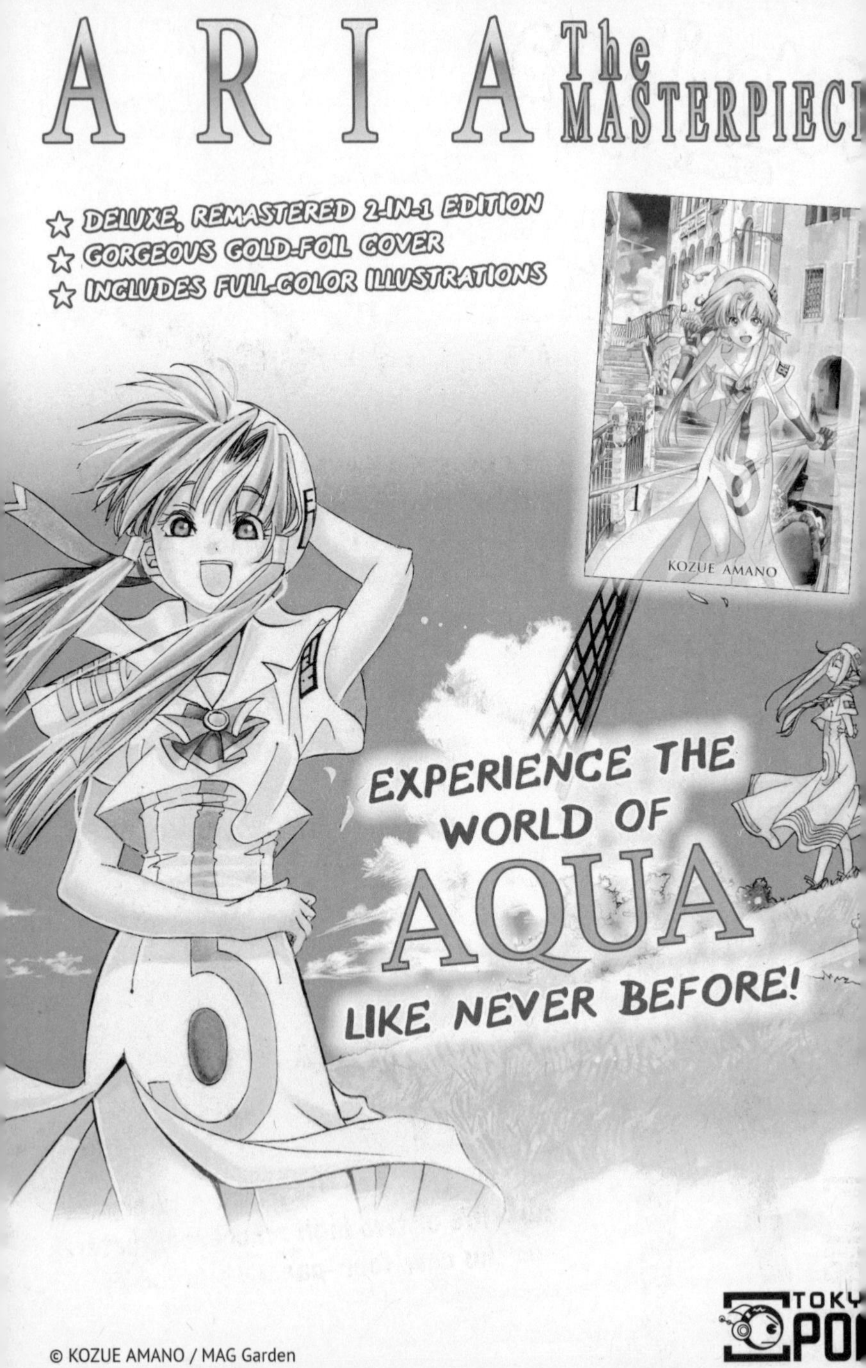
ARIA The MASTERPIECE
DELUXE, REMASTERED 2-IN-1 EDITION
GORGEOUS GOLD-FOIL COVER
INCLUDES FULL-COLOR ILLUSTRATIONS
1
KOZUE AMANO
EXPERIENCE THE WORLD OF AQUA LIKE NEVER BEFORE!
© KOZUE AMANO / MAG Garden
TOKYOPOP

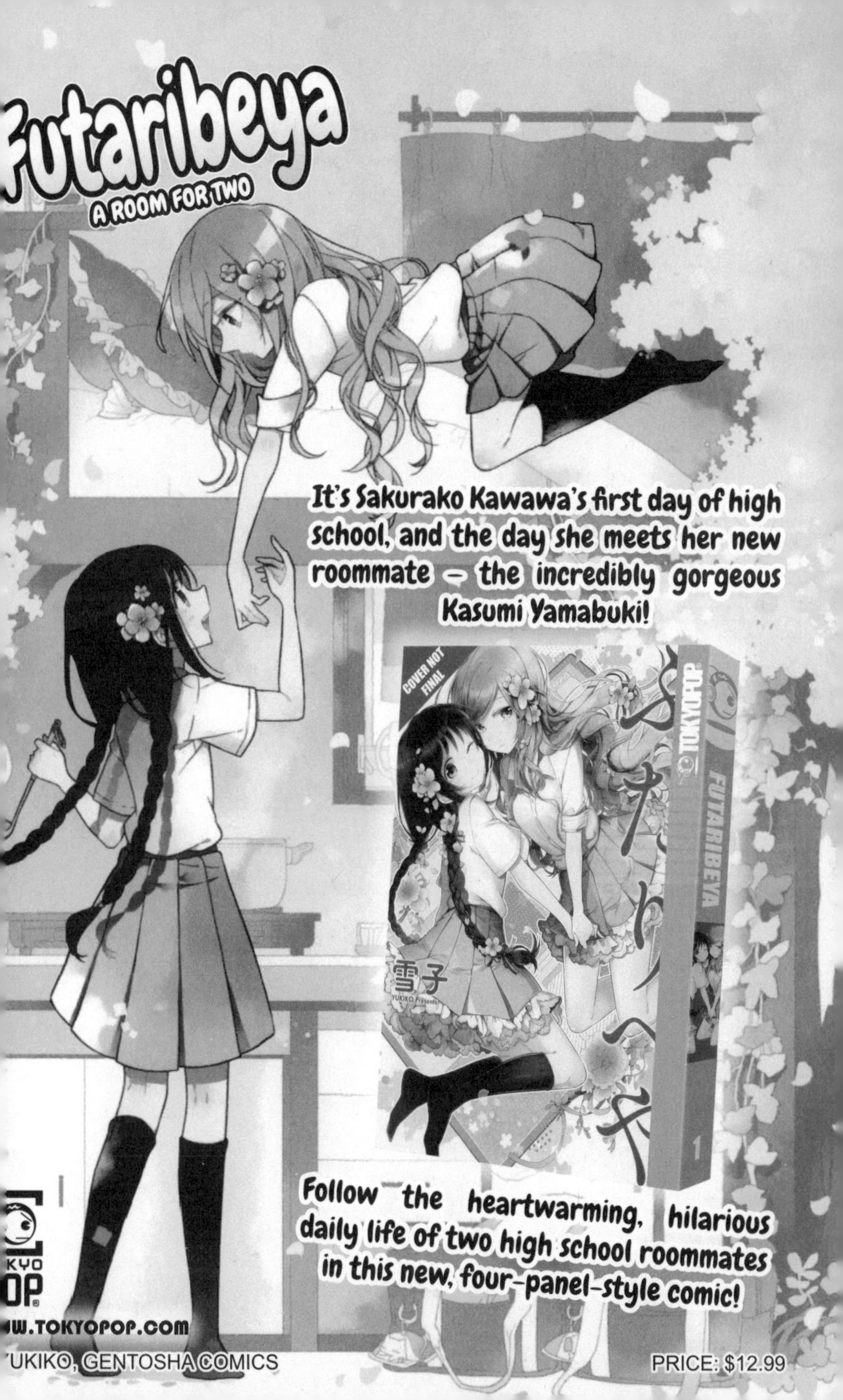
Futaribeya
A ROOM FOR TWO
It's Sakurako Kawawa's first day of high school, and the day she meets her new roommate – the incredibly gorgeous Kasumi Yamabuki!
COVER NOT FINAL
TOKYOPOP
FUTARIBEYA
1
雪子
Follow the heartwarming, hilarious daily life of two high school roommates in this new, four-panel-style comic!
W.TOKYOPOP.COM
UKIKO, GENTOSHA COMICS
PRICE: $12.99

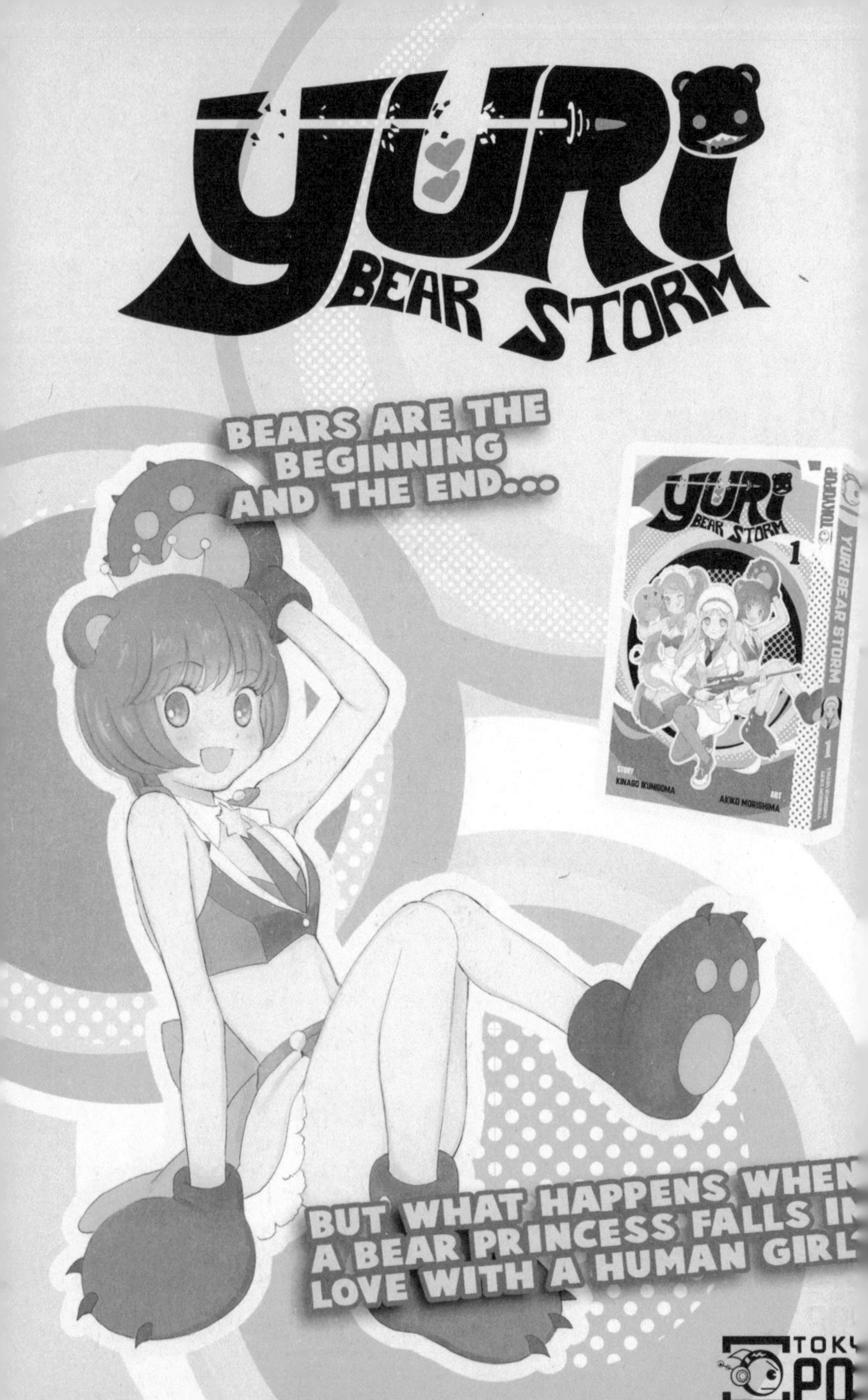
YURI BEAR STORM
BEARS ARE THE BEGINNING AND THE END...
YURI BEAR STORM 1
STORY KINAGO IKUNIGOMA
ART AKIKO MORISHIMA
BUT WHAT HAPPENS WHEN A BEAR PRINCESS FALLS IN LOVE WITH A HUMAN GIRL

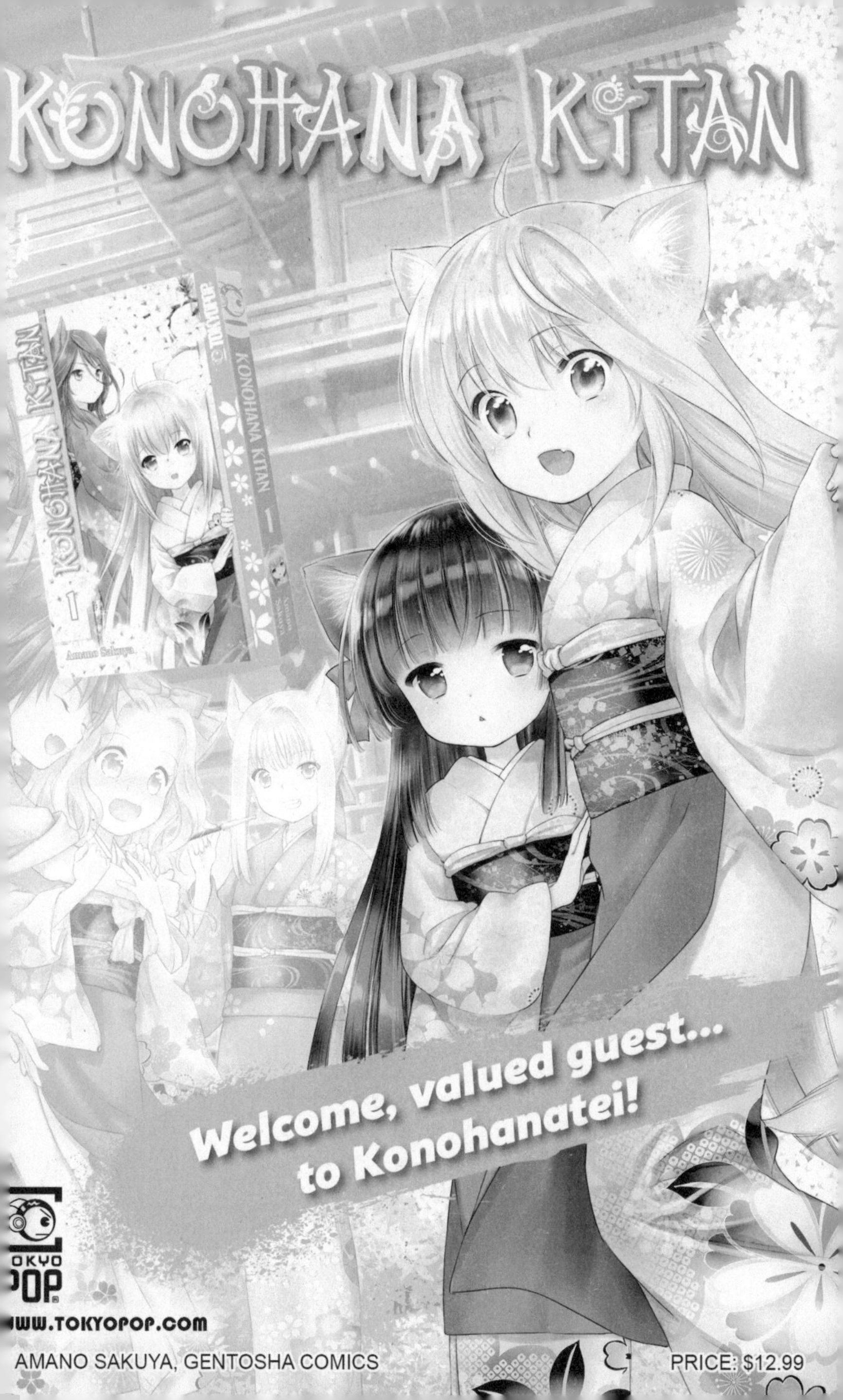
KONOHANA KITAN
KONOHANA KITAN
1
Amano Sakuya
KONOHANA KITAN
1
TOKYOPOP
Welcome, valued guest...
to Konohanatei!
TOKYOPOP
WWW.TOKYOPOP.COM
AMANO SAKUYA, GENTOSHA COMICS
PRICE: $12.99

Sword Princess Amaltea Volume 3
Manga by: Natalia Batista

Book Three Assistants - Catarina Batista, Emil Johansson,
Editorial Associate - Janae Young
Marketing Associate - Kae Winters
Technology and Digital Media Assistant - Phillip Hong
Digital Media Coordinator - Rico Brenner-Quiñonez
Licensing Specialist - Arika Yanaka
Copy Editor - M. Cara Carper
Graphic Designer - Phillip Hong
Retouching and Lettering - Vibrraant Publishing Studio
Editor-in-Chief & Publisher - Stu Levy

A  Manga

TOKYOPOP and ✿ are trademarks or registered trademarks of TOKYOPOP Inc.

TOKYOPOP inc.
5200 W Century Blvd
Suite 705
Los Angeles, CA 90045 USA

E-mail: info@TOKYOPOP.com
Come visit us online at www.TOKYOPOP.com

www.facebook.com/TOKYOPOP
www.twitter.com/TOKYOPOP
www.pinterest.com/TOKYOPOP
www.instagram.com/TOKYOPOP

Copyright ©2018 Natalia Batista All rights reserved. No portion of this book may be
All Rights Reserved reproduced or transmitted in any form or by any means
without written permission from the copyright holders.
This manga is a work of fiction. Any resemblance to
actual events or locales or persons, living or dead, is
entirely coincidental.

ISBN: 978-1-4278-5925-9
First TOKYOPOP Printing: November 2018
10 9 8 7 6 5 4 3 2 1
Printed in CANADA